D0146071

RELIGIOUS BODIES
IN THE UNITED STATES:
A DIRECTORY

Garland Reference Library of the Humanities (Vol. 1568)

Religious Information Systems Series, Vol. 1

RELIGIOUS BODIES IN THE UNITED STATES: A DIRECTORY

by
J. Gordon Melton

RELIGIOUS INFORMATION SYSTEMS

Garland Publishing, Inc.
New York & London
1992

© 1992 by J. Gordon Melton

Library of Congress Cataloging-in-Publication Data
Melton, J. Gordon
  Religious bodies in the United States: a directory / by J. Gordon Melton.
  p.   cm.—(Garland reference library of the humanities; vol. 1568)
  Rev. ed. of: A directory of religious bodies in the United States. 1977.
  Includes bibliographic references and index.
  ISBN 0-8153-0806-X
  1. United States—Religion—Directories. I. Melton, J. Gordon.
Directory of religious bodies in the United States. II. Title. III. Series
BL2525.M452 1992
200' .25' 73—dc20   91-41564
                                                                  CIP

Printed on acid-free, 250-year-life paper
Manufactured in the United States of America

This is a revised, expanded edition of *A Directory of Religious Bodies in the United States* by J. Gordon Melton, first published by Garland in 1977.

TABLE OF CONTENTS

Introduction   vii

Interfaith Organizations   3

Christianity
Intrafaith Organizations   9
Christian Churches   13
Christian Periodicals   115

Buddhism
Intrafaith Organizations   133
Buddhist Centers and Organizations   134
Buddhist Periodicals   149

Hinduism and Related Organizations
Intrafaith Organizations   153
Hindu Centers and Organizations   153
Hindu Temple Associations   169
Hindu Periodicals   175

Islam and Islamic Inspired Organizations
Intrafaith Organizations   179
The Orthodox Muslim Community   180
Islamic and Islamic-Inspired Groups   181
Muslim Periodicals   187

AUG 25 1994

Judaism
Intrafaith Organizations   192
Jewish Congregational and Rabbinical Organizations   193
Other Jewish and Jewish-Inspired Organizations   194
Jewish Periodicals   199

Latter-Day Saints
Latter-day Saint Churches   201
Latter-day Saint Periodicals   207

Metaphysical/Ancient Wisdom/New Age
Intrafaith Organizations   210
Metaphysical/Ancient Wisdom/New Age Organizations   210
Metaphysical/Ancient Wisdom/New Age Periodicals   241

Shinto
Shinto Centers and Organizations   255
Shinto Periodicals   257

Sikhism/Sant Mat
Sikhism/Sant Mat Organizations   259
Sikhism/Sant Mat Periodicals   263

Taoism
Taoist Centers   265
Taoist Periodicals   267

Unclassified Religious Groups
Unclassified Religious Organizations   269
Periodicals of the Unclassified Religious Groups   275

Bibliography   277

Index   279

INTRODUCTION

Some fifteen years ago Garland Publishing, Inc., published a first attempt to compile a *Directory* of religious groups in the United States. This second edition follows the goal of the first in attempting to provide a comprehensive listing of each religious group known to be operating in the United States as of the summer of 1991, along with its headquarters address, and telephone numbers. Not limited to the Christian community, this *Directory* covers the entire spectrum of American religion including the Buddhist, Hindu, Jewish, Muslim, Metaphysical, Occult/Magical, Shintoist, Sikh, and Taoist communities.

The original *Directory* proved most useful and only the perceived need to produce other equally useful reference tools prevented the updating of the *Directory* until now. During that time the need for such a *Directory* has, if anything, markedly increased. The actual number of religious groups functioning in the United States continued to grow during the 1980s at the same remarkable rate noticeable since World War II and especially since 1965. All the indications are that the number will not remain static as population increases, urbanization, and immigration continue to provide a nurturing environment for new religious expressions. The new immigration regulations enacted in November 1990 will have the most dramatic impact on the continued emergence of new religious communities in the next decade. The 1980s have also seen significant changes within the older religious denominations, the most significant related to this *Directory* being their many mergers and movement into new headquarters facilities.

Between 1977 when the first *Directory* was issued, and this new edition, at least three major trends correlative to the production of religious changes have been observed. First, a significant shift in

vii

American religious life has occurred with the rise of Islam, Hinduism, and Buddhism. While the Christian and Jewish communities in the United States trace their history to Colonial times, Islam and the ancient religions of the East arrived in the nineteenth century and only began to make their presence felt after the destruction of immigration barriers in 1965. The largest increase in the number of new religious bodies has come in the establishment of the full range of Muslim, Hindu, and Buddhist religious life in the West. The United States is now home to each of the different Eastern and Middle Eastern religions and to most of their ethnic variations.

Second, in part based upon the influx of Eastern religions, a new wave of metaphysical/occult religion has appeared under the umbrella of what has been termed the New Age movement, the first occult movement to become statistically significant on a national scale in America. Quite apart from its more superficial elements (and the even more superficial comment on it by the media), the New Age Movement is a fitting sign of the movement of the formerly small esoteric and metaphysical religions from the margin to the middle of American society. More than any other community, the New Age has experienced a continuing flux as new religious groups have appeared and passed away only to be replaced by others as a maturing of religious life and a sorting out process of groups occurs.

Third, the Christian community has undergone equally significant changes. A most important shift has occurred as liberal Protestant groups continue their loss of membership and the old religious center of American religion shifts away from them to the more conservative evangelical community. That shift has been best illustrated in the restructuring of the Southern Baptist Convention as in recent years it became the nation's second largest religious body and was placed firmly in the hands of its most conservative leaders. The rise of evangelicalism, a segment of which was somewhat fearful of the older denominations, was accompanied by the production of a number of altogether new denominations, some of which (for example, Calvary Chapel, the Association of Vineyard Churches, and People of Destiny) became national and even international bodies within a few years.

The Nature of this *Directory*

The name, *Religious Bodies in the United States: A Directory*, was carefully chosen for this new edition. It is drawn from the name given the religious censuses previously published by the United States government every decade. These regularly published censuses provided basic data about each religious group, and it is hoped that this new edition will fill an information gap and provide basic data about each religious group and be regularly updated as changes in the religious community dictate (annually or bi-annually).

This edition thus attempts to list the name, headquarters address, and telephone number of every currently active religious group in the United States. In addition, additional addresses of foreign headquarters are given where applicable as are cable and fax numbers for those groups that have these supplementary communications systems.

The *Directory* was compiled from the files and data base at the Institute for the Study of American Religion. These records have been generated over the 22 years of the Institute's existence, first in Chicago and since 1985 in Santa Barbara, California. These files are growing daily and the data base is being corrected as new information is received. The *Directory* represents the state of the data base as of the summer of 1991.

The *Directory* is not seen as a competitor to the *Yearbook of American and Canadian Churches* and is certainly not meant to in any way replace it. The *Yearbook* is a continuing source of valuable information on the several hundred church groups it covers. For those groups, including many of the larger Christian churches, it offers a very detailed listing of national offices and officers. *Religious Bodies in the United States* has a much different focus. It broadens its scope to list over 1300 denominations and religious groups not to be found in the *Yearbook*, while narrowing its focus to include only contact points with the headquarters office. Thus it is hoped that the *Directory* will take its place beside the *Yearbook* as a much-needed additional tool assisting contact with the larger religious community.

For convenience, the *Directory* has been broken down into chapters, each chapter containing the entries for groups of a single major religious community. The first chapter lists interfaith organizations which have attempted to create a dialogue among the different religious communities. Second, since America remains overwhelmingly Christian and well over half of the religious groups in the country are Christian denominations, Christianity is the initial religious community to be listed. It is then followed by each of the other religious communities in alphabetical order—Buddhism,

Hinduism, Islam, Judaism, Latter-day Saints, Metaphysical/Ancient Wisdom/New Age, Shinto, Sikhism/Sant Mat, Taoist, and Unclassified.

The domination of the American religious scene by Christianity creates a problem in any attempted classification of religious groups. There are a number of religious groups, especially the Church of Christ, Scientist, the Church of Jesus Christ of Latter Day Saints, the Unitarian Universalist Association, and a variety of New Age Christian groups, which affirm a relation to the Christian community, but do so in such a way that the larger Christian church groups have refused them recognition. To the observer, these groups obviously hold beliefs not shared by the mainline Christian community and members do not freely associate in Christian ecumenical circles. Thus such groups have been listed within other appropriate chapters. The listing of the Church of Christ Scientist and New Age Christian groups in the metaphysical chapter, the development of a separate chapter for the Church of Jesus Christ of Latter-day Saints (and related Mormon groups), and placement of the Unitarian Universalist Association in the Unclassified chapter should not be taken as either an indication of the group's self-image or a decision on this compiler's part concerning their relation to the Christian faith. Rather, it is an indication of their present observed status within the religious community.

It should also be noted that the Unclassified chapter contains a wide variety of groups from the old and well-known Unitarian Universalist Association to religious traditions which have immigrated here from other countries but have not as yet grown sufficiently to warrant a separate chapter (Zoroastrianism), to groups which have a unique (and hence minority) religious perspective (Satanism). Their inclusion in this final chapter implies no value judgment about either their legitimacy or their relationship to each other, merely their position as not easily fitting into the larger religious communities.

Each chapter contains three divisions. First, any intrafaith organizations that attempt to work with a variety of groups within a religious family are listed. Second, each individual denomination or group is presented. A final section lists the periodicals serving the community. Several of the family groupings have not as yet developed any ecumenical intrafaith organizations.

Each entry for a group contains its name, address, and where known, telephone, fax, and cable numbers. In cases in which the

American group is an outpost or mission of an international organization whose continental or international headquarters are elsewhere, we have attempted to list those foreign headquarters addresses. A short text to each entry briefly identifies it. Most of these groups are covered in more depth in the *Encyclopedia of American Religions* (Gale, 1989) and it is suggested that the reader who wishes more information about any particular group consult the third edition of the *Encyclopedia*.

Bibliography

The sources for this *Directory* have been quite varied. While the files of the Institute for the Study of American Religion, especially material received from direct contact with the different religious groups, have been the main source consulted, we have made reference to a number of published sources to double check data, assist in locating new groups, and track down known groups which have moved. A list of the major published sources is given in the bibliographical section at the end of the text.

Indexing

At the end of this volume is a comprehensive alphabetical listing of all the religious groups mentioned in the *Directory*. Alternate names used by some religions are included in the index to assist the user in locating a particular group.

Future Editions

The dynamic nature of American religion requires that a directory such as this one be constantly updated. New groups regularly appear as old groups go out of existence. It is expected that a new edition will thus be required at least every two years, if not annually. For future editions, the staff of the Institute for the Study of American Religion earnestly desires any information on groups not listed below and corrections/updating of information on groups which are included in this edition. We also encourage any suggestions for improvement of this volume. Please write the author at the Institute:

J. Gordon Melton, Director
Institute for the Study of American Religion
Box 90709
Santa Barbara, California 93190-0709

Acknowledgments

The compiling of this *Directory* would not have been possible without the effort of a number of people. The most important has been Ms. Isotta Poggi, an executive member of the Institute's staff who became the primary assistant in putting this edition together. She has been the key person at every stage from initial keying of entries to proofreading of the final product. Additionally, Michael Koszegi and Suzette Melton worked on various stages of the *Directory*'s production.

Over the years literally hundreds of people from across the country have provided the information which has been compiled into *Religious Bodies in the United States*. Without the constant input of data, such a *Directory* would have been impossible. I want to thank each one who contributed, especially staff people who work for the various religious groups which have answered letters requesting information.

J. Gordon Melton
Santa Barbara, California
August 1991

RELIGIOUS BODIES
IN THE UNITED STATES:
A DIRECTORY

INTERFAITH ORGANIZATIONS

Recognition of the pluralistic religious environment which has emerged in the United States in the decades since World War II has led to the formation of numerous interfaith groups. In the last twenty-five years the older Jewish-Christian dialogue in the United States has been joined by interfaith organizations that limit their task to two or three specific faith communities, as well as some that operate across the broad spectrum of the American religious community.

The list below includes known interfaith groups which operate beyond the reach of a single metropolitan community. There are, of course, many urban centers now hosting interfaith councils, the most well-known being the Berkeley (California) Interfaith Council, but these are beyond the scope of this *Directory*. Also not included in this list are the numerous interfaith offices of the individual churches and religious organizations which have responsibility for their formal contacts with other religions.

American Forum for Jewish-Christian Cooperation
The Forum was founded in 1980 by Rabbi David Z. Ben-Ami to build bridges between the Jews and Christians.

Hq: 1407 Montfort Drive, Windsor Farms, Harrisburg, PA 17110
Tel: (717) 236 0437

American Institute for the Study of Racial and Religious Cooperation
The Institute was founded by Irvin J. Borowsky to work for interreligious and interracial harmony especially between Christians and Jews.

Hq: North American Building, 401 N. Broad Street, Philadelphia, PA 19180
Tel: (215) 238 5307

Associates for Religion and Intellectual Life
ARIL is composed of Jewish and Christian scholars in dialogue.

Hq: c/o Dir. Harold B. Whiteman, College of New Rochelle, New Rochelle, NY 10801
Tel: (914) 632 8852

Centennial Parliament of Religions

Sponsored by the Leyden Tolerants Church, the Parliament is planning a 1993 celebration of the centennial of the first Parliament of the World's Religions for the West Coast of the United States.

Hq: c/o Coordinator Rev. William E. Swailes, Box 1525, Bellevue, WA 98009

Tel: (206) 455 1816

Center for Religious Experience and Study

Hq: Box 4165, Overland Park, KS 66204

Tel: (913) 649 5114

Coalition for Religious Freedom, U.S.A.

The Coalition works on behalf of the religious rights of individuals and religious groups.

Hq: c/o Dir. of Communications Dr. Kathleen Masters, 325 Pennsylvania Avenue, Suite 225, Washington, D.C. 20003

Tel: (202) 544 5160

Council for the World's Religions

The Council was founded in 1984 by a network of scholars who had come to know each other through the various programs sponsored by the Unification Church.

Hq: c/o Dr. Frank Kaufman, JAF Box 2347, New York, NY 10116

Tel: (212) 695 0446

Fax: (212) 244 6739

Telex: 4991393 NWERA

or

481 Eighth Avenue, New York, NY 10001

Tel: (212) 695 0446

Council on Religion and International Affairs

Hq: Mr. R. J. Meyers, 170 East 64th Street, New York, NY 10021

Embrace Foundation

The Embrace Foundation was founded in 1980 to create better understanding between different religious and cultural groups.

Hq: Pres. Ajata N. Sharma, 16 West 22nd Street, New York, NY 10010

Tel: (212) 675 4500

Fellowship in Prayer

The Fellowship in Prayer was founded in 1949 with a basic belief that prayer is a common reality, and hence a uniting bond, among people of all religions.

Hq: c/o Pres. Mr. Paul Walsh, Franklin Office Park, 134 Franklin Corner Road, Lawrenceville, NJ 08648

Tel: (609) 896 3636

Global Congress of the World's Religions

The Global Congress of the World's Religions was founded in 1980 by a network of scholars who had been brought together through the efforts of the Unification Church. See also the entry on the Council for the World's Religions.

Hq: c/o Exec. Sec. Dr. Henry O. Thompson, 7 University Mews, Philadelphia, PA 19104

Tel: (215) 747 2526

or

c/o Pres. Sri Radhnakrishna, Unification Theological Seminary, 10 Dock Road, Barrytown, NY 12507

Tel: (914) 758 6881

Hope Center for Interfaith Understanding

The Center founded by Sister Dr. Marie Goldstein holds dialogues between Christians, Jews and Muslims. The North American branch is led by William Goldstein.

Hq: 177 Southern Boulevard, Danbury, CT 16810
or
International Hq: P. O. Box 491, Bethlehem, Israel

Interfaith Inc.,

The Interfaith Inc. was founded in the early 1970s by Rabbi Dr. Joseph H. Gelberman of the Little Synagogue in New York City. It sponsors interfaith gatherings and a school for training ministers and rabbis in a nonsectarian environment.

Hq: 7 West 96th Street, Suite 19B, New York, NY 10025
Tel: (212) 866 3795

Interfaith Movement

Hq: Pres. Mr. Maurice Blond, 45 East 33rd Street, New York, NY 10016

International Association for Religious Freedom

The Association was founded in 1900 as "The International Council of Unitarians and other Liberal Religious Thinkers and Workers." It promotes the idea of a society of religious communities that recognize and cooperate with each other.

Hq: U.S. Chapter/IARF, 1880 Hemlock Circle, Abington, PA 19001-4706
Tel: (215) 576 1884
or

International Hq: Dreiechstrasse 59, D-6000 Frankfurt 70, Germany

International Council of Religions

The International Council of Religions was founded by Baron William von Blomberg.

Hq: c/o Rt. Rev. J. Stuart Wetmore, Synod House, 1047 Amsterdam Avenue, New York, NY 10025
Tel: (212) 316 7414

Middle East Dialogue Group

The Middle East Dialogue Group, founded in 1981, is a working group of Jewish, Christian, and Muslim background that has created various initiatives for peace in the Middle East, especially as they relate to the conflicts between Israel and the Palestinians.

Hq: c/o T. William Hall, Dept. of Religion, Syracuse University, Syracuse, NY 13201
Tel: (315) 423 3861

National Conference of Christians and Jews

One of the oldest interfaith organizations in the United States, the National Conference was founded in 1928.

Hq: c/o Pres. Dr. Jacqueline G. Wexler, Suite 1100, 71 Fifth Avenue, New York, NY 10003
Tel: (212) 206 0006

National Ecumenical Coalition, U.S.A. (NEC)

The National Ecumenical Coalition, founded in 1976, is an association of different religious groups that work internationally for the civil rights of people of all countries.

Hq: c/o Chairman Rev. Mgr. William E. Hibbs, P. O. Box 3554, Georgetown Station, Washington, D.C.
Tel: (703) 524 4503
or
2059 North Woodstock Street, Suite 305, Arlington, VA

National Workshops on Christian-Jewish Relations

The National Workshops on Christian-Jewish Relations are held every few years and bring together a wide range of speakers on contemporary issues.

Hq: 915 Chemical Building, 721 Olive Street, St. Louis, MO 63101

New Ecumenical Research Association, Inc. (New ERA)

The New Ecumenical Research Association was founded in 1980 by a network of scholars who had originally been brought together through the programs sponsored by the Unification Church. See also the entry on the Council for the World's Religions.

Hq: c/o Exec. Dir. Dr. Jonathan Wells, 481 Eighth Avenue, New York, NY 10001
Tel: (212) 695 0446

North American Interfaith Network Project

The North American Interfaith Network Project was founded in 1960 by Judith Hollister with the goal of establishing interfaith networks throughout North America.

Hq: c/o Dir. Mr. Dan Anderson, Temple of Understanding, 1047 Amsterdam Avenue at 112th Street, New York, NY 10025
Tel: (212) 865 9117

Office of Christian-Muslim Concerns

This major structure for Muslim-Christian dialogue is jointly sponsored by the National Council of Churches of Christ and the Duncan Black MacDonald Center for the Study of Islam and Christian-Muslim Religions at Hartford Seminary.

Hq: Hartford Seminary, 77 Sherman Street, Hartford, CT 06105
Tel: (203) 232 4451

Religious Liberty Association of America

The Association is sponsored by the Seventh-day Adventist Church.

Hq: 6840 Eastern Avenue N.W., Washington, D.C. 20012
Tel: (202) 722 6000

Religious Youth Service

The Religious Youth Service was founded in 1985 and grew out of previous interfaith work sponsored by the Unification Church. See also the entry on the Council for the World's Religions.

Hq: Project Dir. Mr. Gary Young, JAF Box 2347, New York, NY 10116
Tel: (212) 695 0446
Fax: (212) 244 6739

Summit: A Forum for Inter-Religious Dialogue

The Summit: A Forum for Inter-Religious Dialogue was founded in 1984 by Rabbi Rami M. Shapiro with the aim of promoting the evolution of human spirituality through inter-religious dialogue.

Hq: P. O. Box 160081, Miami, FL 33116
Tel: (305) 596 4523

World Conference on Religion and Peace

The World Conference on Religion and Peace was founded in 1970 with an activist interfaith constituency who work for peace and human dignity.

Hq: Assistant Sec. Gen. Dr. William Thompson, 12th Floor, 777 United Nations Plaza, New York, NY 10017
Tel: (212) 687 2163
   or
International Hq: c/o Sec. Gen. Dr. John B. Taylor, 14 Chemin Auguste-Vilbert, 1218 Grand Saconnex, Geneva, Switzerland
Tel: (022) 985 162

World Fellowship of Religions

Founded in the 1950s in India by Jain leader H. H. Acharya Sushil Kumarji Maharaj, the Fellowship pro-motes peace, just human relationships, and understanding among peoples.

Hq: c/o Siddhachalam, RD 4, Box 374, Mud Pond Road, Blairstown, NJ 07825
   or
International Hq: c-599 Chetna Marg, New Delhi, India

World Parliament of Religions-Centenary Celebration Planning Group

The Group is planning a centennial program in recognition of the first World's Parliament of Religions in Chicago in 1893.

Hq: Dr. Gene Reeves, 5701 South Woodlawn Avenue, Chicago, IL 60637
Tel: (312) 753 0892

CHRISTIANITY

INTRAFAITH ORGANIZATIONS

Listed below are international, continental, and national Christian ecumenical organizations in which American churches participate. Some are traditional family groupings in which, for example, American Baptists will participate with Baptists around the world in creating the Baptist World Alliance. Others, such as the World Council of Churches, draw members from across denominational family lines. The spectrum of American Protestantism is represented in the National Council of Churches (liberal Protestantism), National Association of Evangelicals (Evangelicalism), and American Council of Christian Churches (separatist Fundamentalism).

Alliance World Fellowship

The Alliance World Fellowship was founded in 1975 to provide a worldwide network for churches which originated in the missionary activity of the Christian and Missionary Alliance.

Hq: 350 North Highland Avenue, Nyack, NY 10960
Tel: (914) 353 0750

American Council of Christian Churches

The American Council of Christian Churches was founded in 1941 as a fellowship of fundamentalist Protestant Christian denominations. It is a member of the Council of Bible Believing Churches International.

Hq: c/o Executive Secretary: B. Robert Biscoe, P. O. Box 816, Valley Forge, PA 19482
Tel: (215) 566 8154

Anglican Consultative Council

The Anglican Consultative Council is the coordinating body and service agency for the leadership of the churches of the worldwide Anglican Communion, i.e., those churches historically connected and in communion with the Church of England. In the United States, the Episcopal Church is the primary member.

International Hq: The Archbishop of Canterbury, London, SE1 7JU, England
Tel: (01) 222 2851/2

9

Associated Gospel Churches

The Associated Gospel Churches, founded in 1939, has served as a networking organization for conservative fundamentalist churches and includes among its duties the representation of its associated denominations with the chaplains' offices in the armed forces.

Hq: c/o Pres. Col. H. P. Kissinger, 3209 Norfolk Street, Hopewell, VA 23860
Tel: (804) 541 2879

Baptist World Alliance

The Baptist World Alliance, founded in 1905, is an international network of Baptist conventions and unions.

Hq: 6733 Curran Street, McLean, VA 22101
Tel: (703) 790 8980

Christian Holiness Association

The Christian Holiness Association grew out of the former National Camp Meeting Association for the Promotion of Holiness founded in 1867. It includes a number of holiness bodies and congregations among its members.

Hq: CHA Center, S. Walnut Street, Box 100, Wilmore, KY 40380
Tel: (606) 858 3581

Consultation on Church Union

The Consultation on Church Union was founded in 1962 and has worked toward an organic union of a number of liberal Protestant churches.

Hq: c/o Gen. Sec. Dr. David W. A. Taylor, Research Park, 151 Wall Street, Princeton, NJ 08540
Tel: (609) 921 7866

Council of Bible Believing Churches International (CBBC)

The CBBC was founded in 1987 in the United States. It is an international organization related to the American Council of Christian Churches.

Hq: P. O. Box 816, Valley Forge, PA 19482
Tel: (215) 566 8154

Friends World Committee for Consultation

The Committee, founded in 1937, provides a network for the various branches of the Society of Friends. There is an American, European, and African Section.

Hq: 1506 Race St., Philadelphia, PA 19102
Tel: (215) 241 7250

International Council of Christian Churches

The ICCC was founded in 1948. Originally connected to the American Council of Christian Churches, it broke that connection in 1969 when the ACCC dropped the council's founder Rev. Carl McIntire from its board.

Hq: c/o Sec. Suzanne L. DiCanio, 756 Haddon Avenue, Collingswood, NJ 08108
Tel: (609) 854 8464

Lutheran World Federation

The Lutheran World Federation was founded in 1947 as the successor to the Lutheran World Convention, an international Lutheran organization founded in 1923. The Federation first turned its attention to the problems left by the end of World War II and has remained to foster

Lutheran cooperation worldwide. International headquarters are located in the World Council of Churches building in Geneva.

Hq: c/o Gen. Sec. Mr. Harold T. Hanson, Office of Ecumenical Affairs - Evangelical Lutheran Church in America - U.S. National Committee, 8765 W. Higgins Rd., Chicago, IL 60631
Tel: (312) 380 2700
or
International Hq: 150 Route de Ferney, 1211 Geneva 20, Switzerland

Mennonite World Conference

The Mennonite World Conference gathers periodically to provide fellowship and a forum for dialogue among the Mennonite churches of the world.

Hq: c/o Pres. Ross T. Bender, 11480 W. Virginia Avenue, Lakewood, CO 80226.
Tel: (312) 690 9666

National Association of Evangelicals

The National Association of Evangelicals was founded in 1942 as a fellowship of conservative Evangelical churches.

Hq: 450 Gundersen Dr., Carol Stream, IL 60188
Tel: (312) 665 0500

National Council of the Churches of Christ in the United States of America

The National Council of Churches was founded in 1950 as a successor to the Federal Council of Churches, which had been created at the beginning of the twentieth century, and several other ecumenical agencies. It's membership consists of both Protestant and Orthodox churches.

Hq: c/o Pres. Rev. Patricia A. McClurg, 465 Riverside Dr., New York, NY 10115
Tel: (212) 870 2200

North American Baptist Fellowship

The North American Baptist Fellowship, founded in 1964, is a fellowship of American, Canadian, and Mexican Baptist conventions and unions.

Hq: c/o Pres. Pastor Dr. V. Simpson Turner, 6733 Curran St., McClean, VA 22101
Tel: (703) 790 8980
or
Mt. Carmel Baptist Church, 714 Quincy Street, Brooklyn, NY 11221
Tel: (718) 452 3500

Pentecostal Fellowship of North America

The Pentecostal Fellowship of North America was founded in 1948, following the first Pentecostal World Conference.

Hq: c/o Chairperson G. Raymond Carlson, 1445 Boonville Ave., Springfield, MO 65802
Tel: (417) 862 2781

Pentecostal World Conference

The Pentecostal World Conference was founded in 1947 as an international network and fellowship association for Pentecostal churches.

Hq: P. O. Box 904 HSJ, Springfield, MO 65801
Tel: (417) 862 2781

Standing Conference of Canonical Orthodox Bishops in the Americas

The Standing Conference of Canonical Orthodox Bishops in the Americas was founded in 1960 and includes those bishops in communion with the ancient Orthodox Patriarchates in Europe and the Middle East.

Hq: c/o Sec. V. Rev. R. W. Schneirla, 8-10 East 79th Street, New York, NY 10021
Tel: (212) 628 2500

World Alliance of Reformed Churches (Presbyterian and Congregational)

The World Alliance was founded in 1970 as a network of Reformed, Presbyterian, and Congregational churches worldwide. Its international offices are located in the World Council of Churches building in Geneva.

Hq: c/o Chpsn. Rev. R. Stanley Wood, 226 Church St. NW, Huntsville, AL 35801
or
Rev. James E. Andrews, North American Secretary, 100 Witherspoon St., Louisville, KY 40202
Tel: (215) 627 1852
or
International Hq: 150 route de Ferney, 1211 Geneva 20, Switzerland

World Council of Churches

The World Council of Churches was founded in 1948 but was an outgrowth of many decades of ecumenical dialog and cooperative activity. Its membership includes both Protestant and Orthodox churches from every continent.

Hq: c/o Gen. Sec. Emilio Castro, 475 Riverside Dr., Rm. 1062, New York, NY 10115
Tel: (212) 870 2533
or
777 United Nations Plaza, New York, NY 10117
Tel: (212) 867 5890
or
International Hq: 150 Route de Ferney, (P. O. Box 66), 1211 Geneva 20, Switzerland

World Evangelical Fellowship

The World Evangelical Fellowship, founded in 1951, actually began in Great Britain in 1846 as the Evangelical Alliance. As the Alliance grew internationally, national organizations were formed. These national organizations created the World Fellowship.

Hq: P. O. Box WEF, Wheaton, IL 60189
Tel: (312) 668 0440
or
International Hq: c/o Dir. Dr. David M. Howard, 1 Sophia Road, 07-09 Peace Centre, Singapore 0922

World Methodist Council

The World Methodist Council grew out of the Ecumenical Methodists Conferences which began to meet every ten years in 1881. The Council was formally established in 1951.

Hq: c/o Gen. Sec. Dr. Joe Hale, P. O. Box 518, Lake Junaluska, NC 28745
Tel: (405) 456 9432

CHRISTIAN CHURCHES

The largest number of religious groups in the United States are Christian, and the larger Christian bodies (Baptist, Catholic, Congregational, Episcopal, Methodist, Lutheran, Orthodox, Presbyterian, and Reformed) essentially represent mainstream religion in America. Included below are those church bodies which fall within the major traditional denominational families of Christianity. They share a broad agreement on basic doctrines, including the authority of the Bible, though each group might dissent on one or two particular issues. Their practices vary widely, especially in worship style and organization.

This chapter does not include those churches which, while drawing heavily on Christian traditions and symbols, have significantly reinterpreted them to the point that their relation to the larger Christian community is somewhat ambiguous, and hence the major Christian Church groups have not recognized them as a part of the tradition. Thus groups related to the Church of Jesus Christ of Latter-day Saints, the Church of Christ, Scientist, the Liberal Catholic Church, and the various New Thought and New Age churches which affirm their Christian roots will be found in other chapters in this directory.

Advent Christian Church

The Advent Christian Church is one of several churches which grew out of the Adventist movement initiated by William Miller in the 1840s and which adheres to Sunday (rather than Saturday) worship. The church was formally organized in 1860.

Hq: c/o Exec. Vice-Pres. David H. Northup, Box 23152, Charlotte, NC 28212
Tel: (704) 545 6161

African-American Catholic Congregation

The African-American Catholic Congregation was founded in 1990 by Most Rev. George Augustus Stallings, a former priest in the Roman Catholic Church.

Hq: Pro-Cathedral of Our Lady of Africa, 1134 Third Street N.E., Washington, D.C.
Tel: (202) 371 0800
Fax: (202) 371 0808

13

African Methodist Episcopal Church

The African Methodist Episcopal Church was founded in 1787 by Rev. Richard Allen and former members of the Methodist Episcopal Church.

Hq: 500 8th Avenue, S., Nashville, TN 37203
Tel: (615) 242 6814 or 242 1420

African Methodist Episcopal Zion Church

The African Methodist Episcopal Zion Church was founded in 1796 by former members of the Methodist Episcopal Church.

Hq: Box 23843, Charlotte, NC 28232
Tel: (704) 332 3851

African Orthodox Church

The African Orthodox Church was founded in 1921 by Bishop George A. McGuire.

Hq: Rt. Rev. James A. Ford, 137 Allston Street, Cambridge, MA 02139

African Orthodox Church of the West

The African Orthodox Church of the West was founded in 1984 by Most Rev. D. Duncan Hinkson, formerly a bishop with the African Orthodox Church.

Hq: St. Augustine's African Orthodox Church, 5831 Indiana Street, Chicago, IL 60637
Tel: (312) 324 1096

African Union First Colored Methodist Protestant Church

The African Union First Colored Methodist Protestant Church is a predominantly black church founded in 1913 by Peter Spencer and William Anderson.

Hq: 2611 N. Claymont Street, Wilmington, DE 19802

African Universal Church

The African Universal Church was founded in 1927 by Archbishop Clarence A. Addison.

Hq: Hollywood, FL

Alaska Yearly Meeting

The Alaska Yearly Meeting of the Society of Friends was founded in 1982.

Hq: Walter E. Outwater, Box 687, Kotzebue, AK 99752
Tel: (907) 442 3906

Albanian Orthodox Archdiocese of America

The Albanian Orthodox Archdiocese of America dates to the arrival of Albanian Christians in the United States early in this century. The Archdiocese was organized in the 1930s. It became independent after Albania fell under Communist rule.

Hq: Metropolitan Theodosius, 529 E. Broadway, Boston, MA 02127
Tel: (617) 268 1275

Albanian Orthodox Diocese of America

The Albanian Orthodox Diocese was organized in 1905 by His Grace Mark I. Lipa. The church is in communion with the ecumenical Patriarchate, and its leadership participates in the Standing Conference of Canonical Orthodox Bishops in America.

Christian Churches 15

Hq: c/o Vicar Gen. Rev. Ik. Ilia Katre,
270 Cabot Street, Newton, MA
02160
Tel: (617) 731 3500

All Faiths Ecumenical Diocese of the South and Southwest
The Diocese is a small independent Catholic jurisdiction.

Hq: c/o Mt. Rev. Leo E. Rondeau,
1204-1206 House St., El Paso,
TX 79903

Allegheny Wesleyan Methodist Connection (Original Allegheny Conference)
The Allegheny Wesleyan Methodist Connection was founded in 1968 by H. C. Van Wormer, T. A. Robertson, J. N. Markey, F. E. Mansell, and members of the Wesleyan Methodist Church who rejected its merger with the Pilgrim Holiness Church.

Hq: c/o Pres. Rev. John B. Durfee,
1827 Allen Dr., Salem, OH
44460

Alpha and Omega Christian Church
The Alpha and Omega Christian Church is a Pentecostal church founded in 1962 by Alezandro B. Faquaragon.

Hq: 96-171 Kamahamaha Hwy., Pearl
City, HI 96782

Alpha and Omega Pentecostal Church of God of America, Inc.
The Alpha and Omega Pentecostal Church of God of America is a predominantly black Pentecostal church founded in 1945 by Rev. Magdalene Mabe Phillips.

Hq: 3023 Clifton Avenue, Baltimore,
MD 21216
Tel: (301) 462 6959 or 366 2253

Amana Church Society (Church of True Inspiration)
The Amana Church Society (Church of True Inspiration) was founded in 1714 by Eberhard Ludwig Gruber and John Friedrich Rock.

Hq: c/o Pres. Charles L. Selzer,
Homestead, IA 52236

American Association of Lutheran Churches
The American Association of Lutheran Churches was formed by conservative Lutheran ministers and lay people who did not wish to participate in the merger which created the Evangelical Lutheran Church in America in 1988.

Hq: c/o Dr. Dwane R. Lindberg,
Presiding Pastor, 611 1/2 West
5th St., Waterloo, IA 50702
Tel: (319) 232 3971
or
Hq: P. O. Box 17097, Minneapolis, MN
55417
Tel: (612) 623 3611

American Baptist Association
The American Baptist Association grew out of the "landmark" movement among Southern Baptists in the 1850s. The movement, which emphasized the role of the local church, was led by James R. Graves and J. M. Pendleton. A merger of two landmark associations in 1924 created the American Baptist Association.

Hq: 4605 N. State Line Avenue,
Texarkana, TX 75501
Tel: (214) 792 2783

American Baptist Churches in the U.S.A.

The American Baptist Churches in the U.S.A. continue the oldest organization of Baptists in the United States. Having existed under various names, the present name was adopted in 1972.

Hq: c/o Pres. Harold Davis, P. O. Box 851, Valley Forge, PA 19482
Tel: (215) 768 2000

American Carpatho-Russian Orthodox Greek Catholic Church

This church was founded in 1938 by former members of the Roman Catholic church who returned to Eastern Orthodoxy under the leadership of Bishop Orestes P. Chornock.

Hq: c/o Rt. Rev. Nicolas Smisko, 312 Garfield Street, Johnstown, PA 15906
Tel: (814) 536 4207

American Catholic Church of Antioch

The American Catholic Church is a small independent Catholic jurisdiction.

Hq: c/o Rt. Rev. Leonard I. Bacon, P.O. Box 21674, Long Beach, CA 90802

American Catholic Church— Old Catholic

The American Catholic Church— Old Catholic was founded in 1990 by Bishop E. Paul Raible.

Hq: c/o Pastor Fr. Peter E. Hickman, St. Matthew Old Catholic Church, 2207 W. Orangewood Avenue, Orange, CA 92668
Tel: (714) 385 1007

American Catholic Church (Syro-Antiochean)

The American Catholic Church (Syro-Antiochean) was founded during the 1940s by Ernest Leopold Peterson.

Hq: Current address unavailable for this edition

American Coalition of Unregistered Churches

The American Coalition of Unregistered Churches is an informal network of fundamentalist Christian churches.

Hq: 2560 Sylvan Rd., East Point, GA 30344

American Eastern Orthodox Catholic Church

The American Eastern Orthodox Church is a small liturgical jurisdiction operating in southern California.

Hq: c/o Most Rev. Martin De Porres, 103 Camino Algarve, Camarillo, CA 93010

American Episcopal Church

The American Episcopal Church was founded in 1968 by Indian bishop James Charles Ryan (K. C. Pillai) and former priests and members of the Episcopal Church.

Hq: 155 Riverbend Dr. #4, Charlottesville, VA 22901

American Episcopal Diocese, South

The American Episcopal Diocese, South was formed by congregations under the leadership of Bishop Frank H. Benning who withdrew from the American Episcopal Church.

Hq: Rt. Rev. Frank H. Benning, P. O.
Box 52702, Atlanta, GA 30355

American Evangelical Christian Churches

The American Evangelical Christian Churches is an independent evangelical fellowship founded in 1944.

Hq: c/o Moderator Dr. G. W. Hyatt, Waterfront Dr., Pineland, FL 33945
Tel: (813) 283 0519

American Evangelistic Association

The American Evangelistic Association is a Pentecostal fellowship founded in 1954 by Rev. John E. Douglas. It sponsors a global missionary program, World Evangelism.

Hq: c/o World Evangelism, Box 660800, Dallas, TX 75266
Tel: (214) 942 1678

American Hebrew Eastern Orthodox Greek Catholic Church

The American Hebrew Eastern Orthodox Greek Catholic Church was founded by its bishop, the Rt. Rev. Gregory David Michael Voris.

Hq: Address unavailable for this edition

American Indian Evangelical Church

The American Indian Evangelical Church is a Pentecostal church founded in 1945 as the American Indian Mission.

Hq: c/o Pres. Iver C. Grover, Box 25019, Minneapolis, MN 55440-6019
Tel: (612) 522 6018

American Mission for Opening Churches

The American Mission for Opening Churches is a fundamentalist group founded in 1943 dedicated to acquiring abandoned church buildings and starting new congregations.

Hq: 6419 E. Lake Road, Olcott, NY 14126
Tel: (716) 778 8568

American Orthodox Catholic Church

Previously known as the Church of God in the Lord Jesus Christ, the American Orthodox Catholic Church is a liturgical body which has absorbed some emphases from Pentecostalism.

Hq: c/o Bishop Steven A. Kochones, 810 E. Walnut Street, Pasadena, CA 91101
Tel: (213) 681 2168 or 356 9144

American Orthodox Catholic Church (Irene)

The American Orthodox Catholic Church (Irene) was founded in 1962. The Archbishop is Irene and Bishop Emeritus is Most Rev. Milton A. Pritts.

Hq: 851 Leyden Street, Denver, CO 80220

American Orthodox Catholic Church (Propheta)

The American Orthodox Catholic Church (Propheta) was founded in 1965 by Archbishop Walter A. Propheta (1912-1972).

Hq: Most Rev. Dom Lorenzo, O.S.B., Holy Trinity Monastery, P. O. Box 323, Shirley, NY 11967
or

God's Benevolence Institute, c/o Rt.
Rev. Patrick McReynolds, E.
628 Everett, Spokane, WA
99207
Tel: (509) 487 1390

American Orthodox Catholic Church-Western Rite Mission, Diocese of New York

The Diocese of New York was founded in 1976 by Most Rev. Joseph J. Raffaele.

Hq: 318 Expressway Dr. S., Medford, NY 11763
Tel: (516) 475 0605

American Orthodox Church

The American Orthodox Church was founded in 1981 by Archbishop Aftimios Harold Donovan.

International Hq: San Antonio, Los Vanos, Laguna 3732, Philippines

American Orthodox Exarchate: Archdiocese of North America

The American Orthodox Exarchate was founded by Mt. Rev. Donald L. Locke, formerly with the Western Orthodox Church under Mt. Rev. James L. Mondok. Around 1990 he left to establish the Exarchate.

Hq: Mt. Rev. Donald L. Locke, P. O. Box 5374, Youngstown, OH 44504

American Prelature

The American Prelature (formerly the Old Roman Catholic Church) is a liturgical church founded in 1941 by Archbishop Richard A. Marchenna.

Hq: Most Rev. Derek Lang, 2103 S. Portland Street, Los Angeles, CA 90007

American Rescue Workers

The American Rescue Workers was founded in 1884 by Thomas E. Moore and former members of the Salvation Army.

Hq: c/o Commander in Chief Gen. Paul E. Martin, 2827 Frankford Avenue, Philadelphia, PA 19134
Tel: (215) 739 6524

American World Patriarchs

The American World Patriarchs is an Eastern liturgical church founded in 1967 by Uladyslau Ryzy-Ryski.

Hq: Most Rev. Emigidius J. Ryzy, 19 Aqueduct Street, Ossining, NY 10562

Anchor Bay Evangelistic Association

The Anchor Bay Evangelistic Association was founded in 1940 by Roy John and Blanche Turner.

Hq: Box 188, New Baltimore, MI 48047

Ancient Tridentine Catholic Church

The Ancient Tridentine Catholic Church was founded in 1983 by Most Rev. Thadeus B. J. Alioto.

Hq: P. O. Box 26414, San Francisco, CA 94126
Tel: (416) 751 0066 or 585 2404

Anglican Catholic Church

The Anglican Catholic Church was founded in 1979 by former members of the Episcopal Church.

Hq: c/o First Bishop Most Rev. Louis W. Falk, 4807 Aspen Dr., West Des Moines, IA 50265
Tel: (515) 223 1591

Anglican Church of North America

The Anglican Church of North America dates to the formation of the Independent Anglican Church in the 1930s in Canada. Over the years it passed through several alternations, which included name changes, before emerging in the 1980s as the North American Episcopal Church. It adopted its present name in 1984.

Hq: c/o Bishop Rt. Rev. Robert T. Shepherd, Chapel of St. Augustine of Canterbury, 1906 Forest Green Dr., N.E., Atlanta, GA 30329
Tel: (404) 634 2939

Anglican Episcopal Church of North America

The Anglican Episcopal Church of North America was founded in 1972 by Walter Hollis Adams and other former members of the Episcopal Church.

Hq: Most Rev. Walter Hollis Adams, 789 Allen Ct., Palo Alto, CA 94303
Tel: (415) 493 2927

Anglican Orthodox Church

The Anglican Orthodox Church was founded in 1963 by Most Rev. James P. Dees (d. 1990), a former priest in the Episcopal Church.

Hq: 323 E. Walnut Street, P. O. Box 128, Statesville, NC 28677
Tel: (704) 873 8365

Anglican Rite Jurisdiction

The Anglican Rite Jurisdiction was founded in 1989 by Bishops Larry lee Shaver, formerly a bishop of the Holy Catholic Church, Anglican Rite Jurisdiction of the Americas, along with David Marion Davis, and William Thompson.

Hq: c/o Rt. Rev. Larry Lee Shaver, 195 East 68th Place, Merrillville, IN 46410

Anglo-Catholic Church in America

The Anglo-Catholic Church is a small liturgical jurisdiction.

Hq: Rt. Rev. Arthur J. Threipland Erazo, 1439 E. St., Napa, CA 49559

Anglo-Saxon Federation of America

The Anglo-Saxon Federation of America was founded in 1928 by Howard B. Rand.

Hq: Box 177, Merrimac, MA 01860

Antiochian Orthodox Christian Archdiocese of North America

The Antiochian Orthodox Christian Archdiocese of North America dates to the beginning of an Orthodox mission among Arab-American Christians by the Russian Orthodox Church in 1892. The Mission became independent in 1925.

Hq: c/o Primate Metropolitan Philip Saliba, 358 Mountain Road, Englewood, NJ 07631
Tel: (201) 871 1355

Apostolic Assemblies of Christ, Inc.

The Apostolic Assemblies of Christ, Inc., a predominantly black Oneness Pentecostal church, was founded in 1970 by Bishop G. N. Boone, formerly with the Pentecostal Churches of the Apostolic Faith.

Hq: Current address unavailable for this edition

Apostolic Catholic Assyrian Church of the East, North American Diocese

The Church of the East, the ancient Christian Church of Iran, was organized in America in 1940.

Eastern Hq: c/o Bishop His Grace Mar Aprim Khamis, 890 Birch Avenue, Morton Grove, IL 60053
Tel: (312) 966 0009
or
Western Hq: c/o Bishop His Grace Mar Bawai, P. O. Box 32035, San Jose, CA 95152
Tel: (408) 923 1752
or
International Hq: c/o Patriarch H.H. Mar Dinkha IV, Box 3257, Sadoun, Baghdad, Iraq

Apostolic Catholic Church of the Americas

The Apostolic Catholic Church of the Americas was founded in 1976 by Bishops Robert S. Zeiger and Gordon DaCosta.

Hq: Most Rev. C. F. Quinn Jr., Archbishop Primate, 4201 Fairmont, Dallas, TX 75219
Tel: (214) 526 7529

Apostolic Christian Church (Nazarean)

The Apostolic Christian Church (Nazarean) was founded in 1906/7 by former members of the Apostolic Christian Churches of America.

Hq: c/o Gen. Sec. Eugene R. Galat, Apostolic Christian Church Foundation, P. O. Box 151, Tremont, IL 61568
Tel: (309) 925 5162

Apostolic Christian Churches, International

The Apostolic Christian Churches, International is an independent fellowship.

Hq: P. O. Box 3966, Florence, SC 29502

Apostolic Christian Churches of America

The Apostolic Christian Churches of America is the American branch of the movement founded in the 1830s by former Swiss Reformed minister Samuel Heinrich Froelich.

Hq: Bishop Dale Eisenmann, 6913 Wilmette, Darien, IL 60559
Tel: (312) 969 7021

The Apostolic Church

The Apostolic Church was founded in 1916 by Rev. Daniel Powell Williams, a British minister with the Apostolic Faith Church, one of England's first Pentecostal churches. It came to America in 1924.

Hq: 142 N. 17th Street, Philadelphia, PA 19103
or
International Hq: Bryncwar Road, Penygroes, Llanelli, Dyfed SA14 7PA, Wales, U.K.
Tel: (0269) 842 349

Apostolic Church of Christ

The Apostolic Church of Christ is a predominantly black Oneness Pentecostal church founded in 1969 by Bishop Johnnie Draft and Elder Wallace Snow, both former ministers with the Church of God (Apostolic).

Hq: 2044 Stadium Dr., Winston-Salem, NC 27107
Tel: (919) 788 2539

Apostolic Church of Christ in God

The Apostolic Church of Christ in God is a predominantly black Oneness Pentecostal church organized in 1943. Founders included the Revs. J. W. Audrey, J.C. Richardson, J. Jenkins, W. R. Bryant, and J. M. Williams, all former leaders with the Church of God (Apostolic).

Hq: 1217 E. 15th Street, Winston-Salem, NC 27105
Tel: (919) 722 1032

Apostolic Church of Jesus

The Apostolic Church of Jesus is a Oneness Pentecostal church founded in 1927 by Antonio and George Sanches to work among Spanish-speaking people.

Hq: Current address unavailable for this edition

Apostolic Church of Jesus Christ

The Apostolic Church of Jesus Christ is a Oneness pentecostal church founded by former members of the Pentecostal Assemblies of the World in the 1930s.

Hq: Current address unavailable for this edition

Apostolic Episcopal Church (Holy Eastern Catholic and Orthodox Church)

The Apostolic Episcopal Church (Holy Eastern Catholic and Orthodox Church) is an Old Catholic body founded in 1930 by Arthur Wolfort Brooks, formerly a minister in the Episcopal Church.

Hq: c/o Mt. Rev. Paul Schultz, P. O. Box 6, Glendale, CA 91209
or

International Hq: Archbishop Bertill Persson, P. O. Box 7048, S-17107 Solna, Sweden

Apostolic Faith (Hawaii)

The Apostolic Faith (Hawaii) is a Oneness Pentecostal church founded in 1923 by Rev. Charles and Ada Lochbaum.

Hq: 1043 Middle Street, Honolulu, HI 96819

Apostolic Faith (Kansas)

The Apostolic Faith (Kansas) is the original Pentecostal church founded at the beginning of this century by Rev. Charles Fox Parham, formerly a Methodist minister.

Hq: 1009 Lincoln Avenue, Baxter Springs, KS 66713
Tel: (316) 856 5281

Apostolic Faith Church of America

The Apostolic Faith Church of America is a predominantly black Pentecostal church founded by Bishop Isaac Ryles, formerly a member of the Apostolic Faith Church of God.

Hq: c/o Bishop Isaac Ryles, Fremont, NC 27830
Tel: (919) 242 6208

Apostolic Faith Church of God

The Apostolic Faith Church of God is a predominantly black Pentecostal Church founded in 1909 by Elder Charles W. Lowe. The church was chartered in 1938 and reorganized in 1946. It grew out of the original Apostolic Faith Mission headed by William Seymour in Los Angeles.

Hq: 5211 "A" Street, S.E., Washington, DC 20019

or
841 Griggs Road, Jefferson, Ohio 44047
Tel: (216) 993 8339

Apostolic Faith Church of God and True Holiness

The Apostolic Faith Church of God and True Holiness was founded in 1946 by Bishop Charles W. Lowe, previously the founder of the Apostolic Faith Church of God.

Hq: c/o Bishop O. Key, 825 Gregg Road, Jefferson, OH 44047

Apostolic Faith Church of God Giving Grace

The Apostolic Faith Church of God Giving Grace is a predominantly black Pentecostal church founded in Virginia in the 1960s by Mother Lillie P. Williams and Bishop Rufus A. Easter.

Hq: c/o Bishop Geanie Perry, Rt. 3, Box 111A, Warrenton, NC 17589
Tel: (919) 257 2120

Apostolic Faith Church of God Live On

The Apostolic Faith Church of God Live On is a predominantly black Pentecostal Church founded in Virginia in 1952 by Bishop Jesse Handshaw, formerly a minister with the Apostolic Faith Church of God.

Hq: c/o Bishop Richard Cross, 2300 Trenton Street, Hopewell, VA 23868.

Apostolic Faith Churches of God in Christ

The Apostolic Faith Churches of God in Christ is a predominantly black Oneness Pentecostal church.

Hq: 330 King Street, Hertford, NC 27944

Apostolic Faith Mission Church of God

The Apostolic Faith Mission Church of God is a predominantly black Oneness Pentecostal church founded in 1906 by Bishop F. W. Williams.

Hq: 3344 Pearl Avenue N., Birmingham, AL 36101
or
Bishop Houston Ward, P. O. Box 551, Cantonment, FL 32522
Tel: (904) 587 2332

The Apostolic Faith Mission of Portland, Oregon, Inc.

The Apostolic Faith Mission of Portland, Oregon, is a Pentecostal church founded in 1907 by Mrs. Florence L. Crawford.

Hq: c/o Gen. Overseer Rev. Loyce C. Carver, 6615 S.E. 52nd Avenue, Portland, OR 97206
Tel: (503) 777 1741

Apostolic Gospel Church of Jesus Christ

The Apostolic Gospel Church of Jesus Christ is a predominantly black Oneness Pentecostal church founded in 1963 by Rev. Donald Abernathy.

Hq: Current address unavailable for this edition

Apostolic Holiness Church of America

The Apostolic Holiness Church of America is a predominantly black Pentecostal church founded in 1927 in Mount Olive, North Carolina, by a group of independent ministers and lay people.

Hq: P. O. Box 353, Fremont, NC 27830
Tel: (919) 242 6208

Apostolic Lutheran Church of America

The Apostolic Lutheran Church of America is a Finnish-American church founded in 1872 as the Solomon Korteniemi Lutheran Society. It adopted its present name in 1962.

Hq: c/o Pres. Richard E. Sakrisson, 7606 NE Vancouver Mall Dr. 14, Vancouver, WA 98662

Apostolic Lutherans (Church of the First Born)

The Apostolic Lutherans (Church of the First Born) is one of several branches of the Finnish-American Apostolic Lutheran movement.

International Hq: Gellivara, Finland

Apostolic Lutherans (Evangelicals No. 1)

The Apostolic Lutherans (Evangelicals No. 1), one of several branches of the Finnish-American Apostolic Lutheran Movement, was founded in 1940 under the leadership of Arthur Leopold Heideman.

Hq: Current address unavailable for this edition

Apostolic Lutherans (Evangelicals No. 2)

The Apostolic Lutherans (Evangelicals No. 2) is one branch of the Finnish-American Apostolic Lutheran movement. It was begun in 1940 by members of the Apostolic Lutherans (Evangelicals No. 1).

Hq: Current address unavailable for this edition

Apostolic Lutherans (The Heidemans)

The Apostolic Lutherans (The Heidemans) is one branch of the Finnish-American Apostolic Lutheran movement. It started in 1921-22 under the leadership of Arthur Leopold Heideman.

Hq: Current address unavailable for this edition

Apostolic Lutherans (New Awakening)

The Apostolic Lutherans (New Awakening) is one branch of the Finnish-American Apostolic Lutheran movement originally begun in Finland under the leadership of Lars Levi.

Hq: Current address unavailable for this edition

Apostolic Methodist Church

The Apostolic Methodist Church was founded in 1932 by E. H. Crowson, a former minister of the Methodist Episcopal Church, South.

Hq: Current address unavailable for this edition

Apostolic Old Catholic Church

The Apostolic Old Catholic Church is a small liturgical body centered upon Los Angeles.

Hq: c/o Mt. Rev. Hans B. Kroneberg, 1157 N. Bronson Av., Los Angeles, CA 90038

Apostolic Orthodox Catholic Church

The Apostolic Orthodox Catholic Church was founded in the 1980s by several independent Catholic bishops, most of whom had been members of the Western Orthodox Church in America.

Hq: Most Rev. Charles W. Ingram, Greater Pacific Diocese, P. O. Box 1834, Glendora, CA 91740
Tel: (818) 335 7369

Apostolic Orthodox Old Catholic Church

The Apostolic Orthodox Old Catholic Church is a small independent Catholic jurisdiction founded in 1985 which works primarily among Spanish-speaking peoples.

Hq: c/o Most Rev. Jorge Rodriguez, Presiding Bishop, P. O. Box 879, Chicago, IL 60690

Apostolic Overcoming Holy Church of God, Inc.

The Apostolic Overcoming Holy Church of God, Inc., is a predominantly black Oneness Pentecostal church founded in 1920 by William Thomas Phillips.

Hq: Bishop Jasper C. Roby, 1120 N. 24th Street, Birmingham, AL 35234
Tel: (205) 324 2202

Armenian Apostolic Church of America

The ancient Christian church in Armenia has two branches. The Armenian Apostolic Church of America was founded in 1930, after the installation of a Communist government in Armenia. The Archbishop of the North American Diocese is Mesrob Ashjian. The Church is under the jurisdiction of Catholicos of Cilicia (Lebanon), His Holiness Karekin II.

Hq: 138 E. 39th Street, New York, NY 10016
Tel: (212) 689 7810
or
International Hq: Holy See-Armenian Catholicossate of Cilicia, Antelas, Lebanon
Tel: 410 001-3
Telex: Cilcat 44501 LE

Armenian Church of America, Diocese of

The Armenian Church dates to the first century C.E., and is currently led by the Supreme Patriarch and Catholicos of All Armenians, His Holiness Vasken I. The Church was established in the United States in 1889.

Hq: c/o Primate, His Eminence Torkom Manoogian, 630 Second Avenue, New York, NY 10016
Tel: (212) 686 0710
or
International Hq: c/o Holy See, Etchmiadzin, Armenia

Armenian Evangelical Brethren

The Armenian Evangelical Brethren was founded in 1948. It is an outgrowth of nineteenth century Protestant missions in Armenia.

Hq: c/o Rev. Dikran Shanlian, 3200 W. London Street, Los Angeles, CA 90026
Tel: (213) 483 7265

Armenian Evangelical Church

The Armenian Evangelical Church was founded in 1960 by Armenian immigrants who settled in the United States.

Hq: c/o Rev. Vahan Toutigian, 3922 Yorba Linda, Royal Oak, MI 48072

Asbury Bible Churches

The Asbury Bible Churches was founded in 1971 by former members of the Southern Methodist Church.

Hq: Rev. Jack Tondee, Box 1021, Dublin, GA 31021

Assemblies of God, General Council of the

The General Council of the Assemblies of God was established in 1914 at a gathering of Pentecostal ministers in Hot Springs, Arkansas.

Hq: c/o Gen. Superintendent G. Raymond Carlson, 1445 Boonville Avenue, Springfield, MO 65802
Tel: (417) 862 2781

Assemblies of God International Fellowship (Independent/ Not Affiliated)

The Assemblies of God International Fellowship (Independent/Not Affiliated) was founded in 1935 by a merger of the Independent Assemblies of God (Scandinavian) with the Independent Assemblies of God of the U.S. and Canada.

Hq: c/o Exec. Dir. Rev. T. A. Lanes, 8504 Commerce Avenue, San Diego, CA 92121
Tel: (619) 530 1727

Assemblies of the Called Out Ones of Yah

The Assemblies of the Called Out Ones of Yah is a Sacred Name organization founded in 1974 by Sam Surratt.

Hq: 231 Cedar Street, Jackson, TN 38301
Tel: (901) 422 3623

Assemblies of the Lord Jesus Christ, Inc.

The Assemblies of the Lord Jesus Christ was founded in 1952 by a merger of three Oneness Pentecostal churches: the Assemblies of the Church of Jesus Christ, Jesus Only Church of God, and the Church of the Lord Jesus Christ.

Hq: 875 N. White Station Road, Memphis, TN 38122
Tel: (901) 685 1969

Assemblies of Yahweh

The Assemblies of Yahweh is a Sacred Name organization founded in 1969 by Jacob O. Meyer.

Hq: Bethel, PA 19507
Tel: (717) 933 4518 or 933 4880

Assemblies of Yahweh (Eaton Rapids, Michigan)

The Assemblies of Yahweh (Eaton Rapids, Michigan) is an early Sacred Name Church founded in 1939.

Hq: P. O. Box 102, Holt, MI 48842
Tel: (517) 663 3724

Assembly of Christian Soldiers

The Assembly of Christian Soldiers is a small church based in the Ku Klux Klan founded in 1971 by Jessie L. Thrift.

Hq: Current address unavailable for this edition

Assembly of Yahvah

The Assembly of Yahvah was founded in 1949 by Lorenzo Dow Snow.

Hq: Box 89, Winfield, AL 35594
Tel: (205) 487 6997

Assembly of YHWHHOSHUA

The Assembly of YHWHHOSHUA is a Sacred Name Adventist organization which has also accepted some emphases from the Pentecostal movement.

Hq: David K. Johnson, 50006 Olson Road, Boone, CO 81025

Associate Reformed Presbyterian Church (General Synod)

The Associate Reformed Presbyterian Church (General Synod) grew out of the Seceder Movement which broke with the Church of Scotland in the 1740s. It was organized in the United States in 1790.

Hq: c/o Mod. E. Benton Johnson, One Cleveland Street, Greenville, SC 29601
Tel: (803) 232 8297

Associated Brotherhood of Christians

The Associated Brotherhood of Christians is a Pentecostal body which was founded during World War II by E. E. Partridge and H. A. Riley.

Hq: Current address unavailable for this edition

Associated Churches Inc.

The Associated Churches Inc. was founded in 1974 by former members of the Worldwide Church of God.

Hq: Box 4455, Rolling Bay, WA 98061
Tel: (206) 842 5511

Associated Churches of Christ (Holiness)

The Associated Churches of Christ (Holiness) is a predominantly black holiness church founded in 1947 by Bishop William Washington.

Hq: 1302 E. Adams Blvd., Los Angeles, CA 90011

Associated Gospel Churches

The Associated Gospel Churches started in 1939 under the leadership of W. O. H. Garman.

Hq: 1919 Beach Street, Pittsburgh, PA 15221

Associates for Scriptural Knowledge

The Associates for Scriptural Knowledge was founded in 1984 by Ernest L. Martin.

Hq: Box 7777, Alhambra, CA 91802

Association of American Laestadian Congregations

The Association of American Laestadian Congregations, a more conservative branch of the Apostolic Lutheran Movement, emerged in the 1970s among Finnish Lutherans.

Hq: 13030 47th Street, Plymouth, MN 55442

Association of Evangelical Gospel Assemblies

The Association is a fellowship of independent Pentecostal ministers and congregations.

Hq: 4403 Sterlington Rd., Monroe, LA 71203
Tel: (800) 842 5176

Association of Evangelicals for Italian Missions

The Association of Evangelicals for Italian Missions was founded in 1899 by a group of Italian-American Baptists.

Hq: 314 Richfield Road, Upper Darby, PA 19082

Association of Free Lutheran Congregations

The Association of Free Lutheran Congregations was founded in 1962 by Rev. John P. Strand and other members of the Lutheran Free Church who rejected that church's merger with the American Lutheran Church.

Hq: 3110 E. Medicine Lake Blvd., Minneapolis, MN 55441
Tel: (612) 545 5631

Association of Fundamental Gospel Churches

The Association of Fundamental Gospel Churches is a fellowship of congregations in the German Brethren tradition. It was founded in 1954 by G. Henry Besse as a merger of the Calvary Chapel of Hartsville, Ohio, the Webster Mills Free Brethren Church of McConnellsburg, Pennsylvania, and the Little Country Chapel of Myersburg, Maryland.

Hq: 9189 Grubb Court, Canton, OH 44721

Association of Fundamental Ministries and Churches

The Association of Fundamental Ministries and Churches was founded in 1931 by Rev. Fred and Hallie Bruffett, Rev. Paul Bennett, Rev. George Fisher, and former ministers of the Church of God (Anderson, Indiana).

Hq: Current address unavailable for this edition

Association of Independent Methodists

The Association of Independent Methodists was founded in 1965 by former members of the Methodist Church (1939-1968).

Hq: Box 4274, Jackson, MS 39216
Tel: (601) 362 1301

Association of Occidental Orthodox Parishes

The Association of Occidental Orthodox Parishes was founded in 1981 by Father Stephen Empson.

Hq: 57 Saint Marks Place, New York, NY 10003

Association of Seventh-Day Pentecostal Assemblies

The Association of Seventh-Day Pentecostal Assemblies was founded in 1967.

Hq: c/o Chairman Elder Garver C. Gray, 4700 N.E. 119th Street, Vancouver, WA 98686
Tel: (206) 693 9095

Association of Vineyard Churches

The Association of Vineyard Churches was founded in 1986 by John Wimber.

Hq: 902 E. Yorba Linda Blvd., Box 909, Placentia, CA 92670
Tel: (800) 852 8463

Autocephalous Slavonic Orthodox Catholic Church (In Exile)

The Autocephalous Slavonic Orthodox Catholic Church (In Exile) was founded in 1620 in what is now Czechoslovakia and was established in the United States in 1968.

Hq: 2237 Hunter Avenue, New York,
NY 10475

Autocephalous Syro-Chaldean Church of North America

The Autocephalous Syro-Chaldean Church of North America was founded in 1977. The Northeastern Diocese Bishop is Mar Uzziah (Most Rev. Bertram S. Schlossberg).

Hq: c/o Metropolitan Mar Uzziah, 9 Ellington Avenue, Rockville, CT 06066
Tel: (203) 872 4300

Baptist Bible Fellowship

The Baptist Bible Fellowship was founded in 1950 by Rev. Beuchamp Vick with former members of the World Baptist Fellowship.

Hq: c/o Pres. Harold Henninger, Box 191, Springfield, MO 65801
Tel: (417) 862 5001 or 831 3996

Baptist General Conference

The Baptist General Conference was founded among Swedish-Americans in 1852 by Gustaf Palmquist.

Hq: c/o Pres. Dr. Robert S. Ricker, 2002 S. Arlington Heights Rd., Arlington Heights, IL 60005
Tel: (312) 228 0200 or (800) 323 4215

Baptist Missionary Association of America

The Baptist Missionary Association of America was founded in 1950 by former members of the American Baptist Association. It was originally named the North American Baptist Association and took the present name in 1969.

Hq: c/o Pres. Rev. Gary D. Divine, 2617 Brookcrest Dr., Garland, TX 75040, or 716 Main Street, Little Rock, AR 72201

Beachy Amish Mennonite Churches

The Beachy Amish Mennonite Churches started when Bishop Moses Beachy refused to pronounce the ban against some former Old Order Amish members.

Hq: 9650 Iams Road, Plain City, OH 43064
or
Ervin N. Hershberger, R.D. 1, Meyersdale, PA 15552
Tel: (814) 662 2483

Berachah Church

The Berachah Church is a fundamentalist evangelical church founded in 1936 by C. Y. Colgan.

Hq: 5139 W. Alabama, Houston, TX 77056
Tel: (713) 622 6922

Berean Bible Fellowship

The Berean Bible Fellowship is a association of fundamentalist "Grace Gospel" believers.

Hq: 52nd & E. Virginia Sts., Phoenix, AZ 85008

Berean Bible Fellowship (Chicago)

The Berean Bible Fellowship (Chicago) is a fundamentalist "Grace Gospel" association founded in 1966 by Cornelius R. Stam.

Hq: 7609 W. Belmont, Chicago, IL 60635
Tel: (312) 456 7889

Berean Fundamental Church

The Berean Fundamental Church is an independent fundamentalist fellowship of churches founded in 1936 by Ivan E. Olsen.

Hq: c/o Pres. Rev. Curt Lehman, Box 549, North Platte, NE 69101
Tel: (308) 532 7448

Bethany Bible Church and Related Independent Bible Churches of the Phoenix, Arizona, Area

This Church was founded during the 1950s by John Mitchell and others who had chosen to leave their denominational congregations.

Hq: 6060 N. Seventh Avenue, Phoenix, AZ 85013
Tel: (602) 246 9788

Bethel Ministerial Association

The Bethel Ministerial Association was founded in 1934 by Rev. Albert Franklin Varnell.

Hq: 4350 Lincoln Avenue, Evansville, IN 47715

Bethel Temple

The Bethel Temple, founded in 1914, was the first Pentecostal church in the state of Washington. Other congregations soon formed and have become associated with it.

Hq: 2033 Second Avenue, Seattle, WA 98121
Tel: (206) 448 9983 or 441 0444

Bible Brethren

The Bible Brethren were formed in 1948 by some members of the Church of the Brethren under the leadership of Clair H. Alspaugh.

Hq: Current address unavailable for this edition

Bible Church of Christ

The Bible Church of Christ is a pentecostal church founded in 1961 by Bishop Roy Bryant, Sr.

Hq: c/o Pres. Bishop Roy Bryant, 1358 Morris Avenue, Bronx, NY 10456
Tel: (212) 588 2284

Bible Churches (Classics Expositor)

This fundamentalist "Grace Gospel" association was formed around the periodical, *Classics Expositor*.

Hq: 1429 N.W. 100th Street, Oklahoma City, OK 73114

Bible Fellowship Church

The Bible Fellowship Church was founded in 1947 as a split from the Church of the Mennonite Brethren in Christ.

Hq: Pastor W. B. Hottel, 404 W. Main Street, Terre Hill, PA 17581

Bible Holiness Church

The Bible Holiness Church is a conservative holiness church founded as a split from the Bible Methodist Connection of Tennessee.

Hq: Current address unavailable for this edition

Bible Methodist Connection of Churches

The Bible Methodist Connection of Churches is a conservative Holiness church founded in 1970 as a merger of Bible Methodist Church with Wesleyan Connection of Churches.

Hq: Rev. V. O. Agan, Box 523, Pell City, AL 35125

Bible Methodist Connection of Tennessee

The Bible Methodist Connection of Tennessee is a conservative holiness church founded in 1966 by Rev. D. P. Denton who opposed the merger of the Wesleyan Methodist Church and the Pilgrim Holiness Church (now the Wesleyan Church).

Hq: c/o Pres. Rev. D. P. Denton, Evangelist of Truth, Box 22309, Knoxville, TN 37933

Bible Missionary Church

The Bible Missionary Church is a holiness church founded in 1956 by Rev. Glenn Griffith and other former members of the Church of the Nazarene.

Hq: 822 S. Simms, Denver, CO 80211
Tel: (303) 986 5866

Bible Presbyterian Church

The Bible Presbyterian Church is a conservative fundamentalist church founded in 1938 by Rev. Carl McIntire, formerly a minister in the Presbyterian Church in the U.S.A.

Hq: Haddon and Cuthbert Blvd. S., Collingswood, NJ 08108

Bible Way Church of Our Lord Jesus Christ World Wide, Inc.

The Bible Way Church of Our Lord Jesus Christ World Wide is a predominantly black Oneness Pentecostal church founded in 1957 by Smallwood E. Williams and former members of the Church of Our Lord Jesus Christ of the Apostolic Faith.

Hq: c/o Presiding Bishop Smallwood E. Williams, 1130 New Jersey Avenue NW, Washington, D.C. 20001
Tel: (202) 789 0700

Bible Way Pentecostal Church

The Bible Way Pentecostal Church is a predominantly black Oneness Pentecostal church founded in 1960 by Curtis P. Jones, a former member of the Church of Our Lord Jesus Christ of the Apostolic Faith.

Hq: Current address unavailable for this edition

Biblical Church of God

The Biblical Church of God was founded in 1979 by Fred Coulter, a former member of the Worldwide Church of God.

Hq: Box 1234, Santa Cruz, CA 95061
Tel: (415) 829 2795

Black Primitive Baptists

Following the Civil War, black members of the primitive Baptist Church began to form their own associations, among the first being the Indian Creek Association in Alabama. Currently a string of such associations exist across the Southern United States.

Hq: No central address. For information contact: Primitive Baptist Library, Rte. 2, Elon College, NC 27244.

B'Nai Shalom

B'Nai Shalom is a Pentecostal association founded in the 1950s by Reynolds Edward Dawkins who had been associated with the Gospel Assemblies (Sowders).

Hq: Current address unavailable for this edition

Body of Christ Movement

The Body of Christ Movement is a Pentecostal-Charismatic movement founded during the 1970s by Charles P. Schmitt and his wife, Dorothy E. Schmitt.

Hq: c/o *Foundational Teachings*, Box 6598, Silver Spring, MD 20916

Boston Church of Christ

The Boston Church of Christ and its related congregations represent a distinct circle of fellowship which emerged in the 1980s within the Church of Christ (Non-Instrumental) movement. They originated within the discipling movement which began at the Crossroads Church of Christ in Gainesville, Florida, but have now separated from Crossroads and become a distinct grouping.

Hq: Boston Church of Christ, Boston Gardens, 150 Causeway Street, Box 144, Lexington, MA 02173
Tel: (617) 862 5921

Branch SDA's

Branch SDA's was founded in 1930 by Victor T. Houteff and other former members of the Seventh-day Adventist Church.

Hq: Box 4098, Waco, TX 76705
Tel: (817) 863 5325

Branham Tabernacle and Related Assemblies

The Branham Tabernacle and its associated assemblies around the world grew out of the ministry of Pentecostal healer William Marrion Branham in the middle of this century.

Hq: William Branham Evangelistic Association and the Branham Tabernacle, Box 325, Jefferson, IN 47130
or
Hq: Voice of God recordings, P. O. Box 950, Jeffersonville, IN 47131
Tel: (812) 288 8811

Brethren Church (Ashland, Ohio)

The Brethren Church (Ashland, Ohio) was founded in 1882 by Henry R. Holsinger and former members of the Church of the Brethren.

Hq: 524 College Avenue, Ashland, OH 44805
Tel: (419) 289 1708

Brethren in Christ Church

The Brethren in Christ Church, a church out of the Mennonite tradition, was founded 1778 in Pennsylvania. It took its present name in 1863.

Hq: c/o Gen. Sec. Dr. R. Donald Shafer, P. O. Box 245, Upland, CA 91786

Bulgarian Eastern Orthodox Church, Diocese of North and South America

This branch of the Bulgarian Eastern Orthodox Church was founded in 1964 by members of the Church who refused to associate with the Bulgarian government.

Hq: 519 Brynhaven Dr., Oregon, OH 45054

Bulgarian Eastern Orthodox Church (Diocese of North and South America and Australia)

The Bulgarian Eastern Orthodox Church (Diocese of North and South

America and Australia), an Eastern Rite liturgical church, was established in America in 1907.

Hq: c/o Metropolitan Ghelasiy, 550 A, W. 50th Street, New York, NY 10019

Tel: (212) 581 3756

or

International Hq: Bulgarian Patriarchate, Holy Synod, 4 Oborishte Street, P. O. Box 376, 1090 Sofia

Byelorussian Autocephalic Orthodox Church in the U.S.A.

The Byelorussian Autocephalic Orthodox Church in the U.S.A. was founded in 1949 in the United States. The Primate is Archbishop Mikalay who was elected in 1984.

International Hq: c/o Archbishop Mikalay, Church of St. Cyril of Turau, 524 St. Clarens Avenue, Toronto, ON, Canada

Byelorussian Orthodox Church

The Byelorussian Orthodox Church was founded after 1948. It is in communion with the Greek Orthodox Archdiocese of North and South America.

Hq: 190 Turnpike Road, South River, NJ 08882

Byzantine Catholic Church

The Byzantine Catholic Church was founded in 1984 as a merger of the Byzantine Old Catholic Church (Bishop Mark I. Miller) and the Holy Orthodox Catholic Church, Eastern and Apostolic.

Hq: Most Rev. Mark I. Miller, P. O. Box 3682, Los Angeles, CA 90078

Byzantine Orthodox Church

The Byzantine Orthodox Church is an independent Eastern Orthodox jurisdiction.

Hq: Rt. Rev. Paul Lemmen, 505 U.S. 195, Apt. 12-266, Clearwater, FL 34624

California Evangelistic Association

The California Evangelistic Association was founded in 1933 as Colonial Tabernacle of Long Beach California by Oscar C. Harms.

Hq: Current address unavailable for this edition

Calvary Chapel Church

From its founding in 1965, by Chuck Smith, the Calvary Chapel Church, a Pentecostal-Charismatic fellowship of churches, has grown into a national organization.

Hq: Box 8000, Costa Mesa, CA 92626
Tel: (714) 979 4422

Calvary Fellowship, Inc.

The Calvary Fellowship, Inc., is a British-Israelite association founded during the 1960s.

Hq: Box 128, Rainier, WA 98576
Tel: (206) 446 2482

Calvary Holiness Church

The Calvary Holiness Church, a Mennonite holiness church was founded in 1964 by William L. Rosenberry as a split from the Brethren in Christ.

Hq: 3415-19 N. Second Street, Philadelphia, PA 19140
Tel: (215) 634 6431

Calvary Ministries Inc., International

The Calvary Ministries Inc., International is a Pentecostal group founded in 1978 by Dr. Paul E. Paino, a former minister with the Assemblies of God.

Hq: 1400 W. Washington Center Road, Fort Wayne, IN 46825
Tel: (219) 489 5562

Calvary Pentecostal Church

The Calvary Pentecostal Church was founded in 1931 by a group of Pentecostal ministers who formed a fellowship in Olympia, Washington. The fellowship eventually became a denomination, as churches began to affiliate.

Hq: Rev. Leroy Holman, 1775 Yew, NE, Olympia, WA 98506

Carolina Evangelistic Association

The Carolina Evangelistic Association was founded in 1930 by Dr. A. G. Garr.

Hq: Cannon Cathedral, Box 31773, Charlotte, NC 28231-1773

Catholic Apostolic Church at Davis

The Catholic Apostolic Church at Davis was founded in 1972 by Albert Ronald Coady.

Hq: Gates of Praise Center, 921 W. 8th Street, Davis, CA 95616

Catholic Apostolic Church in North America (Patriarchate of Brazil)

The Catholic Church in America was founded in 1950 by Stephen Meyer Corradi-Scarella as an outpost of the Catholic Apostolic Church in Brazil, originally founded in 1946 by former Roman Catholic Bishop Dom Carlos Duarte Costa. The Church was officially reconstituted in 1983 by Archbishop Jerome Joachim.

Hq: Most Rev. Jerome Joachim, 130 Lincoln Av., Ste. 782, Santa Fe, NM 87501
Tel: (505) 983 2885

Catholic Life Church

The Catholic Life Church is an independent Catholic jurisdiction founded in 1971 by Rev. A. L. Mark Harding and by Rev. Peter A. Tonella.

Hq: Most Rev. A. L. Mark Harding, 1955 Arapahoe Street, Suite 1603, Denver, Colorado 80202

Celtic Evangelical Church

The Celtic Evangelical Church is an independent Anglican jurisdiction founded in 1981 by Rev. Wayne W. Gau.

Hq: Box 90880, Honolulu, HI 96835-0880

Central Yearly Meeting of Friends

In 1926 the Central Yearly Meeting of Friends disassociated itself from the Five Years Meeting.

Hq: Supt: Ollie McCune, Route 1, Box 226, Alexandria, IN 46001
Tel: (317) 724 3583

Charismatic Catholic Church: Independent Rite of America

Hq: c/o Mt/ Rev. Daniel C. Braun, 102 Freya Rd., Rocky Point, NY 11128

Charismatic Catholic Church of Canada

The Charismatic Catholic Church of Canada is an independent Catholic jurisdiction founded in 1957 by Archbishop André L. Barbeau, formerly a priest of the Roman Catholic Church. It is headquartered in Canada, but has an American diocese.

Hq: c/o Mt. Rev. Ray W. Renville, 1853 W. 183rd St., Homewood, IL 60430
or
International Hq: c/o Mt. Rev. André L. Barbeau, Vite do Mari II, 141 Rte. 148 RR Ste Scholastique, Mirabel, PQ, Canada J0N 1S0
Tel: (514) 258 4419

Christ Catholic Church

The Christ Catholic Church is an independent Catholic jurisdiction founded in 1968 by Most Rev. Karl Pruter.

Hq: Cathedral Church, P. O. Box 98, Highlandsville, MO 65669
Tel: (417) 587 3951

Christ Faith Mission

The Christ Faith Mission is an independent evangelical ministry originally founded in 1908 by Dr. Finis E. Yoakum.

Hq: 6026 Echo Street, Los Angeles, CA 90042
Tel: (213) 255 4783

Christ Family

The Christ Family was founded in the early 1960s by Charles Franklin Hughes, also better known by his religious name Lightning Amen.

Hq: Current address unavailable for this edition

Christ Holy Sanctified Church of America

Christ Holy Sanctified Church of America, a predominantly black Pentecostal church, was founded in 1919 in Keatchie, Louisiana.

Hq: 5204 Willie Street, Fort Worth, TX 76105

Christadelphians-Amended

The Christadelphian movement, an evangelical movement founded in 1844 by John Thomas, divided in the 1890s over some proposed changes in the group's statement of faith. Those who agreed to amend the doctrinal position became known as the Amended Christadelphians.

Hq: No central address. For information: Christadelphian Book Supply, 14651 Livonia, Detroit, MI 48154

Christadelphians-Unamended

The Christadelphians movement, founded in 1844, split in the 1890s over a proposed amendment to the statement of faith. Those who rejected the proposed changes became known as the Unamended Christadelphians.

Hq: No central address. For information: Lawrence Dodl, 5104 Cavedo Lane, Richmond, VA 23231

Christian Apostolic Church (Forest, Illinois)

The Christian Apostolic Church (Forest, Illinois) was founded in 1950s by Peter Schaffer, Sr., as a split from the German Apostolic Christian Church.

Hq: Forest, IL 91741

Christian Apostolic Church (Sabetha, Kansas)

The Christian Apostolic Church (Sabetha, Kansas) was founded in the early 1960s by William Edelman as a split from the German Apostolic Christian Church.

Hq: Sabetha, KS 66534

Christian Assemblies (Gene Edwards)

Gene Edwards is an independent Evangelical minister who has developed a national following among people who have read his many books. The following is focused upon a worshipping community in Maine and his many books.

Hq: c/o Christian Books Publishing House, Box 959, Gardiner, ME 04345
Tel: (207) 737 8267

Christian Assemblies (George Geftakys)

The set of Christian assemblies for whom George Geftakys is the central teacher is very similar in belief and practice to the Local Church movement.

Hq: c/o Torch and Testimony Publications, P. O. Box 3596, Fullerton, CA 92631

Christian Brethren (Plymouth Brethren)

The Christian or Open Brethren is that branch of the movement (popularly called the Plymouth Brethren) begun by John Nelson Darby in England in the 1820s which has been more open to cooperation with Evangelical Christians of non-Brethren organizations.

Hq: No central address. For information contact: Interest, Box 294, Wheaton, IL 60187
Tel: (312) 653 6573

Christian Catholic Church (Evangelical-Protestant)

The Christian Catholic Church (Evangelical-Protestant) was founded in 1896 by John Alexander Dowie (1847-1907).

Hq: Dowie Memorial Dr., Zion, IL 60099
Tel: (312) 746 1411

Christian Church (Disciples of Christ)

The Christian Church (Disciples of Christ) is one of several large groups which has grown out of the Restoration Movement begun in the early nineteenth century by Barton Stone, and Thomas and Alexander Campbell.

Hq: 222 S. Downey Avenue, Box 1986, Indianapolis, IN 46206
Tel: (317) 353 1491

Christian Church of North America, General Council

The Christian Church of North America, General Council, grew out of the work of pioneer Italian-American Pentecostals (Luigi Francesconi, Massimiliano Tosetto, Peter Ottolini, Giacomo Lombardi and Giuseppe Petrelli).

Hq: Rt. 18 & Rutledge Rd., Box 141-A, R.D. #1, Transfer, PA 16154
Tel: (412) 962 3501

Christian Churches and Churches of Christ

The Christian Churches and Churches of Christ are one of the larger branches of the Restoration Movement begun in the early nineteenth century by Barton Stone and Thomas and Alexander Campbell.

Hq: No central address. For information: North American Christian Convention, 3533 Epley Rd., Cincinnati, OH 45239
Tel: (513) 385 2470

Christian Congregation

The Christian Congregation is an evangelical organization which dates to 1798. After a brief association with the Christian Church movement of Barton Stone, it incorporated in 1887.

Hq: c/o Gen. Superintendent Rev. Ora Wilbert Eads, 804 W. Hemlock Street, La Follette, TN 37766

Christian Conservative Churches of America

The Christian Conservative Churches of America was founded in 1959 by John R. Harrell.

Hq: Box 575, Flora, IL 62839
Tel: (618) 665 3937

Christian Convention Church

The Christian Convention Church is a name used by a church which has no name to conduct its necessary business with the government. This conservative separatist group, founded in 1903 by William Irvine, has a number of names given them by others, including: the Two-by-Twos, Cooneyites, and the No-name Church.

Hq: No central address. No current address for information available for this edition

Christian Identity Church

The Christian Identity Church, a British-Israelite association founded in 1982 by Pastor Charles Jennings, grew out of the prior ministry work of Wesley Swift.

Hq: c/o Pastor Fred Demoret, Box 1779, Harrison, AK 72601

Christian International Network of Prophetic Ministries

The Christian International Network is an association of Latter Rain Pentecostal ministers and churches founded by Bill Hamon.

Hq: P. O. Box 9000, Santa Rosa Beach, FL 32459
Tel: (904) 231 5308 or (800) 388 5308

Christian Israelite Church

The Christian Israelite Church, founded in England in 1822 by John Wroe (1782-1863), grew out of the prophetic revelations of Joanna Southcott (1750-1815).

Hq: 1204 N. Rural Street, Indianapolis, IN 46201
Tel: (317) 589 3221
or
International Hq: 193 Fitzroy Street, Fitzroy, Victoria, Australia 3065

Christian Methodist Episcopal Church

The Christian Methodist Episcopal Church (formerly the Colored Methodist Church) was founded in 1870 by black former members of the Methodist Episcopal Church, South. It took its present name in 1956.

Hq: c/o Gen. Sec. Rev. Edgar L. Wade, 564 Frank Avenue, P. O. Box 3403, Memphis, TN 38101
Tel: (901) 947 3135

Christian and Missionary Alliance

The Christian and Missionary Alliance was founded in 1897 as a merger of the Christian Alliance and the Evangelical Missionary Alliance both founded by Albert B. Simpson.

Hq: c/o Pres. David L. Rambo, 350 N. Highland Avenue, Nyack, NY 10960
Tel: (914) 353 0750

Christian Millennial Fellowship

The Christian Millennial Fellowship, founded in 1986 by Gaetano Boccaccio, grew out of the Bible Student Movement which originated with Charles Taze Russell in the late nineteenth century.

Hq: 307 White Street, Hartford, CT 06106

Christian Nation Church U.S.A.

The Christian Nation Church U.S.A., an evangelical Protestant body, was founded in 1895 and incorporated with the present name in 1961.

Hq: c/o Gen. Overseer Rev. Harvey Monjar, Box 513, South Lebanon, Ohio 45036
Tel: (513) 932 0360

Christian Orthodox Catholic Church

The Christian Orthodox Catholic Church is an independent Catholic jurisdiction founded by Rt. Rev. Richard Lane, formerly a member of the North American Old Roman Catholic Church (Utrecht Succession).

Hq: Chancellery Office, 750 La Playa St., Ste. 914, San Francisco, CA 94121-3258

Christian Pilgrim Church

The Christian Pilgrim Church was founded in 1937 by Fannie and Tracy Alldaffer and Rev. C. W. Cripps.

Hq: (Current address unavailable for this edition)

Christian Prophets of Jehovah

The Christian Prophets of Jehovah is an Adventist group founded in the 1970s by Timothy Tauver, a former member of the Jehovah's Witnesses who began to feel that he was a prophet.

Hq: Box 8302, San Jose, CA 95555

Christian Reformed Church in North America

The Christian Reformed Church in North America continues the conservative Reformed tradition of the Netherlands. It was founded in the United States in 1857.

Hq: 2850 Kalamazoo Avenue SE, Grand Rapids, MI 49560
Tel: (616) 246 0744

Christian Research, Inc.

The Christian Research, Inc., is a British-Israel group founded by Greta Koch.

Hq: Box 385, Eureka Springs, AR 72632

Christian Union

The Christian Union is an evangelical Protestant body organized in 1864.

Hq: c/o Pres. Rev. Hearold McElwee, 220 W. Excelsior Street, P. O. Box 397, Excelsior Springs, MO 64024
Tel: (816) 637 4668

Christian Unity Baptist Association

The Christian Unity Baptist Association emerged out of a controversy on open community within the Mountain Union Regular Baptist Association in 1901.

Hq: Elder Thomas T. Reynolds, Thomasville, NC 27360

Christ's Ambassadors

The Christ's Ambassadors was founded in 1968 by Paul Beidler and other former members of the Dunkard Brethren Church.

Hq: Current address unavailable for this edition

Christ's Assembly

The Christ's Assembly was founded in 1967 by Danish minister Johannes Thalitzer who drew members from several of the groups which had originated from the Church of the Brethren.

Hq: Current address unavailable for this edition

Christ's Sanctified Holy Church (Louisiana)

The Christ's Sanctified Holy Church (Louisiana), a holiness church of predominantly black membership, was founded in 1904 by Dempsey and Leggie Perkins, A. C. Mitchell, James Briller, Sr., and others.

Hq: S. Cutting Avenue at E., Spencer Street, Jennings, LA 70546

Christ's Sanctified Holy Church (South Carolina)

The Christ's Sanctified Holy Church (South Carolina) is a conservative holiness church founded in 1892 by Joseph Lynch.

Hq: Box 1376, CSHC Campgrounds and Home for the Aged, Perry, GA 31068

Church for the Fellowship of All People

The Church for the Fellowship of All People was founded in 1943 by Dr. Albert G. Fisk.

Hq: 2041 Larkin Street, San Francisco, CA 94109
Tel: (415) 776 4910

Church of Bible Understanding

The Church of Bible Understanding, one branch of the Jesus People Movement of the late-1960s, was founded in 1971 by Stewart Traill.

Hq: Box 841, Radio City Station, New York, NY 10019-0841
Tel: (212) 246 4370

Church of Christ Holiness unto the Lord

The Church of Christ Holiness unto the Lord is a predominantly black Pentecostal church founded in 1926 in Savannah, Georgia, by Bishop Milton Solomon Bennett, his wife, and others, former Methodists who had received the Pentecostal message.

Hq: 1650 Smart Street, Savannah, GA 31401

Church of Christ (Holiness) U.S.A.

The Church of Christ (Holiness) U.S.A., a predominantly black holiness church, was founded in 1894 by C. P. Jones and Charles H. Mason.

Hq: 329 E. Monument Street, Jackson,
    MS 39202
Tel: (601) 353 4033

Church of Christian Liberty

The Church of Christian Liberty is
a fundamentalist Christian church
founded in 1965 by Paul Lindstrom.

Hq: 502 W. Euclid Avenue, Arlington
    Heights, IL 60004

Church of Daniel's Band

The Church of Daniel's Band was
founded in 1893 by former members
of the Methodist Episcopal Church.

Hq: c/o Pres. Rev. Jim Seaman, Adam
    Street, Coleman, MI 48618
Tel: (517) 465 6059

Church of God and True Holiness

The Church of God and True
Holiness is a predominantly black
Pentecostal church founded in
Wilson, North Carolina, in 1960 by
Robert Allen Carr.

Hq: 1225 North Roxboro Road, Wilson,
    NC 27707

Church of God (Anderson, Indiana)

The Church of God (Anderson,
Indiana) is a holiness church founded
in 1881 by Daniel S. Warner.

Hq: c/o Exec. Sec. Edward L. Foggs,
    Box 2420, Anderson, IN 46018
Tel: (317) 642 0256

Church of God (Apostolic)

The Church of God (Apostolic) is a
predominantly black Oneness
Pentecostal church founded originally
as the Christian Faith Band in 1877
by Thomas J. Cox.

Hq: 11th & Highland Avenue, Winston-
    Salem, NC 27101
Tel: (919) 722 2285

Church of God, Body of Christ

The Church of God, Body of Christ
is a sabbatarian adventist group.

Hq: Rte. 1, Mocksville, NC 27028

Church of God by Faith, Inc.

The Church of God by Faith, Inc.
is a holiness Pentecostal church
founded in 1914 by John Bright.

Hq: 3220 Haines Street, Jacksonville,
    FL 32206
Tel: (904) 353 5111

Church of God (Cleveland, Tennessee)

The Church of God (Cleveland,
Tennessee) was founded in 1886 as
a holiness church, the Christian
Union. It assumed its present name
in 1907 after members accepted a
new Pentecostal perspective.

Hq: P. O. Box 2430, Cleveland, TN
    37320
Tel: (615) 472 3361

Church of God, the Eternal

The Church of God, the Eternal,
was founded in 1975 by Raymond C.
Cole and other former members of
the Worldwide Church of God.

Hq: Box 755, Eugene, OR 97440

Church of God Evangelistic Association

The Church of God Evangelistic
Association was founded in 1980 by
David J. Smith and other former
members of the Worldwide Church of
God.

Hq: 11824 Beaverton, Bridgeton, MO
   63044
Tel: (314) 739 4490

Church of God General Conference (Abrahamic Faith)

The Church of God General Conference (Abrahamic Faith) emerged as older Church of God congregations were affected by the Adventist movement and organized in the late nineteenth century.

Hq: 131 N. Third Street, Box 100,
   Oregon, IL 61061
Tel: (815) 732 7991

Church of God (Guthrie, Oklahoma)

The Church of God (Guthrie, Oklahoma) was founded in 1910-11 by former members of the Church of God (Anderson, Indiana) under the leadership of C. E. Orr.

Hq: c/o Faith Publishing House, 7415
   W. Monsur Avenue, Guthrie,
   OK 73044
Tel: (405) 282 1479

Church of God (Holiness)

The Church of God (Holiness) is a holiness church founded in 1922 by A. M. Kiergan.

Hq: 7415 Metcalf, Overland Park, KS
   66204
Tel: (913) 432 0331

Church of God (Huntsville, Alabama)

The Church of God (Huntsville, Alabama) was founded in 1943 by Homer Tomlinson following a disagreement with his brother Milton Tomlinson who had taken control of the Church of God of Prophecy.

Hq: Bishop Voy M. Bullen, 1270
   Willow Brook SE, Apt.2,
   Huntsville, AL 35802
Tel: (205) 881 9629

Church of God in Christ

The Church of God in Christ, the largest of the several predominantly black Pentecostal churches, was founded in 1894 by Charles H. Mason.

Hq: 272 S. Main Street, P. O. Box 320,
   M_mphis, TN 38103
Tel: (90?) 578 3838

Church of God in Christ, Congregational

The Church of God in Christ, Congregational, was founded in 1932 in Hot Springs, Arkansas, by Bishop J. Bowe, a former minister in the Church of God in Christ.

Hq: 1905 Bond Avenue, East St. Louis,
   IL 62201
Tel: (618) 271 7780

Church of God in Christ, International

The Church of God in Christ, International was founded in 1969 by Bishop Illie L. Jefferson, and other former members of the Church of God in Christ.

Hq: c/o Presiding Bishop Rt. Rev. Carl
   E. Williams, 170 Adelphi Street,
   Brooklyn, NY 11025
Tel: (718) 625 9175

Church of God in Christ, Mennonite

The Church of God in Christ, Mennonite, was founded in 1859 by John Holdeman, a former member of the Mennonite Church.

Hq: 420 N. Wedel, Mountridge, KS
  67107
Tel: (316) 345 2532

Church of God International

The Church of God International was founded in 1978 by Garner Ted Armstrong, son of the founder and formerly a minister with the Worldwide Church of God.

Hq: Box 2525, Tyler, TX 75710
Tel: (214) 561 2525

Church of God (Jerusalem)

The Church of God (Jerusalem) is a sabbatarian Sacred Name Adventist group founded in the 1950s by A. N. Dugger. While the membership is largely in the United States, the headquarters was moved to Israel.

International Hq: Box 10184, Jerusalem
  91101, Israel

Church of God (Jerusalem Acres)

The Church of God (Jerusalem Acres) is a holiness Pentecostal church founded in 1957 by Grady R. Kent, a former leader in the Church of God of Prophecy.

Hq: c/o Chief Bishop John A. Looper,
  Box 1207, 1826 Dalton Pike,
  (Jerusalem Acres), Cleveland,
  TN 37364-1207
Tel: (615) 472 1597

Church of God (Jesus Christ the Head)

The Church of God (Jesus Christ the Head) was founded in 1972 by a group of Sabbatarian Church of God members.

Hq: c/o Pastor M. L. Bartholomew, Box
  02026, Cleveland, OH 44102

Church of God (O'Beirn)

The Church of God (O'Beirn) was founded in 1970 by Carl O'Beirn.

Hq: P. O. Box 81224, Cleveland, OH
  44181

Church of God of Prophecy

The Church of God of Prophecy is a holiness Pentecostal church founded by Ambrose J. Tomlinson in 1921 as Tomlinson Church of God and took the present name in 1952.

Hq: Bible Place, P. O. Box 2910,
  Cleveland, TN 37320
Tel: (615) 479 8511

Church of God of the Apostolic Faith

The Church of God of the Apostolic Faith is a Pentecostal holiness church founded in 1914 by Reverends James O. McKenzie, Edwin A. Buckles, Oscar H. Myers, and Joseph P. Rhoades.

Hq: Current address unavailable for
  this edition

Church of God of the Mountain Assembly

The Church of God of the Mountain Assembly is a holiness Pentecostal church founded in 1906 by Reverends J. H. Parks, Steve Bryant, Tom Moses, and William O. Douglas.

Hq: c/o Gen. Overseer Rev. Kenneth
  E. Massingel, Florence Avenue,
  Jellico, TN 37762
Tel: (615) 784 8260

Church of God of the Original Mountain Assembly

The Church of God of the Original Mountain Assembly was founded in

1946 by A. J. Long and former members of the Church of God of the Mountain Assembly. The Church has a strong belief in healing.

Hq: Williamsburg, KY 40769

Church of God of the Union Assembly

The Church of God of the Union Assembly is a holiness Pentecostal body founded in 1920 by former members of the Church of God of the Mountain Assembly.

Hq: c/o Jesse Pratt, Box 1323, Dalton, GA 30720

Church of God (Sabbatarian)

The Church of God (Sabbatarian) was founded in 1969 by Roy Marrs.

Hq: Current address unavailable for this edition

Church of God (Sanctified Church)

The Church of God (Sanctified Church) is a predominantly black holiness church founded in 1907 by Charles W. Gray.

Hq: 1037 Jefferson Street, Nashville, TN 37208
Tel: (615) 255 5579

Church of God (Seventh Day, Denver, Colorado)

See: General Conference of the Church of God (Seventh Day)

Church of God (Seventh Day, Salem, West Virginia)

The Church of God (Seventh Day, Salem, West Virginia) was founded in 1933 by former members of the General Conference of the Church of God (Seventh Day).

Hq: 79 Water Street, Salem, WV 26426

Church of God, the House of Prayer

The Church of God, the House of Prayer is a predominantly black Pentecostal church founded in 1939 by Harrison W. Poteat.

Hq: Rev. Charles Mackenin, Markleysburg, PA 15459

Church of God with Signs Following

The Church of God with Signs Following, one of several Pentecostal churches known for its members handling snakes, was founded in 1914 by George Went Hensley.

Hq: No central headquarters.

Church of God (Which He Purchased with His Own Blood)

The Church of God (Which He Purchased with His Own Blood) is a predominantly black Pentecostal church founded in 1953 by William Jordan Fizer, formerly a minister with the Church of the Living God (Christian Workers for Fellowship).

Hq: 1628 N.E. 50th, Oklahoma City, OK 73111
Tel: (405) 427 8264

Church of Israel

The Church of Israel was founded by Dan Gayman in the 1970s as a split from the Church of Christ at Halley's Bluff (which is also known as Church of Christ at Zion's Retreat).

Hq: Box 62 B3, Schell City, MO 64783

Church of Jesus Christ Christian, Aryan Nations

The Church of Jesus Christ Christian, Aryan Nations was founded in the late 1940s (as Church of Jesus Christ Christian) by Wesley A. Swift. It has become known for its stance on racial issues and its association with the Ku Klux Klan and American Nazi Party.

Hq: Box 362, Hayden Lake, ID 83835

Church of Our Lord Jesus Christ of the Apostolic Faith, Inc.

The Church of Our Lord Jesus Christ of the Apostolic Faith, Inc. was founded in 1919 by Robert Clarence Lawson, formerly a minister with the Pentecostal Assemblies of the World.

Hq: 2081 Adam Clayton Powell Jr. Blvd., New York, NY 10027
Tel: (212) 866 1700

Church of Saint Joseph

The Church of Saint Joseph is a traditionalist Catholic church founded during the 1960s by Fr. Henry Lovett.

Hq: 2307 S. Laramie, Cicero, IL 60650

Church of the Bible Covenant

The Church of the Bible Covenant was founded in 1967 by Marvin Powers, Amos Hann, Donald Hicks, and Granville Rogers.

Hq: Rte. 8, Box 214, 450 N. Fortville Pike, Greenfield, IN 46140

Church of the Brethren

The Church of the Brethren grew out of the eighteenth century pietist movement which spread among German Lutherans who rejected the state church. It was founded in 1723 in USA by Alexander Mack Sr., Christopher Sauer II, Alexander Mack Jr., and Peter Becker.

Hq: 1451 Dundee Avenue, Elgin, IL 60120
Tel: (312) 742 5100

Church of the Christian Crusade

The Church of the Christian Crusade is a conservative evangelical church founded in 1950 by Billy James Hargis.

Hq: Box 977, Tulsa, OK 74102

Church of the Gospel

See: Churches of Christ in Christian Union

Church of the Holy Trinity

The Church of the Holy Trinity is a predominantly black Pentecostal church founded in 1910 in Washington, D.C., by Lewis T. Chapman.

Hq: 1618 11th Street, N.W., Washington, DC 20001

Church of the Kingdom of God

The Church of the Kingdom of God is a predominantly black Pentecostal church founded in 1955 in Eustis, Florida, by William H. Bryant, popularly known as Bishop Noah Nothing.

Hq: P. O. Box 577, Eustis, FL 32727
Tel: (904) 357 3348

Church of the Little Children

The Church of the Little Children is a Pentecostal church founded in 1916 by John Quincy Adams.

Hq: Current address unavailable for this
edition

Church of the Living God (Christian Workers for Fellowship)

The Church of the Living God (Christian Workers for Fellowship) is a predominantly black Pentecostal church founded in 1889 by Rev. William Christian (1856-1928).

Hq: Bishop W. E. Crumes, 434 Forest
Avenue, Cincinnati, OH 45229
Tel: (405) 427 3701 or (513) 221 1685

Church of the Living God (Hawaii)

The Church of the Living God (which is also known as Hoomana O Ke Akua Ola) is one of several evangelical churches which developed among native Hawaiians. It was founded in 1911 as a split from the Hoomana Naauoa O Hawaii.

Hq: 632 Mokauea, Honolulu, HI 96819

Church of the Living God (North Carolina)

The Church of the Living God is a predominantly black Pentecostal church founded in Winston-Salem, North Carolina, in 1917 by Bishop J. S. Cranfill.

Hq: Current address unavailable for this
edition

Church of the Living God, the Pillar and Ground of the Truth

The Church of the Living God, the Pillar and Ground of the Truth is a predominantly black Pentecostal church founded in 1903 by Mother Mary L. Tate, a pioneer female Pentecostal evangelist in the South.

Hq: 4520 Hydes Ferry Pike, Box 5735,
Nashville, TN 37208
Tel: (615) 255 0401

Church of the Living Word

The Church of the Living Word (which is also known as "The Walk") is a Pentecostal church founded in 1951 by John Robert Stevens, formerly a member of the International Church of the Foursquare Gospel.

Hq: Box 858, North Hollywood, CA
91063

Church of The Lord Jesus Christ of the Apostolic Faith

The Church of The Lord Jesus Christ of the Apostolic Faith was founded in 1933 by Bishop Sherrod C. Johnson, formerly a minister with the Church of Our Lord Jesus Christ of the Apostolic Faith.

Hq: 22nd & Bainbridge Sts., Philadelphia, PA 19146
Tel: (215) 735 8982

Church of the Lutheran Brethren of America

The Church of the Lutheran Brethren of America was founded in 1900 by a group of Norwegian-American Lutherans under the leadership of Rev. Kurt O. Lundeberg.

Hq: c/o Pres. Rev. Robert M.
Overgard, 1007 Westside Dr.,
Box 655, Fergus Falls, MN
56537
Tel: (218) 739 3336

Church of the Lutheran Confession

The Church of the Lutheran Confession was founded in 1957 by former ministers and members of the Wisconsin Evangelical Lutheran Synod.

Hq: c/o Pres. Rev. Daniel Fleischer, 460 75th Avenue NE, Minneapolis, MN 55432
Tel: (612) 784 8784

Church of the Nazarene

The Church of the Nazarene is a holiness church founded in 1908 by Phineas Bresee, a former superintendent in the Methodist Episcopal Church. It assumed its present name in 1919.

Hq: 6401 The Paseo, Kansas City, MO 64131
Tel: (816) 333 7000

Church of the United Brethren in Christ

The Church of the United Brethren in Christ was founded by conservative members of the United Brethren in Christ who rejected the new constitution adopted by its general conference in 1889.

Hq: 302 Lake Street, Huntington, IN 46750
Tel: (219) 356 2312

Church of True Inspiration

See: Amana Church Society

Church of Universal Triumph/ the Dominion of God

The Church of Universal Triumph/the Dominion of God is a predominantly black Pentecostal church founded in the 1940s by Rev. James Francis Marion Jones, more popularly known as Prophet Jones.

Hq: Rev. James Shaffer, 8317 LaSalle Blvd., Detroit, MI 48206

Church on the Rock North America

The Church on the Rock North America is a Pentecostal church which grew out of the charismatic movement of the 1970s. It is led by Dr. Lawrence Kennedy and popular evangelist Larry Lea.

Hq: c/o 12700 Park Central Drive, #1414, Dallas, TX 75251
Tel: (214) 701 8887
Fax: (214) 701 0738

The Church Which is Christ's Body

The Church Which is Christ's Body is a fundamentalist church founded in the 1920s by Maurice M. Johnson.

Hq: Current address unavailable for this edition

Churches in the Lord Jesus Christ of the Apostolic Faith

The Churches in the Lord Jesus Christ of the Apostolic Faith was founded in 1946 in Hartsville, South Carolina by Bishop L. Hunter, the Chief Apostle, formerly a minister in the Church of the Lord Jesus christ of the Apostolic Faith.

Hq: Rt. 2, Box 469C-1, Hartsville, SC 29550
Tel: (803) 332 5661

Churches of Christ in Christian Union

The Churches of Christ in Christian Union is a holiness church founded in 1909 by former members of the Christian Union.

Hq: c/o Gen. Superintendent Rev. Robert Kline, 1427 Lancaster Pike, P. O. Box 30, Circleville, OH 43113

Churches of Christ (Non-Instrumental)

The Churches of Christ (Non-Instrumental) is one of the major branches of the Restoration movement begun in the early nineteenth century by Barton Stone and Thomas and Alexander Campbell. Originating primarily among those Restorationist congregations in the South, it has become a national movement. It has been most identified for its disavowal of the use of instrumental music in worship and ultra congregational organization. Over the years the decentralized polity has allowed for a number of factions to develop over various beliefs and practices not accepted by the majority of churches. The Church of Christ (Non-instrumental) represent the largest faction of the movement.

Hq: No central headquarters. For information: *Firm Foundation*, P. O. Box 17200, Pensacola, FL 32522
or
Gospel Advocate, Box 150, Nashville, TN 37202
Tel: (615) 254 8781 or (800) 251 8446

Churches of Christ (Non-Instrumental, Conservative)

The Churches of Christ (Non-Instrumental, Conservative), who represent the most conservative wing of the Churches of Christ Movement, emerged in the South in the late-nineteenth century. It became a visible branch of the Movement in the 1950s. It follows the Movement in most respects but is distinguished from the larger body by its conservative approach to the support of institutions above and beyond the local church.

Hq: No central headquarters. For information: Florida College, 119 Glen Arven Avenue, Tampa, FL 33617
or
Guardian of Truth Foundation, P. O. Box 9670, Bowling Green, KY 42101

Churches of Christ (Non-Instrumental, Discipling)

During the 1970s some congregations of the Churches of Christ adopted the practice of membership training usually termed "discipling." The practice spread originally from the Crossroads Church of Christ in Gainesville, Florida. See also the entry on the Boston Church of Christ.

Hq: No central headquarters. For information: Crossroads Church of Christ, 2720 S.W. 2nd Avenue, Gainesville, FL 32607
Tel: (904) 378 1471

Churches of Christ (Non-Instrumental, Ecumenical)

The most liberal wing of the Churches of Christ, these churches advocate a broadly accepting attitude toward all the church groups which have grown out of the Restoration movement begun by Barton Stone and Thomas and Alexander Campbell.

Hq: No central headquarters. For information: *Restoration Review*, 1201 Windsor Dr., Denton, TX 76201

Churches of Christ (Non-Instrumental, Non-Class, One Cup)

The Churches of Christ (Non-Instrumental, Non-Class, One Cup) emerged in the twentieth century to oppose the introduction of individual communion cups in the Lord's Supper and Sunday schools.

Hq: No central headquarters. For information: *Old Paths Advocate*, Box 10811, Springfield, MO 65808

Churches of Christ (Non-Instrumental, Non-Sunday School)

Early in the twentieth century, a movement opposing sunday schools within the Churches of Christ became focused in 1936 in a magazine, *Gospel Tidings*, founded by G. B. Shelburne.

Hq: No central headquarters. For information: *Gospel Tidings*, 500 E. Henry, Hamilton, TX 76531

Churches of Christ (Non-Instrumental, Premillennial)

The debate within the Churches of Christ over premillennialism, the belief in Christ's imminent appearance to establish a millennial rule on earth, was focused upon the writings of R. H. Boll. During the 1930s, those congregations which accepted the premillennialist perspective became focused upon a magazine, *Word and Work*, published in Louisville, Kentucky.

Hq: Current address unavailable for this edition

Churches of Christ (Pentecostal)

During the 1970s many congregations of the Churches of Christ (Non-Instrumental) were affected by the Charismatic Movement and accepted its emphases upon the gifts of the Spirit, especially the practices of speaking-in-tongues and spiritual healing.

Hq: No central headquarters. For information: Conference on Spiritual Renewal, Box 457, Missouri City, TX 77459

Churches of God, General Conference

The Churches of God, General Conference was founded in 1825 by John Winebrenner, formerly a minister with the German Reformed Church in southeastern Pennsylvania.

Hq: United Church Center, Rm. 200, 900 S. Arlington Av., Harrisburg, PA 17109
Tel: (717) 652 0255

Churches of God, Holiness

The Churches of God, Holiness is a predominantly black holiness church founded in 1920 by Bishop King Hezekiah Burruss.

Hq: 170 Ashby Street, N.W., Atlanta, GA 30314

Churches of God (Independent Holiness People)

The Churches of God (Independent Holiness People) is a holiness church founded in 1922 as a split from the Church of God (Holiness).

Hq: 1225 E. First Street, Fort Scott, KS 66701

Churches of God in the British Isles and Overseas (Needed Truth)

The Churches of God in the British Isles and Overseas (Needed Truth) were founded in the 1890s by a group of Plymouth (or Open) Brethren.

Hq: Current address unavailable for this edition

Colonial Village Pentecostal Church of the Nazarene

The Colonial Village Pentecostal Church of the Nazarene was founded in 1968 by Bernard Gill and a small group of former members of the Church of the Nazarene.

Hq: Current address unavailable for this edition

Colorado Reform Baptist Church

The Colorado Reform Baptist Church is a loose association of Arminian (free will) Baptists founded in 1981. The church has an active social ministry.

Hq: Bishop William T. Conklin, Box 12514, Denver, CO 80212

Community Chapel and Bible Training Center

The Community Chapel and Bible Training Center is a Pentecostal-Charismatic fellowship founded in 1967 by Donald Lee Barnett.

Hq: 18635 8th Avenue S., Seattle, WA 98148
Tel: (206) 431 3100

Community Churches, International Council of

See: International Council of Community Churches

Community of Catholic Churches

The Community of Catholic Churches is an independent Catholic jurisdiction founded in 1971 by several Old Catholic bishops and priests under the leadership of Archbishop Thomas Sargent.

Hq: Most Rev. Thomas Sargent, 3 Columbia Street, Hartford, CT 06106

Community of the Love of Christ (Evangelical Catholic)

The Community of the Love of Christ (Evangelical Catholic), best known for its active support of the gay and lesbian community in San Francisco, was founded in 1959 (as the Primitive Catholic Church Evangelical Catholic) by Most Rev. Mikhail Francis Itkin.

Hq: 1546 Hayes St., San Francisco, CA 94117
Tel: (415) 864 2799

Concilio Olazabal de Iglesias Latino Americano

The Concilio Olazabal de Iglesias Latino Americano was founded in 1936 by Rev. Francisco Olazabal.

Hq: 1925 E. First Street, Los Angeles, CA 90033
Tel: (213) 267 8579

Concordant Publishing Concern

The Concordant Publishing Concern is a fundamentalist Bible student group founded by Adolph Ernst Knoch. Knoch developed a new way of dividing the periods of Bible history into "eons" which informed his interprepation of the Scriptures.

Hq: 15570 W. Knochaven Drive, Canyon Country, CA 91351
Tel: (805) 252 2112

Concordia Lutheran Conference

The Concordia Lutheran Conference is a conservative Lutheran body founded in 1956 by former ministers and members of the Lutheran Church-Missouri Synod.

Hq: Central Avenue at 171th Place,
  Tinley Park, IL 60477
Tel: (312) 532 4288

Conference of the Evangelical Mennonite Church

The Conference of the Evangelical Mennonite Church was founded in 1948 by Henry Egli.

Hq: Rev. Gary Gates, 1420 Kerrway
  Court, Fort Wayne, IN 46805
Tel: (219) 423 3649

Confraternity of Christian Doctrine, Saint Pius X

The Confraternity of Christian Doctrine, Saint Pius X is an independent Catholic jurisdiction founded in 1958 (as the Puerto Rican National Catholic Church) by Hector Gonzales.

Hq: Most Rev. Msgr. Hector Gonzales,
  10 Stagg Street, Brooklyn, New
  York 11206
Tel: (718) 338 3542

Congregation of Yah

The Congregation of Yah was founded in 1973 as Church of God Seventh Era by Larry Johnson, formerly of the Worldwide Church of God.

Hq: Current address unavailable for this
  edition

Congregational Bible Church

The Congregational Bible Church was founded by former members of the Mennonite Church in 1951 as the Congregational Mennonite Church, and took the present name in 1969.

Hq: Congregational Bible Church,
  Marietta, PA 17547
Tel: (215) 426 1345

Congregational Christian Churches, National Association of

See: National Association of Congregational Christian Churches

Congregational Holiness Church

The Congregational Holiness Church was founded in 1920 by Rev. Watson Sorrow and Hugh Bowling.

Hq: 3888 Fayetteville Hwy., Griffin, GA
  30223
Tel: (404) 228 4833

Congregational Methodist Church

The Congregational Methodist Church was founded in 1852 by members of the Georgia Conference protesting the episcopal structure of the Methodist Episcopal Church, South.

Hq: Box 155, Florence, MS 39073

Conservative Baptist Association of America

The Conservative Baptist Association of America was founded in 1947 by former ministers and members of the Northern Baptist Convention (now the American Baptist Churches in the U.S.A.).

Hq: c/o Gen. Dir. Dr. Tim Blanchard,
  Box 66, 25 W 560 Geneva Rd.,
  Wheaton, IL 60189
Tel: (312) 653 5350

Conservative Congregational Christian Conference

The Conservative Congregational Christian Conference was founded in 1945 by conservative ministers and members of the Congregational

Christian Churches who opposed the merger that created the United Church of Christ.

Hq: c/o 7582 Currell Blvd., St. Paul, MN 55125
Tel: (612) 739 1474

Conservative German Baptist Brethren

The Conservative German Baptist Brethren was founded in 1931 by members of the Dunkard Brethren Church who withdrew under the leadership of Clayton F. Weaver and Ervin J. Kenney.

Hq: Current address unavailable for this edition

Conservative Lutheran Association

See: World Confessional Lutheran Association

Conservative Mennonite Conference

The Conservative Mennonite Conference was founded in 1910 as an association of liberal Amish Mennonite congregations.

Hq: c/o Ivan J. Miller, Granstville, MD 21536

Conservative Mennonite Fellowship (Non-Conference)

The Conservative Mennonite Fellowship (Non-Conference) was founded in 1956 as a split from the Mennonite Church.

Hq: Box 36, Hartville, OH 44632

Continuing Episcopal Church

The Continuing Episcopal Church is an independent Anglican jurisdiction which formed in reaction to the Episcopal Church's ordaining of female ministers.

Hq: Rt. Rev. Henry C. Robbins, Ste. 722, 60 Skiff Street, Hamden, CT 06517

Coptic Orthodox Church

The Coptic Orthodox Church was organized in 1962 to serve Egyptian-American Christians who had migrated to the United States.

Hq: Archpriest Fr. Gabriel Abdelsayed, 427 West Side Avenue, Jersey City, NJ 07304
Tel: (201) 333 0004

Coptic Orthodox Church (Western Hemisphere)

The Coptic Orthodox Church (Western Hemisphere) is a small independent jurisdiction founded in the 1970s. Bishop Samuel T. Garner had been consecrated in 1976 by Archbishop James Francis Augustine Lashley of the American Catholic Church, Archdiocese of New York.

Hq: Mt. Rev. Samuel T. Garner, 117-38, 141 St., South Ozone Park, NY 11420

Cumberland Presbyterian Church

The Cumberland Presbyterian Church began on the Western frontier in the early nineteenth century. The present church is the continuing remnant which stayed out of the merger with the Presbyterian Church in the U.S.A. in 1906.

Hq: Cumberland Presbyterian Center, 1978 Union Avenue, Memphis, TN 38104
Tel: (901) 276 4572

Damascus Christian Church

The Damascus Christian Church is a Spanish-speaking Pentecostal church founded in 1939 by Francisco and Leoncai Rosado.

Hq: Rev. Enrique Melendez, 170 Mt. Eden Parkway, Bronx, NY 10473
Tel: (212) 583 5550

Davidian Seventh-Day Adventist Association

The Davidian Seventh-Day Adventist Association is one of several branches of the movement founded in 1934 by Victor T. Houteff.

Hq: Bashan Hill, Exeter, MO 65647
Tel: (417) 835 4922

Dawn Bible Students Association

The Dawn Bible Students Association was founded in the 1920s by some members of the Pastoral Bible Institute, one of several branches of the Bible Student movement founded by Charles Taze Russell.

Hq: 199 Railroad Avenue, East Rutherford, NJ 07073
Tel: (201) 438 6421

Defenders of the Truth

Defenders of the Truth was started in 1925 by Baptist evangelist Dr. Gerald B. Winrod.

Hq: Current address unavailable for this edition

Deliverance Evangelistic Centers

The Deliverance Evangelistic Centers is an independent Pentecostal fellowship founded in the 1950s by Arturo Skinner.

Hq: 505 Central Avenue, Newark, NJ 07017
or
621 Clinton Avenue, Newark, NJ
Tel: (210) 824 7300

Diocese of Christ the King

The Diocese of Christ the King is an independent Anglican jurisdiction founded in 1977 by Bishop Robert S. Morse in reaction to the liberalizing trends in the Episcopal Church.

Hq: c/o Rt. Rev. Robert S. Morse, 2316 Bowditch St., Box 40020, Berkeley, CA 94704
Tel: (415) 841 3083

Disciples of the Lord Jesus Christ

The Disciples of the Lord Jesus Christ is an independent evangelical movement founded in 1974 and headed by Rama Behera, a Christian teacher from India.

Hq: Rama Behera, Shawano, WI 54166

Door of Faith Church and Bible School

The Door of Faith Church and Bible School is a holiness Pentecostal church founded in 1940 by Mildred Johnson Brostek, formerly a minister with the Pentecostal Holiness Church.

Hq: 1161 Young Street, Honolulu, HI 96814

Duck River (and Kindred) Association of Baptists

The Duck River (and Kindred) Association of Baptists was founded in 1825 as a split from the Elk River Baptist Association in Tennessee.

Hq: Moderator Morris Broyler, Rt. 1, Readyville, TN 37149

Dunkard Brethren Church

The Dunkard Brethren Church was founded in 1922 by B. E. Kesler and former members of the Church of the Brethren.

Hq: Chairman Dale E. Jamison, Board of Trustees, Quinter, KS 67752

Eastern Orthodox Catholic Church in America

The Eastern Orthodox Catholic Church in America was founded in 1951 by John Chrysostom More-Moreno.

Hq: Most Rev. Dismas Markle, 321 S. Magnolia Avenue, Sanford, FL 32771

Ecumenical Catholic Church

The Ecumenical Catholic Church is a small independent Catholic jurisdiction.

Hq: c/o Dr. Mark S. Shirilau, Prime Bishop, P.O. Box 182, Villa Grande, CA 95486
Tel: (707) 865 1880
Fax: (707) 865 2437

Ecumenical Catholic Diocese of America

The Ecumenical Catholic Diocese of America is an independent Catholic jurisdiction founded in 1984 by Fr. Peter Brennan and former members of the Roman Catholic Church.

Hq: 151 Regent Place, W. Hensted, NY 11552
Tel: (516) 485 0616

Ecumenical Orthodox Catholic Church-Autocephalous

See: Holy Eastern Orthodox Catholic and Apostolic Church in North America

Elim Fellowship

The Elim Fellowship is a Pentecostal church founded by Rev. and Mrs. Ivan Q. Spencer in 1932 as the Elim Minister Fellowship. It took its present name in 1972.

Hq: 7245 College Street, Lima, NY 14485
Tel: (716) 582 2790

Emmanuel Association

The Emmanuel Association is a holiness church founded in 1937 by Ralph G. Finch.

Hq: West Cucharas at 27th Street, Colorado Springs, CO 80904

Emmanuel's Fellowship

The Emmanuel's Fellowship was founded in 1966 by Paul Goodling as a split from the Old Order River Brethren.

Hq: Current address unavailable for this edition

Emmanuel Holiness Church

The Emmanuel Holiness Church is a Pentecostal church founded in 1953 as a split from the Pentecostal Fire-Baptized Holiness Church.

Hq: Box 818, Bladenboro, NC 28320

Epiphany Bible Students Association

The Epiphany Bible Students Association is one of several smaller branches of the Bible Students Movement founded by Charles Taze Russell in the late-nineteenth century. It was founded in 1968 by John J. Hoefle, formerly of the Laymen's Home Missionary Movement.

Hq: Box 97, Mount Dora, FL 32757

Episcopal Church

The Episcopal Church continues the mission established by the Church of England in the American Colonies in the seventeenth century. Becoming independent after the American Revolution, the church was known for many years as the Protestant Episcopal Church in the U.S.A. and more recently took its popular shorter name as its official name.

Hq: 815 Second Avenue, New York, NY 10017
Tel: (212) 867 8400

Estonian Evangelical Lutheran Church

The Estonian Evangelical Lutheran Church was reorganized by Estonian refugees during World War II and brought to North America soon after the war.

Hq: Rev. Karl Raudsepp, Bishop of North America, 30 Sunrise Avenue, Apt. 216, Toronto, ON, Canada M4A 2R3
or
International Hq: Wallingatan 32, Box 45074, 10430 Stockholm 45, Sweden

Estonian Orthodox Church in Exile

The Estonian Orthodox Church in Exile was founded by Estonian refugees following the overrun of their country during World War II. The church was established in the United States in 1949.

Hq: c/o Rev. Sergius Samon, 5332 Fountain Avenue, Los Angeles, CA 90029
or
International Hq: c/o Rev. Nikolai Suursot, Fridhemsgatan 2-4 V, 112 40 Stockholm, Sweden

Ethiopian Orthodox Church in the United States of America

The Ethiopian Orthodox Church in the United States of America is a branch of the Ethiopian Orthodox Church headquartered in Addis Ababa, Ethiopia. It came to the United States in 1959 under the leadership of Archbishop Laike Mandrefo.

Hq: c/o His Eminence Abuna Yeshaq, Archbishop, 140-142 W. 176th Street, Bronx, NY 10453
Tel: (212) 299 2741
or
International Hq: His Holiness Abuna Tekle Haimanot, Box 1283, Addis Ababa, Ethiopia

Ethiopian Orthodox Coptic Church, Diocese of North and South America

The Ethiopian Orthodox Coptic Church, Diocese of North and South America was founded in 1959 by Abuna Gabre Kristos Mikael, an independent Ethiopian-American bishop.

Hq: 1255 Bedford Avenue, Brooklyn, NY 11216

Eucharistic Catholic Church

The Eucharistic Catholic Church was founded in 1970 by Fr. Robert Clement who was consecrated in 1974 by Archbishop Richard A. Marchenna of the Old Roman Catholic Church.

Hq: Bishop Robert Clement, 348 W. 144 Street, New York, NY 10011

Evangelical Bible Church

The Evangelical Bible Church is a pentecostal church founded in 1947 by Rev. Frederick B. Marine.

Hq: 2444 Washington Blvd., Baltimore,
      MD 21230
Tel: (301) 644 3185

Evangelical Catholic Church

The Evangelical Catholic Church is an independent Catholic jurisdiction which attempts to include some Lutheran emphases. It was established in the 1970s by Archbishop Mark Robert Hakes.

Hq: c/o Mt. Rev. Karl J. Berwin,
      Presiding Bishop,   P.O. Box
      6821, Phoenix, AZ 85005

Evangelical Catholic Communion

The Evangelical Catholic Communion is an independent Catholic jurisdiction founded in 1960 by Michael A. Itkin and reorganized in 1968 by Archbishop Ballard.

Hq: Most Rev. Marlin Paul Bausum
      Ballard, P. O. Box 8484,
      Baltimore, MD 21234
Tel: (301) 665 6587

Evangelical Christian Church (Wesleyan)

The Evangelical Christian Church (Wesleyan) is a holiness church founded in 1889 as the Heavenly Recruit Association.

Hq: Box 277, Birdsboro, PA 19508

Evangelical Church of Christ (Holiness)

The Evangelical Church of Christ (Holiness) is a predominantly black holiness church founded in 1947 in Washington, D.C., by Bishop Holman E. Williams, formerly of the Church of Christ (Holiness).

Hq: 1938 Sanannah Place, Washington,
      DC 20020

Evangelical Church of North America

The Evangelical Church of North America was founded in 1968 by former members of the Evangelical United Brethren who rejected that church's merger into the United Methodist Church.

Hq: c/o Gen. Superintendent Dr.
      George K. Millen, 7525 S.E.
      Lake Rd., Suite 7, Milwaukee,
      OR 97267
Tel: (503) 652 1029

Evangelical Congregational Church

The Evangelical Congregational Church was formed by members of the United Evangelical Church who did not approve of the merger of that church into the Evangelical Association in 1922. The Evangelical Association is now a constituent part of the United Methodist Church.

Hq: Evangelical Congregational Church
      Center, 100 W. Park Avenue,
      Box 186, Myerstown, PA 17067

Evangelical Covenant Church of America

The Evangelical Covenant Church of America, Swedish pietist church, was founded in 1885 as a merger of the Swedish Lutheran Mission Synod and the Swedish Lutheran Ansgarius Synod. It took the present name in 1957.

Hq: 5101 N. Francisco Avenue,
      Chicago, IL 60625
Tel: (312) 784 3000

Evangelical Episcopal Church

The Evangelical Episcopal Church is a small independent Anglican jurisdiction.

Hq: c/o Rt. Rev. Edward H. Marshall, 600 West 113th Street, New York, NY 10025

Evangelical Free Church of America

The Evangelical Free Church of America was founded in 1950 as a merger of the Swedish Evangelical Free Church and the Norwegian-Danish Evangelical Free Church.

Hq: 1551 E. 66th Street, Minneapolis, MN 55423
Tel: (612) 866 3343

Evangelical Friends Church, Eastern Division

The Evangelical Friends Church, Eastern Division was formed in 1913 as the Ohio Yearly Meeting of Friends. It follows a conservative holiness faith.

Hq: 1201 30th St., N.W., Canton, OH 44709
Tel: (216) 493 1660

Evangelical Lutheran Church in America

The Evangelical Lutheran Church in America is a small Lutheran jurisdiction founded in 1846 by Elling Eielsen among Norwegian-Americans.

Hq: c/o Truman Larson, Rte. 1, Jackson, MN 56143

Evangelical Lutheran Church in America (1988)

The Evangelical Lutheran Church in America (1988), the largest Lutheran body in the United States, continues the first Lutheran churches in America. It was founded in 1988 as a merger of the Lutheran Church in America, the American Lutheran Church, and the Association of Evangelical Lutheran Churches.

Hq: c/o Exec. Adm. Rev. Dr. Robert N. Bacher, 8765 W. Higgins Rd., Chicago, IL 60631
Tel: (312) 380 2700

Evangelical Lutheran Synod

The Evangelical Lutheran Synod was founded in 1918 by conservative members of the Norwegian Lutheran Church.

Hq: c/o Pres. Rev. George Orvick, 447 N. Division Street, Mankato, MN 56001

Evangelical Mennonite Brethren Conference

See: Fellowship of Evangelical Bible Churches

Evangelical Mennonite Church, Inc.

See: Conference of the Evangelical Mennonite Church

Evangelical Methodist Church

The Evangelical Methodist Church is a conservative evangelical church founded in 1946 by a group of former members of the Methodist Church (1939-1968) under the leadership of Dr. J. H. Hamblen.

Hq: 3000 W. Kellogg, Wichita, KS 67213
Tel: (316) 943 3278

Evangelical Methodist Church of America

The Evangelical Methodist Church of America was founded in 1952 by former members of the Evangelical Methodist Church under the leadership of Rev. W. W. Beckbill.

Hq: Box 751, Kingsport, TN 37662

Evangelical Ministers and Churches, International, Inc.

The Evangelical Ministers and Churches, International was founded in 1950 by a group of independent ministers.

Hq: 105 Madison, Chicago, IL 60602

Evangelical Orthodox (Catholic) Church in America (Non-Papal Catholic)

The Evangelical Orthodox (Catholic) Church in America (Non-Papal Catholic) is a church combining Roman Catholic and Lutheran emphases. It was founded by Bishop Wilhelm Waterstraat in 1938 as Protestant Orthodox Western Church and took the present name in 1948 under Archbishop Frederick L. Pyman.

Hq: Current address unavailable for this edition

Evangelical Presbyterian Church

The Evangelical Presbyterian Church is a conservative Presbyterian Church founded in 1981.

Hq: 26049 Five Mile Rd., Detroit, MI 48239
Tel: (313) 532 9555

Evangelical Wesleyan Church

The Evangelical Wesleyan Church is a conservative holiness church founded in 1963 as a merger of the Wesleyan Church of North America and of the Midwest Holiness Association.

Hq: Current address unavailable for this edition

Evangelistic Church of God

The Evangelistic Church of God is a Pentecostal church founded in 1949 by Norman L. Chase and former members of the Church of God (Cleveland, Tennessee)

Hq: Current address unavailable for this edition

Faith Assembly

Faith Assembly is a Pentecostal association founded in 1978 by Hobart E. Freeman.

Hq: Wilmot, IN 46590

Faith Mission Church

The Faith Mission Church is a holiness church founded in 1963 by Rev. Ray Snow.

Hq: Pastor Leonard Sankey, 1813 26th Street, Bedford, IN 47421

Faith Tabernacle Corporation of Churches

The Faith Tabernacle Corporation of Churches, a predominantly black Pentecostal church, was founded in 1962 in Portland, Oregon, by Johnnie Welsh-Castle.

Hq: 7015 N. E. 23rd Avenue, Portland, OR 97211
Tel: (505) 282 8071

Family of Love (Children of God)

The Family of Love was founded in California in 1969 by David Berg and originally known as the Children of God. In the 1970s the headquarters shifted to England.

International Hq: BM Box 8440, London, UK WC1N 3XX

Fellowship of Christian Assemblies

The Fellowship of Christian Assemblies is an independent Pentecostal church founded in 1922 as the Independent Assemblies of God. It assumed its present name in 1973.

Hq: Current address unavailable for this edition

Fellowship of Evangelical Bible Churches

The Fellowship of Evangelical Bible Churches can be traced to work organized in 1889 by Isaac Peters and Aaron Walls. Going through a variety of name changes, prior to 1987, the group was known as the Evangelical Mennonite Brethren Conference.

Hq: 5800 S. 14th Street, Omaha, NE 68107
Tel: (402) 731 4780

Fellowship of Fundamental Bible Churches

The Fellowship of Fundamental Bible Churches was formed by former members of the Methodist Protestant Church in New Jersey who opposed their church's merger into the Methodist Church in 1939. For many years they retained the name Methodist Protestant Church, but adopted their present name in 1985

Hq: Rev. Howard E. Haines, Box 43, Glassboro, NJ 08028

Fellowship of Grace Brethren Churches

The Fellowship of Grace Brethren Churches was founded in 1930s by former members of the Brethren Church (Ashland, Ohio).

Hq: P. O. Box 386, Winona Lake, IN 46590
Tel: (219) 267 5566 or 267 6623

Fellowship of Independent Evangelical Churches

The Fellowship of Independent Evangelical Churches was founded in 1949 by Dr. L. P. McClenny and other independent fundamentalist ministers.

Hq: Current address unavailable for this edition

Filipino Assemblies of the First Born

The Filipino Assemblies of the First Born founded in 1933 by Rev. Julian Barnabe, is a Pentecostal church serving Filipino-Americans.

Hq: 1229 Glenwood, Delano, CA 93215

Filipino Community Churches

The Filipino Community Churches was founded in 1947 by Rev. N. Z. Dizon.

Hq: Current address unavailable for this edition

Finnish Orthodox Church

From the small Orthodox community in Finland, a first group of American adherents of the Finnish Orthodox Church was organized in Michigan in 1955.

Hq: Current address unavailable for this edition

Fire-Baptized Holiness Church of God of the Americas

The Fire-Baptized Holiness Church of God of the Americas is a predominantly black Pentecostal church founded in 1908 by W. E. Fuller.

Hq: 901 Anderson Road, Greenville, SC 20743
or
c/o The Fuller Press, 130 Jackson Street, N.E., Atlanta, GA 30312

Fire-Baptized Holiness Church (Wesleyan)

The Fire-Baptized Holiness Church (Wesleyan) was founded in 1890 as the Southeast Kansas Fire Baptized Holiness Associations by former members of the Methodist Episcopal Church. It assumed its present name in 1945.

Hq: c/o Gen. Superintendent Gerald Broadway, 600 College Avenue, Independence, KS 67301
Tel: (316) 331 3049

First Assembly Holiness Church of God in Christ

The First Assembly Holiness Church of God in Christ is a predominantly black Oneness Pentecostal church founded in Trenton, Florida, in the late 1940s by Prophet Richard Lee Jones.

Hq: P. O. Box 503, Trenton, FL 32693
Tel: (904) 463 2613

First Born Church of the Living God

The First Born Church of the Living God, a predominantly black Pentecostal church, was founded in 1913 in Waycross, Georgia, by a Bishop Echols, an early member of the Church of the Living God, The Pillar and Ground of Truth.

Hq: Current address unavailable for this edition.

First Congregational Methodist Church of the U.S.A.

The First Congregational Methodist Church of the U.S.A. was founded in 1941 by former members of the Congregational Methodist Church.

Hq: Decatur, MS 39327

First Deliverance Church of Atlanta

The First Deliverance Church of Atlanta is a Pentecostal church founded in 1956 by Reverends Lillian G. and William Fitch.

Hq: Current address unavailable for this edition

First Interdenominational Christian Association

The First Interdenominational Christian Association is a holiness church founded in 1946 by Rev. Watson Sorrow.

Hq: Calvary Temple, Holiness Church, 1061 Memorial Dr., S.E., Atlanta, GA 30315
Tel: (404) 522 1995

Followers of Christ

The Followers of Christ is a small Bible-oriented movement founded by a Mr. Riess.

Hq: Elder Marion Morris, Ringwood, OK 73768

For My God and My Country

"For My God and My Country" is an independent Catholic group oriented on the messages from the Blessed Virgin Mary which it claims had been received by Mary Ann Van Hoof, a visionary.

Hq: Necedah, WI 54646

Foundation for Biblical Research

The Foundation for Biblical Research was founded in 1985 by Dr. Ernest L. Martin, formerly a professor at Ambassador College, the school sponsored by the Worldwide Church of God.

Hq: Box 499, Pasadena, CA 91102

Fountain of Life Fellowship

The Fountain of Life Fellowship, a Church of God Adventist association, was founded in 1970 by James L. Porter, formerly a minister with the Worldwide Church of God.

Hq: Valley Center, KS 67147
Tel: (316) 755 0576

Free and Old Christian Reformed Church of Canada and America

The Free and Old Christian Reformed Church of Canada and America was founded in 1926 as the Free Reformed Church. This conservative Reformed group assumed its present name in 1949.

Hq: Jacob Tamminga, 950 Ball Avenue, N.E., Grand Rapids, MI 49503

Free Anglican Church in America

The Free Anglican Church in America is a small independent Anglican jurisdiction.

Hq: c/o Rt. Rev. Joseph Lampl, 9537 Helen Avenue, Sunland, CA 91040

Free Christian Zion Church of Christ

The Free Christian Zion Church of Christ is a predominantly black Methodist church founded in 1905 by Rev. E. D. Brown.

Hq: c/o Chief Pastor Willie Benson, 1315 Hutchinson, Nashville, AR 71852

Free Church of God in Christ

The Free Church of God in Christ is a predominantly black Pentecostal Church founded in 1915 by J. H. Morris and former members of the Church of God in Christ.

Hq: Current address unavailable for this edition

Free Church of God in Christ in Jesus' Name

The Free Church of God in Christ in Jesus' Name is a predominantly black sabbatarian Oneness Pentecostal church founded in 1927 in Austin, Texas, by Bishop Earl Evans and Elizabeth Evans.

Hq: 1904 East Weir Avenue, Phoenix, AZ 85401
Tel: (602) 276 5902

Free Church of God True Holiness

The Free Church of God True Holiness, a predominantly black holiness church, was founded in Kansas City, Kansas, in the 1920s.

Hq: 1900 N. 3rd Street, Kansas City, KS 66101

Free Gospel Church, Inc.

The Free Gospel Church is an early Pentecostal church founded in 1916 by Reverends Frank Casley and William Casley. Originally known as the United Free Gospel and Missionary Society, it assumed its present name in 1958.

Hq: Rev. Chester H. Heath, Box 477, Export, PA 15632

Free Lutheran Congregations, Association of

See: Association of Free Lutheran Congregations

Free Methodist Church of North America

The Free Methodist Church of North America was founded in 1860 as the result of a split in the Genesee Conference of the Methodist Episcopal Church.

Hq: Bishop Robert F. Andrews, 901 College Avenue, Winona Lake, IN 46590
Tel: (219) 267 7656

Free Protestant Episcopal Church

The Free Protestant Episcopal Church was founded in 1897 by the union of the Ancient British Church, the Nazarene Episcopal Ecclesia, and the Free Protestant Church of England. In 1958 the Church was established in USA.

Hq: c/o Mt. Rev. Edwin D. Follick, 6435 Jumilla Avenue, Woodland Hills, CA 91367
Tel: (818) 346 6228

Free Serbian Orthodox Church- Diocese for the U.S.A. and Canada

The Free Serbian Orthodox Church-Diocese for the U.S.A. and Canada was founded in 1984 after a successful effort to gain control of the Serbian Orthodox Church in America by representatives of the Patriarch of Belgrade (Yugoslavia) from the followers of Bishop Dionisji (Milivojevich).

Hq: Metropolitan Ireney (Kovachevich), P. O. Box 371, Grayslake, IL 60030
Tel: (312) 223 4300

Free Will Baptist Church of the Pentecostal Faith

The Free Will Baptist Church of the Pentecostal Faith was founded in the 1950s as a split from the South Carolina Pentecostal Free Will Baptist Church.

Hq: Current address unavailable for this edition

Friends General Conference

The Friends General Conference, founded in 1900, brought together the many yearly meetings of the Society of Friends who followed the unprogrammed and free spirit of the Quakers associated with Friends minister Elias Hicks (1748-1830).

Hq: 1520-B Race Street, Philadelphia, PA 19102
Tel: (215) 241 7270

Friends United Meeting

The Friends United Meeting was founded by the more programmed and "orthodox" tradition among Friends in 1902. At first known as the Five Years Meeting, it assumed its present name in 1965.

Hq: 101 Quaker Hill Dr., Richmond, IN 47374
Tel: (317) 962 7573

Full Gospel Assemblies International

Full Gospel Assemblies International is a Pentecostal body started in 1972 under the leadership of Dr. Charles E. Strauser.

Hq: Pres. Dr. Charles E. Strauser, P.O. Box 1230, Coatesville, PA 19320
Tel: (215) 857 2357

Full Gospel Church Association

The Full Gospel Church Association is an independent Pentecostal church founded in 1952 by Rev. Dennis W. Thorn.

Hq: Box 265, Amarillo, TX 79105

Full Gospel Evangelistic Association

The Full Gospel Evangelistic Association is a Pentecostal church established in the 1940s by former members of the Apostolic Faith Church.

Hq: 5828 Chippewa Blvd., Houston, TX 70086
Tel: (713) 448 5125

Full Gospel Fellowship of Churches and Ministers International

The Full Gospel Fellowship of Churches and Ministers International was founded in 1962 by a group of independent Pentecostal ministers under the leadership of Gordon Lindsey. The Fellowship has a special emphasis upon divine healing.

Hq: 1545 W. Mockingbird Ln., Suite 1012, Dallas, TX 75235
Tel: (214) 630 1949

Full Gospel Pentecostal Association

The Full Gospel Pentecostal Association is a predominantly black Pentecostal church founded in 1970 in Portland, Oregon, by Bishops Adolph Well, Pastor Edna Travis, and Elder S. D. Leffall.

Hq: 1032 North Sumer, Portland, OR 97217
or
Tabernacle Evangelism Community Church, 1300 N. La Brea Avenue, Inglewood, CA 90302
Tel: (213) 678 0135

Full Salvation Union

The Full Salvation Union was founded in 1934 by James F. Andrews.

Hq: Northville, MI 48167

Fundamental Baptist Fellowship

The Fundamental Baptist Fellowship was founded in 1961 as a split from the Conservative Baptist Association.

Hq: Current address unavailable for this edition

Fundamental Baptist Fellowship Association

The Fundamental Baptist Fellowship Association was founded in 1962 by black members of the General Association of Regular Baptist Churches (GARBC).

Hq: Current address unavailable for this edition

Fundamental Brethren Church

The Fundamental Brethren Church was founded in 1962 as a split from the Church of the Brethren.

Hq: Current address unavailable for this edition

Fundamental Methodist Church, Inc.

The Fundamental Methodist Church, Inc. was founded in 1942 by Rev. Roy Keith and former members of the Methodist Protestant Church who rejected that church's merger into the Methodist Church (1993-1968).

Hq: 1034 N. Broadway, Springfield, MO 65802

General Assemblies and Church of the First Born

The General Assemblies and Church of the First Born is one of the early Pentecostal bodies founded in 1907.

Hq: Current address unavailable for this edition

General Association of Davidian Seventh-Day Adventists

The General Association of Davidian Seventh-Day Adventists was one of several groups that formed when the movement, founded by Victor T. Houteff, splintered following his death.

Hq: Route 1, Box 384, Salem, SC 29676
Tel: (803) 944 1254

General Association of General Baptists

The General Association of General Baptists was founded in the 1820s by Benoni Stinson.

Hq: 100 Stinson Dr., Poplar Bluff, MO 63901

General Association of Regular Baptist Churches

The General Association of Regular Baptist Churches grew out of the Baptist Bible Union created by fundamentalist members of the Northern Baptist Convention in 1922. Despaired of turning the Convention

from its liberalizing tendencies, many members of the Union left the Convention in 1932 to form the GARBC.

Hq: 1300 N. Meacham Rd., Schaumburg, IL 60173
Tel: (312) 843 1600

General Conference of Mennonite Brethren Churches

See: Mennonite Brethren Church of North America

General Conference Mennonite Church

The General Conference Mennonite Church was founded in 1860 by a union of more liberal and innovative Mennonite congregations under the leadership of John H. Oberholtzer.

Hq: c/o Gen. Sec. Vern Preheim, 722 Main Street, Newton, KS 67114
Tel: (316) 283 5100

General Conference of the Church of God (Seventh Day)

The General Conference of the Church of God (Seventh Day) grew out of the movement of those Adventists who in the 1850s rejected the visions and messages of Ellen G. White (founder of the Seventh-day Adventist Church), who had accepted the idea of worship on the Sabbath.

Hq: 330 W. 152nd Avenue, P. O. Box 33677, Denver, CO 80233
Tel: (303) 452 7973

General Conference of the Evangelical Baptist Church, Inc.

The General Conference of the Evangelical Baptist Church was founded in 1935 as Church of the Full Gospel, Inc.

Hq: 1601 E. Rose St., Goldsboro, NC 27530
Tel: (919) 734 2482

General Council of the Churches of God

The General Council of the Churches of God was founded in 1949 as a split from the General Conference of the Church of God (Seventh Day).

Hq: 1827 W. 3rd Street, Meridian, ID 83642-1653
Tel: (208) 888 3380

General Six-Principle Baptists

The General Six-Principle Baptists, one of the earliest of Baptist organizations in America, was founded in 1652.

Hq: c/o Pres. Rev. Edgar S. Kirk, Rhode Island Conference, 350 Davisville Rd., North Kingstown, RI 02852
Tel: (401) 884 2750

German Apostolic Christian Church

The German Apostolic Christian Church was founded in the 1930s by Martin Steidinger as a split from the Apostolic Christian Churches of America.

Hq: Current address unavailable for this edition

Glorious Church of God in Christ Apostolic Faith

The Glorious Church of God in Christ Apostolic Faith is a predominantly black Oneness Pentecostal church founded by C. H. Stokes in 1921. Passing through a crisis in 1952, it emerged under the leadership of S. C. Bass.

Hq: Current address unavailable for this edition

God's House of Prayer for All Nations

The God's House of Prayer for All Nations is a predominantly black Pentecostal church founded in 1964 by Bishop Tommie Lawrence, formerly a member of the Church of God in Christ.

Hq: Current address unavailable for this edition

God's Missionary Church

The God's Missionary Church is a conservative holiness church founded in 1935 by former members of the Pilgrim Holiness Church.

Hq: c/o Rev. Paul Miller, Swengal, PA 17880

Gospel Assemblies (Jolly)

The Gospel Assemblies (Jolly) is one of several groups which grew out of the early Pentecostal ministry of William Sowders in the South and Midwest. It was founded in 1965 by Tom M. Jolly.

Hq: Current address unavailable for this edition

Gospel Assemblies (Sowders/Goodwin)

The Gospel Assemblies (Sowders/Goodwin) traces its history to the ministry of pioneer Pentecostal minister, William Sowders. In the splintering of the movement in the years following Sowders' death, Lloyd L. Godwin, pastor of the Gospel Assembly Church in Des Moines, became the center of the largest network of churches and ministers.

Hq: Gospel Assembly Church, 7135 Meredith Dr., Des Moines, IA 50322
Tel: (515) 276 1331

Gospel Harvesters Evangelistic Association (Atlanta)

The Gospel Harvesters Evangelistic Association (Atlanta), a Charismatic fellowship of churches, was founded in 1961 by Earl P. Paulk Jr. and Harry A. Mushegan, both former ministers with the Church of God (Cleveland, Tennessee).

Hq: 1521 Hurt Road, S.W., Marietta, GA 30060
Tel: (404) 435 1152

Gospel Mission Corps

The Gospel Mission Corps is a holiness church founded in 1962 by Obert S. Tarton II, a former member of the Pillar of Fire.

Hq: Box 175, Highstown, MD 08520

Gospel Spreading Church

The Gospel Spreading Church is a predominantly black holiness church founded in 1922 by evangelist Lightfoot Solomon Michaux, who became a nationally syndicated radio minister in the 1950s.

Hq: 2030 Georgia Avenue, N.W., Washington, D.C. 20003
Tel: (202) 387 1471

Grace and Hope Mission

The Grace and Hope Mission is a holiness church founded in 1914 by Mamie E. Caske and Jennie E. Goranflo.

Hq: 4 S. Gay Street, Baltimore, MD 21202
Tel: (301) 685 5252

Grace Brethren Churches, Fellowship of

See: Fellowship of Grace Brethren Churches

Grace Gospel Fellowship

The Grace Gospel Fellowship is a "ultra"-dispensationalist fundamentalist association founded in 1944 by Pastor J. C. O'Hair and Charles Baker.

Hq: c/o Pres. Charles E. O'Connor, 1011 Aldon Street, S.W., Grand Rapids, MI 49509
Tel: (616) 531 0046

Greek Archdiocese of Vasiloupolis

The Greek Archdiocese of Vasiloupolis is a conservative "old calendar" Orthodox church founded in 1970 by Archimandrite Pangratios Vrionis.

Hq: 44-02 48th Avenue, Sunnyside/Woodside, NY 11377

Greek Orthodox Archdiocese of North and South America

Greek immigrants settled in America in the nineteenth century and organized parishes under the jurisdiction of the Russian Orthodox Church. In 1918, they established a separate ethnic diocese, which eventaully became the Greek Orthodox Archdiocese of North and South America.

Hq: His Eminence Archbishop Iakovos, 8-10 E. 79th Street, New York, NY 10021
Tel: (212) 570 3500
    or
International Hq: Ecumenical Patriarchate of Constantinople, Rum Patrikhanesi, Fener, Istanbul

Greek Orthodox Church of America

The Greek Orthodox Church of America was founded in 1971 by Father Theodore Kyritsis, a former priest in the Greek Orthodox Archdiocese of North and South America.

Hq: Current address unavailable for this edition

Greek Orthodox Diocese of New York

The Greek Orthodox Diocese of New York was founded in 1964 by Bishop Photios and former members of the Greek Orthodox Archdiocese of North and South America.

Hq: Current address unavailable for this edition

Hall Deliverance Foundation

The Hall Deliverance Foundation is a pentecostal fellowship founded in 1956 by Rev. Franklin Hall.

Hq: Box 9910, Phoenix, AZ 85068
Tel: (602) 944 5711

Healing Temple Church

The Healing Temple Church is a predominantly black Pentecostal church founded in Macon, Georgia, by Bishop P. J. Welch. Welch traveled for many years as a Pentecostal healing evangelist.

Hq: 660 William Street, Macon, GA 31201
Tel: (912) 742 5308

Highway Christian Church of Christ

The Highway Christian Church of Christ is a predominantly black One-ness Pentecostal church founded in 1929 by James Thomas Morris, formerly a minister with the Pentecostal Assemblies of the World.

Hq: 436 W St. N.W., Washington, D.C. 20001
Tel: (202) 234 3940

Holiness Baptist Association

The Holiness Baptist Association is a Pentecostal church founded in 1894 as a split from the Little River Baptist Association.

Hq: Current address unavailable for this edition

Holiness Church of God, Inc.

The Holiness Church of God is a Pentecostal church founded in 1920 by holiness believers under the leadership of Elder James A. Frost.

Hq: Box 541, Galax, VA 24333
Tel: (919) 227 2755

Holiness Gospel Church

The Holiness Gospel Church is a conservative holiness church founded in 1945 by former members of the Evangelical United Brethren and of the Church in God.

Hq: Rte. 2, Box 13, Etters, PA 17319

Holy Apostolic-Catholic Church of the East (Chaldean-Syrian)

The Holy Apostolic-Catholic Church of the East (Chaldean-Syrian) is an independent Orthodox jurisdiction founded in late 1970s by Mar Mikhael (Michael Rice).

Hq: Metropolitan Mikhael, 190 Palisades Dr., Daly City, CA 94015
Tel: (415) 755-4447

Holy Catholic Church, Anglican Rite Jurisdiction of the Americas
The Holy Catholic Church, Anglican Rite Jurisdiction of the Americas, is an independent Anglican jurisdiction founded in 1980.

Hq: Archbishop Most Rev. G. Wayne Craig, P. O. Box 14352, Columbus, OH 43214
Tel: (614) 476-4191

Holy Eastern Orthodox Catholic and Apostolic Church in North America (THEOCACNA)
The Holy Eastern Orthodox Catholic and Apostolic Church in North America was founded in the 1970s by Archbishop Francis J. Ryan as the Ecumenical Orthodox Catholic Church-Autocephalous. It assumed its present designation in 1988.

Hq: c/o Archbishop Seraphim Holdridge, P.O. Box 21451, Baltimore, MD 21208-0451

Holy Eastern Orthodox Church of the United States
The Holy Eastern Orthodox Church of the United States, formed in 1971, continues the tradition of Bishop Aftimios Ofiesh under Metropolitan Trevor Wyatt Moore who formed the Orthodox Catholic Archdiocese of Philadelphia. The Church assumed its present name in 1976.

Hq: Most Rev. Trevor W. Moore, 1611 Wallace Street, Philadelphia, PA 19130
Tel: (215) 232 1780

Holy Episcopal Church in America
The Holy Episcopal Church in America is an independent liturgical jurisdiction.

Hq: c/o Mt. Rev. George C. Lyon, 707 Chillingworth Drive, West Palm Beach, FL 33409

Holy Orthodox Catholic Apostolic Church in the Philippines
The Holy Orthodox Catholic Apostolic Church in the Philippines is an independent Orthodox jurisdiction based in the Philippines and affiliated with the Catholic Apostolic Church of Brazil. Bishop Forest Barber is the church's American liaison.

Hq: c/o Rt. Rev. Forest E. Barber, 2552 San Francisco Avenue, Long Beach, CA 90806

Holy Orthodox Catholic Church
The Holy Orthodox Catholic Church is an independent Orthodox jurisdiction founded in 1965 as the American Orthodox Church by Bishop Paul G. Russell. It assumed its present name in 1972.

Hq: c/o Most Rev. Paul G. Russell, 5831 Tremont, Dallas, TX 75214

Holy Orthodox Catholic Church, Eastern and Apostolic
The Holy Orthodox Catholic Church, Eastern and Apostolic is an independent Orthodox jurisdiction founded in 1984 by Richard Bruce Morrill (Mar Apriam) (d. 1991).

Hq: Current address unavailable for this edition

Holy Orthodox Catholic Church in America
The Holy Orthodox Catholic Church in America is a small independent Orthodox jurisdiction.

Hq: Rt. Rev. Richard McFarland, 127 Broad St., Groton, CT 06340

Holy Orthodox Church in America

The Holy Orthodox Church in America is an independent Orthodox jurisdiction founded in 1934 by George Winslow Plummer. The church is intimately connected with the Rosicrucian Society in America.

Hq: 10 E. Chestnut, Kingston, NY 12401
Tel: (914) 339 6335 or (518) 239 4349

Holy Orthodox Church, American Jurisdiction

The Holy Orthodox Church, American Jurisdiction is an independent Orthodox jurisdiction which grew out of the former Western Rite parishes of the Antiochean Orthodox Church. It was founded in 1974 by Archbishop William Francis Forbes.

Hq: Most Rev. W. Francis Forbes, P. O. Box 400, 138 Overby Dr., Antioch, TX 37013
Tel: (615) 833 9564

Holy Orthodox Old Catholic Church

The Holy Orthodox Old Catholic Church is a small independent Catholic jurisdiction.

Hq: Rt. Rev. Paul I. French, Long Beach, CA

Holy Temple of God, Inc.

The Holy Temple of God, a predominantly black Pentecostal church, was founded by Bishop Walter Camps, a popular evangelist formerly with the Church of God by Faith.

Hq: Big Apple Road, East Palatka, FL 32077

Holy Ukrainian Autocephalic Orthodox Church in Exile

The Holy Ukrainian Autocephalic Orthodox Church in Exile was founded in 1951 by Archbishops Palladios Rudenko and Ihor Huba.

Hq: c/o Adm. Rt. Rev. Serhij K. Pastukhiv, 103 Evergreen St. W., Babylon, NY 11704
Tel: (516) 669 7402

Hoomana Naauoa O Hawaii

The Hoomana Naauoa O Hawaii is an evangelical church founded in 1853 by Rev. J. H. Poliwailehua and others.

Hq: 910 Cooke St., Honolulu, HI 96813

House of God, Holy Church of the Living God, The Pillar and Ground of Truth, the House of Prayer for All People

The House of God is a predominantly black Pentecostal Church founded in 1914 in Beaufort, South Carolina, by Bishop R. A. R. Johnson.

Hq: 548 Georgetown Street, Lexington, KY 50608

House of God Which is the Church of the Living God, The Pillar and Ground of Truth, Inc.

The House of God Which is the Church of the Living God, The Pillar and Ground of Truth is a predominantly black Pentecostal church. It was created by the 1926 merger of several groups which had split from the Church of the Living God (Christian Workers for Fellowship). Work in Philadelphia is traced to Rev. E. J. Cain in 1919. This group is not to be confused with the church of the same name which derived from the ministry of Mary L. Tate.

Hq: 1301 N. 58th Street, Philadelphia, PA 19131
or
3943 Fairmount Avenue, Philadelphia, PA 19104

House of God Which is the Church of the Living God, The Pillar and Ground of Truth, Inc.

The House of God Which is the Church of the Living God, The Pillar and Ground of Truth, a predominantly black Pentecostal church, was founded in 1919 when the Philadelphia congregation of the Church of the Living God, The Pillar and Ground of Truth (founded by Mary L. Tate) became independent. Subsequently other congregations were founded and a new denomination arose. It is not to be confused with the church of the same name which derives from the Church of the Living God (Christian Workers for Fellowship).

Hq: Bishop Raymond W. White, 6107 Cobbs Creek Pkwy., Philadelphia, PA 19143
Tel: (215) 748 6338

House of God Which is the Church of the Living God, The Pillar and Ground of Truth without Controversy (Keith Dominion)

The House of God Which is the Church of the Living God, The Pillar and Ground of Truth without Controversy (Keith Dominion), a predominantly black Pentecostal church, emerged in the 1930s. Following founder Mary L. Tate's

death in 1931, the Church of the Living God, The Pillar and Ground of Truth, which she founded, was divided into three districts. One district was headed by Tate's daughter-in-law, M. F. L. Keith. It gradually became independent of the other districts and assumed its present name.

Hq: c/o Chief Overseer Bishop H. L. Harrison, Box 9113, Montgomery, AL 36108

House of Prayer, Church of God

The House of Prayer, Church of God is a predominantly black Pentecostal church founded in 1929 by Bishop James P. Simms, formerly of the United House of Prayer for all People.

Hq: Rt. 9, Box 131, Charleston, WV 25311

House of Prayer for All People

The House of Prayer for All People is an independent ministry founded in 1941 by William Lester Blessing, formerly a member of the Church of the United Brethren in Christ.

Hq: Box 837, Denver, CO 80201
Tel: (303) 778 0733

House of the Lord

The House of the Lord was founded in 1925 by Bishop W. H. Johnson.

Hq: Current address unavailable for this edition

House of the Lord Pentecostal Church

The House of the Lord Pentecostal Church is a predominantly black Pentecostal church founded in 1930 by A. A. Daughtry, formerly of the United House of Prayer for All People.

Hq: 415 Atlantic Avenue, Brooklyn, NY 11217
Tel: (212) 596 1991

House of Yahweh
(Abilene, Texas)

The House of Yahweh (Abilene, Texas) is a sabbatarian Sacred Name group founded in 1980 by Ysrayl B. Hawkins, the brother of Jacob Hawkins, founder of the House of Yahweh (Odessa, Texas).

Hq: Box 242, Abilene, TX 79604
Tel: (15) 529 3627 or 672 5420

House of Yahweh
(Odessa, Texas)

The House of Yahweh (Odessa, Texas) is a sabbatarian Sacred Name group founded in 1973 in Israel by Jacob Hawkins. It was established in the United States in 1975.

Hq: Jacob Hawkins, Box 4983, Odessa, TX 79760
Tel: (915) 337 9644 or 337 4267

Hungarian Reformed Church
in America

The Hungarian Reformed Church in America was founded in 1922 by those Hungarian Reformed congregations which did not follow the majority into a merger with the Reformed Church in the U. S. The congregations reorganized as the Free Magyar Reformed Church in America, taking its present name in 1958.

Hq: Rt. Rev. Dr. Andrew Harsanyi, P.O. Box D, Hipatcong, NY 07843

Hutterian Brethren-Dariusleut

The Hutterian Brethren movement, named for Jacob Hutter, an early leader, is a German Anabaptist movement which adopted a communal lifestyle. The Hutterian Brethren-Dariusleut (Darius' People) is one of four branches of the movement in the United States with colonies throughout the Plains and Northwest.

Hq: Rev. Elias Walter, Surprise Creek Colony, Stanford, MT 59479

Hutterian Brethren-Lehreleut

The Hutterian Brethren-Lehreleut is one of four branches of the Hutterian movement. It has colonies scattered from Minnesota to Washington.

Hq: Rev. Joseph Kleinsasser, Milford Colony, Wolf Creek, MT 59648

Hutterian Brethren-Schmiedeleut

The Hutterian Brethren-Schmiedeleut is one of four branches of the Hutterian movement. It has colonies scattered from Minnesota to Washington.

Hq: Rev. David D. Decker, Tachetter Colony, Olivet, SD 57052

Hutterian Brethren of
New York, Inc.

The Hutterian Brethren of New York is one of four branches of the Hutterian movement and the only one founded in the twentieth century. It began in Germany as the Society of Brothers and slowly found their identification with the Hutterian way of life. Colonies are primarily in the Northeast.

Hq: P. O. Woodcrest, Rte. 213, Rifton, NY 12471
Tel: (914) 658 3141

Independent Assemblies of God, International

The Independent Assemblies of God, International was founded in 1935 as a merger of the Scandinavian Assemblies of God in the U.S., Canada and Other Lands, and the Scandinavian Independent Assemblies.

Hq: 24411 Ridge Route Dr., Laguna Hills, CA 92653
Tel: (619) 464 8995

Independent Baptist Church of America

The Independent Baptist Church of America was founded in 1927 as a merger of the Scandinavian Independent Baptist Denomination in the U.S.A., and the Scandinavian Free Baptist Society of the U.S.A.

Hq: Current address unavailable for this edition

Independent Bible Church Movement

The Independent Bible Church Movement was founded in 1977 by a group of independent Bible churches.

Hq: Church Multiplication Inc., Box 79203, Houston, TX 77279
Tel: (713) 465 3473

Independent Brethren Church

The Independent Brethren Church was founded in 1972 as a merger of two congregations in southeastern Pennsylvania who left the Church of the Brethren.

Hq: Current address unavailable for this edition

Independent Catholic Church in Montana

The Independent Catholic Church in Montana is a small Catholic jurisdiction.

Hq: Mt. Rev. Bert Joseph Rauber, West Glacier, MT 59936

Independent Catholic Church International

The Independent Catholic Church International is an independent Catholic jurisdiction founded in 1981 by the merger of several small Catholic and Anglican churches.

Hq: Mt. Rev. R.V. Bernard Dawe, 1260 American Canyon Rd., 148, Vallejo, CA 94589

Independent Christian Churches, International

The Independent Christian Churches, International was founded in 1984 by Dr. Donald Ned Hicks and others.

Hq: Current address unavailable for this edition

Independent Fundamental Churches of America

The Independent Fundamental Churches of America is a fundamentalist Protestant church founded in 1930 by R. Lee Kirkland and others.

Hq: Box 810, Grandville, MI 49468
Tel: (616) 878 1285 or 531 1840
or
3520 Fairlanes, Grandville, MI 49418

Independent Fundamentalist Bible Churches

The Independent Fundamentalist Bible Churches was founded in 1965 by a group of leaders of the American Council of Christian Churches (Marion H. Reynolds, Rev. W. E. Standridge, Rev. Henry Campbell, and Rev. Kenneth L. Barth).

Hq: Dr. M. H. McReynolds, Jr., 205 N. Union Avenue, Los Angeles, CA 90026

Independent Old Roman Catholic Hungarian Orthodox Church of America

The Independent Old Roman Catholic Hungarian Orthodox Church of America is an autonomous Orthodox-Old Catholic jurisdiction founded in 1970 (as the Independent Catholic Church of America) by Archbishop Edward C. Payne.

Hq: Catholicos-Metropolitan Most Rev. Edward C. Payne, P. O. Box 261, Wethersfield, CT 06109

Infant Jesus of Prague Catholic Church

The Infant Jesus of Prague Catholic Church is an independent Catholic jurisdiction founded in 1979 by Archbishop John Gabriel.

Hq: Mt. Rev. John Gabriel, 3442 W. Woodlawn St., San Antonio, TX 78228
Tel: (512) 432 1544

Integrity Communications (and Related Ministries)

The Integrity Communications (and Related Ministries) is a Pentecostal-Charismatic fellowship of churches founded in 1978 by Charles Simpson and other Charismatic ministers.

Hq: Box Z, Mobile, AL 36616
Tel: (205) 633 9000

Intermountain Yearly Meeting of the Society of Friends

The Intermountain Yearly Meeting of the Society of Friends was founded in 1975 by congregation of Friends.

Hq: Ms. Anne White, 624 Pearl Street, No. 302, Boulder, CO 80302
Tel: (303) 444 0169

International Association of Lutheran Churches

The International Association of Lutheran Churches is an independent fellowship of conservative Lutheran ministers and churches.

Hq: 387 E. Brandon Dr., Bismarck, ND 58501
Tel: (701) 255 0519

International Christian Churches

The International Christian Churches is a Pentecostal fellowship founded in 1943 by Rev. Franco Manuel and former members of the Christian Church (Disciples of Christ).

Hq: 2322-22 Kanealii Avenue, Honolulu, HI 96813

International Church of the Foursquare Gospel

The International Church of the Foursquare Gospel is a Pentecostal church founded in 1927 by evangelist Aimee Semple McPherson.

Hq: c/o Pres. Dr. John R. Holland, Angelus Temple, 1100 Glendale Blvd., Los Angeles, CA 90026
Tel: (213) 484 1100

International Convention of Faith Churches and Ministers

The International Convention of Faith Churches and Ministers is a

Charismatic fellowship founded in 1979 by Dr. Doyle Harrison.

Hq: 3840 S. 103 E. Avenue, #132, Tulsa, OK 74146-2445

International Council of Community Churches

The International Council of Community Churches was founded in 1946 as an association of interdenominational community (mostly liberal Protestant) congregations. Originally known as the National Council of Community Churches, it assumed its present name in 1950.

Hq: c/o Exec. Dir. Rev. J. Ralph Shotwell, 900 Ridge Rd., Suite LL 1, Homewood, IL 60430
Tel: (312) 798 2264

International Deliverance Churches

International Deliverance Churches is a fellowship of independent Pentecostal congregations which emphasize the healing ministry. It was founded in 1962 by W. V. Grant.

Hq: Box 353, Dallas, TX 75221
Tel: (214) 337 9152

International Evangelical Church and Missionary Association

The International Evangelical Church and Missionary Association is a predominantly black Pentecostal church founded in the early 1980s by John Meares, a white minister formerly with the Church of God (Cleveland, Tennessee).

Hq: Evangel Temple, 610 Rhode Island Avenue, N.E., Washington, D.C. 20002
Tel: (202) 635 8000

International Evangelism Crusades

The International Evangelism Crusades is a Pentecostal fellowship founded in 1959 by Dr. Frank E. Stranges, Revs. Natale Stranges, Bernice Stranges, and Warren MacKall.

Hq: c/o Pres. Dr. Frank E. Stranges, 14617 Victory Blvd., Van Nuys, CA 91411
Tel: (818) 989 5942

International Minister Association

The International Minister Association was founded in 1954 by W. E. Kidson and former members of the United Pentecostal Church.

Hq: Current address unavailable for this edition

International Ministerial Federation, Inc.

The International Ministerial Federation is a fundamentalist fellowship founded in 1930 by Dr. J. Kellog and Dr. W. E. Opie.

Hq: Current address unavailable for this edition

International Ministerial Fellowship

The International Ministerial Fellowship is an independent pentecostal group founded in 1958.

Hq: P. O. Box 32364, Minneapolis, MN 55432

International Pentecostal Church of Christ

The International Pentecostal Church of Christ was founded in

1976 as a merger of the International Pentecostal Assemblies and the Pentecostal Church of Christ.

Hq: c/o Gen. Overseer Tom G. Grinder, Box 439, 2245 U.S. 42, S.W., London, OH 43140
Tel: (614) 852 0348

International Pentecostal Holiness Church

The International Pentecostal Holiness Church was founded in 1911 as the Pentecostal Holiness Church.

Hq: P. O. Box 12609, Oklahoma City, OK 73157
Tel: (405) 787 7110

Iowa Yearly Meeting of Friends

The Iowa Yearly Meeting of Friends was founded in 1877 by a group of conservative Friends.

Hq: Gen. Supt. Stephen Main, Box 703, Oskaloosa, IA 52577
Tel: (515) 673 9717

Israelite House of David

The Israelite House of David, founded in 1903 by Adventist preacher Benjamin Purnell.

Hq: P. O. Box 1067, Benton Harbor, MI 49022
Tel: (616) 926 6695

Israelite House of David as Reorganized by Mary Purnell

The Israelite House of David as Reorganized by Mary Purnell was founded in 1927 by Mary Purnell.

Hq: Box 187, Benton Harbor, MI 49022

Jehovah's Witnesses

The Jehovah's Witnesses emerged out of the Bible Student movement begun by Charles Taze Russell who founded the Watch Tower Bible and Tract Society in the 1880s. They assumed their present name in 1931 during the presidency of Joseph F. Rutherford.

Hq: c/o Pres. Frederick W. Franz, 25 Columbia Heights, Brooklyn, NY 11201
Tel: (718) 625 3600

Jesus People Church

The Jesus People Church is an evangelical church founded in the 1970s by Dennis Worre, Roger Vann, and others.

Hq: 2924 Rahn Way, St. Paul, MN 55122-2329

John Wesley Fellowship and the Francis Asbury Society of Ministers

The Fellowship and the Society of Ministers were founded in 1971 by former members of the Southern Methodist Church.

Hq: Current address unavailable for this edition

Ka Hale Hoano Hou O Ke Akua (Hallowed House of God, King of Kings and Lord of Lords)

The Ka Hale Hoano Hou O Ke Akua was founded in 1948 by Lt. Com. W. H. Abbey by former members of the Hoomana Naauoa O Hawaii.

Hq: 1760 Nalani, Honolulu, HI 96819
Tel: (808) 845 2897

Kealaokamalamalama (Way of Light)

Kealaokamalamalama, a Hawaiian Protestant church, was founded in

1935 as a split from the Kawaiaho (Congregational) Church.

Hq: 1207 Prospect, Honolulu, HI 96822
Tel: (808) 533 3201

Kentucky Mountain Holiness Association

The Kentucky Mountain Holiness Association was founded in 1925 by Lela G. McConnell.

Hq: Star Rte. 1, Box 350, Jackson, KY
    41339
Tel: (606) 666 5008

Kodesh Church of Emmanuel

The Kodesh Church of Emmanuel is a predominantly black holiness church founded in 1929 by Rev. Frank Russell Killingsworth.

Hq: Dr. Kenneth O. Barber, 932 Logan
    Road, Bethel Park, PA 15102
Tel: (412) 833 1351

Korean Presbyterian Church in America, General Assembly of the

The General Assembly of the Korean Presbyterian Church in America was founded in 1976 in the USA by Korean-Americans, most post-1965 first generation.

Hq: c/o Mod. Rev. Kwang Soo Choi,
    1251 Crenshaw Blvd., Los
    Angeles, CA 90019
Tel: (213) 857 0361

Kyova Association of Regular Baptists

The Kyova Association of Regular Baptists was founded in 1924 as a split from the New Salem Association of Regular Baptists.

Hq: Current address unavailable for
    this edition

Lake Erie Yearly Meeting

The Lake Erie Yearly Meeting was founded in 1939 as the Association of Friends Meetings. It assumed its present name in 1969.

Hq: c/o Clerk Richard W. Taylor, 492
    Miller Street, Kent, OH 44240
Tel: (216) 673 6477

Lamb of God Church

The Lamb of God Church is a Pentecostal church founded in 1942 by Rev. Rose Soares.

Hq: 612 Isenburg Street, Honolulu, HI
    96817

Laodicean Home Missionary Movement

The Laodicean Home Missionary Movement emerged out of the larger Bible Student movement began in the 1880s by Pastor Charles Taze Russell. It was founded in 1955 by John W. Krewson, a former member of the Layman's Home Missionary Movement.

Hq: Rte. 38, 9021 Temple Rd., W. Fort
    Myers, FL 33912
Tel: (813) 267 1388

Last Day Messenger Assemblies

The Last Day Messenger Assemblies is a grace-gospel fundamentalist group founded in the early twentieth century by Nels Thompson, a former member of the Plymouth Brethren.

Hq: Box 17406, Portland, OR 97217

Latin-American Council of the Pentecostal Church of God of New York

The Latin-American Council of the Pentecostal Church of God of New York (also known as Concilio Latino-

Americano de la Iglesia de Dios Pentecostal de New York, Incorporado) was founded in 1957 by former members of the Latin American Council of the Pentecostal Church of God.

Hq: 115 E. 125th Street, New York, NY 10035
Tel: (212) 427 2447

Latter House of the Lord for All People and the Church of the Mountain, Apostolic Faith

The Latter House of the Lord for All People and the Church of the Mountain, Apostolic Faith is a predominantly black Pentecostal church founded in 1936 by Bishop L. W. Williams.

Hq: Current address unavailable for this edition

Latvian Evangelical Lutheran Church in America

The Latvian Evangelical Lutheran Church in America was founded in 1939 and came to the USA in 1957. It took the present name in 1976.

Hq: c/o Pres. Rev. Vilis Varsberg, 6551 W. Montrose, Chicago, IL 60634
Tel: (312) 725 3820
or
International Hq: Latvijas Evangeliski Luteriska Baznica Eksila (Evangelical Lutheran Church in Exile), 5 Valleymede Road, Toronto, Ontario M6S 1G8
Tel: (416) 767 2310

Layman's Home Missionary Movement

The Layman's Home Missionary Movement grew out of the Bible Students movement founded in the 1880s by Pastor Charles Taze Russell.

It was founded after 1918 by Paul S. L. Johnson.

Hq: Chester Springs, PA 19425

Leroy Jenkins Evangelistic Association

The Leroy Jenkins Evangelistic Association, spearhead of a Pentecostal healing ministry, was founded in 1960 by evangelist Leroy Jenkins.

Hq: Current address unavailable for this edition

Liberty Baptist Fellowship

The Liberty Baptist Fellowship is an association of fundamentalist Baptist churches and ministers which emerged out of the congregation and television ministry initiated by independent Baptist minister Jerry Falwell and the college and seminary he founded.

Hq: c/o Exec. Dir. Elmer L. Towns, Candler's Mountain Rd., Lynchburg, VA 24506
Tel: (804) 237 5961, ext. 325

Liberty Fellowship of Churches and Ministers

The Liberty Fellowship of Churches and Ministers is a loosely-confederated fellowship of independent Pentecostal-Charismatic churches and ministers founded in 1975 by Ken Sumrall and others.

Hq: 2732 Old Rocky Ridge Rd., Birmingham, AL 35216
Tel: (205) 987 9978

Lighthouse Gospel Fellowship

The Lighthouse Gospel Fellowship is a Pentecostal church founded in 1958 by Drs. H. A. and Thelma Chaney.

Hq: Current address unavailable for this edition

Lithuanian Evangelical Lutheran Church in Exile

The Lithuanian Evangelical Lutheran Church in Exile was formed by refugees following World War II.

Hq: 6620 S. Saint Louis Avenue, Chicago, IL 60629

The (Local) Church

The (Local) Church is a fundamentalist movement founded in the early 1920s in China by Watchman Nee (Nyi Shutsu) and developed in the United States by his disciple Witness Lee.

Hq: Living Stream Ministry, 1853 West Ball Rd., Anaheim, CA 92804
Tel: (714) 991 4681

Lower Lights Church

The Lower Lights Church is a holiness church founded in 1940 in Michigan.

Hq: Current address unavailable for this edition

Lumber River Annual Conference of the Holiness Methodist Church

The Lumber River Annual Conference was founded in 1900 by members of the Methodist Episcopal Church, South.

Hq: Bishop C. N. Lowry, Rowland, NC 28383

Lutheran Church—Missouri Synod

The Lutheran Church—Missouri Synod is a conservative Lutheran church founded in 1847 by immi-grants from Prussia who had rejected the Prussian state's attempt to mix Lutheran and Reformed churches into a national union church.

Hq: 1333 S. Kirkwood Rd., St. Louis, MO 63122
Tel: (314) 965 9000

Lutheran Churches of the Reformation

The Lutheran Churches of the Reformation is a conservative Lutheran body founded in 1964 by former members of the Lutheran Church—Missouri Synod.

Hq: Route 2, Box 47, Delano, MN 55328

Macedonian Orthodox Church

The Macedonian Orthodox Church was established as a new autonomous jurisdiction in 1947 by former members of the Serbian Orthodox Church in Yugoslavia. It was brought to the United States in 1961.

Hq: c/o Rev. Spiro Tanaskaki, 51st & Virginia Sts., Gary, IN 46409

Malankara Orthodox (Syrian) Church

The Malankara Orthodox (Syrian) Church traces its beginning to the work of the Apostle St. Thomas who, according to tradition, arrived in India in 52 A.D. to begin his preaching mission. It was brought to the United States in the 1960s.

Hq: His Grace Dr. Thomas Makarios, Episcopal Diocesan House, 1114 Delaware Avenue, Buffalo, NY 14209
or
International Hq: Malankara Mar Thoma Suriani Sabha (Mar Thoma Syrian Church of Malabar), His

Holiness Moran Mar, Basilius Mar Thoma Mathews I, Catholicate Palace, Poolatheen, Tiruvalla, Kottayam, Kerala 689 101, India

Maranatha Christian Churches

The Maranatha Christian Churches was founded in 1972 by Bob and Rose Weiner.

Hq: Box 1799, Gainesville, FL 32602

Mariavite Old Catholic Church, Province of North America

The Mariavite Old Catholic Church was founded by Robert R. J. M. Zaborowski in 1972 (as American Orthodox Catholic Church) and took the present name in 1974.

Hq: His Eminence Most Rev. Robert R. J. M. Zaborowski, 2803 10th Street, Wyandotte, MI 48192

Tel: (313) 281 3082

Mary Immaculate Queen of the Universe Center

The Mary Immaculate Queen of the Universe Center is the one of a group of associated organizations representing a traditionalist Roman Catholic group whose orders derive from Roman Catholic Archbishop Pierre Martin Ngo-Dinh-Thuc. Associated with the Center are the Our Lady of Fatima Crusade, Our Lady of Fatima Cell Movement, and the Congregation of Mary Immaculate Queen.

Hq: P. O. Box 40025, Spokane, WA 99202

Tel: (509) 467 0986

Megiddo Mission

The Megiddo Mission was founded in 1901 by L. T. Nichols.

Hq: 478 Thurston Rd., Rochester, NY 14619

Mennonite Brethren Church of North America (Bruedergemeinde)

The Mennonite Brethren Church of North America (Bruedergemeinde) was founded by Pastor Edward Wuest in 1860 and came to the United States in 1879 under the leadership of Abraham Schellenberg.

Hq: Hillsboro, KS 67063

Mennonite Church

The Mennonite Church grew out of the sixteenth century Swiss Brethren and were named for one of their leaders Menno Simons.

Hq: 421 S. Second St., Ste. 600, Elkhart, IN 46516

Tel: (219) 294 7131

Mennonite Church, General Conference

See: General Conference Mennonite Church

Mercian Rite Catholic Church

The Mercian Rite Catholic Church traces its history to Archbishop Rene Vilatte who brought independent Catholic orders to North America, but appeared as a separate jurisdiction in the 1970s with the emergence of Archbishop Joseph G. Sokolowski (consecrated in 1970).

Hq: Primatal Diocese of SS. Peter and Paul, 3366 Parade Circle East, Colorado Springs, CO 80917

Tel: (719) 591 2766

Methodist Protestant Church

The Methodist Protestant Church was founded in 1939 by former members of the Mississippi Conference of the Methodist Protestant Church which in 1939 merged with the Methodist Episcopal Church and the Methodist Episcopal Church, South to become the Methodist Church (1939-1968).

Hq: Rev. F. E. Sellers, Monticello, MS 55362

Metropolitan Church Association

The Metropolitan Church Association is a holiness church founded in 1894 (as Metropolitan Holiness Church). It took its present name in 1899.

Hq: 323 Broad Street, Lake Geneva, WI 53147
Tel: (414) 248 6786

Metropolitan Community Churches, Universal Fellowship of

The Universal Fellowship of Metropolitan Community Churches, the largest of the several churches primarily serving the homosexual community, was founded in 1968 by Troy Perry, formerly a minister in the Church of God of Prophecy.

Hq: Mod: Elder Rev. Troy D. Perry, 5300 Santa Monica Blvd. 304, Los Angeles, CA 90029
Tel: (213) 464 5100

Mexican National Catholic Church

The Mexican National Catholic Church, an independent Catholic jurisdiction, was founded in the 1920s as part of a nationalistic wave which swept Mexico. It received episcopal orders from the North American Old Roman Catholic Church. An initial congregation was established in Los Angeles among Mexican-Americans in the late 1920s.

Hq: Rt. Rev. Emile F. Rodriguez Fairfield, 4011 E. Brooklyn Avenue, East Los Angeles, CA 90022

Mid-America Yearly Meeting (of Friends)

The Mid-America Yearly Meeting (of Friends) was founded in 1872 as the Kansas Yearly Meeting. It recently assumed its present name.

Hq: 2018 Maple, Wichita, KS 67213
Tel: (316) 267 0391

Midwest Congregational Christian Church

The Midwest Congregational Christian Church was founded in 1958 by former members of the Congregational and Christian Churches who did not approve of that church's merger into the new United Church of Christ.

Hq: Current address unavailable for this edition

Ministry of Christ Church

The Ministry of Christ Church, a British-Israel Identity church, was founded in the 1970s by William Potter Gale.

Hq: 4241 Usona Rd., Mariposa, CA 95338
Tel: (209) 966 2269

Minnesota Baptist Association

The Minnesota Baptist Association was founded by fundamentalist Baptists who voted to separate the Minnesota Convention from the Northern Baptist Convention in 1948. The Minnesota Convention assumed its present name in 1974.

Hq: c/o Exec. Sec. Dr. Richard L.
Paige, 5000 Golden Valley Rd.,
Minneapolis, MN 55422
Tel: (612) 588 2755

Miracle Life Fellowship International

The Miracle Life Fellowship International was founded in 1951 by Asa Alonzo Allen among independent Pentecostal ministers who had come to support his evangelistic work. It took its present name in 1970.

Hq: 11052 N. 24th Avenue, Phoenix, AZ 85029

Miracle Life Revival

The Miracle Life Revival, a Pentecostal healing/deliverance ministry headed by independent evangelist Neal Frisby, was founded in 1972.

Hq: Box 20707, Phoenix, AZ 85036
Tel: (602) 996 3187

Missionary Christian and Soul Winning Fellowship

The Missionary Christian and Soul Winning Fellowship was founded in 1957 by Rev. Lee Shelley and former members of the Christian and Missionary Alliance.

Hq: 350 E. Market Street, Long Beach, CA 90805

Missionary Church

The Missionary Church is a holiness church out of the Mennonite tradition. It was founded in 1969 as a merger of the United Missionary Church and the Missionary Church Association.

Hq: 3901 S. Wayne Avenue, Fort Wayne, IN 46807
Tel: (219) 456 4502

Missionary Diocese of the Holy Spirit

The Missionary Diocese of the Holy Spirit is a small independent Catholic jurisdiction founded in the late 1980s by Bishop Richard Saint John, formerly a bishop in the Orthodox Catholic Church.

Hq: c/o Mt. Rev. Richard Saint John, 1217 Lagonda Av., Fort Worth, TX 76106

Missionary Dispensary Bible Research

The Missionary Dispensary Bible Research is a sabbatarian Sacred Name Adventist group associated with the Assemblies of Yahvah.

Hq: Box 5296, Buena Park, CA 90622

Missionary Methodist Church of America

The Missionary Methodist Church of America was founded in 1913 by Rev. H. C. Sisk and other members of the Wesleyan Methodist Church.

Hq: Rte. 7, Morganton, CA 28655

Missouri Valley Friends Conference

The Missouri Valley Friends Conference was founded in 1955 by a group of Friends of the Midwest.

Hq: John Griffith, 5745 Charlotte, Kansas City, MO 64110
Tel: (816) 444 2543

Mita Movement

The Mita Movement is a Spanish-speaking Pentecostal church founded in 1940 by Juanita Garcia Peraga.

Hq: Calle Duarte 235, Hata Rey, PR 60919

Molokan Spiritual Christians (Postojannye)

The Molokan Spiritual Christians (Postojannye) is a free church movement founded in the 1830s in Russia. This branch resulted from a split within the Molokan Spiritual Christians (Pryguny). It came to the U.S.A. in 1905.

Hq: 841 Carolina Street, San Francisco, CA 94107

Molokan Spiritual Christians (Pryguny)

The Molokan Spiritual Christians (Pryguny) is a free church movement founded in the eighteenth century in Russia by Simeon Uklein. Followers arrived in the United States in the late-nineteenth century.

Hq: 944 Ormer Street, Los Angeles, CA 99923

Moody Church

The Moody Church was founded by fundamentalist evangelist Dwight L. Moody in 1864 as the Illinois Street Church in Chicago. It was renamed in 1901, shortly after Moody's death. During the twentieth century it has remained a prominent fundamentalist pulpit.

Hq: 1609 N. LaSalle, IL 60614
Tel: (312) 943 0466

Moravian Church in America (Unitas Fratrum)

The Moravian Church in America (Unitas Fratrum) traces its origins to the reforming activity of John Hus in the fifteenth century in Czechoslovakia. It was brought to America in 1735 by a group under the leadership of Bishop August Gottlieb Spangenberg.

Hq: Northern Province, 1021 Center Street, Box 1245, Bethlehem, PA 18016-1245
Tel: (215) 867 7566
or
Southern Province, 459 S. Church Street, Winston-Salem, NC 27108
Tel: (919) 725 5811

Mount Calvary Holy Church of America

The Mount Calvary Holy Church of America is a predominantly black Pentecostal church founded in 1927 by Bishop Blumfield Johnson, formerly of the United Holy Church of America.

Hq: Bishop Harold Williams, 1214 Chowan Street, Durham, NC 27713

Mount Calvary United Church of God

The Mount Calvary United Church of God is a predominantly black Pentecostal Church founded in 1919 in Albaramare, North Carolina.

Hq: 223-25 First Street, Elizabeth, NJ 07201
Tel: (201) 354 6221

Mount Hebron Apostolic Temple of Our Lord Jesus of the Apostolic Faith

The Mount Hebron Apostolic Temple of Our Lord Jesus of the Apostolic Faith, a predominantly black Oneness Pentecostal church, was founded in 1963 by George H. Wiley III, formerly a minister in the Apostolic Church of Christ in God.

Hq: Mount Hebron Apostolic Temple, 27 Vineyard Avenue, Yonkers, NY 10703
Tel: (914) 963 5372

Mount Sinai Holy Church of America

The Mount Sinai Holy Church of America is a predominantly black Pentecostal church founded in 1924 by Bishop Ida Robinson, formerly of the United Holy Church of America.

Hq: 1601 N. Broad Street, Philadelphia, PA 19148
Tel: (215) 763 9409

Mt. Zion Sanctuary

The Mt. Zion Sanctuary was founded in 1882 by Mrs. Antoinette Jackson.

Hq: 21 Dayton Street, Elizabeth, NJ 07202

Music Square Church

The Music Square Church was founded in 1969 (also known as Holy Alamo Christian Church Consecrated) by Susan and Tony Alamo (Edith Opal Horn and Bernie Lazar Hoffman).

Hq: Box 398, Alma, AK 72921

National Anglican Church

The National Anglican Church is a small Anglican jurisdiction headed by Bishop Montgomery Griffith-Mair.

Hq: c/o George Evers, P. O. Box 111, Wentworth, NH 03282

National Association of Congregational Christian Churches

The National Association of Congregational Christian Churches was founded in 1955 by members of the Congregational Christian Churches who rejected the merger of that church into the United Church of Christ.

Hq: P. O. Box 1620, 8473 S. Howell Avenue, Oak Creek, WI 53154
Tel: (414) 764 1620

National Association of Free Will Baptists

The National Association of Free Will Baptists dates to the ministry of Paul Palmer in the American South in the eighteenth century.

Hq: 1134 Murfreesboro Rd., Nashville, TN 37217
Tel: (615) 361 1010

National Association of Holiness Churches

The National Association of Holiness Churches was founded in 1967 by H. Robb French.

Hq: 351 S. Park Dr., Griffith, IN 46319

National Baptist Convention of America

The National Baptist Convention of America, a predominantly black church, was founded in 1915 by Rev. R. H. Boyd and his supporters within the National Baptist Convention.

Hq: c/o President E. Edward Jones, National Baptist Publishing Board, 7145 Centennial Blvd., Nashville, TN 37209
Tel: (615) 228 6292
or
1450 Pierre Avenue, Shreveport, LA 71103

National Baptist Convention of the U.S.A., Inc.

The National Baptist Convention of the U.S.A., the largest predominantly black denomination in America, was founded in 1895 as a merger of the Foreign Mission Baptist Convention of the U.S.A., the American National Baptist Convention, and the Baptist

National Educational Convention. President is Dr. T. G. Jemison.

Hq: 915 Spain Street, Baton Rouge, LA 70802
Tel: (504) 383 4501

National Baptist Evangelical Life and Soul Saving Assembly of the U.S.A.

The National Baptist Evangelical Life and Soul Saving Assembly of the U.S.A., a predominantly black church, was founded in 1920 by A. A. Banks.

Hq: 441-61 Monroe Avenue, Detroit, MI 48226

National Primitive Baptist Convention, Inc.

The National Primitive Baptist Convention was founded in 1907 as a fellowship for a group of black Primitive Baptist associations.

Hq: Box 2355, Tallahassee, FL 32301

Nestorian Apostolic Church

The Nestorian Apostolic Church was founded by Bishop James H. Hess who had been consecrated in 1984 by Bishop Brian Glenn Turkington, then of the Free Anglican Church in America.

Hq: c/o Bishop James H. Hess, 2410 Derry Street, Harrisburg, PA 17111-1141
Tel: (717) 564 9407

Netherlands Reformed Congregations

The Netherlands Reformed Congregations was founded in 1907 in Netherlands by Rev. G. H. Kersten as a merger of two Reformed groups, the Churches under the Cross and the Ledeboerian Churches.

Hq: c/o Clerk of the Synod Dr. J. R. Beeke, 2116 Romence Avenue, N.E., Grand Rapids, MI 49503

The Neverdies

The Neverdies (also known as Church of the Living Gospel or Church of Everlasting Gospel) is an elusive movement reported to exist in the hills of West Virginia among some who believe themselves to be (potentially) physically immortal.

Hq: Current address unavailable for this edition

New Apostolic Church of North America

The New Apostolic Church of North America was founded in 1863 in Germany as a split from the Catholic Apostolic Church.

Hq: 3753 N. Troy St., Chicago, IL 60618
Tel: (312) 539 3652

New Bethel Church of God in Christ (Pentecostal)

The New Bethel Church of God in Christ (Pentecostal) was founded in 1927 by Rev. A. D. Bradley, his wife and Lonnie Bates.

Hq: Current address unavailable for this edition

New Christian Crusade Church

The New Christian Crusade Church was founded in 1971 by James K. Warner.

Hq: Box 426, Metairie, LA 70004

New Congregational Methodist Church

The New Congregational Methodist Church was founded in 1881 by former members of the Methodist Episcopal Church, South.

Hq: c/o Bishop Joe E. Kelley, 354 E. 9th Street, Jacksonville, FL 32206

New Covenant Churches of Maryland

The New Covenant Churches of Maryland is a Pentecostal-Charismatic fellowship founded in the mid-1970s by Robert Wright (New Life Christian Center).

Hq: 804 Windsor Rd., Arnold, MD 21012

New England Evangelical Baptist Fellowship

The New England Evangelical Baptist Fellowship is a small conservative baptist church.

Hq: c/o Dr. John Viall, 40 Bridge Street, Newton, MA 02158

New Life Fellowship

The New Life Fellowship is a small sabbatarian Sacred Name Adventist organization.

Hq: Box 75, Natural Dam, AR 72948

New Testament Association of Independent Baptist Churches

The New Testament Association of Independent Baptist Churches is a conservative fundamentalist Baptist fellowship founded in 1965 by Dr. Richard V. Clearwaters.

Hq: 1079 Westview Dr., Rochelle, IL 61068

New Testament Church of God

The New Testament Church of God is a holiness church founded in 1942 by G. W. and Martha Pendleton, and former members of the Church of God (Anderson, Indiana).

Hq: Box 611, Mountain Home, AR 72653

North American Baptist Conference

The North American Baptist Conference was founded in 1843 as a German-American Baptist fellowship.

Hq: Mod. Rev. Harvey Mehlhaff, 1 S. 210 Summit Avenue, Oakbrook Terrace, IL 60181
Tel: (312) 495 2000

North American Old Roman Catholic Archdiocese of Saint Mary Orthodox Catholic Churches

The North American Old Roman Catholic Archdiocese of Saint Mary Orthodox Catholic Churches is a small independent Catholic jurisdiction founded and headed by Mt. Rev. Roland A. Lucier.

Hq: Mt. Rev. Roland A. Lucier, 140 Linden Av., Ste. 279, Long Beach, CA 90802
Tel: (213) 435 7508
Fax: (213) 436 4721

North American Old Roman Catholic Church

The North American Old Roman Catholic Church was founded in 1916 by Archbishop Carmel Henry Carfora. It is an independent Catholic jurisdiction which rejects the idea of the infallibility of the Pope.

Hq: c/o Most Rev. Edward J. Ford, 200 Emerson Street, So. Boston, MA 02127
Tel: (617) 268 0511

North American Old Roman Catholic Church—Utrecht Succession

The North American Old Roman Catholic Church—Utrecht Succession is an independent Catholic jurisdiction founded in 1936 by Bishop A. D. Bell.

Hq: 3519 Roosevelt Avenue, Richmond, CA 94805

North American Traditional Old Roman Catholic Church (Chicago)

The North American Traditional Old Roman Catholic Church claims to be the successor organization to the North American Old Roman Catholic Church founded in 1916 by Carmel Henry Carfora. The first bishop of this jurisdiction was Archbishop John E. Schweikert. In 1988, following Schweikert's death, Theodore Joseph Rematt became the new archbishop and gave the church its present name.

Hq: Archbishop Most Rev. Theodore J. Rematt, 4200 N. Kedvale, Chicago, IL 60641

North Carolina Yearly Meeting of Friends (Conservative)

The North Carolina Yearly Meeting of Friends (Conservative) was founded in 1904 as a split among Friends in North Carolina.

Hq: c/o Clerk Louise B. Wilson, 113 Pinewood Rd., Virginia Beach, VA 23451
Tel: (804) 428 7853

North Pacific Yearly Meeting of the Religious Society of Friends

The North Pacific Yearly Meeting of the Religious Society of Friends was founded in 1972 by Friends of Oregon and Washington states.

Hq: c/o Susan Dimitroff, Steering Committee Clerk, 503E. "W" Street, Tumwater, WA 98501
Tel: (206) 484 7966

Northwest Yearly Meeting of Friends Church

The Northwest Yearly Meeting of Friends Church was founded in 1893 (as Oregon Yearly Meeting of Friends) as an independent from the Iowa Yearly Meeting Friends.

Hq: Evangelical Friends Alliance, General Supt. Howard Harmon, Box 190, Newberg, OR 97132
Tel: (503) 538 9419

Norwegian Seaman's Church (Mission)

The Norwegian Seaman's Church was founded in 1864 in Norway as a mission to assist Lutheran seamen when they landed at the world's ports.

Hq: c/o Gen. Sec. Rev. Halfdan T. Bondevik, 1035 Beacon Street, San Pedro, CA 90731
Tel: (213) 832 6800
or
International Hq: Strandgaten 198, N-5000 Bergen, Norway

Ohio Bible Fellowship

The Ohio Bible Fellowship was founded in 1968 by former members of the Independent Fundamental Church of America.

Hq: Rev. John Ashbrook, 5733 Hopkins Rd., Mentor, OH 44060

Ohio Yearly Meeting of the Society of Friends

The Ohio Yearly Meeting of the Society of Friends was founded in

1813 by Friends who had absorbed Methodist ideas and manners.

Hq: 61830 Sandy Ridge Rd., Barnesville, OH 43712

Old Brethren Church

The Old Brethren Church was founded in 1913 as a split from the Old German Baptist Brethren.

Hq: Current address unavailable for this edition

Old Brethren German Baptist Church

The Old Brethren German Baptist Church was founded in 1939 by the more conservative members of the Old Brethren Church.

Hq: Current address unavailable for this edition

Old Catholic Church, Archepiscopate of Healing Arts, Missionaries and Chaplains of America

The Old Catholic Church, Archepiscopate of Healing Arts, Missionaries and Chaplains of America is a small independent Catholic jurisdiction. It was formed by Mt. Rev. Paul Garrow who had been consecrated by Archbishop Paul G. W. Schultz of the Philippine Independent Catholic Church.

Hq: Chancery Office, Mt. Rev. Arthur J. Garrow, P. O. Box 1077, 68-121 1st St., Cathedral City, CA 92234

Old Catholic Church in America

The Old Catholic Church in America is an independent Catholic Jurisdiction founded in 1917 by Archbishop W. H. Francis Brothers.

Hq: Metropolitan Hilarion, 1905 S. Third Street, Austin, TX 78704
Tel: (512) 442-2289

Old Catholic Church in North America (Catholicate of the West)

The Old Catholic Church in North America (Catholicate of the West) was founded in 1950 by Grant Timothy Billet and others.

Hq: Rev. Dr. Charles V. Hearn, 2210 Wilshire Blvd., Suite 582, Santa Monica, CA 90403

Old Episcopal Church

The Old Episcopal Church is an independent Anglican jurisdiction founded in 1971 by Rt. Rev. Jack C. Adam.

Hq: Rt. Rev. Jack C. Adam, Box 2424, Mesa, AZ 85204

Old Episcopal Church of Scotland

The Old Episcopal Church of Scotland is an independent Anglican jurisdiction that traces its history to the mid-eighteenth century and to some Scottish Episcopalian clergy who refused to swear allegiance to William of Orange as the new king of England. They formed an independent jurisdiction, and later some members migrated to Canada from whence they spread into the United States.

Hq: Chancery Office, 20505, US Highway 19 North, Clearwater, FL 34624-7303
Tel: (813) 443 5645

Old German Baptist Brethren

The Old German Baptist Brethren was founded in 1881 as a split from the Church of the Brethren.

Hq: Elder Clement Skiles, Rte. 1, Box
140, Bringhurst, IN 46913
Tel: (219) 967 3367

Old Holy Catholic Church of the Netherlands

The Old Holy Catholic Church of the Netherlands is an independent Catholic jurisdiction that came to the United States from Holland by way of Canada in 1979.

Hq: Diocese of Pennsylvania, Mt. Rev.
William H. Bushnell, 1529
Hastings Mill Rd., Upper St.
Clair, PA 15241
Tel: (412) 833 8473
or
International Hq: Oud Heilig Katholieke
Kerk van Nederland, Mt. Rev.
Theodorus P. N. Groenenijk,
Gerard ter Borchstraat 98, 4903
NP Roosendaal, Netherlands

Old Order Amish Mennonite Church

The Old Order Amish Mennonite Church was founded in Switzerland in the seventeenth century by Mennonites under the leadership of Jacob Amman. Amish first came to America in the eighteenth century and have become known for the horse and buggy culture they perpetuate.

Hq: No central address. For
information: Der Neue
Amerikanische Calendar,
Raber's Book Store, 2467 C R
600 Baltic, OH 43804

Old Order German Baptist Church

The Old Order German Baptist Church was founded in 1921 as a split from the Old German Baptist Brethren.

Hq: Current address unavailable for this
edition

Old Order (or Yorker) River Brethren

The Old Order (or Yorker) River Brethren was founded in 1843 by Bishop Jacob Strickler as a split from the Brethren in Christ.

Hq: Current address unavailable for this
edition

Old Order (Reidenbach) Mennonites

The Old Order (Reidenbach) Mennonites was founded during World War II as a split from the Old Order (Wenger) Mennonites.

Hq: For information: Henry W. Riehl,
Rte. 1, Columbiana, OH 44408

Old Order (Wenger) Mennonites

The Old Order (Wenger) Mennonites, one of several factions among the Old Order Mennonites, originated among the Wisler Mennonites in the 1930s.

Hq: For information: Henry W. Riehl,
Rte. 1, Columbiana, OH 44408

Old Order (Wisler) Mennonites

The Old Order (Wisler) Mennonites, one of several factions of the Old Order Mennonites, was founded in 1870 by Jacob Wisler.

Hq: No central address. For
information: Arthur Van Pelt,
13550 Germantown Road,
Columbiana, OH 44408
Tel: (216) 482 3691

Old Orthodox Catholic Patriarchate of America

The Old Orthodox Catholic Patriarchate of America originated in 1930 as the Polish Old Catholic

Church under the leadership of Bishop Joseph Zielonka. The present name was chosen by Zielonka's successor, Archbishop Peter A. Zurawetsky, in hopes of broadening the ethnic base of the church.

Hq: 66 N. Brookfield Street, Vineland, NJ 08360

Old Roman Catholic Church

The Old Roman Catholic Church continues the original Old Catholic Church established in England early in this century by Arnold Harris Mathew

Hq: Mt. Rev. Carl Howard, 4603 Hunt Club Drive, Apt. 2D, Ypsilanti, MI 48197
or
International Hq: c/o Rt. Rev. Frederick G. Linale, 10 Barnmead Rd., Beckenham, Kent, England

Old Roman Catholic Church Archidiocese of Chicago (Fris)

The Old Roman Catholic Church Archidiocese of Chicago (Fris) is an independent Old Catholic jurisdiction founded in 1974 by Howard Fris.

Hq: Current address unavailable for this edition

Old Roman Catholic Church (English Rite) and the Roman Catholic Church of the Ultrajectine Tradition

The Old Roman Catholic Church (English Rite) also known as the Roman Catholic Church of the Ultrajectine Tradition is an Old Catholic jurisdiction founded in 1974 by Bishop Robert W. Lane.

Hq: Rev. Robert Lane, 1000 N. LaSalle, Chicago, IL 60610

Old Roman Catholic Church in North America

The Old Roman Catholic Church in North America is an independent Catholic jurisdiction founded in 1963 as the Old Roman Catholic Church-English Rite by Bishop Robert Alfred Burns.

Hq: Most Rev. Francis P. Facione, 3827 Old Creek Road, Troy, MI 48084
Tel: (313) 435 0933 or 552 7207

Old Roman Catholic Church-Utrecht Succession

The Old Roman Catholic Church-Utrecht Succession is an independent old Catholic jurisdiction founded in 1977 by Archbishop Roy G. Bauer.

Hq: c/o Most Rev. Roy G. Bauer, 21 Aaron Street, Melrose, MA 02176

Open Bible Standard Churches, Inc.

The Open Bible Standard Churches is a Pentecostal fellowship founded in 1935 as a merger of the Open Bible Evangelistic Association and Bible Standard Inc. General Superintendent is Ray E. Smith.

Hq: 2020 Bell Avenue, Des Moines, IA 50315-1096
Tel: (515) 288 6761

Order of St. Francis

The Order of St. Francis is a traditionalist Roman Catholic jurisdiction led by Bishop Louis Vezelis whose episcopal orders derive from traditionalist Roman Catholic Archbishop Pierre Martin Ngo-Dinh-Thuc.

Hq: Box 16194, Rochester, NY 14616

Oriental Missionary Society Holiness Church of North America

The Oriental Missionary Society Holiness Church of North America, an evangelical church operating primarily within the Japanese-American community, was founded in 1920 by a group of young Japanese Christians.

Hq: 3660 S. Gramercy Pl., Los Angeles, CA 90018

(Original) Church of God, Inc.

The (Original) Church of God is a holiness Pentecostal church founded in 1917 by Rev. Joseph L. Scott, a former minister in the Church of God (Cleveland, Tennessee).

Hq: c/o Gen. Overseer Rev. W. D. Sawyer, Box 3086, Chattanooga, TN 37404
Tel: (615) 629 4505

Original Free Will Baptists, North Carolina State Convention

The Original Free Will Baptists, North Carolina State Convention was founded in 1961 by former members of the National Association of Free Will Baptists.

Hq: Box 39, Ayden, NC 28513

Original Glorious Church of God in Christ Apostolic Faith

The Original Glorious Church of God in Christ Apostolic Faith is a predominantly black Oneness Pentecostal church founded in 1952 by W. O. Howard as a split from the Glorious Church of God.

Hq: Current address unavailable for this edition

Original Pentecostal Church of God

The Original Pentecostal Church of God was founded in the 1910s by Tom Perry and Tom Austin.

Hq: Current address unavailable for this edition

Original United Holy Church International

The Original United Holy Church International was founded in 1977 by Bishop James Alexander Forbes as a split from the United Holy Church of America.

Hq: Bishop H. W. Field, Box 263, Durham, NC 27702
Tel: (919) 682 3498

Orthodox Catholic Autocephalous Church (USA)

The Orthodox Catholic Autocephalous Church (USA) is an independent Eastern Orthodox jurisdiction founded by Rt. Rev. James E. Henderson, formerly bishop with the Holy Eastern Orthodox Church of the United States.

Hq: Rt. Rev. James E. Henderson, 4741 No. 9th St., Philadelphia, PA 19040

Orthodox Catholic Church

The Orthodox Catholic Church is an independent Catholic jurisdiction founded by Rt. Rev. Carlos A. Florido who had been consecrated in 1983 by Lewis S. Keizer of the Independent Church of Antioch.

Hq: U.S. Chancery Office, Mt. Rev. Carlos A. Florido, 485 Dolores St., San Francisco, CA 94110
Tel: (415) 431 9965

Orthodox Catholic Church in America (Brown)

The Orthodox Catholic Church in America (Brown) is an independent Catholic jurisdiction founded in 1941 by Bishop Francis Xavier Resch. It was previously known as the Archdiocese of the Old Catholic Church of America.

Hq: c/o Most Rev. Walter X. Brown, 2450 N. 50th Street, Milwaukee, WI 53210
Tel: (414) 442 5990

Orthodox Catholic Church in America (Verra)

The Orthodox Catholic Church in America (Verra), originally known as the American Catholic Church, Archdiocese of New York, was founded in 1927 by James F. A. Lashley. It assumed its present name in 1982.

Hq: Most Rev. Michael Edward Verra, 238 Mott Street, New York, NY 10012
Tel: (212) 925 5238

Orthodox Catholic Church of America

The Orthodox Catholic Church of America is an independent Eastern Orthodox jurisdiction founded in 1960 by George A. Hyde.

Hq: c/o Most Rev. Alfred Lankenau, P.O. Box 1222, Indianapolis, IN 45206

Orthodox Catholic Church of North and South America

The Orthodox Catholic Church of North and South America was founded by Bishop Joseph W. Alisauskas, Jr., in 1969 (as Orthodox Catholic Diocese of Connecticut and New England) and took its present name in 1971.

Hq: P. O. Box 1213, Akron, OH 44309

Orthodox Catholic Synod of the Syro-Chaldean Rite

The Orthodox Catholic Synod of the Syro-Chaldean Rite is an independent Eastern Orthodox church founded in 1970 by Bishop Bashir Ahmed (Mar Nazarim).

Hq: c/o Most Rev. Bashir Ahmed, 100 Los Banos Avenue, Daly City, CA 94014

Orthodox Church in America

The Orthodox Church in America is the original Eastern Orthodox body to establish work in the United States. It was founded in 1794 by a group of monks as the American mission of the Russian Orthodox Church. It assumed its present name in 1970.

Hq: c/o Chancellor Very Rev. Robert Kondratick, P. O. Box 675, Syosset, NY 11791
Tel: (516) 922 0550

Orthodox Church of America

The Orthodox Church of America is an independent Eastern Orthodox jurisdiction founded in 1970 by Bishop David Baxter.

Hq: Most Rev. David Baxter, 502 East Childress, Morrilton, AZ 72110

Orthodox Church of the East

The Orthodox Church of the East (also known as Church of the East in America) was founded in 1959 by Bishop John Marion Stanley.

Hq: Archbishop John Marion Stanley, Rte. 4, Box 322, Vashon, WA 98070

or
c/o Rev. Floyd W. Newman, 417 Crystal
Dr., Cotati, CA 94931
Tel: (707) 792 0279

Orthodox Episcopal Church of God

The Orthodox Episcopal Church of God, an independent Catholic jurisdiction which has focused its work in the homosexual community of San Francisco, was founded in 1966 by Rev. Ray Broshears.

Hq: Box 1528, San Francisco, CA 94101

Orthodox Presbyterian Church

The Orthodox Presbyterian Church was founded after 1932 by J. Gresham Machen, previously an outstanding theologian of the Presbyterian Church in the U.S.A.

Hq: 303 Horsham Road, Ste G., Horsham, PA 19044
Tel: (215) 956 0123

Orthodox Reformed Church

The Orthodox Reformed Church was founded in 1970 by former members protesting what they felt were unfair actions by the Protestant Reformed Churches in America.

Hq: 3836 30th Street, Grandville, MI 49418
or
1900 Greenleaf, S.E., Grand Rapids, MI
Tel: (616) 452 6295

Our Lady of the Roses, Mary Help of Mothers Shrine

The Our Lady of the Roses, Mary Help of Mothers Shrine is an independent Catholic group founded in the 1970s by Veronica Lueken.

Hq: P. O. Box 52, Bayside, NY 11361
Tel: (718) 961 8865

Overcoming Saints of God

The Overcoming Saints of God, a predominantly black Pentecostal church, was organized in 1959 in Archer, Florida, by Pastor Anna Thompson Mobley.

Hq: P. O. Box 879, Gainesville, FL
Tel: (904) 377 6725 or 375 2687

Pacific Yearly Meeting of Friends

The Pacific Yearly Meeting of Friends was founded by Howard H. and Mary Brinton in 1931 as the Pacific Coast Association of Friends. It took the present name in 1972.

Hq: Stratton Jaquette, 258 Cherry Avenue, Los Altos, CA 94022
Tel: (415) 941 9562

Pastoral Bible Institute

The Pastoral Bible Institute is one of several groups to emerge from the Bible Student movement founded in the 1880s by Pastor Charles Taze Russell. The Institute was established in 1918 by R. H. Hirsh, I.F. Hoskins, A. I. Ritchie, and J. D. Wright, all formerly affiliated with the Watch Tower Bible and Tract Society.

Hq: 4454 S. 14th St., Suite 2, Milwaukee, WI 53221-0539
Tel: (414) 282 1076

Pentecostal Assemblies of the World

The Pentecostal Assemblies of the World, the first of the Oneness Pentecostal churches, was founded in 1906 by J. J. Frazee. The church has attempted to remain a functionally integrated church through the years.

Hq: 3939 Meadows Dr., Indianapolis, IN 46205
Tel: (317) 547 9541

Pentecostal Church of God

The Pentecostal Church of God, a predominantly black Oneness Pentecostal church, was founded in 1955 by Apostle Willie James Peterson, Jr.

Hq: 9244 Delmar, Detroit, MI 48211
Tel: (313) 865 0510

Pentecostal Church of God of America

The Pentecostal Church of God of America was founded by Rev. John C. Sinclair in 1919 and took the present name in 1922.

Hq: c/o Gen. Superintendent Dr. James D. Gee, 4901 Pennsylvania, Box 850, Joplin, MO 64802

Pentecostal Church of the Living God, The Pillar and Ground of Truth

The Pentecostal Church of the Living God is a predominantly black Pentecostal church founded in 1952 in Pennsgrove, New Jersey, by Bishop M.L. Benn.

Hq: 3909 Brown Street, Philadelphia, PA 19401

Pentecostal Church of Zion

The Pentecostal Church of Zion was founded in 1954 by Luther S. Howard.

Hq: Zion College of Theology, Box 110, French Lick, IN 47432

Pentecostal Churches of Apostolic Faith

The Pentecostal Churches of Apostolic Faith was founded in 1957 by Bishop Samuel N. Hancock, formerly of the Pentecostal Assemblies of the World.

Hq: Current address unavailable for this edition

Pentecostal Evangelical Church

The Pentecostal Evangelical Church was founded in 1936 by G. F. C. Fons.

Hq: Rev. Ernest Beroth, Box 4218, Spokane, WA 99202

Pentecostal Evangelical Church of God, National and International

The Pentecostal Evangelical Church of God, National and International is a Pentecostal church founded in 1960.

Hq: Riddle, OR 97469

Pentecostal Fire-Baptized Holiness Church

The Pentecostal Fire-Baptized Holiness Church was founded in 1918 as a split from the International Pentecostal Holiness Church.

Hq: c/o Gen. Mod. Steve E. Johnson, Rt. 2 Box 204, Dry Fork, VA 24549
Tel: (804) 724 4879

Pentecostal Free Will Baptist Church, Inc.

The Pentecostal Free Will Baptist Church was founded in 1959 as a merger of a number of Free Will Baptist Associations.

Hq: c/o Gen. Supt, Rev. Don Sauls, Box 1568, Dunn, NC 28334
Tel: (919) 892 4161

People of Destiny International

The People of Destiny International is a Pentecostal-Charismatic church founded in the early 1980s by Larry

Tomczak and several independent Charismatic ministers.

Hq: 7881-B Beechcraft Avenue, Gaithersburg, MD 20879
Tel: (301) 948 4891 or 933 6500

People's Christian Church
The People's Christian Church is an Adventist church founded in 1916 by Elmer E. Franke, formerly a member of the Seventh-day Adventist Church.

Hq: 402 Melrose Street, Schenectady, NY 12306

People's Methodist Church
The People's Methodist Church was founded in 1939 as a split from the Methodist Episcopal Church, South.

Hq: Current address unavailable for this edition

Philanthropic Assembly
The Philanthropic Assembly grew out of the Bible Student Movement begun by Pastor Charles Taze Russell in the 1880s. It was founded in Switzerland in 1921 by Alexander Freytag.

Hq: 709 74th Street, North Bergen, NJ 07047
Tel: (201) 868 5655

Philippine Independent Catholic Church
The Church is a splinter from the Philippine Independent Church.

Hq: c/o Most Rev. Paul Schultz, P. O. Box 6, Glendale, CA 91209

Philippine Independent Church
The Philippine Independent Church was founded in the Philippine Islands in 1899 by Gregorio Aglipay, a former Roman Catholic.

Hq: St. Andrew's Episcopal Cathedral, Queen Emma Sq., Honolulu, HI 96813

Pilgrim Assemblies International
The Pilgrim Assemblies International is an independent Pentecostal fellowship.

Hq: c/o Bishop Roy E. Brown, Brooklyn, NY
Tel: (718) 452 5180

Pilgrim Holiness Church of New York
The Pilgrim Holiness Church of New York is a conservative holiness church founded by former members of the Pilgrim Holiness Church who did not wish to participate in the 1968 merger of that church with the Wesleyan Methodist Church.

Hq: 32 Cadillac Avenue, Albany, NY 12205
Tel: (518) 235 1662

Pilgrim Holiness Church of the Midwest
The Pilgrim Holiness Church of the Midwest is a conservative holiness church founded by members of the Pilgrim Holiness Church who rejected its 1968 merger with the Wesleyan Methodist Church.

Hq: Union Bible Seminary, 434 S. Union Street, Westfield, IN 46074
Tel: (317) 896 9324

Pillar of Fire
The Pillar of Fire is a holiness church founded in 1917 by Alma White.

Hq: Bishop Donald J. Wolfram, Zarephath, NJ 08890
Tel: (201) 356 0102

Plymouth Brethren (Exclusive: Ames Brethren)

One of several factions of the fundamentalist Plymouth Brethren, the Plymouth Brethren (Exclusive: Ames Brethren) originated from the activity of a preacher named Ames in England in the 1940s.

Hq: Christian Literature, Box 23082, Minneapolis, MN 55423

Plymouth Brethren (Exclusive: Ex-Taylor Brethren)

One of several factions of the fundamentalist Plymouth Brethren, the Plymouth Brethren (Exclusive: Ex-Taylor Brethren) was founded in 1960 as a split from the Plymouth Brethren (Ex-Taylor Brethren).

Hq: Current address unavailable for this edition

Plymouth Brethren (Exclusive: Raven-Taylor Brethren)

One of several factions of the fundamentalist Plymouth Brethren, the Plymouth Brethren (Exclusive: Raven-Taylor Brethren) originated from the ministry of F. E. Raven and his successor, James Taylor, Sr.

Hq: Current address unavailable for this edition

Plymouth Brethren (Exclusive: Reunited Brethren)

In 1974 several factions of the divided Plymouth Brethren completed a process of merger which created The Plymouth Brethren (Exclusive: Reunited Brethren).

Hq: No central address. For information: Grace and Truth, 210 Chestnut Street, Danville, IL 61832

Plymouth Brethren (Exclusive: The Tunbridge Well Brethren)

One of several factions of the Plymouth Brethren, the Plymouth Brethren (Exclusive: The Tunbridge Well Brethren) originated in England in 1909.

Hq: No central address. For information: Bible Truth Publishers, 59 Industrial Dr., Addison, IL 60101

Polish National Catholic Church of America

The Polish National Catholic Church of America is an independent Old Catholic jurisdiction founded in the 1890s by former members of the Roman Catholic Church of Polish ancestry under the leadership of Bishop Francis Hodur.

Hq: Most Rev. John F. Swantek, 1002 Pittston Avenue, Scranton, PA 18505
Tel: (717) 345 9131

Prayer Band Fellowship Union

The Prayer Band Fellowship Union, a predominantly black Pentecostal church, was founded in 1976 in Bridgeport, Connecticut, by Bishop Curtis Mouning and Rev. Lucille Fogg.

Hq: Gospel Temple Community Holiness Church, P. O. Box 9109, Bridgeport, CT 06601

Presbyterian Church in America

The Presbyterian Church in America was founded in 1974 by conservative members of the Presbyterian Church in the United States who rejected that church's merger with the United Presbyterian Church in the U.S.A.

Hq: c/o Stated Clerk Dr. Paul R. Gilchrist, 1852 Century Plaza, Suite 202, Atlanta, GA 30345
Tel: (404) 320 3366

Presbyterian Church (U.S.A.)

The Presbyterian Church (U.S.A.), the largest of several Presbyterian churches in America, was founded in 1983 as a merger of the United Presbyterian Church in the U.S.A. and the Presbyterian Church in the United States.

Hq: 100 Witherspoon St., Louisville, KY 40202
Tel: (502) 569 5000

Primitive Advent Christian Church

The Primitive Advent Christian Church was founded by former members of the Advent Christian Church.

Hq: c/o Pres. Donald Young, 1640 Clay Avenue, South Charleston, WV 25312

Primitive Baptists-Absolute Predestinarians

The most conservative branch of the Primitive Baptists, the Absolute Predestinarians believe and teach that each person was predestined by God for either eternal salvation or damnation.

Hq: No central headquarters. For information: c/o Primitive Baptist Library, Rte. 2, Elon College, NC 27244

Primitive Baptists-Moderates

The central branch of the Primitive Baptists, the Moderates are Calvinist in doctrine and emphasize God's election of the saved from the foundation of the earth.

Hq: No central headquarters. For information: c/o Primitive Baptist Library, Rte. 2, Elon College, NC 27244
or
c/o Cayce Publishing Co., Thornton, AR 71766
Tel: (501) 352 3694

Primitive Baptists-Progressive

The most liberal branch of the Primitive Baptists, the Progressives have instituted a number of innovations including the support of a varied youth ministry, Bible conferences, and two homes for the elderly.

Hq: Manner Bookstore, Box 4, Jesup, GA 31545

Primitive Methodist Church

The Primitive Methodist Church grew out of the revivalist impulse in England in the early nineteenth century. It was founded in 1811 by Revs. Hugh Bourne and William Clowes and was brought to the United States in the 1820s.

Hq: c/o Gen. Sec. Rev. K. Gene Carroll, 223 Austin Avenue, Wilkes-Barre, PA 18702

Progressive National Baptist Convention, Inc.

The Progressive National Baptist Convention, a predominantly black Baptist church, was founded in 1961 by formers members of the National Baptist Convention who supported the Civil Rights Movement under the leadership of Dr. Martin Luther King. The National Baptists had refused to support the Movement actively.

Hq: 601 50th Street, N.E., Washington, D.C. 20019
Tel: (202) 396 0558

The Protes'tant Conference

The Protes'tant Conference is a conservative Lutheran church founded in 1928 by former members of the Wisconsin Evangelical Lutheran Synod.

Hq: Rec. Sec. Pastor Gerald Hinz, P. O. Box 86, Shiocton, WI 54170
Tel: (414) 986 3918

Protestant Reformed Churches in America

The Protestant Reformed Churches in America was founded in 1926 as a split from the Christian Reformed Church.

Hq: 15615 S. Park Avenue, South Holland, IL 60473
Tel: (312) 333 1314

Pure Holiness Church of God

The Pure Holiness Church of God is a predominantly black Oneness Pentecostal church founded in Anniston, Alabama, in 1911 by Bishop John Isaac Woodly.

Hq: Saint Timothy's Pure Holiness Church, 408 McDonough Blvd. SE, Atlanta, GA 30315
Tel: (404) 627 3791

Redeemed Assembly of Jesus Christ, Apostolic

The Redeemed Assembly of Jesus Christ, Apostolic is a predominantly black Pentecostal church founded in 1979 by James Frank Harris and Douglas Williams, both formerly of the Highway Christian Church of Christ.

Hq: Bishop Douglas Williams, 734 1st St., S.W., Washington, D.C. 20024
Tel: (202) 646 0010

Reform Catholic Church

The Reform Catholic Church is a small independent Catholic jurisdiction founded in the 1980s.

Hq: Most Rev. S. Trivoli-Johnson, 124 Casitas Av., San Francisco, CA 94127

Reformed Church in America

The Reformed Church in America, the oldest continuously existing Protestant church in the United States, continues the first Dutch Reformed settlement of New Amsterdam (New York) in the seventeenth century.

Hq: 475 Riverside Dr., Rm. 1811, New York, NY 10115
Tel: (212) 870 2841

Reformed Church in the United States

The Reformed Church in the United States was founded in 1934 by the Eureka Classis of South Dakota whose leadership refused to join the merger of the (German) Reformed Church in the United States with the Evangelical Synod.

Hq: c/o Pres. Rev. Robert Stuebbe, 401 Cherry Hill Dr., Bakersfield, CA 93309

Reformed Episcopal Church

The Reformed Episcopal Church is an independent Anglican church founded in 1873 by Rt. Rev. George David Cummins and former members of the evangelical wing of the Episcopal Church.

Hq: Presiding Bishop Rev. William H. S. Jerdan, Jr. 414 W. Second South St., Summerville, SC 29483

Reformed Mennonite Church

The Reformed Mennonite Church, a very conservative Mennonite body known for its use of shunning (or avoidance) against deviating members, was founded in 1812 by John Herr and former members of the Mennonite Church.

Hq: Bishop Earl Basinger, 1036 Lincoln Heights Avenue, Ephrata, PA 17522

Reformed Methodist Union Episcopal Church

The Reformed Methodist Union Episcopal Church is a predominantly black church founded in 1885 by former members of the African Methodist Episcopal Church.

Hq: Rt. Rev. Leroy Gethers, 1136 Brody Avenue, Charleston, SC 29407
Tel: (803) 766 3534

Reformed Orthodox Church in America

The Reformed Orthodox Church in America is an independent Eastern Orthodox church formed by Bishop Richard E. Drews shortly after his consecration in 1969.

Hq: Rt. Rev. Richard E. Drews, 800 W. Sunrise Blvd., Ft. Lauderdale, FL 33311

Reformed Orthodox Church (Slavonic)

The Reformed Orthodox Church (Slavonic) is a small independent Catholic jurisdiction.

Hq: c/o Most Rev. Thomas Ephriam, 1674 Palm Av., #21, San Diego, CA 92154

Reformed Presbyterian Church of North America

The Reformed Presbyterian Church of North America trace their history to the 1643 Solemn League and Covenant, a document issued by a group (the Covenanters) which separated from the Church of Scotland. The Church remains today the only Covenanter branch which has not merged into one of the other Presbyterian churches.

Hq: c/o Stated Clerk Louis D. Hutmire, 7418 Penn Avenue, Pittsburgh, PA 15208
Tel: (412) 731 1177

Reformed Zion Union Apostolic Church

The Reformed Zion Union Apostolic Church was founded in 1869 by Rev. James Howell as a split from the African Methodist Episcopal Church.

Hq: c/o Deacon James C. Feggins, 416 South Hill Avenue, South Hill, VA 23970
Tel: (804) 447 3374

The Registry

The Registry is an Adventist fellowship founded in 1967 by Cecil Shrock, a former member of the Seventh-day Adventist Church.

Hq: Box 279, Leslie, AR 72645

Regular Baptists

The Regular Baptist church dates to the 1854 organization of the New Salem Association of Regular Baptists by Baptists who rejected the innovations introduced among American Baptists during the nineteenth century.

Hq: Current address unavailable for this edition

Regular Baptists (Predestinarian)

The Regular Baptists (Predestinarian) church was founded in the 1890s by members who separated from the Union Association, the Sandlick Association, and the Mages Creek Association of Regular Baptists.

Hq: Current address unavailable for this edition

Remnant Church

The Remnant Church was founded in 1957 by Tracy B. Bizich and Elsworth Thomas Kaiser.

Hq: Current address unavailable for this edition

Remnant of Israel

The Remnant of Israel is a small organization founded in 1915 by Adventist minister G. G. Rupert, a believer in Anglo-Israelism.

Hq: 11303 E. 7th, Opportunity, WA 99206
Tel: (206) 926 6767

Restored Israel of Yahweh

The Restored Israel of Yahweh was founded in 1973 by Leo Volpe.

Hq: Mrs. Nancy Micsko, 649 2nd Street, Somers Point, NJ 08244

Rex Humbard Ministry

The Rex Humbard Ministry was founded in 1958 by popular television evangelist Rex Humbard and continues his ministry from the Cathedral of Tomorrow, an independent church in Akron, Ohio.

Hq: Box 3063, Boca Raton, FL 33431

Rocky Mountain Yearly Meeting

The Rocky Mountain Yearly Meeting (of Friends) was founded in 1957 as a split from the Nebraska Yearly Meeting.

Hq: Box 9629, Colorado Springs, CO 80932
Tel: (303) 570 1267

Roman Catholic Church

The Roman Catholic Church first colonized what was to become the United States in 1565. Through processes of immigration and evangelism, by the 1840s it emerged and has remained as the largest denomination in America.

Hq: Apostolic Pro Nuncio to the U.S. Archbishop Pio Laghi, 3339 Massachusetts Avenue NW, Washington, D.C. 20008
Tel: (202) 333 7121
or
National Conference of Catholic Bishops, 1312 Massachusetts Avenue NW, Washington, D.C. 20005
Tel: (202) 659 6600
or
International Hq: Vatican City

Romanian Orthodox Church in America

The first Romanian Orthodox parish in North America was founded in Regina, Saskatchewan. A diocese was formed in 1929. Following World War II, the church was split over ties to the church in Romania. The Romanian Orthodox Church in America remained affiliated to the Church in Romania.

Hq: Archbishop His Eminence The Most Rev. Victorin (Ursache), 19959 Riopelle, Detroit, MI 48203
Tel: (313) 893 7191

or
International Hq: Biserica Ortodoxa Romana, Palatul Patriarhiei, Aleea Marea Adunare Nationala, no.1, 70526 Bucharest I, Romania

Romanian Orthodox Episcopate of America

The Romanian Orthodox Episcopate of America grew out of the split in the Romanian Church in America following World War II. It rejected ties to the church headquarters in Bucharest which it saw dominated by the Communist government.

Hq: Rt. Rev. Nathaniel Popp, 2522 Grey Tower Road, Jackson, MI 49201
Tel: (517) 522 4800

Russian Orthodox Church in the U.S.A., Patriarchal Parishes of the

In 1970, following the creation of the autonomous Orthodox Church in America, which included most of the factions of the Russian Orthodox Church then operating in the United States, a few parishes declined to enter the new church. They wished to remain directly under the Patriarch in Moscow and reorganized as the Patriarchal Parishes of the Russian Orthodox Church in the U.S.A.

Hq: Vicar Bishop Most Rev. Clement, Bishop of Serpukhov, St. Nicholas, Patriarchal Cathedral, 15 E. 97th Street, New York, NY 10029
Tel: (212) 831 6294

Russian Orthodox Church Outside of Russia

The Russian Orthodox Church Outside of Russia was founded in 1921 in reaction to the Russian Revolution. A group of bishops not in Russia at the time rejected the new Russian government and organized to continue their life and organization on pre-Revolutionary patterns.

Hq: Metropolitan His Eminence Vitaly, 75 E. 93rd Street, New York, NY 10028
Tel: (212) 534 1601

Russian-Ukrainian Evangelical Baptist Union of the U.S.A., Inc.

The Russian-Ukrainian Evangelical Baptist Union of the U.S.A. was founded in 1901 by Baptist immigrants to America and have continued as a missionary society to Slavic-speaking peoples.

Hq: Roosevelt Blvd. & 7th Street, Philadelphia, PA 19120

Salvation Army

The Salvation Army was founded in 1868 (as the Christian Mission) in England by William Booth.

Hq: c/o National Commander Commissioner Andrew S. Miller, 799 Bloomfield Avenue, Verona, NJ 07044
Tel: (201) 239 0606
or
International Hq: 101 Queen Victoria Street, London EC4P 4EP, England

Sanctified Church of Christ

The Sanctified Church of Christ was founded in 1937 by Brother E. K. Leary, Sister Jemima Bishop, and former members of the Methodist Episcopal Church.

Hq: 2715 18th Avenue, Columbus, GA 31901

R. W. Schambach Revivals

R. W. Schambach Revivals includes under its care the various congregations which have emerged in response to the evangelistic activity of R. W. Schambach, an independent Pentecostal minister.

Hq: P. O. Box 9009, Tyler, TX 75711

Schwenkfelder Church in America

The Schwenkfelder Church in America was founded in 1782 by followers of Caspar Schwenkfeld, a sixteenth century mystic in Germany.

Hq: Pennsburg, PA 18073

Scripture Research Association

The Scripture Research Association is a sabbatarian Sacred Name organization founded in 1950 by biblicist A. B. Traina, one of the first translators of a *Sacred Name Bible*.

Hq: 14410 S. Springfield Rd., Brandywine, MD 20613

Second Cumberland Presbyterian Church in U.S.

The Second Cumberland Presbyterian Church in U.S. was founded in 1874 by members of the Cumberland Presbyterian Church.

Hq: c/o Stated Clerk Rev. Dr. R. Stanley Wood, 226 Church Street, Huntsville, AL 35801
Tel: (205) 536 7481

Separate Baptists in Christ

The Separate Baptists in Christ trace their history to the "separation" of people from the Congregational Church in the early eighteenth century because of their acceptance of Baptist doctrines and their subsequent migration south to the Allegheny Mountain area. While many of the Separate Baptists were absorbed by other Baptist groups through mergers, a few survived and in 1912 organized the general Association of Separatist Baptists.

Hq: c/o Mod. Rev. Jim Goff, 1020 Gagel Avenue, Louisville, KY 40216

Serbian Eastern Orthodox Church for the U.S.A. and Canada

The Serbian Eastern Orthodox Church for the U.S.A. and Canada was founded in the thirteenth century in Serbia and came in 1892 to the United States under the leadership of Archimandrite Firmilian.

Hq: Rt. Rev. Bishop Firmilian, St. Sava Monastery, P. O. Box 519, Libertyville, IL 60048
Tel: (312) 362 2440

Servant Catholic Church

The Servant Catholic Church is an independent Catholic jurisdiction founded in 1978 by Bishop Primate Robert E. Burns.

Hq: c/o Most Rev. Robert E. Burns, 50 Coventry Lane, Central Islip, NY 11722

Seventh-day Adventist Church

The Seventh-day Adventist Church grew out of the revival led by William Miller who predicted the Second Coming of Christ in 1843. It was founded in 1860 by Ellen G. White and James White.

Hq: 6840 Eastern Avenue, N.W., Washington, D.C. 20012
Tel: (202) 722 6000

Seventh-day Adventist Church, Reform Movement

The Seventh-day Adventist Church, Reform Movement was founded in 1920 by former members of the Seventh-day Adventist Church.

Hq: Box 7239, Roanoke, VA 24019

Seventh Day Baptist General Conference USA and Canada Ltd.

The Seventh Day Baptist General Conference USA and Canada was organized in 1801 and continues the practice of sabbatarianism among English-speaking Baptists.

Hq: Seventh Day Baptist Center, 3120 Kennedy Rd., P. O. Box 1678, Janesville, WI 53547
Tel: (608) 752 5055

Seventh Day Baptists (German)

The Seventh Day Baptists (German) began with the work of Johann Beissel who founded a sabbatarian community at Ephrata, Pennsylvania, in 1764.

Hq: R.D. 1, Box 158, New Enterprise, PA 16664

Seventh Day Christian Conference

The Seventh Day Christian Conference is a predominantly black sabbatarian fellowship founded in 1934 by former members of the Seventh-day Adventist Church.

Hq: 252 W. 138th Street, New York, NY 10030
Tel: (212) 926 6222

Seventh Day Church of God

The Seventh Day Church of God was founded in 1954 by ministers of

the Church of God (Seventh Day).

Hq: Box 804, Caldwell, ID 83606-0804
Tel: (208) 459 9755

Seventh Day Pentecostal Church of the Living God

The Seventh Day Pentecostal Church of the Living God is a sabbatarian Pentecostal church founded by Bishop Charles Gamble.

Hq: 1443 S. Euclid, Washington, D.C. 20009

Shiloh Apostolic Temple

The Shiloh Apostolic Temple, a predominantly black Oneness Pentecostal church, was founded in 1953 by Robert O. Doub, Jr., formerly a minister of the Apostolic Church of Christ in God.

Hq: 1516 W. Master, Philadelphia, PA 19121
Tel: (215) 763 7335

Shiloh True Light Church of Christ

The Shiloh True Light Church of Christ is an independent Adventist church which grew out of the work of former Methodist Cunningham Boyle, a late nineteenth century minister.

Hq: Elder James Rommie Purser, Rt.1, Box 426, Indian Trail, NC 28079
Tel: (704) 753 4180

Social Brethren

The Social Brethren church was founded in 1867 by people who had left several different evangelical churches.

Hq: Rev. John Hancock, RR #3, Box 221, Harrisburg, IL 62946
Tel: (618) 252 0802

Society of St. Pius V

The Society of St. Pius V was founded in 1987 due to a split in the American branch of the Society of Pius X, the movement initiated by French conservative Roman Catholic Archbishop Marcel Lefebvre.

Hq: 8 Pond Place, Oyster Bay Cove, NY 11771
Tel: (516) 922 5430

Society of St. Pius X

The Society of St. Pius X is an independent traditionalist Roman Catholic movement founded in 1969 by Roman Catholic Archbishop Marcel Lefebvre.

Hq: P. O. Box 13077, Dickinson, TX 77539

Soldiers of the Cross of Christ, Evangelical International Church

The Soldiers of the Cross of Christ, Evangelical International Church is a Spanish-speaking Pentecostal church founded in the 1920s in Cuba by Ernest William Sellers, popularly called "Daddy John."

Hq: 636 N.W. 2nd Street, Miami, FL 33128

Sought Out Church of God in Christ

The Sought Out Church of God in Christ is a predominantly black Pentecostal church founded in 1947 by Mother Mozella Cook.

Hq: Current address unavailable for this edition

South Carolina Baptist Fellowship

The South Carolina Baptist Fellowship is a fundamentalist asso-ciation founded in 1954 by Rev. John R. Waters and Rev. Vendyl Jones. Many of its congregations are also members of the Southwide Baptist Fellowship.

Hq: c/o Rev. John R. Waters, Faith Baptist Church, 1600 Greenwood Rd., Laurens, SC 29360

Southeastern Yearly Meeting

The Southeastern Yearly Meeting was founded in 1962 by a group of Friends from Florida.

Hq: Gene E. Beardsley, Route 2, Box 108F, Gainesville, FL 32606
Tel: (904) 462 3201

Southern Appalachian Yearly Meeting and Association

The Southern Appalachian Yearly Meeting and Association was founded in 1970 by Friends congregations in several southern states.

Hq: 902 State Lick Road, Berea, KY 40403
Tel: (606) 986 9256

Southern Baptist Convention

The Southern Baptist Convention was founded in 1845 by southern Baptist congregations who withdrew support from the Northern Baptist Convention.

Hq: Executive Committee, 901 Commerce, Nashville, TN 37203
Tel: (615) 244 2355

Southern Episcopal Church

The Southern Episcopal Church is an independent Anglican church founded in 1953 by a group of members of the All Saints Episcopal Church in Nashville, Tennessee.

Hq: c/o Rt. Rev. Huron C. Manning,
    Jr., 234 Willow Lane, Nashville,
    TN 37211

Southern Methodist Church

The Southern Methodist Church was founded in 1934 by members of the Methodist Episcopal Church, South, who rejected that church's merger with the Methodist Episcopal Church and Methodist Protestant Church consummated in 1939.

Hq: Rev. W. Lynn Corbett, Box 132,
    Orangeburg, SC 29116-0132
Tel: (803) 536 1378

Southwide Baptist Fellowship

The Southwide Baptist Fellowship is an association of fundamentalist Baptist churches formed in 1955. Many of the member churches in South Carolina are also associated with the South Carolina Baptist Fellowship.

Hq: c/o Rev. John Waters, Faith Baptist
    Church, 1600 Greenwood
    Road, Lauren, SC 29360

Sovereign Grace Baptist Churches

The Sovereign Grace Baptist movement emerged in the years following World War II among Baptists and Presbyterians who rejected their several churches' movement away from a close adherence to the Calvinist theological tradition. There is no central authority but a strong sense of doctrinal unity among the various independent centers.

Hq: No central headquarters. For in-
    formation: Pastor Jon Zens,
    P. O. Box 548, St. Croix Falls,
    WI 54024
    or

Calvary Grace Baptist Church, Box
    7464, Pine Bluff, AR 71611-
    7464

Stauffer Mennonite Church

The Stauffer Mennonite Church was founded by a conservative group led by Jacob Stauffer who believed the "ban" against deviating members should be applied more severely. In protest they withdrew from the Mennonite Church.

Hq: Bishop Jacob S. Stauffer, Rte. 3,
    Ephrata, PA 17522

Syrian Orthodox Church of Antioch (Archdiocese of the United States and Canada) (Jacobite)

The Syrian Orthodox Church of Antioch (Jacobite) traces its origins to the group of Christians at Antioch described in the biblical Book of Acts who were the first people to be called Christians. The first priest of the church arrived in the United States in 1907 to organize the then scattered believers. Archbishop Mar Athanasius Y. Samuel moved to America to organize the archdiocese.

Hq: Archbishop Primate Mar
    Athanasius Y. Samuel, 49 Kipp
    Avenue, Lodi, NJ 07644
Tel: (201) 778 0638
    or
International Hq: Greek Orthodox
    Patriarchate of Antioch and All
    the East, Bab Tooma,
    Damascus, Syria

Syrian Orthodox Church of Malabar

The Syrian Orthodox Church of Malabar derives from missionary work by Syrian missionaries in India in the seventeenth century. It came to the United States in the 1960s.

Hq: c/o Vicar in Charge Dr. K. M. Simon, Union Theological Seminary, Broadway and 120th Street, New York, NY 10027

Tel: (212) 662 7100

Tabernacle of Prayer for All People

The Tabernacle of Prayer for All People was founded in Brooklyn, New York, in 1968 by Johnnie Washington.

Hq: Current address unavailable for this edition

Thee Orthodox Old Roman Catholic Church

Thee Orthodox Old Roman Catholic Church is an independent Catholic jurisdiction founded in 1974 by Archbishop Simon Peter (Peter Charles Caine Brown).

Hq: P. O. Box 49314, Chicago, IL 60649

Timely Messenger Fellowship

The Timely Messenger Fellowship is an association of congregations tied together by their acceptance of the perspective of *The Timely Messenger*, a magazine founded in 1939 by Ike T. Sidebottom.

Hq: R. B. Shiflet, Box 473, Mineral Wells, TX 76067

Tioga River Christian Conference

The Tioga River Christian Conference was founded in the 1930s by former members of the Christian Church who rejected that church's merger with the Congregational Church.

Hq: Rev. Calvin Duvall, R.D. 1, Box 134, Cherry Valley, NY 13320

Traditional Catholics of America

The Traditional Catholics of America is an independent traditionalist Roman Catholic fellowship founded in the 1970s by Fr. Frances Fenton.

Hq: P. O. Box 6827, Colorado Springs, CO 80934

Traditional Christian Catholic Church

The Traditional Christian Catholic Church is an independent Catholic jurisdiction founded in the 1960s by Archbishop Thomas Fehervary.

Hq: Current address unavailable for this edition

Traditional Episcopal Church

The Traditional Episcopal Church is an independent Anglican jurisdiction founded by Bishop Juan Solanas.

Hq: Rt. Rev. Juan V. Solanas, Bishop, Diocese of St. James, Rt. 1, Box 150 A, White Post, WA 22663

Traditional Protestant Episcopal Church

The Traditional Protestant Episcopal Church is an independent Anglican church formed in 1986 by Bishop Robert Morley, formerly a bishop in the United Episcopal Church of America.

Hq: c/o Rt. Rev. Charles E. Morley, Presiding Bishop, 6 Derby Lane, Fairhope, AL 36532

Tel: (205) 928 4617

Traditional Roman Catholic Church in the Americas

The Traditional Roman Catholic Church in the Americas is an

independent Catholic jurisdiction founded in 1978 by Most Rev. John D. Fesi, formerly a bishop in the Old Roman Catholic Church.

Hq: Most Rev. John D. Fesi, Friary Press, P. O. Box 470, Chicago, IL 60690

Tridentine Catholic Church

The Tridentine Catholic Church is an independent Catholic jurisdiction founded in 1976 by Bishop Leonard J. Curreri, formerly a bishop of the Traditional Christian Catholic Church.

Hq: Primate Archbishop Leonard J. Curreri, Sacred Heart of Jesus Chapel, 1740 W. Seventh Street, Brooklyn, NY 11223

Tridentine Old Roman Community Catholic Church

The Tridentine Old Roman Community Catholic Church is an independent Catholic jurisdiction founded in 1976 by Fr. Jack Alwin Jones.

Hq: Most Rev. Charles T. Sutter, 1956 Garden Avenue, Long Beach, California 90813

Triumph the Church and the Kingdom of God in Christ (International)

The Triumph the Church and the Kingdom of God in Christ (International) is a predominantly black Pentecostal church founded in 1902 by E. D. Smith.

Hq: c/o Chief Bishop Rt. Rev. A. J. Scott, 1323 N. 36th St., Savannah, GA 31404
Tel: (912) 236 2877
or
Box 77056, Birmingham, AL 35228
Tel: (205) 798 2450

Triumph The Church in Righteousness

Triumph the Church in Righteousness, a predominantly black Pentecostal church, was founded in the early 1950s in Fort Lauderdale, Florida, by Bishop Annie Lizzie Brownlee.

Hq: P. O. Box 1572, Fort Lauderdale, FL 33302

True Fellowship Pentecostal Church of God in America

The True Fellowship Pentecostal Church of God in America is a predominantly black Pentecostal church founded in 1964 by Charles E. Waters, formerly a minister of the Church of God in Christ.

Hq: 4238 Pimlico Road, Baltimore, MD 21215
Tel: (301) 367 7716

True Grace Memorial House of Prayer

The True Grace Memorial House of Prayer is a predominantly black Pentecostal church founded in the 1960s by Thomas O. Johnson, formerly of the True Grace Memorial House of Prayer.

Hq: 205 V Street, N.W., Washington, D.C. 20001
Tel: (202) 232 9387

True Jesus Church

The True Jesus Church is a sabbatarian Pentecostal church founded in China in 1917 and brought to the United States in recent decades.

Hq: 11236 Dale Street, Garden Grove, CA 92641
Tel: (714) 539 0480

True Light Church of Christ

The True Light Church of Christ was founded in 1970 as a split from the Shiloh True Light Church of God. It is led by Bishop Herman Flake Braswell and Elder Clyde M. Huntley.

Hq: Current address unavailable for this edition

True (Old Calendar) Orthodox Church of Greece (Synod of Metropolitan Cyprian), American Exarchate

The True (Old Calendar) Orthodox Church of Greece (Synod of Metropolitan Cyprian), American Exarchate is the American branch of the conservative Greek Orthodox believers who still use the old (Julian) calendar and oppose what they see as the liberal and ecumenical activity of the Church of Greece.

Hq: c/o Synodal Exarch His Grace Bishop Chrysostomos, St. Gregory Palamas Monastery, P. O. Box 398, Etna, CA 96027
Tel: (916) 467 3228

True Vine Pentecostal Churches of Jesus (Apostolic Faith)

The True Vine Pentecostal Churches of Jesus (Apostolic Faith), a predominantly black Oneness Pentecostal church, was founded in 1961 by Dr. Robert L. Hairston. Hairston had been the co-founder of the True Vine Pentecostal Holiness Church but came to accept the non-Trinitarian "Oneness" belief about God and left to found a new church fellowship.

Hq: c/o Dr. Robert L. Hairston, New Bethel Apostolic Church, Martinsville, VA 24112

True Vine Pentecostal Holiness Church

The True Vine Pentecostal Holiness Church, a predominantly black Pentecostal church, was founded in the 1940s by William Monroe Johnson and Robert Leonard Hairston.

Hq: Current address unavailable for this edition

Truth for Today Bible Fellowship

The Truth for Today Bible Fellowship was founded in 1948 by Oscar M. Baker.

Hq: c/o Joseph L. Watkins, Box 6358, Lafayette, IN 47903
Tel: (317) 742 2958

Twentieth Century Church of God

The Twentieth Century Church of God was founded after 1974 by Al Carrozzo, a former member of the Worldwide Church of God.

Hq: Box 4010, Carlsbad, CA 92008

Ukrainian Autocephalous Orthodox Church of America and Europe

The Ukrainian Autocephalous Orthodox Church of America and Europe is an independent Eastern Orthodox jurisdiction.

Hq: Rt. Rev. Christopher Fontaine, 5523 Venetian Blvd., N.E., St. Petersburg, FL 33703

Ukrainian Evangelical Alliance of North America

The Ukrainian Evangelical Alliance of North America was founded in 1922 by a group of Ukrainian Protestants.

Hq: Rev. Vladimir Borosky, 690 Berkeley Avenue, Elmhurst, IL 60126

Ukrainian Evangelical Baptist Convention

The Ukrainian Evangelical Baptist Convention was founded by Rev. Paul Bartkow in 1945 (as Ukrainian Missionary and Bible Society) and took its present name in 1953.

Hq: Olexa R. Barbuiziuk, 6751 Riverside Dr., Berwyn, IL 60402

Ukrainian Orthodox Church in America (Ecumenical Patriarchate)

The Ukrainian Orthodox Church in America (Ecumenical Patriarchate) was founded in 1950 by Bishop Bohdan T. Shpilka.

Hq: St. Andrews Ukrainian Orthodox Diocese, 90-34 139th Street, Jamaica, NY 11435
Tel: (718) 297 2407

Ukrainian Orthodox Church of the U.S.A.

The Ukrainian Orthodox Church of the U.S.A. was founded in 1915 by Ukrainian immigrants who left the jurisdiction of the Russian Orthodox Church.

Hq: c/o Metropolitan Most Rev. Mstyslav S. Skrypnyk, P. O. Box 495, South Bound Brook, NJ 08880

Undenominational Church of the Lord

The Undenominational Church of the Lord, a holiness church, was founded in 1918 by Pastor Jesse N. Blakeley.

Hq: Current address unavailable for this edition

Unification Association of Christian Sabbath Keepers

The Unification Association of Christian Sabbath Keepers, a predominantly black Adventist church, was founded in 1956 by Thomas I. C. Hughes and other former members of the Seventh-day Adventist Church.

Hq: 255 W. 131st Street, New York, NY 10027
Tel: (212) 926 8694

Union of Messianic Jewish Congregations

The Union of Messianic Jewish Congregations was founded in the 1960s by a group of American Jewish converts to evangelical Christianity who wished to retain the outward forms of Jewish ethnic culture while putting Christian content in their worship.

Hq: Rev. David C. Juster, Beth Messiah Congregation, 2208 Rockland Avenue, Rockville, MD 20851
Tel: (301) 926 8652

United American Orthodox Catholic Church

The United American Orthodox Catholic Church is an independent liturgical church.

Hq: Monastery of St. Anthony, Rt. 3, Box 31, Lake Mauner Rd., Excelsior Springs, MO 64024
Tel: (816) 637 1503

United Anglican Church in North America

The United Anglican Church is an independent Anglican jurisdiction founded in the 1980s.

Hq: c/o Mt. Rev. John Riffenbury, 1 Wayside Village, Ste. 312, Marmosa, NV 08223

United Baptists

The United Baptists movement was founded in 1786 by a merger of the Regular Baptists' and Separate Baptists' associations.

Hq: Current address unavailable for this edition

United Christian Church

The United Christian Church was founded in 1877 by George W. Hoffman and former members of the United Brethren in Christ.

Hq: c/o Elder John Ludwig, Jr., 528 W. Walnut Street, Cleona, PA 17042

United Christian Church and Ministerial Association

The United Christian Church and Ministerial Association, a holiness Pentecostal fellowship, was founded in 1956 by evangelist H. Richard Hall, formerly a minister with the Church of God (Cleveland, Tennessee).

Hq: Box 700, Cleveland, TN 37311

United Christian Church of America

The United Christian Church of America, a conservative evangelical church, was founded in 1893 and was reorganized in the 1940s by Bishop Alexander A. Lowande.

Hq: Current address unavailable for this edition

United Church of Christ

The United Church of Christ was founded in 1957 as a merger of the Congregational-Christian Churches and the Evangelical and Reformed Church.

Hq: 105 Madison Avenue, New York, NY 10016
Tel: (212) 683 5656

United Church of Jesus Christ (Apostolic)

The United Church of Jesus Christ (Apostolic), a predominantly black Oneness Pentecostal church, was founded in 1965 by Monroe R. Saunders, formerly a co-founder of the Church of God in Christ Jesus (Apostolic).

Hq: c/o Presiding Bishop Monroe Saunders, 5150 Baltimore National Pike, Baltimore, MD 21229
Tel: (301) 945 0064 or 728 9679

United Church of Jesus Christ Apostolic

The United Church of Jesus Christ Apostolic, a predominantly black Oneness Pentecostal church, was founded in 1963 by Bishop James B. Thornton, formerly a minister with the Church of Our Lord Jesus Christ of the Apostolic Faith.

Hq: 2226 Park Avenue, Baltimore, MD 21217
Tel: (301) 728 9679

United Church of the Living God, The Pillar and Ground of Truth

The United Church of the Living God, a predominantly black Pentecostal church, was founded in Los Angeles in 1946 by Bishop "O. K." Okley Clifton, formerly of the Church of the Living God, The Pillar and Ground of Truth.

Hq: 601 Kentucky Avenue, Fulton, KY 42041
Tel: (502) 472 1453

United Churches of Jesus Christ, Apostolic

The United Churches of Jesus Christ, Apostolic, a predominantly black Oneness Pentecostal church, was founded in 1970 by Bishop J. W. Audrey and other former members of the Apostolic Church of Christ in God.

Hq: Current address unavailable for this edition

United Crusade Fellowship Conference

The United Crusade Fellowship Conference is a predominantly black Pentecostal church founded in Bellevue, Washington, in 1973 by Bishop Richard E. Taylor.

Hq: 15749 N. E. 4th, Bellevue, WA 98008

United Episcopal Church (1945) Anglican/Celtic

The United Episcopal Church (1945) Anglican/Celtic was founded in 1945 by Bishops Julius Massey, Albert Sorensen, and Hinton Pride.

Hq: Office of the Chancery, 526 North Maple, Murfreesboro, TN 37130

United Episcopal Church of North America

The United Episcopal Church of North America was founded in 1985 by C. Dale D. Doren.

Hq: Rt. Rev. Albion W. Knight, Jr., 7005 Radnor Rd., Bethesda, MD 20817

United Free-Will Baptist Church

The United Free-Will Baptist Church is a predominantly black church founded in 1901 by former members of the Free Will Baptists (now the National Association of Free Will Baptists).

Hq: Current address unavailable for this edition

United Full Gospel Ministers and Churches

The United Full Gospel Ministers and Churches is an independent Pentecostal fellowship founded in 1951 by Arthur H. Collins.

Hq: Current address unavailable for this edition

United Fundamentalist Church

The United Fundamentalist Church, a conservative evangelical church, was founded in 1939 by Rev. Leroy M. Kopp.

Hq: Current address unavailable for this edition

United Holiness Church of North America

The United Holiness Church of North America is a conservative holiness body founded in 1955 by former members of the Free Methodist Church.

Hq: Bible College, Cedar Springs, MI 49319

United Holy Church of America

The United Holy Church of America is a predominantly black Pentecostal church founded by Rev. Isaac Cheshier in North Carolina in 1886. It assumed its present name in 1916.

Hq: Route 5, Box 861, Greensboro, NC
Tel: (919) 621 0669
or
Mailing Address: 825 Fairoak Avenue,
Chillum, MD 20783

United House of Prayer
for All People

The United House of Prayer for All
People was founded in the mid-1920s
by Sweet Daddy Grace (Bishop
Marcelino Manoel de Graca).

Hq: 1721 1/2 7th Street, N.W.,
Washington, D.C. 20001
Tel: (202) 387 9267

United Methodist Church

The United Methodist Church, the
third largest church in America,
continues the Methodist movement
founded in the seventeenth century in
England by John Wesley. In 1968, a
long process of consolidation of
various Methodist churches in the
United States was completed in the
formation of the United Methodist
Church by the merger of the
Methodist Church (1939-1968) and
the United Evangelical Brethren.

Hq: 601 W. Riverside Avenue, Dayton,
OH 45406
Tel: (513) 227 9400

United Old Roman Catholic
Church

The United Old Roman Catholic
Church is an independent Catholic
jurisdiction founded in 1963 by Most
Rev. Armand C. Whitehead.

Hq: 527 82nd Street, Brooklyn, NY
11209

United Pentecostal Church
International

The United Pentecostal Church
International, a Oneness Pentecostal

church, was founded in 1945 as a
merger of the Pentecostal Church,
Inc., and the Pentecostal Assemblies
of Jesus Christ. It is the largest of the
predominantly white Oneness
Pentecostal churches.

Hq: c/o Gen. Superintendent Rev.
Nathaniel A. Urshan, 8855
Dunn Road, Hazelwood, MO
63042
Tel: (314) 837 7300

United Pentecostal Council of
the Assemblies of God

The United Pentecostal Council, a
predominantly black Pentecostal
church, dates to the ministry of
Mother Lillian Yates who began
evangelistic work in New York City in
1917.

Hq: 211 Columbia Street, Cambridge,
MA 02139
Tel: (617) 648 0808

United Seventh-Day Brethren

The United Seventh-Day Brethren,
a small sabbatarian Adventist church,
was founded in 1947.

Hq: Myrtle Ortiz, Box 225, Enid, OK
73701

United Way of the Cross
Churches of Christ of the
Apostolic Faith

The United Way of the Cross
Churches of Christ of the Apostolic
Faith, a predominantly black Oneness
Pentecostal church, was founded in
1974 by Bishop Joseph H. Adams,
formerly of the Way of the Cross
Church of Christ, and Harrison J.
Twyman of the Bible Way Churches
of Our Lord Jesus Christ Worldwide.

Hq: Current address unavailable for
this edition

United Wesleyan Methodist Church of America

The United Wesleyan Methodist Church of America was founded in 1905 by former members of the Methodist Church in the Caribbean and the Americas who had migrated to the United States.

Hq: Rev. David S. Bruno, 270 W. 126th Street, New York, NY 10027

United Zion Church

The United Zion Church was founded in 1855 by Matthias Brinser and other former members of the Brethren in Christ.

Hq: c/o Gen. Conf. Mod. Bishop J. Paul Martin, Box 212 D, RD 1, Annville, PA 17003
Tel: (717) 665 6274

Unity of the Brethren

The Unity of the Brethren, a Czechoslovakian pietist movement related to the Moravian Church in America, was founded by Rev. A. Chumsky and H. Juren in the mid-nineteenth century as the Evangelical Union of Bohemian and Moravian Brethren in North America. It assumed its present name in 1919.

Hq: c/o Pres. Unity Dr. Mark L. Labaj, 4202 Ermine, Temple, TX 76501
Tel: (817) 774 8179

Universal Christian Spiritual Faith and Churches for All Nations

The Universal Christian Spiritual Faith and Churches for All Nations, a predominantly black spiritual church, was founded in 1952 as a merger of the National David Spiritual Temple of Christ Church Union (Inc.) U.S.A., the St. Paul's Spiritual Church Convocation, and the King David Spiritual Temple of Truth Association.

Hq: Current address unavailable for this edition

Universal Church of Christ

The Universal Church of Christ, a predominantly black Oneness Pentecostal church, was founded in 1972 by Bishop Robert C. Juggetts and others.

Hq. 19 Park Street, Orange, NJ 107050
Tel: (201) 673 4424

Universal Church, the Mystical Body of Christ

The Universal Church, the Mystical Body of Christ was founded in the 1970s.

Hq: Bishop R. O. Frazier (Current address unavailable for this edition)

Universal Shrine of Divine Guidance

The Universal Shrine of Divine Guidance is an independent Eastern Orthodox jurisdiction founded in 1955 by Most Rev. Mark A. G. Karras.

Hq: Most Rev. Mark A. G. Karras, 30 Malta Street, Brooklyn, NY 11207

Universal World Church

The Universal World Church is an independent Pentecostal church founded in 1952 by evangelist O. L. Jaggers.

Hq: 123 N. Lake Street, Los Angeles, CA 90026
Tel: (213) 413 3030

Upper Cumberland Presbyterian Church

The Upper Cumberland Presbyterian Church was founded in 1955 by H. C. Wakefield, W. M. Dycus, Lum Oliver, and other members of the Cumberland Presbyterians.

Hq: Roaring River, Upper Cumberland Presbyterian Church, Gainesboro, TN 38562

Volunteers of America

The Volunteers of America movement was founded in 1896 by Ballington and Maud Booth, both former leaders in the Salvation Army.

Hq: c/o Pres. Raymond C. Tremont, 3813 N. Causeway Blvd., Metaire, LA 70002
Tel: (504) 837 2652

The Way International

The Way International is an evangelical Bible study fellowship founded in 1942 by Victor Paul Wierwille, a former minister in the Evangelical and Reformed Church.

Hq: Box 328, New Knoxville, OH 45871

Way of the Cross Church of Christ

The Way of the Cross Church of Christ is a predominantly black Oneness Pentecostal church founded in 1927 by Henry C. Brooks, previously a minister in the Church of Our Lord Jesus Christ of the Apostolic Faith.

Hq: 332 4th St., N.E., Washington, D.C. 20003
Tel: (202) 543 0500

Weaver Mennonites

The Weaver Mennonites split from the Stauffer Mennonite Church in 1916.

Hq: Current address unavailable for this edition

Weaverland Conference Old Order (Horning or Black Bumper) Mennonites

The Weaverland Conference Old Order (Horning or Black Bumper) Mennonites was founded by Bishop Moses Horning, formerly a bishop with the Old Order (Wisler) Mennonites.

Hq: Current address unavailable for this edition

Wesleyan Church

The Wesleyan Church continues the tradition of the Wesleyan Methodist Church founded in the 1820s. In 1968 the Wesleyan Methodist Church merged with Pilgrim Holiness Church to form the Wesleyan Church.

Hq: c/o Gen. Sec. Dr. Ronald R. Brannon, Box 50434, Indianapolis, IN 46250-0434
Tel: (317) 674 0444

Wesleyan Holiness Association of Churches

The Wesleyan Holiness Association of Churches is a conservative holiness church founded in 1959 by Rev. Glenn Griffith, previously the founder of the Bible Missionary Church.

Hq: c/o Gen. Superintendent Rev. J. Stevan Manley, 108 Carter Avenue, Dayton, OH 45405
Tel: (513) 278 3770

Wesleyan Tabernacle Association

The Wesleyan Tabernacle Association is a holiness church founded in 1936.

Hq: 626 Elliott Avenue, Cincinnati, OH 45215

Western Orthodox Church

The Western Orthodox Church is a small independent Eastern Orthodox jurisdiction founded in 1972 by Joseph Russell Morse.

Hq: Current address unavailable for this edition

Western Orthodox Church in America

The Western Orthodox Church in America is an independent Catholic jurisdiction which began as the Community of the Good Shepherd Eastern founded in the mid-1970s by C. David Luther.

Hq: Most Rev. C. David Luther, 1529 Pleasant Valley Blvd., Altoona, PA 16602

Westminster Biblical Fellowship

The Westminster Biblical Fellowship is a conservative fundamentalist church founded in 1969 by J. Phillip Clark and other former members of the Bible Presbyterian Church.

Hq: Current address unavailable for this edition

Wisconsin Evangelical Lutheran Synod

The Wisconsin Evangelical Lutheran Synod began with the organization of German Lutheran immigrants in Wisconsin in the 1850s and the organization spread as similar synods from other states associated with it.

It is among the most conservative of Lutheran bodies.

Hq: c/o Pres. of the Synod Rev. Carl H. Mischke, 2929 North Mayfair Rd., Wauwatosa, WI 53222

Tel: (414) 771 9357

Witness and Testimony Literature Trust and Related Centers

The Witness and Testimony Literature Trust was founded by independent fundamentalist Bible teacher Theodore Austin-Sparks in the mid-1920s in England. For many years he published a magazine, *A Witness and Testimony*. Other centers aligned to his perspective emerged in England and the United States.

Hq: Testimony Book Ministry, Box 34241, Bethesda, MD 20817

Workers Together with Elohim

The Workers Together with Elohim, a sabbatarian Adventist movement, was founded by Charles Andy Dugger, the Son of A. N. Dugger, following a split in the Church of God (Jerusalem).

International Hq: P. O. Box 14411, Jerusalem, Israel

World Baptist Fellowship

The World Baptist Fellowship was founded in 1939 by J. Frank Norris and fundamentalist colleagues from both the Southern Baptist Convention and Northern Baptist Convention. The flamboyant Norris was pastor of both First Baptist Church, Fort Worth, and a congregation in Detroit, Michigan.

Hq: 3001 W. Division, Arlington, TX 76012

World Confessional Lutheran Association

The World Confessional Lutheran Association was founded in 1965 as Lutheran's Alert National by a group of conservative Lutheran pastors.

Hq: c/o Pres. Dr. Rueben H. Redal, 3504 N. Pearl Street, P. O. Box 7186, Tacoma, WA 98407
Tel: (206) 759 1891

World Insight International

The World Insight International was founded in 1977 by Kenneth Storey, formerly with the Worldwide Church of God.

Hq: Box 35, Pasadena, CA 91102

Worldwide Church of God

The Worldwide Church of God is a sabbatarian Adventist church founded in 1933 by Herbert W. Armstrong.

Hq: 300 W. Green St., Pasadena, CA 91129
Tel: (818) 304 6111 or (800) 423 4444

Yahweh Assemblies in Messiah

The Yahweh Assemblies in Messiah is a sabbatarian Sacred Name group founded in 1980 by former members of the Assemblies of Yahweh.

Hq: Rte. 1, Box 364, Rocheport, MO 65279
Tel: (314) 698 4335 or 698 4215

Yahweh's Temple

The Yahweh's Temple was founded in 1947 as the Church of Jesus by Bishop Samuel E. Officer, who later absorbed elements of the Sacred Name movement into his Pentecostal beliefs. The church took the present name in 1981.

Hq: Box 652, Cleveland, TN 37311

CHRISTIAN PERIODICALS

Literally thousands of periodicals serve the Christian community and no comprehensive listing of them has been attempted to date. The list below begins such a comprehensive listing with the periodicals produced by the church groups included in this *Directory*. Each entry includes the name of the periodical, the address of its editorial/subscription office, and the name of the sponsoring organization. In the case of the larger denominations, only one or two of the major national periodicals have been listed. (Consult the *Yearbook of American Churches* for a more comprehensive list, especially of local magazines and newspapers.)

A

ACD Newsletter, P. O. Box 4455, Rolling Bay, WA 98061, Associated Churches, Inc.

Activity Bulletin, P. O. Box S, Beebe, AR 72012, Congregation of Yah

Acts, Church of God Publishing House, 1827 W. 3rd St., Meridian, ID 83642-1653, General Council of the Churches of God

Advent Christian News, P. O. Box 23152, Charlotte, NC 28212, Advent Christian Church

Advent Christian Witness, P. O. Box 23152, Charlotte, NC 28212, Advent Christian Church

Adventist Review, 55 W. Oak Ridge Dr., Hagerstown, MD 21740, Seventh-day Adventist Church

The Advocate of Truth, P. O. Box 328, Salem, WV 26426, Church of God (Seventh Day, Salem, West Virginia)

Again, P. O. Box 106, Mt. Hermon, CA 95041, Antiochian Orthodox Christian Archdiocese of North America

The AGC Reporter, 1919 Beach St., Pittsburgh, PA 15221, Associated Gospel Churches

Aglipayian Review, P. O. Box 2484, Manila, Philippines, Philippine Independent Church

A.M.E. Christian Recorder, 500 8th Av. S., Nashville, TN 37203, African Methodist Episcopal Church

A.M.E. Review, 468 Lincoln Drive N.W., Atlanta, GA 30318, African Methodist Episcopal Church

The American Messianic Jew, P. O. Box 1055, Havertown, PA 19083, Union of Messianic Jewish Congregations

America's Promise Newsletter, P. O. Box 30000, Phoenix, AZ 85046, Church Research, Inc.

The Angelus, Box 1307, Dickinson, TX, Society of St. Pius X

Anglican Episcopal Tidings, Box 1693, Deming, NM 88031, Anglican Episcopal Church of North America

The Anglican Evangelist, P. O. Box 785, Rincon, GA 31326, Holy Catholic Church, Anglican Rite Jurisdiction of the Americas

The ASK Exposition, P. O. Box 7777, Alhambra, CA 91802, Associates for Scriptural Knowledge

Assembly Bulletin, 210 Chestnut St., Danville, IL 61835, Plymouth Brethren (Exclusive: Reunited Brethren)

The Associate Reformed Presbyterian, One Cleveland St. , Greenville, SC 29601, Associate Reformed Presbyterian Church (General Synod)

The Augustinian, Box 1647, G.P.O., Brooklyn, NY 11202, North American Old Catholic Church (Rogers)

Awake!, 25 Columbia Heights, Brooklyn, NY 11201, Jehovah's Witnesses

Axios, 800 S. Euclid St., Fullerton, CA 92632, (unofficial publication) Association of Occidental Orthodox Parishes

B

The Banner, 2850 Kalamazoo Av. S.E., Grand Rapids, MI 49560, Christian Reformed Church in North America

Banner of Truth, 1053 Maplegrove N.W., Grand Rapids, MI 49504, Netherlands Reformed Congregations

The Bashan Tidings, Universal Publishing Association, Bashan Hill, Exeter, MO 65647, Davidian Seventh-day Adventist Association

Beginning Anew, P. O. Box 578, Columbia, MO 65205-0578, Yahweh's Assembly in Messiah

Bema, 630 2nd Av., NY, NY 10016, Armenian Church of America

Berean Digest, P. O. Box 213, Basalt, CO 81621, Berean Fundamental Churches

The Berean News, c/o The Berean Bible Students Church, 5930 West 28th St., Cicero, IL 60650, Christian Believers Conference

Berean Searchlight, 7609 W. Belmont, Chicago, IL 60635, Berean Bible Fellowship (Chicago)

Bible Advocate, P. O. Box 33677, Denver, CO 80233, General Conference of the Church of God (Seventh Day)

The Bible Answers Magazine, P. O. Box 1234, Santa Cruz, CA 95061, Biblical Church of God

Bible PR Messenger, Rd 1, P. O. Box 12, Port Jarvis, NY 12771, Fellowship of Fundamental Bible Churches

The Bible Standard Institute and Herald of Christ's Kingdom, Chester Springs, PA 19425, Layman's Home Missionary Movement

Biblical Church of God Newsletter, P. O. Box 1234, Santa Cruz, CA 95061, Biblical Church of God

Bipa (Faith), 201-63 27th St., Bayside, NY 11360, Ukrainian Orthodox Church of the USA

Blessing Letter, P. O. Box 837, Denver, CO 80201, House of Prayer for All People

Brethren Journal, 5905 Carleen Drive, Austin, TX 78731, Unity of the Brethren

The Bulletin, 8 Pond Place, Oyster Bay Cove, NY 11771, Society of St. Pius V

C

Called Out Ones Bible Thought Provoker Messenger, 231 Cedar St., Jackson, TN 38301, Assemblies of the Called Out Ones of Yah

Calling Our Nation, Hayden Lake, ID 83835, Church of Jesus Christ Christian, Aryan Nations

The CDL Report, P. O. Box 426, Metaire, LA 70004, New Christian Crusade Church

Cela Biedrs, 6551 W. Montrose, Chicago, IL 60634, Latvian Evangelical Lutheran Church in America

The Celtic Evangelist, 1666 St. Louis Drive, Honolulu, HI 96816, Celtic Evangelical Church

The Cerkovni Vistnik (Church Messenger), 419 S. Main St., Homer City, PA 15748, American Carpatho-Russian Orthodox Greek Catholic Church

Challenge, Oregon, IL 61061, Church of God General Conference (Abrahamic Faith)

Christ Is the Answer, P. O. Box 128, Rainier, WA 98576, Calvary Fellowship

The Christian Beacon, 756 Haddon Av., Collingswood, NJ 08108, (unofficial publication) Bible Presbyterian Church

The Christian Community, 900 Ridge Rd., Ste. LL1, Homewood, IL 60430, International Council of Community Churches

The Christian Educator, 502 W. Euclid Av., Arlington Heights, IL 60004, Church of Christian Liberty

Christian Index, P. O. Box 665, Memphis, TN 38101, Christian Methodist Episcopal Church

Christian Monthly, Apostolic Book Concern, Rte. 1, P. O. Box 150, New York Mills, MN 56567, Apostolic Lutheran Church of America

Christian Truth for the Household of Faith, 59 Industrial Dr., Addison, IL 60101, Plymouth Brethren (Exclusive: The Tunbridge Well Brethren)

Christian Vanguard, P. O. Box 426, Metaire, LA 70004, New Christian Crusade Church

The Church Advocate, P. O. Box 926, Findlay, OH 45839, Churches of God, General Conference

The Church Herald, 6157 28th St., S.E., Grand Rapids, MI 49506, Reformed Church in America

Church Newsletter, Lindenhurst, NY 11757, United Church of the Apostles

Church of God, The Eternal, Newsletter, P. O. Box 775, Eugene, OR 97440, Church of God, the Eternal

The Circuit Rider, United Methodist Publishing House, P. O. Box 801, Nashville, TN 37202, United Methodist Church

The Classics Expositor, 1429 N.W. 100th, Oklahoma City, OK 73114, Bible Churches (Classics Expositor)

The Communicator, P. O. Box 7777, Alhambra, CA 91802, Associates for Scriptural Knowledge

The Communicator, Universal Publishing Association, Bashan Hill, Exeter, MO 65647, Davidian Seventh-day Adventist Association

The Communicators, P. O. Box 400, Antioch, TN 37013, Holy Orthodox Church, American Jurisdiction

The Concordia Lutheran, Central Av. at 171st St., Tinley Park, IL 60477, Concordia Lutheran Conference

The Congregational Methodist Messenger, P. O. Box 555, Florence, MS 39073, Congregational Methodist Church

The Congregationalist, 8473 So. Howell Av., P. O. Box 1620, Oak Creek, WI 53154, National Association of Congregational Christian Churches

Covenant Companion, 5110 N. Francisco Av., Chicago, IL 60625, Evangelical Covenant Church of America

Covenant Home Altar, 5110 N. Francisco Av., Chicago, IL 60625, Evangelical Covenant Church of America

Covenant Quarterly, 5110 N. Francisco Av., Chicago, IL 60625, Evangelical Covenant Church of America

The Covenanter Witness, 800 Wood St., Pittsburgh, PA 15221, Reformed Presbyterian Church of North America

Credinta-The Faith, 19959 Riopelle, Detroit, MI 48203, Romanian Orthodox Church in America

Crusade, US 24, Postal Drawer 159, St. Mary's, KS 66536, Society of St. Pius X

The Cumberland Flag, 226 Church St., Huntsville, AL 35801, Second Cumberland Presbyterian Church in U.S.

D

The Dawn, East Rutherford, NJ 07073, Dawn Bible Students Association

Diocesean Observer, P. O. Box 371, Grayslake, IL 60030, Free Serbian Orthodox Church-Diocese for the U.S.A. and Canada

The Door, 4201 Fairmount St., Dallas, TX 75219, Apostolic Catholic Church of the Americas

E

Ecclesia, 3206 Heritage Circle, Henderville, NC 28739, American Episcopal Church

Echoes of Grace, 59 Industrial Dr., Addison, IL 60101, Plymouth Brethren (Exclusive: The Tunbridge Well Brethren)

The Elijah Messenger, P. O. Box 89, Winfield, AL 33594, Assembly of Yahvah

EMCI Herald, 106 Madison, Chicago, IL 60602, Evangelical Ministers and Churches, International, Inc.

The Episcopal Recorder, 901 Church Rd., Oreland, PA 19075, Reformed Episcopal Church

The Episcopalian, 1930 Chestnut St., Philadelphia, PA 19103, Episcopal Church in the U.S.A.

The Evangelical Beacon, 1515 E. 66th St., Minneapolis, MN 55423, Evangelical Free Church of America

The Evangelical Methodist, Street, MD 21154, Evangelical Methodist Church of America and Fundamental Methodist Church

The Evangelical Methodist Viewpoint, 3000 W. Kellogg, Wichita, KS 67213, Evangelical Methodist Church

Expression, c/o One Mind Temple, 351 Divisadero St., San Francisco, CA 94117, African Orthodox Church of the West

F

The Faith, P. O. Box 102, Holt, MI 48842, Assembly of Yahweh

Faith and Fellowship, 704 Vernon Av. W., Fergus Falls, MN 56537, Church of the Lutheran Brethren of America

Faith-Life, P. O. Box 2141, LaCrosse, WI 54644, The Protes'tant Conference

The Fellowship Herald, Church of God Publishing House, 1827 W. 3rd St., Meridian, ID 83642-1653, General Council of the Churches of God

Fellowship Letters, c/o Aldridge F. Johnson, Route 1, P. O. Box 33, Isanti, MN 55040, Plymouth Brethren (Exclusive: Ames Brethren)

Foresee, 7582 Currell Blvd., Ste. 108, St. Paul, MN 55125, Conservative Congregational Christian Conference

The Foundation Commentator, P. O. Box 499, Pasadena, CA 91102, Foundation for Biblical Research

Francis Asbury Society Bulletin, John Wesley Fellowship and the Francis Asbury Society of Ministers

G

Glad Tidings, 318 Expressway Drive South, Medford, Long Island, NY 11763, American Orthodox Catholic Church - Western Rite Mission, Diocese of New York

Glad Tidings, P. O. Box 4538, Pensacola, FL 32507, United Episcopal Church of North America

Good News, 300 W. Green St., Pasadena, CA 91129, Worldwide Church of God

Grace and Truth, 210 Chestnut St., Danville, IL 61835, Plymouth Brethren (Exclusive: Reunited Brethren)

H

The Herald, P. O. Box 2733, Des Plaines, IL 60017-2733, Western Orthodox Church in America

The Herald of Christ's Kingdom, 4454 S. 14th St., Ste. 2, Milwaukee, WI 53221-0539, Pastoral Bible Institute

The Herald of Truth, P. O. Box 804, Caldwell, ID 83606-0804, Seventh Day Church of God

The Historical Magazine, P. O. Box 2247, Austin, TX 78705, Episcopal Church

I

Identity, 4241 Usona Rd., Mariposa, CA 95338, Ministry of Christ Church

The Image, 594 5th Av., N.E., Baberton, OH 44203, Orthodox Catholic Church of North and South America

The Independent Catholic, 171 Colby, Hartford, CT 06106, Independent Old Roman Catholic Hungarian Orthodox Church of America

The Independent Methodist Bulletin, P. O. Box 4274, Jackson, MS 39216, Association of Independent Methodists

Insight Into, 4732 East "C" Av., Kalamazoo, MI 49009, Netherlands Reformed Congregations

Interest, Interest Ministries, 218 W. Willow Street, Wheaton, IL 60187, Plymouth Brethren (Open or Christian Brethren)

The International News, P. O. Box 2525, Tyler, TX 75710, Church of God, International

J

Journal Apostolica, 600 Fell St., Ste. 400, San Francisco, CA 94102, Catholic Apostolic Church in America

L

The Larks of Umbria, Friary Press, Box 470, Chicago, IL 60690, Traditional Roman Catholic Church in the Americas

Last Day Messenger, P. O. Box 17056, Portland, OR 97217, Last Day Messenger Assemblies

Light, 401b Melrose St., Schenectady, NY 12306, People's Christian Church

The Living Church, 407 E. Michigan St., Milwaukee, WI 53202, Episcopal Church

The Lutheran, 8765 W. Higgins Rd., Chicago, IL 60631, Evangelical Lutheran Church in America (1988)

The Lutheran Ambassador, 3110 E. Medicine Lake Blvd., Minneapolis, MN 55441, Association of Free Lutheran Congregations

Lutheran Sentinel, Bethany Lutheran College, 734 Marsh St., Mankato, MN 56001, Evangelical Lutheran Synod

The Lutheran Witness, 1333 S. Kirkwood Rd., St. Louis, MO 63122, Lutheran Church-Missouri Synod

M

Magyar Egyaz (Magyar Church), c/o Very Rev. Statan M. Torok, 311 Kirkland Pl., Perth Amboy, NJ 08861, Hungarian Reformed Church in America

Maranatha Devotions, P. O. Box 23152, Charlotte, NC 28212, Advent Christian Church

Maranatha! The Lord Cometh, P. O. Box 3682, Los Angeles, CA 90078, Byzantine Catholic Church

The Mariavita Monthly, 2803 Tenth St., Wyandotte, MI 48192-4994, Mariavite Old Catholic Church, Province of North America

The Master Key, P. O. Box 578, Columbia, MO 65205-0578, Yahweh's Assembly in Messiah

Messages of the Love of God, 59 Industrial Dr., Addison, IL 60101, Plymouth Brethren (Exclusive: The Tunbridge Well Brethren)

The Messenger, 2450 N. 50th St., Milwaukee, WI 53210, Orthodox Catholic Church in America

Messianic Judaism Today, 905713 Gaither Rd., Gaithersburg, MD 20877, Union of Messianic Jewish Congregations

The Messianic Messenger, 3130 Jefferson St. 36, Napa, CA 94558, Orthodox Church of the East

The Messianic Outreach, P. O. Box 37062, Cincinnati, OH 45222, Union of Messianic Jewish Congregations

Ministry, 55 W. Oak Ridge Dr., Hagerstown, MD 21740, Seventh-day Adventist Church

The Missionary Messenger, 1978 Union Av., Memphis, TN 38104, Cumberland Presbyterian Church

The Missionary Signal, P. O. Box 926, Findlay, OH 45839, Churches of God, General Conference

Moments for Youth, P. O. Box 322, Bedford, PA 15522, Plymouth Brethren (Exclusive: Ames Brethren)

Moments with the Bible, P. O. Box 322, Bedford, PA 15522, Plymouth Brethren (Exclusive: Ames Brethren)

The Monarch Messenger, P. O. Box 116, Port Orange, FL 32019, Church of the Holy Monarch

The Monitor of the Reign of Justice, 709 74th St., North Bergen, NJ 07047, Philanthropic Assembly

Monthly Newsletter, P. O. Box 177, Merrimac, MA 01860, Anglo-Saxon Federation of America

Moody Church News, 1609 N. La Salle St., Chicago, IL 60614, Moody Church

The Mother Church, 1201 N. Vine St., Hollywood, CA 90038, Armenian Church of America

The Mount Zion Reporter, P. O. Box 10184, Jerusalem 91101, Israel, Church of God (Jerusalem)

N

Needed Truth, Needed Truth Publishing, Office, Assembly Hall, George Lane, Hayes, Bromley, Kent, U.K., Churches of God in the British Isles and Overseas (Needed Truth)

New Beginnings, P. O. Box 228, Waynesville, NC 28786, New Beginnings

The New Creation, 307 White St., Hartford, CT 06106, Christian Millennial Fellowship

The New Shiloh Messenger, P. O. Box 187, Benton Harbor, MI 49022, Israelite House of David as Reorganized by Mary Purnell

The News, P. O. Box 128, Statesville, NC 28677, Anglican Orthodox Church

News Bulletin, c/o Rev. Wladimir Borosky, 690 Berkeley Av., Elmhurst, IL 60126, Ukrainian Evangelical Alliance of North America

Newsletter, P. O. Box 4693-G, Rolling Bay, WA 98061, American Fellowship Church

Newsletter, P. O. Box 129, Vacaville, CA 95688, Twentieth Century Church of God

The Newsletter, 50 Coventry Lane, Central Islip, NY 11722, Servant Catholic Church

Newsletter for Christian Millennial Church, 307 White St., Hartford, CT 06106, Christian Millennial Fellowship

Newswatch Magazine, 11824 Beaverton, Bridgeton, MO 63044, Church of God Evangelistic Association

The North American Moravian, P. O. Box 1245, Bethlehem, PA 18016-1245, Moravian Church in America

The Northwestern Lutheran, 2929 N. Mayfair Rd., Wauwatosa, WI 53222, Wisconsin Evangelical Lutheran Synod,

Notes from the Church Organ, c/o Stanley Gould, 20 Bourke St., Singleton, N.S.W., Australia 2330, Christian Israelite Church

O

The Ohio Fellowship Visitor, c/o Rev. John Ashbrook, 5733 Hopkins Rd., Mentor, OH 44060, Ohio Bible Fellowship

The Olive Tree, P. O. Box 805, Henryetta, OK 74437, New Life Fellowship

One Church, 727 Miller Av., Youngstown, OH 44502, Russian Orthodox Church in the USA, Patriarchal Parishes of the

The Orthodox Catholic, P. O. Box 389, Ozark, MO 65721, American Orthodox Catholic

The Orthodox Catholic Voice, P. O. Box 1213, Akron, OH 44309, Orthodox Catholic Church of North and South America

The Orthodox Church, P. O. Box 39, Pottstown, PA 19464, Orthodox Church in America

Orthodox Life, Holy Trinity Seminary, Jordanville, NY 13361, Russian Orthodox Church Outside of Russia

Orthodox Observer, 8-10 E. 79th St., NY, NY 10021, Greek Orthodox Archdiocese of North and South America

Our Anglican Heritage, 43 Medina Sq. East, Keswick, Ontario, Canada L4P 1E1, Anglican Church of North America

Our Missionary, 5520 West Dakin, Chicago, IL 60641, Old Catholic Patriarchate of America

The Outreach, 138 E. 39th St., NY, NY 10016, Armenian Apostolic Church of America

P

Paper for All, L'Ange de l'Eternal, Le Chateau, 1236 Cartigny, Switzerland, Philanthropic Assembly

The Pastor's Journal, 900 Ridge Rd., Ste. LL1, Homewood, IL 60430, International Council of Community Churches

The Path of Orthodoxy, P. O. Box 36, Leesdale, PA 15056, Serbian Eastern Orthodox Church for the USA and Canada

The PCA Messenger, 1852 Century Plaza, Atlanta, GA 30345, Presbyterian Church in America

The Plain Truth, 300 W. Green St., Pasadena, CA 91129, Worldwide Church of God

PNCC Studies, 1031 Cedar Avenue, Scranton, PA 18505, Polish National Catholic Church

Polka, 1002 Pittson Avenue, Scranton, PA 18505, Polish National Catholic Church

Presbyterian Survey, 100 Witherspoon Street, Louisville, KY 23261, Presbyterian Church (USA)

The Present Truth of the Apocalypsis, Rte. 38, 9021 Temple Rd., W., Fort Myers, FL 33912, Laodicean Home Missionary Movement

Progress Journal, Oregon, IL 61061, Church of God General Conference (Abrahamic Faith)

The Prophetic Encounter, P. O. Box 7777, Alhambra, CA 91802, Associates for Scriptural Knowledge

The Prophetic Watchman, c/o Jacob Hawkins, P. O. Box 4938, Odessa, TX 79760, House of Yahweh (Odessa, Texas)

The Prophetic Word, P. O. Box 2442, Abilene, TX 79604, House of Yahweh (Abilene, Texas)

Q

Quarterly Review, 1814 Tamarack St. N.W., Washington, DC 20012, African Methodist Episcopal Zion Church

R

Rauhan Tervehdys (Greetings of Peace), Apostolic Lutherans (The Heidmans)

Reformation Herald, P. O. Box 7239, Roanoke, VA 24019, Seventh-day Adventist Church, Reform Movement

The Reformed Episcopalian, South Rd. at Central Avenue, New Providence, NJ 07974, Reformed Episcopal Church

The Reformed Messenger, 15615 South Park Av., South Holland, IL 60473, Protestant Reformed Churches in America

The Reformed Scope, 3268 S. Chestnut, Grandville, MI 49418, Orthodox Reformed Church

The Registry Case-file, P. O. Box 279, Leslie, AR 72645, The Registry

Reporter, 1333 S. Kirkwood Rd., St. Louis, MO 63122, Lutheran Church-Missouri Synod

The Restitution Herald, Oregon, IL 61061, Church of God General Conference (Abrahamic Faith)

Restoring Knowledge of God, 11824 Beaverton, Bridgeton, MO 63044, Church of God Evangelistic Association

Rex Humbard Family Ministry, c/o Rex Humbard, P. O. Box 3063, Boca Raton, FL 33431, Rex Humbard Ministry

Rola Boza, (God's Field), 529 E. Locust St., Scranton, PA 18505, Polish National Catholic Church

The Roman Catholic, Box 217, Oyster Bay Cove, NY 11771, Society of St. Pius V

The Russian Orthodox Messenger, 59 East 2nd St., NY, NY 10003, Orthodox Church in America

S

The Sacred Name Broadcaster, Bethel, PA 19507, Assemblies of Yahweh

Scripture Research, Inc., P. O. Box 518, Atascadero, CA 93423, Berean Bible Fellowship

The Scripture Research Greek Tutor, P. O. Box 518, Atascadero, CA 93423, Berean Bible Fellowship

Shekineh Magazine, P. O. Box 4098, Waco, TX 76705, Branch SDA's

The Shepherd, 929 Lorain Av., Zanesville, OH 43701, Orthodox Catholic Church of North and South America

Shiloh's Messenger, P. O. Box 1067, Benton Harbor, MI 49022, Israelite House of David

Shofar Shalom, Beth Ha Shofar, 13001 37th Av. S., Seattle, WA 98168, Union of Messianic Jewish Congregations

Showers of Blessing, P. O. Box 837, Denver, CO 80201, House of Prayer for All People

Shrine Newsletter, c/o For My God and My Country, Necedah, WI 54646, For My God and My Country

Signs of the Times, Nampa, ID 83707, Seventh-day Adventist Church

SOLIA. The Herald, 146 W. Courtland St., Jackson, MI 49201-2208, Romanian Orthodox Episcopate of America

The Southern Episcopalians, 2315 Valley Brook Rd., Nashville, TN 37215, Southern Episcopal Church

The Southern Methodist, Foundry Press, Orangeburg, SC 29115, Southern Methodist Church

The Standard Bearer, 2016 Tekonsha, S. E., Grand Rapids, MI 49506, Protestant Reformed Churches in America

Star of Zion, P. O. Box 31005, Charlotte, NC 28231, African Methodist Episcopal Zion Church

The Structure of the Church, 140-142 West 176th St., Bronx, NY 10453, Ethiopian Orthodox Church in the United States of America

T

The Timely Messenger, P. O. Box 473, Mineral Wells, TX 76067, Timely Messenger Fellowship

The Timely Truth, Universal Publishing Association, Bashan Hill, Exeter, MO 65647, Davidian Seventh-day Adventists Association

Toward the Mark, 26a Lower Bristol Rd., Weston-Super-Mare, Avon, BS23, London, England S.E.23, Witness and Testimony Literature Trust and Related Centers

The Trinitarian, 3141 South Josephine, Denver, CO 80210, Anglican Catholic Church

The True Gospel Advocate, Route 1, Mocksville, NC 27028, Church of God, Body of Christ

The True Light, 54 Burroughs St., Jamaica Plain, MA 02130, Albanian Orthodox Diocese of America

The Trumpet, c/o Rev. Fr. Harold Furblur, P. O. Box 1925, Boston, MA 02105, African Orthodox Church

Truth, 1011 Aldon St. S.W., Grand Rapids, MI 49509, Grace Gospel Fellowship

The Truth, P. O. Box 14411, Jerusalem, Israel, Workers Together with Elohim

Truth for Today, P. O. Box 6358, Lafayette, IN 47903, Truth for Today Fellowship

Tserkobnost, 1611 Wallace St., Philadelphia, PA 19130, Holy Eastern Orthodox Church of the United States

Twentieth Century Watch, P. O. Box 2525, Tyler, TX 75710, Church of God, International

U

Ukrainian Orthodox Herald, 90-34 139th St., Jamaica, NY 11207, Ukrainian Orthodox Church in America (Ecumenical Patriarchate)

Ukrainian Orthodox Word, P. O. Box 495, South Bond Brook, NJ 08880, Ukrainian Orthodox Church of the USA

The ULC News, 601 Third St., Modesto, CA 95351, Universal Life Church

Unification Leader, 255 W. 131 St., NY, NY 10027, Unification Association of Christian Sabbath Keepers

Union Searchlight, c/o Deacon James C. Feggins, 416 South Hill Avenue, South Hill, VA 23970, Reformed Zion Union Apostolic Church

The United Brethren, 302 Lake St., Huntington, IN 46750, Church of the United Brethren in Christ

United Church News, 105 Madison Av., NY, NY 10016, United Church of Christ

The United Evangelical, Church Center Press, 100 W. Park Av., Myerstown, PA 17067, Evangelical Congregational Church

The Universal Message, Rte. 2, P. O. Box 190, Albany, OR 97321, Crown of Life Fellowship

Unsearchable Riches, 15570 W. Knochaven Dr., Canyon Country, CA 91351, Concordant Publishing Concern

UOL Bulletin, c/o St. Michael Ukrainian Orthodox Church, 7047 Columbia Av., Hammond, IN 46324, Ukrainian Orthodox Church of the USA

V

Verbum, 209 Tackora Trail, Ridgefield, CT 06870, Society of St. Pius X

The Vineyard (Vreshta), 270 Cabot St., Newton, MA 02160, Albanian Orthodox Archdiocese in America

Voice, c/o Living Stream Ministry, P. O. Box 2121, Anaheim, CA 92804, The (Local) Church

The Voice, 3660 S. Gramercy Pl., Los Angeles, CA 90018, Oriental Missionary Society Holiness Church of North America

The Voice, 1860 Mannheim Rd., Westcester, IL 60153, Independent Fundamental Churches of America

Voice from the East, P. O. Box 25264, Chicago, IL 60626, Apostolic Catholic Assyrian Church of the East, North American Diocese

The Voice of Unity, P. O. Box 02026, Cleveland, OH 44102, Church of God (Jesus Christ the Head)

W

De Wachter, 4850 Kalamazoo Av. S.E., Grand Rapids, MI 49560, Christian Reformed Church in North America

The Watchman, P. O. Box 62 B3, Schell City, MO 64783, Church of Israel

The Watchtower Announcing Jehovah's Kingdom, 25 Columbia Heights, Brooklyn, NY 11201, Jehovah's Witnesses

The Way Magazine, P. O. Box 328, New Knoxville, OH 45871, The Way International

The Western Orthodox Catholic, P. O. Box 406, Willow Station, Cleveland, OH 44127, Orthodox Catholic Church of North and South America

Window on Bethany, 6060 N. Seventh Av., Phoenix, AZ 85013, Bethany Bible Church and Related Independent Bible Churches of the Phoenix, Arizona, Area

Wisconsin Lutheran Quarterly, 11831 N. Seminary Dr., 65 W. Mequon, WI 53092, Wisconsin Evangelical Lutheran Synod

A Witness and a Testimony, c/o Witness and Testimony Literature Trust, 39 Honor Oak Rd., London, England S.E.23, Witness and Testimony Literature Trust and Related Centers

The Word, 52 78th St., Brooklyn, NY 11209, Antiochian Orthodox Christian Archdiocese of North America

Words of Truth, Christian Literature, Inc., P. O. Box 23082, Minneapolis, MN 55423, Plymouth Brethren (Exclusive: Ames Brethren)

World Insight, P. O. Box 35, Pasadena, CA 91102, World Insight International

Y

Youth, 300 W. Green St., Pasadena, CA 91129, Worldwide Church of God

Z

Zion Trumphet, c/o 1315 Hutchinson, Nashville, AR 71852, Free Christian Zion Church of Christ

BUDDHISM

Though relatively young, the Buddhist community has moved to form workable ecumenical structures. The first were formed some years ago by the older Japanese Buddhist community. More recently immigrant communities from Korea, China, Tibet, and southeast Asia came together with the new Western Buddhist groups to form the American Buddhist Congress, the Buddhist equivalent of the National Council of Churches.

Since 1965 the Buddhist community has blossomed from its previous confinement largely to the Chinese and Japanese ethnic communities. It not only has found a home among numerous Western converts but is supported by ethnic communities from Japan and Korea to India, across the Buddhist home land. Duirng the 19080s, Taiwanese Buddhists built the largest Buddhist shrine in the West in a California suburb. There are an estimated one to three million Buddhists in America as of 1990.

INTRAFAITH ORGANIZATIONS

American Buddhist Congress
The most representative body of Buddhists, the Congress was founded in Los Angeles in November 1987 at a gathering of delegates of over 50 Buddhist groups.

Hq: 4267 W. Third St., Los Angeles, CA 90020
Tel: (213) 386 8139

Buddhist Sangha Council of Southern California
The Council includes Buddhist groups of a variety of ethnic backgrounds in the greater Los Angeles area. It sponsors the College of Buddhist Studies in Los Angeles and issues a periodical, *Dharma Voice*.

Hq: 933 S. New Hampshire Ave., Los Angeles, CA 90006
Tel: (213) 739 1270

Hawaii Buddhist Council
The council includes the several different (but primarily Japanese) Buddhist groups operating throughout the Hawaiian Islands.

Hq: Current address unavailable for this edition

133

Korean Buddhist Sangha Association of the Western Territory in the U.S.

The Association provides fellowship for the various Korean Buddhist groups operating in the United States.

Hq: 4265 W. 3rd St., Los Angeles, CA 90020
Tel: (213) 380 3303

Los Angeles Buddhist Church Federation

The Federation includes seven Japanese Buddhist groups in the greater Los Angeles area.

Hq: 123 S. Hewitt St., Los Angeles, CA 90012
Tel: (213) 624 8658

Sakyadhita

Founded in 1987, Sakyadhita is an international fellowship of Buddhist women.

Hq: 928 S. New Hampshire Ave., Los Angeles, CA 90006
Tel: (213) 384 0850

BUDDHIST CENTERS AND ORGANIZATIONS

American Buddhist Movement

The American Buddhist Movement is an independent Buddhist order founded in 1980 by Kevin R. O'Neill. It is multi-traditional and includes individuals from various ethnic groups. Among its services is the publishing of a national Buddhist directory.

Hq: 301 W. 45th St., New York, NY 10036
Tel: (212) 489 1075

American Zen College

The American Zen College derives from efforts begun in 1970 by Gosung Shin, a Patriarch in the Korean Zen Lin-Che lineage.

Hq: 16815 Germantown Road (Route 18), Germantown, MD 20767
Tel: (301) 428 0665

Berkeley Zen Center

Founded in 1967 by Shunryu Suzuki-Roshi, the Berkeley Zen Center is a lay community teaching in the Soto Zen tradition.

Hq: 1931 Russell Street, Berkeley, CA 94703
Tel: (415) 845 2403

Bhavana Society

The Bhavana Society is a Theravada Buddhist center founded in 1982 in Washington, D.C., by Bhante Henepola Gunaratana, a monk from Sri Lanka formerly with the Washington Buddhist Vihara.

Hq: Rt. 1, Box 218-3, High View, WV 26808
Tel: (304) 856 3241

Bodaiji Mission

This independent Japanese Buddhist Mission was founded in 1930 by Nisshyo Takao and emphasizes the concept of Dai-O-Kai, filial piety.

Hq: 1251 Elm, Honolulu, HI 96814
Tel: (808) 536 8031

Buddha's Universal Church

Located in the middle of San Francisco's Chinatown, Buddha's Universal Church was founded in the 1920s by Dr. Paul F. Fung and a group of Chinese Buddhists.

Hq: c/o Dr. Frederick Hong, 702 Washington St., San Francisco, CA 94108
Tel: (415) 982 6116

Buddhist Association of the United States

Largest of the Chinese Buddhist organizations in the New York area, the Association was founded in 1964 and attempts to synthesize Ch'an (Zen) and Pure Land Buddhism.

Hq: 3070 Albany Crescent, New York, NY 10463

Buddhist Brotherhood of America

The small Buddhist Brotherhood continues one of the oldest Western Buddhist organizations established originally as the Buddhist Lodge of the Theosophical Society in Los Angeles. Its leader is the Ven. Subhadra (Julius A. Goldwater).

Hq: 2003 Corinth Street, West Los Angeles, CA 90024

Buddhist Churches of America

Outpost of the largest of the many Japanese Buddhist groups, the Buddhist Churches of America was begun by missionaries who arrived in San Francisco in the 1890s. Having the continental United States as its territory, it is in fellowship with the Buddhist Churches of Canada and the Honpa Hongwanji Mission of Hawaii.

Hq: 1710 Octavia St., San Francisco, CA 94109
Tel: (415) 776 5600
Fax: (415) 771 6293
or
Honpa Hongwanji Mission of Hawaii, 1727 Pali Highway, Honolulu, HI 96813
Tel: (808) 538 3805
or
International Hq: Jodo Shinshu Hongwanji Ha, Shimokyo, Kyoto, Japan 600

Buddhist Fellowship of New York

The Fellowship began in 1961 under the leadership of Boris Erwitt to provide fellowship and study for American Buddhists. It publishes a newsletter, *Kantaka*, from its New York headquarters.

Hq: 331 Riverside Dr., New York, NY 10025

California Bosatsukai

The California Bosatsukai grew out of the work of pioneer Zen teacher Nyogen Senzaki (1876-1958) who initiated work in America in 1905.

Hq: 5632 Green Oak Dr., Los Angeles, CA 90068

Cambodian Buddhists

Buddhism was almost wiped out by the government-led massacres in Cambodia in the 1970s. It survived largely through the immigration of many Cambodians to the West. The Venerable Maha Ghosananda has led in reorganizing the scattered community in North America.

Hq: c/o Khmer Buddhist Society of New England, Ven. Maha Ghosananda, 178 Hanover St., Providence, RI 02907
Tel: (401) 273 0969

Cambridge Buddhist Association

This Cambridge Buddhist Association is a Lay-led Zen meditation center. It was inspired by the 1957 visit of Zen teacher Daisetz Teitaro Suzuki (1870-1966) to Harvard University.

Hq: 75 Sparks Street, Cambridge, MA 02138
Tel: (617) 491 8857

Chagdud Gonpa Foundation

Chagdud Gonpa was founded in the 1980s by Lama Chagdud Tulku Rinpoche to continue the Chagdud Nyingpa lineage lost following the Chinese invasion of Tibet. Lama Chagdud Tulku fled to India in 1959 and came to the United States in 1979 where he taught with Yeshe Nyingpo.

Hq: Chagdud Gonpa, 208 N. Rover Road, Cottage Grove, OR 97424
Tel: (503) 942 7270
or
California Hq: 1933-D Delaware, Berkeley, CA 94709
Tel: (415) 849 3300

Ch'an Meditation Center

The Ch'an Meditation Center is headed by the Ven. Dr. Shen Yen and follows the Chinese Zen tradition.

Hq: 90-56 Corona Avenue, Elmhurst, NY
Tel: (718) 592 6593

Chapori-Ling Foundation Sangha

The Foundation is a Nyingmapa Tibetan Buddhist group founded in the 1970s by Dr. Norbu Lompas Chen, formerly of Nepal.

Hq: 766 8th Avenue, San Francisco, CA 94118
Tel: (415) 668 3690

Chinese Buddhist Association

The Association was founded in 1955 by a group of Buddhists from Hong Kong. It was part of the first the wave of Asian immigrants transplanted to the United States.

Hq: 42 Kawananakoa Place, Honolulu, HI 96817
Tel: (808) 536 8458

Cho Ko Long Buddhist Mahayana Center

The center is an independent Tibetan Buddhist organization.

Hq: P. O. Box 236, Dexter, MI 48130
Tel: (313) 426 2314

Chowado Henjo Kyo

The Chowado Henjo Kyo was founded in 1906 by the Rev. Reisai Fugita, a former Shingon Buddhist priest, with a primary interest in spiritual healing.

Hq: c/o Rev. Reisai Fugita, 1757 Algaroba Street, Honolulu, HI 96814

Dharma Friendship Foundation

The Dharma Friendship Foundation is an independent Tibetan center founded in 1985 by B. Allen Walker.

Hq: 3654 Dayton Avenue North, Seattle, WA 98103
Tel: (206) 641 5469 or 547 0053

Dharma Rain Zen Center

The Dharma Rain Zen Center was formed in 1982 by Kyogen Carlson Sensei, formerly associated with Juyi-Kennett Roshi and the Order of Buddhist Contemplatives. The Center became independent of the Order in 1986.

Hq: 2539 S. E. Madison, Portland, OR 97214
Tel: (503) 239 4846

Dharma Realm Buddhist Association

The Dharma Realm Buddhist Association, previously known as the Sino-American Buddhist Association, was formed in 1959 by disciples of Master Hsuan Hua who had migrated to America from Hong Kong.

Hq: City of Ten Thousand Buddhas, Talmage, CA 95481-0217
Tel: (707) 462 0939

Dharma Sangha

Dharma Sangha was formed in 1985 by Richard Baker Roshi, formerly the leader of the Zen center of San Francisco.

Hq: 2255 Mariposa Street, San Francisco, CA 94110

Dharma Zen Center of Hawaii

The Center was founded in 1978 by Dharma Master Ji Kwang, a female Zen master. She teaches her "Social Buddhism" based on the Sutra of the Lotus Flower of the Wonderful Law.

Hq: 99-045 Kauhale Street, P.O. Box 926, Aiea, HI 96701
Tel: (808) 488 6794

Dhiravamsa Foundation

The Foundation, originally called the Vipassana Fellowship of America, was founded in 1969 by Dhiravamsa, a monk from Thailand.

Hq: 1660 Wold Rd., Friday Harbor, San Juan, WA 98250

Diamond Sangha

The Diamond Sangha is a Zen Buddhist group founded by Robert and Anne Aitken in 1969. It is affiliated with the Sanbo Kyodan (Order of the Three Treasures) in Japan. Diamond Sangha practice is based in Soto Zen, but includes elements of Rinzai Zen (i.e., the two main streams of Japanese Zen Buddhism).

Hq: c/o Koko An, 2119 Kaloa Way, Honolulu, HI 96822
Tel: (808) 946 0666
or
California Hq: P. O. Box 2972, Santa Rosa, CA 95405
Tel: (707) 539 6603
or
International Hq: Sanbo Kyodan, 199-10 Hase, Kamakura-shi, Kanagawa-ken, Japan

Drikung Dharma Centers

The Drikung Kagyu Order is a branch of Kagyupa Tibetan Buddhism currently headed by His Holiness Drikung Kyabgon Chetsang Rinpoche. A center was begun in Washington, D.C. in 1978 and a second center, opened a few years later, is now functioning in Los Angeles.

Hq: Drikung Kyabgon, 3454 Macomb Street, N.W., Washington, D.C. 20008
or
Drikung Kaygu Center, 11958 Hartsook Street, No. Hollywood, CA 91607
Tel: (818) 761 0939

Eastern States Buddhist Association of America

The Association was founded in 1963 to serve Chinese-American Buddhists in the greater New York area.

Hq: 64 Mott St., New York, NY 10013
Tel: (212) 966 4753

Ewam Choden

The first Sakya Tibetan Buddhist center in the United States, Ewam Choden was founded in 1971 by Lama Kunga Thartse Rinpoche.

Hq: 254 Cambridge Street, Kensington, CA 94707
Tel: (415) 527 7363

First Zen Institute of America

The Institute was founded by Pioneer American Zen master Sokei-an Sasaki Roshi in New York in 1930. Originally known as the Buddhist Society of America, it assumed its present name in 1944. Since Sokei-an's death, the group has been lay led, with visiting Zen masters supplementing the program.

Hq: 113 E. 30th Street, New York, NY 10016
Tel: (212) 686 2520

Fo Kuang Shan Buddhist Society

The Society is the American branch of a Taiwanese Buddhist group originally established in 1967. During the 1980s it built the Hsi Lai Buddhist Temple complex, the largest Buddhist shrine in the West, in a Los Angeles suburb.

Hq: Hsi Lai Buddhist Temple, 3456 South Glenmark Drive, P. O. Box 5248, Hacienda Heights, CA 991745
Tel: (818) 961 9697

Friends of Buddhism-Washington D.C.

The Friends of Buddhism was founded in the 1930s by Robert Stuart Clifton as a gathering place for western Buddhists.

Hq: c/o Dr. Kurt Leidecker, 306 Caroline Street, Fredericksburg, VA 22401

Friends of the Western Buddhist Order

The Western Buddhist Order was organized in 1967 in the United Kingdom by Ven. Maha Sthavira Sangharakshita. It has subsequently spread around the world and was brought to the United States in 1986.

Hq: Aryaloka   Buddhist   Center, Heartwood Circle, New Market, NH 03857
Tel: (603) 659 5456
or
International Hq: Office of the Western Buddhist Order, Padmalika-Lesinham House, Surlingham, Norwich, England NR14 7AL

Ganden Tekchen Ling

Ganden Tekchen Ling was formed by students of Geshe Sopa, a Tibetan Buddhist teacher and professor at the University of Wisconsin. It is closely related to the branch of Tibetan Buddhism headed by the Dalai Lama.

Hq: Deer Park, 4548 Schneider Dr., Oregon, WI 53575

Gedatsu Church of America

The Gedatsu Church was formed in 1929 by Skoken Okano (now known as Gedatsu Kongo), a former Japanese Shingon Buddhist priest. It was brought to America following World War II and primarily serves the Japanese-American community.

Hq: 353 San Antonio Ave., San Mateo, CA 94401
or
International Hq: 4 Araki-cho, Shinjukuku, Tokyo 160, Japan

Hawaii Chinese Buddhist Society

The Society was founded in 1953 by a group of Buddhists who migrated to America from Hong Kong.

Hq: 1614 Nuuanu Avenue, Honolulu, HI 96817
Tel: (808) 533 6758

Higashi Hongwanji Buddhist Church

One of the two larger Buddhist Pure Land groups in Japan, the Higashi Hongwanji began work in America in 1899 in Honolulu.

Hq: 505 E. Third St., Los Angeles, CA 90013
Tel: (213) 626 4200
or
Higashi Hongwanji Mission of Hawaii, 1685 Alaneo Street, Honolulu, HI 96817
Tel: (808) 531 9088

Insight Meditation Society

The Insight Meditation Society, founded in 1976, is the focus of a network of Theravada Buddhist centers primarily oriented to Burmese teachers.

Hq: Pleasant Street, Barre, MA 01005
Tel: (617) 355 4378

International Buddhist Meditation Center

The oldest Vietnamese Buddhist organization in the United States, the Center was founded by Dr. Thich Thien-An in 1970. It is currently under the leadership of the Ven.

Karuna Dharma, who also leads the Thien An Institute of Buddhist Studies.

Hq: 928 S. New Hampshire, Los Angeles, CA 90006
Tel: (213) 384 0850

International Zen Institute of America

The International Zen Institute was founded by the Ven. Gesshin Prabhasa Dharma Roshi and now has affiliated groups in Holland, Germany, and Spain.

Hq: 3054 West 8th Street, P. O. Box 146, Los Angeles, CA 90005
Tel: (213) 472 5707

Jetsun Sakya Center

The Center was founded in 1977 by Dezhung Rinpoche as a Sakya Tibetan Buddhist organization.

Hq: 623 W. 129th Street, New York, NY 10027

Jodo Mission

The Jodo Mission is the American branch of Japanese Jodo-shu Buddhism, one of several Pure land Buddhists groups. It began in America in 1896 in Hawaii among Japanese immigrants.

Hq: 1429 Makiki Street, Honolulu, HI 96822
Tel: (808) 949 3995
or
International Hq: 3-400 Hayashi Shita-machi, Yamato Oji Higashi-iru, Shinbashi-dori, Higashiyama-ku, Kyoto-shi (605), Japan

Kagyu Dharma

His Eminence Kalu Rinpoche, a Tibetan teacher in the Kargyupa lineage, founded a number of centers around the world which collectively have been referred to as Kagyu Dharma centers. The most active in the United States is the center in San Francisco.

Hq: 1892 Fell Street, San Francisco, CA 94117
Tel: (415) 386 4531

Kanzeonji Zen Buddhist Temple

The Temple was founded in the early 1980s by the Rev. Ryugen Watanabe. Watanabe, also known as Swami Premananda, mixes yoga and soto zen in the practice he teaches and heads the Siva Ashram Yoga Center located at the same address as the Temple.

Hq: 944 Terrace 49, Los Angeles, CA 90042
Tel: (213) 255 5345

Karma Triyana Dharmachakra

Karma Triyana Dharmachakra is the American organization of the Karma Kagya, one of the several branches of Tibetan Buddhism. It was brought to America in 1976 by Khenpo Karthar Rinpoche. The Seat of H. H. Gyalwa Karmapa, the international head of the Karma Kagya, is in Sikkim.

Hq: 352 Meads Mountain Rd., Woodstock, NY 12498
or
International Hq: Dharma Chakra Centre, P.O. Box Rumtek 737 135, Gangtok, Sikkim

Kongosatta-In Tendai Buddhist Temple

The only Tendai Buddhist center in America is headed by the Rev. Jikai, its priest. Tendai, like Nichiren Buddhism, places great emphasis on the Lotus Sutra.

Hq: P. O. Box 212, Cape Girardeau, MO 63702-1212
or
International Hq: Hieizan-Enryakuji, Sakamoto-Honmachi, Otsu-Shi, Shiga-Ken, Japan

Korean Buddhist Bo Moon Order

The Bo Moon Order is one of several Korean Buddhist groups. It came to the United States in the 1970s.

Hq: c/o Rev. Bup Choon, Bul Sim Sa Temple, 5011 N. Damen, Chicago, IL 60625
Tel: (312) 334 8590
or
International Hq: 168 Bomoon-dong, 3-ga, Sungbook-ku, Seoul, Korea

Korean Buddhist Chogye Order

The major school of Buddhism in Korea, the Chogye Order combines Zen meditation and Pure Land Buddhist emphases. It was organized in the United States in the 1970s. This branch works primarily among first generation Korean-Americans.

Hq: c/o Kwan Um Sa Temple, 4265 W. Third St., Los Angeles, CA 90020
Tel: (213) 380 3303
or
International Hq: 45 Kyonji-dong, Chongro-ku, Seoul, Korea

Kunzang Osdal Palyul Changchub Choeling/The World Prayer Center

The Kunzang Osdal Palyul Changchub Choeling was founded in 1983, offering teachings in the Tibetan Nyingma-Palyul tradition.

Hq: 18400 River Road, Poolesville, MD 29837
Tel: (301) 428 8116

Kwan Um Zen School

The Kwan Um Zen School was founded in 1983 but dates to the arrival of Master Seung Sahn Sunim (Soen Sa Nim) in America in 1972. Soen Sa Nim is a Patriarch in the Chogye Korean Buddhist Order and has developed a number of centers primarily serving non-Koreans.

Hq: 528 Pound Road, Cumberland, RI 02864
Tel: (401) 769 6476

Kwan Yin Temple

This Buddhist center is the oldest Chinese temple in America. The group which worships at the temple dates to the 1870s.

Hq: 170 N. Vineyard St., Honolulu, HI 96817
Tel: (808) 533 6361

Lao Buddhist Sangha of the U.S.A.

The Lao Buddhist Sangha is the network of Laotian Buddhists in America.

Hq: 7445 Rail Road St., Highland, CA 92346
Tel: (714) 864 6070

Living Dharma Center

Led by Richard Clark, a teacher in the American Soto and Rinzai Zen tradition of Harada Roshi, Yasutani Roshi, and Philip Kapleau, this lay community also has a branch in Amherst, Massachusetts.

Hq: P.O. Box 513, Bolton, CT 06040
Tel: (203) 742 7049
or
Massachusetts Center: RFD 3, Pratt Corner Road, Amherst, MA 01002-9805
Tel: (413) 259 1611

Longchen Nyingthig Buddhist Society

The Society was established by the Ven. Tsede Lhamo, Rhenock Chamkusko, a female Tibetan Buddhist teacher, shortly after her arrival in the United States in 1969 from Sikkim.

Hq: Box 302, Harris, NY 12742

Los Gatos Zen Group

The Los Gatos Group is a lay group founded in 1963 and led by Arvis Joen Justi.

Hq: 16200 Matilija Drive, Los Gatos, CA 95030
Tel: (408) 354 7506

Mahasiddha Nyingmapa Center

The Mahasiddha Nyingmapa Center is a Nyingmapa Tibetan Buddhist center under the direction of Dodrup Chen Rinpoche.

Hq: Box 87, Charlemont, MA 01339

Mahayana Sutra and Tantra Center

The Center is a Tibetan Buddhist group under the direction of the Ven. Geshe Lobsang Tharchin.

Hq: L'Enfant Plaza, Box 20316, Washington, DC 20024

Maitreya Institute

The Institute, a Tibetan center, carries on an active public program.

Hq: 3315 Sacramento St., Ste. 622, San Francisco, CA 94118
Tel: (415) 781 5590

Mandala Buddhist Center

The Center is an independent Japanese Buddhist temple.

Hq: c/o Rev. Jomyo N. Tanaka, RD 1, Box 2380, Bristol, VT 05443-8841
Tel: (803) 453 5038

Minnesota Zen Meditation Center

The Center was founded in the 1960s by a group of interested Zen students in the Minneapolis area.

Hq: 3343 Calhoun Pkwy., Minneapolis, MN 55408
Tel: (612) 822 5313

Monastery of Tibetan Buddhism

The Monastery began in 1974 as the Sakya Tegchen Choling through the efforts of H. H. Jigdal Dagchen Sakya, the head of the Sakya branch of Tibetan Buddhism.

Hq: 5042 18th Avenue, N.E., Seattle, WA 98105
Tel: (206) 522 6967

Nechung Drayang Ling

Nechung Drayang Ling dates to the arrival in 1972 of H. H. Dudjom Rinpoche (the founder of Yeshe Nyingpo) who introduced Tibetan Buddhism into Hawaii. Three years later the Ven. Nechung Rinpoche began permanent work among those attracted to Tibetan Buddhism.

Hq: Box 250, Pahala, HI 96777
Tel: (808) 928 8539

Nichiren Mission

The Nichiren Mission is an outpost of Japanese Nichiren-shu Buddhism. It organized in Hawaii among Japanese immigrants at the beginning of this century.

Hq: 3058 Pali Hwy., Honolulu, HI 96817
Tel: (808) 595 3517

or
International Hq: Nichiren-shu, 1-31-15 Ikegami, Ota-ku, Tokyo, Japan

Nichiren Shoshu

Nichiren Shoshu resulted from a schism among the followers of Nichiren, the Japanese Buddhist prophet/reformer. Associated with it is its lay organization, the Soka Gakkai.

Hq: 7576 Etiwanda Avenue, Etiwanda, CA 91739
Tel: (714) 899 1708
or
Nichiren Shoshu of America, 525 Wilshire Blvd., Santa Monica, CA 90406
Tel: (213) 451 8811
or
International Hq: Nichiren Shoshu International Centre, 1-22-11 Sendagaya, Shobuya-ku, Tokyo 151, Japan

Nipponzan Myohoji

The Nipponzan Myohoji is one of the Japanese Nichiren sects. It has become well known for its distribution of peace poles which are on display throughout America.

Hq: 4900 16th St., N.W., Washington, DC 20011
Tel: (202) 291 2047
or
International Hq: 8-7 Shinsen-cho, Shibuyaku, Tokyo, 150 Japan

Nyingmapa Institute Center

The Institute is the focus of the work of Tarthang Tulku who had left Tibet following the Chinese invasion and settled in California in 1968. The center has built Oyidan, a monastery near Jenner, California.

Hq: 1815 Highland Place, Berkeley, CA 94709
Tel: (415) 843 6812

Order of Buddhist Contemplatives

The Order was founded in 1969 as the Zen Mission Society by Rev. Jiyu Kennett Roshi, a British-born Zen master who studied in Japan. The Order follows the Soto tradition.

Hq: Box 199, 3612 Summit Dr., Mt.
    Shasta, CA 96067-0199
Tel: (916) 926 4208

Ordinary Dharma

Ordinary Dharma is a Vipassana Insight Meditation center founded by Christopher Reed in the 1980s.

Hq: 247 Horizon Avenue, Venice, CA
    90291
Tel: (213) 396 5054

Paia Montukuji Mission

Founded by a Japanese missionary in 1921, the Mission is directed by Rev. Shuko Ueoka and affiliated with the Eheiji Monastery.

Hq: 253-C Hana Highway, P.O. Box
    207, Paia, Maui, HI 96779
Tel: (800) 579 8051

Palolo Kwannon Temple (Tendai Sect)

The Temple is a small Japanese Buddhist center founded in 1935 for the veneration of Kannon (Kwan Yin), the goddess of mercy.

Hq: 3326 Paalea Street, Honolulu, HI
    96816

Pansophic Institute

The Pansophic Institute is a Tibetan Buddhist center founded in 1973 by Simon Grimes. It follows the Gelugpa school of the Dalai Lama, the teachings of which it seeks to integrate into Western thought.

Associated with the Institute is the Church of Universal Light.

Hq: Box 2422, Reno, NV 89505

Philadelphia Buddhist Association

The Association was founded in 1985 as a nonsectarian center emphasizing sitting.

Hq: 138 Gorgas Lane, Philadelphia, PA
    19119
Tel: (215) 247 3516

Reiyukai America

Reiyukai America is the American branch of a Nichiren Buddhist group which emerged in the 1920s in Japan. It was organized in the United States in the 1970s.

Hq: 2741 Sunset Blvd., Los Angeles,
    CA 90026
Tel: (213) 413 1771
    or
International Hq: 1-7-8 Azabudai,
    Minato-ku, Tokyo, Japan

Rigpa Fellowship

The Rigpa Fellowship is a Tibetan Buddhist group founded in England in the late 1970s. It was brought to America by its founder, the Ven. Sogyal Rinpoche, during the early 1980s.

Hq: Box 7326, Santa Cruz, CA 94707
Tel: (408) 688 2208
    or
International Hq: 44 St. Paul's
    Crescent, London NW1 9TN,
    U.K.

Rinzai-Ji, Inc.

Rinzai-Ji is an association of Zen centers founded by Joshu Sasaki Roshi in 1968. Included in the association are the Cimarron Zen

Center in Los Angeles, Mt. Baldy Zen Center, and the Jemez Bodhi Mandala, Jemez Springs, New Mexico.

Hq: Jemez Bodhi Mandala, Box 8, Jemez Springs, NM 87025
Tel: (505) 829 3854
or
Ithaca Zen Center, 312 Auburn Street, Ithaca, NY 14850
Tel: (607) 273 3190

Rissho Kosei Kai

The Rissho Kosei Kai (literally the Society for the Establishment of Righteous and Friendly Intercourse) is a Nichiren Buddhist group organized in Japan in the 1930s by Nikkyo Niwano and Naganuma Myoko. It came to the United States in 1959.

Hq: c/o Rev. Kazuhiko K. Nagamoto, 118 N. Mott, Los Angeles, CA 90033
Tel: (213) 269 4741
or
International Hq: 11-1, Wada 2-chrome, Suginami-ku, Tokyo, 166 Japan

Sakya Monastery of Tibetan Buddhism

The Monastery was founded in 1974 as a nonsectarian center for Tibetan Buddhist studies and practice.

Hq: 108 Northwest 83rd Street, Seattle, WA 98117
Tel: (206) 789 2573

Sakya Phuntsok Ling Center for Tibetan Buddhist Studies and Meditation

Led by the Ven. Kalsang Gyaltsen, the Center offers textual study of classical Buddhist texts as well as the meditations associated with them.

Hq: 8715 First Avenue, #1501 D, Silver Springs, MD 20910
Tel: (301) 589 3115

Sakya Thupten Dargye Ling

Sakya Thupten Dargye Ling is a Tibetan Buddhist center founded in 1979 by H. H. Sakya Trizin and under the leadership of the Ven. Deshung Rinpoche.

For information call: (612) 722 7460 or (612) 633 0019

Shingon Mission

Shingon Buddhist is a form of Buddhism emphasizing the esoteric aspect of life. It was founded in China in the ninth century by Ku Kai, more popularly known as Kobo Daishi and came to the Hawaiian islands at the beginning of this century.

Hq: Bishop Tetsuei Katoda, 915 Sheridan Street, Honolulu, HI 96810
Tel: (808) 941 5663
or
International Hq: 132 Oaza Koyasan, Koya-machi, Ito-gun, Wakayama-ken, 648-01 Japan

Shinnyo-en

Shinnyo-en was founded in 1936 by Archbishop Shinjo Ito, a former Shingon priest. The first American center opened in Hawaii in 1972.

Hq: 1400 Jefferson Street, San Francisco, CA 94123
Tel: (415) 346 0209
or
International Hq: 2-13 Shibazaki-cho 1-chome, Tachikawa, Tokyo, 190 Japan

Shinshu Kyokai Mission

The Mission is an independent center which follows the Japanese

Pure Land Buddhist tradition.

Hq: c/o Bentenshu Hawaii Kyokai, 3871 Old Pali Rd., Honolulu, HI 86817

Sonoma Mountain Zen Center

The Center was founded in 1974 to continue the Soto Zen lineage of Shunryu Suzuki-Roshi, the Zen master who had originally inspired the Zen center of San Francisco.

Hq: 6267 Sonoma Mountain Road, Santa Rosa, CA 95404
Tel: (707) 545 8105

Soto Mission

The oldest Zen group in the United States, the Mission began in Hawaii in 1903 with the arrival of Senyei Kawahara. It is affiliated with the Soto-shu, the major Soto organization in Japan.

Hq: Soto Zen Buddhist Temple, 1708 Nuuanu Avenue, Honolulu, HI 96817
Tel: (808) 537 9409
or
Zenshuji Soto Mission, 123 S. Hewitt St., Los Angeles, CA 90012
Tel: (213) 624 8658
or
Sokoji Temple, 1691 Laguna Street, San Francisco, CA
Tel: (415) 346 7540
or
International Hq: Soto Shu, 2-21-34 Nishi Azabu, Minato-ku, Tokyo 105, Japan

Sri Lankan Sangha Council of North America

Sri Lankan Sangha council was formed in 1987 as a network of Sri Lankan Buddhist centers and monks. Prominent centers are located in New York City, Washington, D.C., and Los Angeles.

Hq: No central headquarters. For information: American Sri-Lanka Buddhist Association, Inc., 84-32 126th St., Kew Gardens, New York, NY 11415
Tel: (718) 849 2637

Stillpoint Institute

The Stillpoint Institute is a Theravada Buddhist center founded in 1971 as the Susana Yeiktha Meditation Center and Buddhist Society by Anagarika Sujata.

Hq: 2740 Greenwich, #416, San Francisco, CA 94123

Sunray Meditation Society

The Sunray Meditation Society, founded in 1968 by the native American holy woman Ven. Dhyani Ywahoo, was acknowledged as a Tibetan Buddhist Dharma Center of the Nyingma School in 1983 by Dudjom Rinpoche and has become an international organization blending native American and Tibetan Buddhist teachings.

Hq: P.O. Box 398, Bristol, VT 05443
Tel: (802) 453 4610

Taungpupu Kaba-aye Dharma Center

The Taungpupu Kaba-aye Dharma Center, founded in 1971 by the Ven. Kaba-Aye Sayadaw, a Burmese meditation master, is the focus of Burmese Theravada Buddhism in America.

Hq: 18335 Big Basin Way, Boulder Creek, CA 95006
Tel: (408) 338 4050
or
Burma-America Buddhist Association, 1708 Powder Mill Road, Silver Spring, MD 20903
Tel: (301) 439 4035

Thai-American Buddhist Association

Thais began to migrate to the United States in numbers in the late 1960s and temples emerged across the United States during the 1970s. The Association provides a network for cooperation among the various temples.

Hq: Wat Thai of Los Angeles, 12909 Cantara Street, North Hollywood, CA 91506
Tel: (818) 997 9657

Thubten Dhargye Ling

Thubten Dhargye Ling (literally the Land of Increasing Buddha's Teachings) was founded in 1979 by Geshe Tsultrim Gyeltsen. It is a Tibetan Buddhist center of the Gelupga order closely associated with the Dalai Lama.

Hq: 2658 La Cienga Avenue, Los Angeles, CA 90034
Tel: (213) 838 1232

Tibetan Buddhist Learning Center

The first Tibetan Buddhist group to settle in America, the Tibetan Buddhist Learning Center dates to 1951 and the arrival of approximately 200 Mongolians. Their leader, the Ven. Geshe Wangyal, migrated four years later. The Lamaist Buddhist Monastery of America was founded in 1958 and assumed its present name in 1984.

Hq: R.D. 1, Box 306 A, Washington, NJ 07882-9767

Todaiji Hawaii Bekkaku Honzan

The Todaiji Hawaii Bekkaku Honzan is the only Kegon Buddhist center in the United States. It was organized after World War II in Hawaii.

Hq: c/o Bishop Tatsusho Hirai, 2426 Luakini Street, Honolulu, HI 96814
Tel: (808) 595 2083
or
International Hq: Kegon Shu, 406 Zoshi-machi, Nara-shi, 630 Japan

Vajradhatu

The largest of the several Tibetan Buddhist groups in America, Vajradhatu was founded by Chogyam Trungpa Rinpoche in 1970. It is an outpost of the Kagyupa sect.

Hq: 1345 Spruce St., Boulder, CO 80302
Tel: (303) 444 8686
Fax: (303) 443 2975
or
International Hq: Vajradathu International, 1084 Tower Rd., Halifax, NS, Canada B3H 2Y8

Vajrapani Institute for Wisdom Culture

Vajrapani Institute is the American affiliate of the Foundation for the Preservation of the Mahayana Tradition, an international Tibetan Buddhist organization founded as a response to the Chinese invasion of Tibet. The Institute was founded in 1977. The affiliated Wisdom Publications had produced a number of high-quality Buddhist books and prints.

Hq: Box I, Boulder Creek, CA 95006
Tel: (408) 338 3655
or
Wisdom Publications, 361 Newbury Street, 4th Fl., Boston, MA 02115
Tel: (617) 421 9668
or

International Hq: Foundation for the Preservation of Mahayana Buddhism, Istituto Mahayana Internazionale, c/o Harvey Horrocks, Via Poggiberna 9, 56040 Pomaia (Pisa), Italy

Vietnamese United Buddhist Churches in the United States

The largest of the several organizations serving the Vietnamese Buddhist Community, the Vietnamese Buddhists were organized after the arrival of thousands of immigrants in the 1970s.

Hq: c/o Ven. Thich Man Giac, 863 S. Berendo, Los Angeles, CA 90005
Tel: (213) 384 9638 or 480 8693

Western Son Academy

The Academy was organized in 1976 in Mission Viejo, California, by Myo Bong S'nim, a Chogye Zen Buddhist master from Korea who migrated to America.

Hq: P. O. Box 4080, Irvine, CA 92716
Tel: (714) 786 9586

Won Buddhism

Won Buddhism is one of several Korean Buddhist groups which have emerged in the United States since 1965.

Hq: Won Buddhism of America, 1761 Crenshaw Blvd., Los Angeles, CA 90019
Tel: (213) 731 6733
or
International Hq: 344-2, Shinyong-dong, Iri City, Chonpuk, Korea

Yeshe Nyingpo

Yeshe Nyingpo is a Tibetan Nyingmapa Buddhist group founded in 1976 by Dudjom Rinpoche.

Hq: 19 W. 16th St., New York, NY 10011
Tel: (212) 691 8523

Zen Buddhist Temple of Chicago

The Zen Buddhist Temple was established in the late 1950s by Soto Zen instructor the Rev. Soyu Matsuoka. He later began associated centers in Long Beach, California, and Detroit, Michigan.

Hq: 865 Bittersweet Dr., Northbrook, IL 60062-3701
Tel: (312) 272 2070 or 2727 2071

Zen Center of Los Angeles

The Center was initiated in 1967 by students of Hakuyu Taizan Maezumi Roshi, a teacher formerly affiliated with the Zenshuji Soto Mission of Los Angeles.

Hq: 923 S. Normandie Avenue, Los Angeles, CA 90006
Tel: (213) 387 2351

Zen Center of Rochester

The Center was founded in 1966 by Philip Kapleau Roshi. There are now several affiliated centers both in North America and Europe.

Hq: Seven Arnold Park, Rochester, NY 14607
Tel: (716) 473 9180

Zen Center of San Francisco

The Center was begun by non-Japanese students of Shunryu Suzuki Roshi, then the Zen master at the Sokoji Temple in San Francisco, California. Affiliated with the Center is the Tassajara Mountain Center near Carmel Valley, California.

Hq: 300 Page St., San Francisco, CA 94102
Tel: (415) 863 3136

Zen Center of Sonoma Mountain

The Center was started in 1965 by a group under the leadership of Jakusho Kwong Sensei, then a student of Shunrei Suzuki Roshi of the Zen center of San Francisco, with which the Sonoma Mountain Center was affiliated for a number of years.

Hq: Genjo-Ji, 6367 Sonoma Mountain Road, Santa Rosa, CA 95404
Tel: (707) 545 8105

Zen Lotus Society

The Zen Lotus Society was founded in Canada in 1973 by Samu Sunim, a Korean Buddhist monk. The single center in the United States, located at Ann Arbor, Michigan, opened in 1981.

Hq: 1214 Packard Road, Ann Arbor, MI 48104
Tel: (313) 761 6520
or
International Hq: 86 Vaughn Road, Toronto, ON, Canada M6C 2M1

Zen Mountain Monastery

The Monastery was founded in 1980 by Sensei John Daido Loori as the headquarters of Mountain and River Order, which teaches Soto and Rinzai Zen.

Hq: Box 197, South Plank Road, Mount Tremper, NY 12457
Tel: (914) 688 2228

Zen Studies Society

The Society, founded by Cornelius Cane in 1956, emerged in response to the work of Daisetz Teitaro Suzuki who was teaching at Columbia University in the 1950s. Affiliated with the society is the Dai Bosatsu Zendo, a retreat center in the Catskill Mountains.

Hq: 223 E. 67th Street, New York, NY 10021
Tel: (212) 861 3333
or
Dai Bosatsu Zendo, Beecher Lake, HCR 1, Box 80, Lew Beach, NY 12753
Tel: (914) 439 4566

Zen Studies Society of Philadelphia

This Society was founded in 1986 and teaches Rinzai Zen.

Hq: 214 Monroe Street, Philadelphia, PA 19147
Tel: (215) 625 2601

Zen Temple of Cresskill

Founded in 1988, the Temple teaches Zen dance and movement techniques in the Korean Son (Zen) tradition.

Hq: 185 6th Street, Cresskill, NJ 07626
Tel: (201) 567 7468

Zen Wind

This independent center was founded by Zen Master Tundra Wind, a former teacher in the Chogye (Korean) work of Seung Sahn, but who has also received transmission in other Zen traditions.

Hq: P. O. Box 429, Monte Rio CA 95462

BUDDHIST PERIODICALS

The young American Buddhist community is producing a surprising number of periodicals, only a few of which were begun before 1965. Many of the ethnic groups still struggle with English, and a number of periodicals serving the community come from Asia in the various Asian languages. Some are bilingual, symbolic of the change the community is undergoing. Listed below are the English and bilingual publications and their sponsoring organizations.

American Buddhist Newsletter, 301 West 45th Street, New York, NY 10036, American Buddhist Movement

Blind Donkey, 2119 Kaloa Way, Honolulu 96822, Diamond Sangha

Blissful Rays of the Mandala, Australia and New Zealand, Regional Office, 111 Little Lonsdale Street, Melbourne, Victoria 3000, Australia, Vajrapani Institute for Wisdom Culture

Buddha World, American Zen College, 16815 Germantown Road (Route 118), MD 20767, American Zen College

Buddhist Peace Fellowship Newsletter, P. O. Box 4650, Berkeley, CA 94704, Buddhist Peace Fellowship

Buddhist Times, 4267 W. 3rd Street, Los Angeles, CA 90020, Korean Buddhist Chogye Order

California Diamond Sangha Newsletter, P. O. Box 216, Berkeley, CA 94701, Diamond Sangha

Center of Gravity, Jemez Bodhi Mandala, Box 8, Jemez Springs, NM 87025, Rinzai-ji, Inc.

Clear Light, Box 2422, Reno, NV 89505, Pansophic Institute

The Dai Bosatsu News, Beecher Zendo, HCR I, Box 80, Lew Beach, NY 12753, The Zen Studies Society, Inc.

Densal, Karma Triyana Dharmachakra, 352 Meads Mountain Rd., Woodstock, NY 12498, Karma Triyana Dharmachakra

Dharma Season, 223 East 67th Street, New York, NY 10021, The Zen Studies Society

Dharma Voice, 933 So. New Hampshire Avenue, Los Angeles, CA 90006, Buddhist Sangha Council of Southern California/College of Buddhist Studies, Los Angeles

Dharma World, c/o Kosei Publishing Co., 2-7-1 Wada, Suginami, Tokyo 166, Japan, Rissho Kosei Kai

Diamond Sword, 865 Bittersweet Dr., Northbrook, IL 60062-3701, Zen Buddhist Temple of Chicago

Duangprateep, 8225 Coldwater Canyon Av., North Hollywood, CA 91605-1198, Wat Thai-American Buddhist Association

Dundrub Yong (Song of Fulfillment), Kagyu Droden Kunchab, 3476 21st Street, San Francisco, CA 94110, Kagyu Dharma

Horin, 1710 Octavia Street, San Francisco, CA 94109, Buddhist Churches of America

Inner Quest, 2741 Sunset Blvd., Los Angeles, CA 90026, Reiyukai America

Insight Meditation Society Newsletter, Pleasant Street, Barre, MS 01005, Insight Meditation Society

Journal of the Order of Buddhist Contemplatives, Box 199, Mt. Shasta, CA 96067, Order of Buddhist Contemplatives

Jushin, 45-520 Keaahala Road, Kaneohe, HI 96744, Kaneohe Higashi Hongwanji

Kahawa: Journal of Women and Zen, 2119 Kaloa Way, Honolulu, HI 96822, Diamond Sangha

Kaleo O'Dharma, 291 S. Puunene Avenue, Kahului, Maui, HI 96732, Kahului Hongwanji Mission

Kantaka, 331 Riverside Drive, New York, NY 10025, Buddhist Fellowship of New York

Lotus in the West, 939 South New Hampshire Av., Los Angeles, CA 90006 University of Oriental Studies and The International Buddhist Meditation Center

Monthly Guide, 928 S. New Hampshire Avenue, Los Angeles, CA 90006, International Buddhist Meditation Center

M.Z.M.C. Newsletter, 3343 East Calhoun Pkwy., Minneapolis, MN 55408, Minnesota Zen Meditation Center

Newsletter, Box 250, Pahala, HI 96777, Nechung Drayang Ling

Newsletter, 944 Terrace 49, Los Angeles, CA 90042, Kanzeonji Zen Buddhist Temple

The Newsletter, Nichiren Mission of Hawaii, 3058 Pali Highway, Honolulu, HI 96817, Nichiren Sect Mission

Newsletter of the Kwan Um Zen School, 528 Pound Rd., Cumberland, RI 02864, Kwan Um Zen School

News Tibet, Office of Tibet, 107 East 31 Street, New York, NY 10016

New York Buddhist Vihara, 84-32 124th St., Kew Gardens, New York, NY 11415, American Sri Lanka Association

The Nirvana, 2-13 Shibazaki-cho i-chome, Tachikawa, Tokyo 190, Japan, Shinnyo-en

Pacific World, 1710 Octavia Street, San Francisco, CA 94109, Buddhist Churches of America

Primary Point, K.B.C. Hong Poep Won, 528 Pund Rd., Cumberland, RI 02864, Kwan Um Zen School

The Proper Dharma Seal, City of Ten Thousand Buddhas, Box 217, Talmage, CA 95481, Dharma Realm Buddhist Association

Sakya Tegchen Choeling Newsletter, 5042 18th Avenue NE, Seattle, WA 98105, Monastery of Tibetan Buddhism

Seikyo Times, 525 Wilshire Blvd., Box 1427, Santa Monica, CA 90406, Nichiren Shoshu Temple

Soka Gakkai News, 32 Shinano-machi, Shinjuku-ku, Tokyo 160, Japan, Nichiren Shoshu Temple

Temple Notes, 1214 Packard Rd., Ann Arbor, MI 48104, Zen Lotus Society

The Ten Directions, 923 South Normandie Avenue, Los Angeles, CA 90006, Zen Center of Los Angeles and the Kuroda Institute

Thubten Dargye Ling Newsletter, 2658 La Cienga Avenue, Los Angeles, CA 90034, Thubten Dargye Ling

Udumbara, 3343 East Calhoun Pkwy., Minneapolis, MN 55408, Minnesota Zen Meditation Center

Vajra Bodhi Sea, Gold Mountain Monastery, 800 Sacramento Street, San Francisco, CA 94108, Dharma Realm Buddhist Association

The Vajradhatu Sun, 1345 Spruce Street, Boulder, CO 80302, Vajradhatu

Wa, 1685 Alaneo Street, Honolulu, HI 96817, Higashi Hongwanji Mission

Washington Buddhist, c/o Washington Buddhist Vihara, 5017 16th Street N.W., Washington, D.C. 20011, Washington Buddhist Vihara, American Sri Lanka Association

The Way, 505 E. 3rd Street, Los Angeles, CA 90013, Higashi Hongwanji Betsuin

Wind Bell, 300 Page Street, San Francisco, CA 94102, Zen Center of San Francisco

Wisdom: Magazine of the FPMT, Wisdom Publications, 23 Dering Street, London W1, England, U.K., Vajrapani Institute for Wisdom Culture

World Tribune, 525 Wilshire Blvd. Box 1427, Santa Monica, CA 90406, Nichiren Shoshu of America

Zazenkai News, 123 South Hewitt Street, Los Angeles, CA 90012, Zenshuji Soto Mission

Zen Bow Newsletter, 7 Arnold Park, Rochester, NY 14607, Zen Center of Rochester

Zen Notes, 113 E. 30th Street, New York, NY 10016, The First Zen Institute of America, Inc.

HINDUISM AND RELATED ORGANIZATIONS

Hinduism is one of the hardest religions to define. The term usually refers to those religions which exist in the country of India, though generally the Sikh, Sant Mat, Jain and, of course, Muslim faiths are now distinguished from it. Until a more accepted typology of Indian religion is developed we are using the term in its generally accepted sense as referring to those religions which have come to the United States from India. This chapter thus lists everything from "orthodox" Hindus who worship in temples built according to strict Indian standards to gurus (teachers) whose idea are greatly at variance with popular Hindu thought (such as Rajneesh [Osho]).

It should be noted that while the Sikh and Sant Mat communities have developed a large following and thus have a chapter unto themselves, the Jain community remains small, and its several organizations are listed below.

INTRAFAITH ORGANIZATIONS

Vishwa Hindu Parishad of America

The international Vishwa Hindu Parishad was formed to network among Hindus and unite the Hindu community especially as it has emerged outside of India.

Hq: 217 Deerfield Drive, Berlin, CT 06037
Tel: (203) 828 360

HINDU CENTERS, TEMPLE ASSOCIATIONS, AND ORGANIZATIONS

Adhyatma Yoga Dharma

Adhyatma Yoga Dharma is headed by an American spiritual teacher Bhagavan Sri Babajhan-Al-Kahlil, the Friend, described as the Kalki Mahaavatara Satguru of the Age.

Hq: Address unavailable for this edition
Tel: (213) 530 0577 or 534 1965

Adhyatmic Sadhana Sangh, U.S.A.

Adhyatmic Sadhana Sangh was founded in the 1980s by Yogi Kamal.

Hq: c/o Swami Yogiraj Nanak, 20345 Arminta Street, Canoga Park, CA 91306
Tel: (818) 882 8828
or
International Hq: Dhyanyog Ashram, C-Block, Naraina Residential Scheme, New Delhi 110028, India

Advaita Fellowship

The Fellowship was incorporated in 1988 by students of Ramesh S. Balsekar, a teacher of Advaita Vedanta and student of Indian teacher Nissagadatta Maharaj.

Hq: 221-B Indianapolis Street, Huntington Beach, CA 92648
Tel: (714) 960 3529

Agni Dhatu Samadhi Yoga

Agni Dhatu Samadhi Yoga, with centers in Southern California, teaches a system for experiencing infinity as a sheet of white fires (agni dhatu).

Hq: Current address unavailable for this edition
Tel: (714) 670 1705 or (213) 202 4307

Ajapa Yoga Foundation

The Foundation was founded by followers of Guru Janardan Paramahansa, who first came to America in the 1970s.

Hq: Shri Janardan Yoga Ashram, Box 1731, Placerville, CA 95667
or

International Hq: Sri Purnanand Ajapa Yoga Sanstham, Dimna, P. O. Mango, Jamshedpur 831012, Bihar, India

American Haidakhan Samaj

The American Haidakhan Samaj was formed to perpetuate acknowledgment of a young man who appeared in 1970 in Haidakhan, India, as Babaji, the fabled incarnation of Shiva first described to Western audiences in Swami Paramahansa's *Autobiography of a Yogi.*

Hq: 324-15th Avenue, E. #201, Seattle, WA 98112
or
Haidakhandi Universal Ashram, Box 9, Crestone, CO 81131
Tel: (719) 256 4108
or
International Hq: Haidakhan Ashram, P. O. Haidakhan, via Kathgodam, Dist. Nainital, Utter Predesh 263126, India

American Meditation Society

The American Meditation Society was founded in 1977 as a branch of the International Foundation for Spiritual Unfoldment, under the spiritual leadership of Guru Ananda Yogi (Purusshotten Narshinhran).

Hq: Box 314, Dresher, PA 19025
or
International Hq: South African Meditation Society, P. O. Box 202, Gatesville, Athlone, Capetown 7764, S. Africa

American Vegan Society

The Society was founded in 1960 by H. Jay Dinshah and grew out of the work of his father Dinshah P. Ghadiali.

Hq: 501 Old Harding Hwy., Malaga,
NJ 08328

Amrita Foundation

The Amrita Foundation is an independent association of followers of Swami Paramahansa Yogananda.

Hq: c/o Priscilla Jackson, P. O. Box 8080, Dallas, TX 75205
Tel: (214) 521 1072

Ananda

Ananda was founded in 1968 by Swami Kriyananda (J. Donald Walters), a disciple of Swami Paramahansa Yogananda and former member of the board of Self-Realization Fellowship.

Hq: 14618 Tyler Foote Rd., Nevada City, CA 95959
Tel: (916) 292 3065 or 292 3464

Ananda Ashrama and Vedanta Centre

The Ananda Ashrama grew out of the work of Swami Paramananda, a monk with the Vedanta Society. The Ashrama became independent in 1940.

Hq: Box 8555, 5301 Pennsylvania Av., La Crescenta, CA 91214-0555
Tel: (818) 248 1931

Ananda Marga Yoga Society

The Ananda Marga Yoga Society was founded in 1955 in India by Shrii Shrii Anandamurtiji (Prabhat Ranjan Sarkar) and was brought to the United States in 1969.

Hq: 97-38 42nd Ave., Corona, NY 11368
Tel: (718) 898 1603
or

International Hq: c/o Global Office, E. M. Bypass, V.I.P. Nagar, Tiljala, Calcutta 700039, India

Arsha Vidya Pitham

For many years an associate of Swami Chinmayananda, Swami Dayananda became independent in the late 1980s and founded Arsha Vidya through which he continues his work as a teacher of Vedanta.

Hq: Arsha Vidya, P. O. Box 1059, Saylorburg, PA 18353
Tel: (717) 992 2339

Arunchala Ashrama

Arunchala Ashrama is a North American focus for disciples of Indian teacher Ramana Maharshi.

Hq: 72-63 Yellowstone Blvd., Forest Hills, NY 11375
Tel: (718) 575 3215
or
International Hq: Sri Ramanasramam, Tiruvannamalai 606603, Tumil Nadu, India

Atmaniketan Ashram

Atmaniketan Ashram is an independent association of centers in Europe and America founded by Sadhu Loncontirth, a disciple of Sri Aurobindo.

Hq: 1291 Weber St., Pomona, CA 91768
Tel: (714) 629 8255
or
Marschstrasse 49, D-4715 Ascheberg-Herbern, Germany

Aum Namo Bhagavate Vasudevaya Foundation

The Foundation was founded in 1981 by Swami Prem Paramahansa Mahaprabho.

Hq: Box 73, Harbor City, CA 90710-0073
Tel: (213) YOG ANBV

Aurobindo, Disciples of

The disciples of Indian Tantric yoga master Sri Aurobindo Ghose have formed a number of autonomous centers linked in a loose network to the international village he began in French India.

Hq: Sri Aurobindo Association, Box 372, High Falls, NY 12440
Tel: (914) 687 9222
or
East West Cultural Center, 12392 Marshall St., Culver City, CA 53192
Tel: (213) 390 9083
or
Auroville International USA, Box 162489, Sacramento, CA: 95816
Tel: (916) 452 4013
or
California Institute of Integral Studies, 765 Ashbury Street, San Francisco, CA 94117
Tel: (415) 753 6100
or
International Hq: Auroville Trust, Auroville 605104, Kottakuppam, India

Avadhut Ashram

The Ashram was founded by Sage Bhagavan Nome, considered to be an enlightened disciple of famed Indian spiritual teacher Ramana Maharshi.

Hq: Box 8080, Santa Cruz, CA 95061
Tel: (408) 338 9493

Blue Mountain Center of Meditation

The Center was founded in 1960 by students of Indian spiritual teacher Eknath Easwaran.

Hq: Box 477, Petaluma, CA 94953
Tel: (707) 878 2369

Brahma Kumaris World Spiritual University

The World Spiritual University was established in 1937 by Dada Lekh Raj (Sri Prajapita Brahma). Leadership passed to his female disciples, the Brahma Kumaris.

Hq: c/o N.G.O. Offices, Church Center, 777 U.N. Plaza, New York, NY 10017
Tel: (718) 565 5133
or
International Hq: Pandau Bhavan, Mt. Abu, Rajasthan, India

Center of Being

The Center was founded in 1979 by Baba Prem Ananda (Anandaji) and Her Holiness Sri Marashama Devi (Mataji). Mataji, an American-born black woman, is considered to be an avatar (incarnation of the deity).

Hq: 3272 Purdue Avenue, Los Angeles, CA 90066

Sri Chaitanya Saraswat Mandal

The Sri Chaitanya Saraswat Mandal was founded by reform-minded former members of the International Society for Krishna Consciousness following the death of ISKCON's founder, A. C. Bhaktivedanta Swami Prabhupada (1896-1977).

Hq: c/o Guardian of Devotion Press, 62 S. 13th Street, San Jose, CA 95112
or
International Hq: Nabadwip Dham, District Nadia, West Bengal, India

Chinmaya Mission (West)

The Mission is the focus of the work in North America of Indian vedandist teacher Sri Chinmayananda, a disciple of the late Swami Sivananda Saraswati.

Hq: Sandeepany West, Box 129, Piercy, CA 95467
Tel: (707) 247 3488
or
International Hq: Central Chinmaya Trust, Powai Park Drive, Bombay 400072, India

Sri Chinmoy Centres

The Centres grew up in the 1960s around the work of Sri Chinmoy Ghose, an Indian meditation teacher who had grown up in the ashram of Sri Aurobindo Ghose.

Hq: Box 32433, Jamaica, NY 11431
Tel: (212) 523 3471

Church of the Christian Spiritual Alliance

Founded in 1962, the Church is currently under the leadership of Eugene Roy Davis, a former disciple of Swami Paramahansa Yogananda.

Hq: Lake Rabun Road, P. O. Box 7, Lakemont, GA 30552
Tel: (404) 782 4723

Datta Yoga Centers

The Datta Yoga Centers were founded in the 1980s by H. H. Sri Ganapathi Sachchidananda Swamiji, an Indian spiritual teacher from Mysore, India.

Hq: R.D. #2, Box 2084, Moniteau Road, West Sudbury, PA 16061
Tel: (412) 637 3169

or
International Hq: S. G. S. Ashrama, Nanjangud Road, Dattanagar, Mysore 570004, India

Deva Foundation

The Foundation was founded in Sweden in the early 1980s by Dr. Deva Maharaj.

Hq: 336 S. Doheny Drive #7, Beverly Hills, CA 90211
Tel: (213) 276 6777

Devatma Shakti Society

The Society was formed in 1976 by Swami Shivom Tirth, a disciple of Swami Vishnu Tirth Maharaj (d. 1969).

Hq: Rte. 1, Box 150 C-2, Paige, TX 78659

Dhyanyoga Centers

The Dhyanyoga Centers have grown up around Dhyanyoga Mahant Madhusuadndasji Maharaj, a teacher of raja and kundalini yoga who made his first visit to the United States in 1976.

Hq: P. O. Box 3194, Antioch, CA 94531
Tel: (415) 757 9361
or
International Hq: Hanumanji Temple, Bandhvad via, Radhanpur, Dist. Banaskantha, N. Gujarat, India

Fivefold Path

The Fivefold Path was founded in 1973 by Indian teacher Vesant Paranjpe, a teacher of kriya yoga, a practice for purification of self and the environment.

Hq: RFD #1, Box 121-C, Madison, VA

Foundation of Revelation

The Foundation was created in 1970 by students of an obscure Indian holy man who is believed to be an embodiment of perfect knowledge and practical omnipotence.

Hq: c/o Charlotte Wallace, 59 Scott St., San Francisco, CA 94117

Free Daist Communion

The Free Daist Communion was founded in 1970 as the Dawn Horse Fellowship. Its founder, Franklin Jones, is known by his religious name, Heart Master Da Love Ananda.

Hq: The Mountain of Attention Sanctuary, 12040 Seigler Canyon Road, Middletown, CA 95461
Tel: (707) 928 4931
Fax: (707) 987 0137

Gaudiya Vaishnava Society

The Gaudiya Vaishnava Society is a Krishna Consciousness group founded by former members of the International Society for Krishna Consciousness.

Hq: 1307 Church Street, San Francisco, CA 94114
Tel: (415) 695 9864

Golden Lotus Inc.

Golden Lotus is an independent fellowship of followers of Swami Paramahansa Yogananda.

Hq: 9607 E. Sturgeon Valley Rd., Vanderbilt, MI 49795
Tel: (517) 983 4107

Hanuman Foundation

The Hanuman Foundation was incorporated in 1974 as an umbrella for the various activities of Baba Ram Dass (Richard Alpert), among which is the support of a temple to Hanuman, a popular Hindu deity, especially the object of attention by Ram Dass' guru, Neem Karoli Baba.

Hq: 445 Summit Rd., Watsonville, CA 95076
Tel: (408) 847 0406, or 722 7175
or
Hanuman Foundation Tape Library, P. O. Box 2320, Del Ray Beach, FL 33447

Himalayan International Institute of Yoga Science and Philosophy

The Institute was brought to the United States in 1970 by its founder Swami Rama, most well-known for his demonstration of his yogic skills in the laboratory at Menninger Clinic.

Hq: RD 1, Box 400, Honesdale, PA 18431
Tel: (800) 444 5772

Hohm Community

Hohm was founded in the early 1970s by Lee Lozowick, an eclectic spiritual teacher who draws from both Hinduism and Buddhism.

Hq: Box 4272, Prescott Valley, AZ 86302
Tel: (602) 778 5947 or 778 9189

Holy Shankaracharya Order

The Order dates to the 1968 founding of the Sivananda Ashram of Yoga One Science by Swami Lakshmy Devyashram.

Hq: RD 8, Box 8116, Stroudsburg, PA 18360
Tel: (717) 629 0481

Indo-American Yoga-Vedanta Society

The Society was founded in the early 1970s by Swami Bua Ji (H. H. Sri Swami Satchidananda Bua Ji), who moved to the United States from India in 1972.

Hq: 330 West 58th Street, Apt. 11-J, New York, NY 10019
Tel: (212) 265 7719

Integral Yoga International

Integral Yoga International, formerly known as the Integral Yoga Institute, was formed in the late 1960s by Swami Satchidananda, a disciple of Indian yogi Swami Sivananda Saraswati.

Hq: Satchidananda Ashram, Rte. 1, Box 172, Buckingham, VA 23921
Tel: (804) 969 3121

Intercosmic Center of Spiritual Awareness

I.C.S.A. was founded by yoga teacher Dr. Rammurti Sriram Mishra (Swami Brahmananda), a student of Indian Spiritual teacher Sri Ramana Maharshi.

Hq: Ananda Ashram, R.D. 3, Box 141, Monroe, NY 10950
Tel: (914) 782 5575
or
Nada-Brahmananda Ashram, Yoga Society of San Francisco, 2872 Folson St., San Francisco, CA 94110
Tel: (415) 285 5537

International Babaji Kriya Yoga

International Babaji Kriya Yoga was founded in 1952 by Yogi S. A. A. Ramaiah and brought to the United States in the 1960s.

Hq: 595 W. Bedford Rd., Imperial City, CA 92251
Tel: (714) 355 2126
or
International Hq: No 1-A, Arulananda Mudali St., San Thome, Madras-4, Tamil Nada 600004, India

International Nahavir Jain Mission

The Mission was founded in 1970 by Guruji Mini Sushul Kumar.

Hq: Acharya Sushil Jain Ashram, 722 Tomkins Avenue, Staten Island, NY 10305
Tel: (212) 447 9505
or
International Hq: Ahimsa Vihar, C-599 Cetna Harq, Defence Colony, New Delhi, 110024, India

International Society for Krishna Consciousness

Among the most controversial of the new Hindu groups in North America, the International Society for Krishna Consciousness (ISKCON) is a Vaishnava group founded in 1965 in New York by A. C. Bhaktivedanta Swami Prabhupada.

Hq: No central headquarters. For Information: BTG Resource Service, P. O. Box 90946, San Diego, CA 92169
Tel: (619) 272 7384
Fax: (619) 272 3673
or
Gita Nagari Village, ISKCON Farm, Route 1, Box 839, Port Royal, PA 17082
Tel: (717) 527 4101
or
Secretary, Governing Body Commission, P. O. Box 16146, Circus Avenue Office, Calcutta 70017, India

International Society for Krishna Consciousness of West Virginia

ISKCON of West Virginia grew out of the New Vrindaban ashram farm established in the late 1960s by Kirtanananda Swami Bhaktipada, a disciple of A. C. Bhaktivedanta Swami Prabhupada. The center, its associated ashrams, and leader broke with the larger ISKCON organization in the late 1980s.

Hq: R.D. 1, Box 320, Moundsville, WV 26041
Tel: (304) 843 1600 or 845 2290

International Society of Divine Love

The Society was founded in 1972 by Swami H. D. Prakashanand Saraswati to spread Krishna Consciousness. During the 1980s, Swami Prakashanand was quite active in the founding of centers in the West.

Hq: 234 W. Upsal Street, Philadelphia, PA 19119
Tel: (215) 842 0300

Jain Meditation International Center

The Jain Meditation International Center was founded in 1974 by Gurudev Shree Chtrabhanu.

Hq: Current address unavailable for this edition

Jean Klein Foundation

The Foundation was created in the 1980s to network among students of Austrian Advaita Vedanta teacher and writer Jean Klein. Associated with it is Third Millennium Publications.

Hq: P. O. Box 940, Larkspur, CA 94939
Tel: (415) 454 5036

Keshavashram International Meditation Center

The Center was founded in 1968 by Sister Gita, a disciple of Shri Krishna Gopal Cyasji Maharaj of Jaipur, India.

Hq: P. O. Box 260, Warrenton, VA 22186
Tel: (703) 347 9009

Kripalu Center for Yoga and Health

The Kripalu Center was founded in 1966 as the Yoga Society of Pennsylvania by Yogi Amrit Desai who in 1970 developed a new form of yoga, which he named after his guru, Swami Shri Kripalvanandji.

Hq: Box 973, Lenox, MA 01240
Tel: (413) 637 3280

Krishnamurti Foundation of America

The American Foundation, founded in 1969, is part of an international network of centers devoted to the teachings of the late teacher Jiddu Krishnamurti.

Hq: Box 1560, Ojai, CA 93023-0216
Tel: (805) 646 2726
Fax: (805) 646 6674

Kriya Yoga Ashrama, Inc.

Kriya Yoga Ashrama was founded by Swami Hariharananda Giri, a student of Swami Paramahansa Yogananda of the Self-Realization Fellowship. He currently heads the ashram in India founded by Yogananda's guru, Sri Yukteswar.

Hq: Kriya Yoga Center, 1201 Fern Street, N.W., Washington, DC 20012

or

Kriya Yoga Center of California, P.O. Box 9127, Santa Rosa, CA 95404

or

International Hq: Karar Ashram, Puri, Orissa, India

Kundalini Research Foundation

The Foundation was founded in 1970 by American followers of the teachings of Gopi Krishna, an Indian master of kundalini yoga.

Hq: Box 2248, Noroton Heights, CT 06820

Ma Yogi Shakti International Mission

The Mission was founded in 1979 by Ma Yogashakti Saraswati, an Indian female guru.

Hq: 114-23 Lefferts Blvd., South Ozone, NY 11420
Tel: (718) 641 0402, or 322 5856

or

International Hq: 11 Jaldarsham, 51 Napean Sea Rd., Bombay 400036, India

Manujothi Ashram

Hq: P. O. Box 32, Medway, OH 45341-0032

or

International Hq: Odaimarichan Post, (Via) Papagudi Tirunelveli 627-602
Tel: Gandhinagar - 3770 or Mukkudal - 43, India

Mata Amritanandamayi Mission

Mata Amritanandamayi is an Indian spiritual teacher who began to establish centers in both Europe and the United States during the 1980s.

Hq: P.O. Box 613, San Ramon, CA 94583-0613
Tel: (415) 537 9417

or

International Hq: Vallikkavu, Kuzhithura P. O., Via Adinad, Quilon, Kerala 690542, India

Matri Satsang

The Matri Satsang is an American organization following the teachings of Indian spiritual teacher Sri Anandamayi Ma, a renowned female guru. Though not directly affiliated with Anandamayi Ma's centers in India, the Matri Satsang circulates their materials.

Hq: 967a Allegheny Star Route, Nevada City, CA 95959

Meher Baba, Lovers of

Meher Baba, an eclectic Indian spiritual teacher, has become one of the most influential figures in the West. His very loosely organized followers have created a number of independent centers to distribute Baba material, but have found some focus in the center in South Carolina.

Hq: Meher Spiritual Center, 10200 Hwy. 17 No., Myrtle Beach, SC 29577

or

Meher Baba Archives, 704 41st Avenue South, Bldg. 18, No. Myrtle Beach, SC 29882
Tel: (803) 272 8524

or

International Hq: Avatar Meher Baba Trust, King's Road, Ahmednagar, Maharashtra India

Moksha Foundation

The Foundation was founded in 1976 as the Self-Enlightenment Meditation Society by Tantracharya Nityananda (Bishwanath Singh).

Hq: 745 31st St., Boulder, CO 80303
Tel: (303) 449 9915

Narayanananda Universal Yoga Trust

The Trust was founded in 1947 by Swami Narayanananda Maharaj. The first American center opened in 1977.

Hq: N.U. Yoga Ashram, 2937 N. Southport Avenue, Chicago, IL 60657
Tel: (312) 327 3650
or
International Hq: N. U. Yoga Ashrama, Gylling, DK-8300 Odder, Denmark

Nityananda Institute, Inc.

The Institute was founded in 1971 as the Shree Gurudev Rudrananda Yoga Ashram by Swami Rudrananda (Albert Rudolph). Following Rudrananda's death in 1973, his centers splintered under various leaders, the most substantive emerging as the Nityananda Institute under Swami Chetanananda.

Hq: 6 Linnaean Street, Cambridge, MA 02138
Tel: (617) 497 6263

Osho International

Osho International succeeded Rajneesh International, the organization founded to guide the activities of disciples of Bhagavan Rajneesh who shortly before his death in 1990 changed his name to Osho.

Hq: Viha Osho Meditation Center, P.O. Box 352, Mill Valley, CA 94942
Tel: (415) 381 9861
or
International Hq: Rajneeshdham, 17 Koregaon Park, Poona 411001, India

Prana Yoga Ashram

The Prana Yoga Ashram dates to the arrival in the United States of Indian yoga teacher Swami Sivalingam, formerly a teacher at Swami Sivananda's Yoga Vedanta Forest Academy in Rishikish, India.

Hq: 488 Spruce Street, Berkeley, CA 94708
Tel: (415) 655 3664

Rajneesh, Followers of Bhagwan

See: Osho International

Raj-Yoga Math and Retreat

The Raj-Yoga monastery/retreat center, presided over by Fr. Satchakrananda Bodhisattveguru, was founded in 1974.

Hq: Box 547, Deming, WA 98244

Ram Ananda Ashram

The Ashram was founded by Master Ram, an American Hindu teacher of kundalini yoga who has the power to transmit shaktipat (which raises the kundalini energies in each person) to others.

Hq: 218 Pestana Avenue, Santa Cruz, CA 95065
Tel: (213) 652 2563 or 659 8555

Shri Ram Chandra Mission

Followers of Ram Chandra began to appear in North America in the 1980s.

Hq: Address unavailable for this edition

Tel: (408) 646 9749

or

International Hq: Shri Ram Chandra Mission, Shajahanpar, Utter Predesh 242001, India

Rama Seminars

Rama Seminars was founded by Tantric Zen Master Rama (Frederick Lenz), a former disciple of Sri Chinmoy. Rama broke with Chinmoy in the early 1970s and founded Lakshmi, since 1985 known as Rama Seminars.

Hq: 1015 Gayley Avenue, Suite 1116, Los Angeles, CA 90024

Tel: (213) 273 2672

Sadhana Ashram

The Ashram was founded by Shankar Das, an American yogi, following a vision of the Divine Mother in 1981.

Hq: Route 6, Box 359A, Sevierville, TN 37862

Sahaja Yoga

During the 1980s Sahaja Yoga centers were established across the United States by followers of Shri Mataji Nirmala Devi.

Hq: 13659 Victory Blvd., Ste #684, Van Nuys, CA 91401

Tel: (818) 989 0794

S. A. I. Foundation

S. A. I. Foundation is the focus of the American network of followers of Satya Sai Baba, a prominent Indian guru and miracle worker.

Hq: 14849 Lull Street, Van Nuys, CA 91405

or

Sathya Sai Book Center of America, 305 W. First Street, Tustin, CA 92680

Tel: (714) 669 0522

or

International Hq: Sri Sathya Sai Books, P. O. Prasanthi Nilayam, District Anantapur, Andhra Pradesh 575134, India

Saiva Siddhanta Church

The Saiva Siddhanta Church, a Saivite Hindu group, was founded in 1957 as the Subramuniya Yoga Order by Master Subramuniya, an American student of Siva Yogiswami, a Sri Lankan guru.

Hq: Box 10, Kapaa, HI 96746

Tel: (808) 822 7032

Sanskrit Classics

Sanskrit Classics, an imprint for the writings of Swami Satyeswarananda Giri, a guru in the same lineage as Swami Paramahansa Yogananda, also serves as an umbrella for his teaching activity.

Hq: c/o Himalayan Yogi, P. O. Box 5368, San Diego, CA 92105

Tel: (619) 284 7779

Sarvamangala Mission

The Sarvamangala Mission is headed by Sri Rajagopala Anandanatha, a tantric teacher from India.

Hq: 366 Grapevine Drive, Diamond Bar, CA 91765

Tel: (714) 229 0444

Sat Yoga Self Transformation Center

Hq: 2815 La Cienega Avenue, Los Angeles, CA 90034

Tel: (213) 271 4848

Satyananda Ashrams, U.S.A.

Swami Satyananda Saraswati, a former student of Swami Sivananda Saraswati, founded his own ashram in Bihar, India, in 1964. His movement spread to America in the 1970s where it primarily serves the Indian-American community. It took its present name in 1980.

Hq: 1157 Ramblewood Way, San Mateo, CA 94403
or
International Hq: c/o Bihar School, Lal Darwaja, Monghyr 811201, Bihar, India

School of the Natural Order, Inc.

Hq: Dir. Mabel B. Hayden, P. O. Box 578, Baker, NV 89311
Tel: (213) 225 2471

Self-Realization Church of Absolute Monism

The Self-Realization Church began as the Washington, D.C., center of the Self-Realization Fellowship. It later became independent under its leader Swami Premananda.

Hq: c/o Srimata Kamala, 4748 Western Avenue, N.W., Washington, D.C. 20016
Tel: (301) 229-3871

Self-Realization Fellowship

The Self-Realization fellowship was founded by Swami Paramahansa Yogananda in 1917 as the Yogoda Satsang Society of India. He brought the society with him to America in 1922 where it assumed its present name in the 1930s. The Society, currently led by Daya Mata, teaches a form of kriya yoga.

Hq: 3880 San Rafael Avenue, Los Angeles, CA 90065
Tel: (213) 225 2471

Shanti Mandir

Shanti Mandir was founded in 1986 by Swami Nityananda, formerly a leader of the Siddha Yoga Dham and brother of Swami Chidvalasananda.

Hq: P. O. Box 1110, Pine Brush, NY 12566
Tel: (914) 744 6462
Fax: (914) 744 6492

Shanti Temple

The Temple is led by Swami Shantananda Saraswati.

Hq: 43 S. Main Street, Spring Valley, NY 10977

Shanti Yoga Institute and Yoga Retreat

The Shanti Yoga Institute and Yoga Retreat was founded in 1973 by Shanti Desai, a disciple of Swami Kripalvanandji.

Hq: 943 Central Avenue, Ocean City, NJ 08226
Tel: (609) 399 1974

Shiva-Shakti Ashram

The Shiva-Shakti Ashram was founded by Swami Savitripriya, a teacher of Maha Siddha Yoga.

Hq: P. O. Box 1130, Groveland, CA 95321
Tel: (209) 962 6883

Shri Shiva Balayogi Maharaj Trust

Shri Shiva Balayogi Maharaj Trust was founded in the early 1960s by Shri Shri Shri Shivabalayogi Maharaj (Sathyarayu

Alakka), an Indian Spiritual teacher.

Hq: c/o Sally Moberg, 724 Fellowship Road, Santa Barbara, CA 93109
Tel: (805) 966 6238
or
International Hq: J. P. Nagar, Bangalore 560078, India

Shri Vishnu Seva Ashram

The Ashram was established in India in 1966 by H. H. Shri Vishna Hitaishiji and has since been brought to the United States.

Hq: 45-37 Bowne Street, Flushing, New York 11355
Tel: (212) 939 3549 or 539 4202

Siddha Yoga Dham Associates

The Siddha Yoga Dham Associates grew out of the work of Swami Muktananda Paramahansa, a teacher of kundalini yoga, who first came to the United States in 1970. The group is currently led by his designated successor, Swami Chidvalasananada.

Hq: Box 600, South Fallsburg, NY 12779
Tel: (914) 434 2000
or
International Hq: Gurudev Siddha Peeth, P. Ganeshpuri, Dist. Thoma, Maharastra, India

Sivananda Yoga Vedanta Centers

The Sivananda Yoga Vedanta Centers, founded in 1957 by Swami Vishnu Devananda, is the American affiliate of the Divine Life Society founded in 1936 in India by the famous yogi Swami Sivananda Saraswati.

Hq: No central headquarters for the U.S. For information: 1600 Sawtelle Blvd., West Los Angeles, CA 90025
Tel: (213) 478 0202
or
International Hq: 673 8th Avenue, Val Morin, PQ, Canada J0T 2R0

Sri Rama Foundation

The Foundation was founded in 1971 by students of Baba Hari Dass, a teacher from India.

Hq: c/o Mount Madonna Center, 445 Summit Road, Watsonville, CA 95076
Tel: (408) 847 0406 or 722 7175

Swami Kuvalayananda Yoga (SKY) Foundation

The Foundation was founded by Dr. Vijayendra Pratap, a student of Swami Kuvalayanandaji, the founder of Kaivalyadharma, the hatha yoga center in Bombay.

Hq: c/o Garland of Letters Bookstore, 527 South St., Philadelphia, PA 19147
Tel: (215) 923 5946

Swaminarayan Mission and Fellowship

The Swaminarayan Mission, also known as the Akshar Purushottam Sanstha, began in India in the nineteenth century under the leadership of Shree Swaminarayan. It came to the United States with the first wave of Indian immigrants in the late 1960s.

Hq: c/o Ganesha Temple, 43-38 Bowne St., Flushing, NY 11355
Tel: (718) 961 1199 or 539 1587
or

International Hq: Shree Aksharpurushottan Swaminarayan Temple, Shahibaug, Ahmedabad 4, India

Temple of Cosmic Religion

The Temple was founded in 1968 by Sant Keshavadas, a guru from Bangalore, India, known for the hymns (kirtans) and music he has composed and performed.

Hq: 174 Santa Clara Avenue, Oakland, CA 94610
Tel: (415) 654 4683
or
International Hq: Viswa Shanti Ashram, 24 Kim Arasinakunte, Timkur Rd., Nelamangala Taluk, Desanapura Post, Bangalore 562123, India

Temple of Kriya Yoga

The Temple of Kriya Yoga was founded in the 1960s by Swami Kriyananda (Melvin Higgins), an American teacher of yoga in the same lineage as Swami Paramahansa Yogananda.

Hq: 2414 N. Kedzie, Chicago, IL 60647
Tel: (312) 392 4600

Truth Consciousness

Truth Consciousness was founded by Swami Amar Jyotir (Pabhushri Samaji) following his visit to the United States in 1973. There are associated centers in India and New Zealand.

Hq: Sacred Mountain Ashram, 3305 County Road 96, Ward, CO 80481-9606
Tel: (303) 447 1637
or
International Hq: Jyotir Ashram, 87 Lulla Nagar, Pune, Maharasthra 411040, India

Valley Light Center

The Valley Light Center was founded by John Ernst, a disciple of Paramahansa Yogananda.

Hq: P. O. Box 355, Oak View, CA 93022-0355

Vedanta Society

The Vedanta Society, the first Hindu organization in America, was founded in 1894 by Swami Vivekananda, who had come to the United States to speak at the World's Parliament of Religions. Each center in America is autonomous and relates directly to the international headquarters in India.

Hq: 34 W. 71st St., New York, NY 10023
Tel: (212) 877 9197
or
International Hq: Sri Ramakrisna Math, 11 Ramakrishna Math Road, Madras 600004, India

Vedantic Center

The Vedantic Center was founded by Swami Turiyasangitananda (Alice Coltrane), a former student of Swami Satchidananda of the Integral Yoga International. Drawing most of its following from the black community, the Center represents a major thrust to relate Hinduism to Afro-Americans.

Hq: 3528 N. Triunfo Canyon Rd., Agoura, CA 91301
Tel: (818) 706 9478

Vimala Thakar, Friends of

A teacher in the tradition of Jiddu Krishnamurti, Vimala Thakar has built an international following. Like Krishnamurti, she avoids organization, which has remained at a minimum.

Hq: Current address unavailable for this edition
or
International Hq: Vimala Thakar Foundation, Iepenlaan 111, 3723 XG Bilthoven, Netherlands

Viniyoga America

Viniyoga America was founded in 1986 to further the teachings of yoga masters Sri T. Krishnamacharya and T. K. V. Desikachar.

Hq: 1005 Moreno Drive, Ojai, CA 93023
Tel: (805) 646 7054
or
International Hq: Sri Krishnamacharya Yoga Mandiram, c/o T. K. V. Desikachar, 10-B 4th Cross Street, Ramakrishna Nagar, Madras 600028, India

Shri Vishva Seva Ashram

The Shri Vishva Seva Ashram was established in India in 1966 and in the United States in the early 1980s by its founder Shri Vishva Hitaishi.

Hq: 45-37 Bowne Street, Flushing, NY
Tel: (212) 939 3549 or 539 4202

World Community

The World Community was founded in the 1970s by Vasudevadas and Devaki-Ma as Prema Dharmasala. It assumed its present name in 1984.

Hq: Route 4, Box 265, Bedford, VA 24523
Tel: (703) 297 5982

World Community Service

World Community Service was founded in India in 1958 by Yogiraj Vethathiri Maharaj, a teacher of kundalini yoga. He brought his movement to America in 1972.

Hq: 926 La Rambala, Burbank, CA 91501
Tel: (818) 848 1509
or
International Hq: 6 Gopalakrishna Iyer Street, T. Nagar, Madras 600017, India

World Plan Executive Council

The World Plan Executive Council can be dated to 1958 when Maharishi Mehesh Yogi emerged from a period of seclusion to lead a Spiritual Regeneration Movement that took him around the globe (including stops in the United States) the following year to introduce the practice of Transcendental Meditation. In 1972 he announced the World Plan which now guides the movement of global transformation and gave the council its name.

The Council does not consider TM to be a religious teaching, but it tends to function as a religion for its followers and has been so treated by the American court system.

Hq: 5000 14th Street, NW, Washington, DC 20011
Tel: (202) 291 0035
or
Maharishi International Movement, Fairfield, IA 52556
Tel: (515) 472 1166
or
International Hq: CH-6446 Seelisberg, Switzerland

Yasodhara Ashram Society

The Society was founded in 1956 in Vancouver, British, Columbia, by Swami Sivananda Radha (Sylvia Hilman), a disciple of Indian teacher Swami Sivananda Saraswati. The Society has many American members from the Northwest and established its primary American center in Idaho.

Hq: Association for the Development of Human Potential/Timeless Books, Box 160, Porthill, ID 83853

or

International Hq: Box 9, Kootenay Bay, BC, Canada V0B 1X0

Yoga Research Foundation

YRF was founded in 1962 by Swami Jyotir Maya Nanda as Sanantan Dharma Mandir. It assumed its present name in 1969.

Hq: 6111 S.W. 74th Avenue, Miami, FL 33143

Tel: (305) 666 2006

Yogi Gupta Association

One of the early yoga groups, the Association was founded in 1954 by Swami Kailashananda (Yogi Gupta).

Hq: 94-15 51st Street, Elmhurst, NY 11373

HINDU TEMPLE ASSOCIATIONS

The Indian-American Hindu community has tended to gather in urban areas and create temples for communal worship. That task is frequently complicated by the natural divisions of Indian religious life. The major division is between north and south India where two distinct calendars prescribe the major festivals to be celebrated on different days. A second major division is between Saivites (who worship Shiva as their main deity) and Vaishnavas (who worship Vishnu). Temples tend first to be built to accommodate either northern or southern worship and then to be dedicated to either an incarnation of Vishnu (such as Rama, Krishna, or Venkateswara) or Shiva. It is easier to accommodate Saivites at a Vaishnava temple and vice-versa, but difficult to accommodate both northern and southern schedules for festivals. In those cities with the larger Indian communities, several temple complexes will generally be built to accommodate the major types of Hindu temple worship, and often sectarian temples (Shaktaite, Swaminarayan, Krishna Consciousness) will appear.

Listed below are functioning temples serving primarily the Indian-American Hindu community. They are listed alphabetically by state.

ARIZONA

Babaji Lingam Temple
5750 W. 8th Street
Yuma, AZ 85364

Hindu Society of Arizona
4725 W. Palo Verde Avenue
Glendale, AZ 85302
Tel: (602) 931 8332

CALIFORNIA

Badarikashrama
15602 Maubert Avenue
San Leandro, CA 94578
Tel: (415) 278 2444

Bellflower Vedic Dharma Samaj
Om Center
9999 Palm Street
Bellflower, CA 90706

Devi Mandir
3100 Pacheco Blvd.
Martinez, CA 94553
Tel: (415) 370 9099

169

**Hindu Community and
Cultural Center**
1395 Heather Lane
Livermore, CA 94550
Tel: (415) 449 6255

Hindu Temple Cultural Center
3676 Delaware Dr.
Fremont, CA 94538
Tel: (415) 659 0655
or 490 9597

**Hindu Temple Society of
Southern California**
1600 Las Virgenes Canyon Rd.
Calabasas, CA 91302

Om Guru Narayanaya Ashram
11896 Firebrand Cr.
Garden Grove, CA 92640
Tel: (714) 750 3356

Palaniswami Sivan Temple
1819 Second St.
Concord, CA 94519
Tel: (415) 827 0127

Radha-Raman Vedic Temple
1022 N. Bradford Avenue
Placentia, CA 92670
Tel: (714) 996 RAMA

Sacramento Hindu Temple
7495 Older Creek Road
Sacramento, CA 95824
Tel: (916) 383 4206
or 927 9147

SAVC Sri Radha-Krishna Temple
2011 E. Chapman Avenue
Fullerton, CA 92631
Tel: (714) 870 1156

**Shree Venkateswara
Swami Temple**
See above: Hindu Temple
Society of S. California

Vedanta Society of Sacramento
1337 Mission Avenue
Carmichael, CA 95608
Tel: (916) 489 5137

Vishwa Shanti Ashram
1901 Fruitvale Avenue
Oakland, CA 94602
Tel: (415) 534 1753

COLORADO

**Hindu Temple Society
of Colorado**
2001 N. Havana
Aurora, CO 80010
Tel: (303) 779 9034

CONNECTICUT

**Connecticut Valley Hindu
Temple Society**
P. O. Box 3201
Hartford, CT 06103
Tel: (203) 658 9319

DISTRICT OF COLUMBIA

Shri Mangal Mandir
Washington, D.C.
Tel: (301) 989 0581,
or 833 0659

FLORIDA

**Hindu Sanatan Dharma
of America, Inc.**
Shanti Temple
1137 31st Street
Orlando, FL 32806
Tel: (407) 648 9003

Hindu Temple of South Florida
5661 Dykes Rd.
Davie, FL 33331
Tel: (305) 680 8571

Sivananda Yoga Vedanta Center
2216 NW 8th Terrace
Fort Lauderdale, FL 33311
Tel: (305) 563 4946

Voice of the Vedas
Florida Vishnu Mandir
4070 S. Golden Rod Road
Orlando, FL 32707

GEORGIA

Hindu Temple
Priest: Dr. Naresh Shastriji
Rt. 2 Luke Rd., Box 3388
Augusta, GA 30909
Tel: (404) 860 3864

Hindu Temple of Atlanta (Balaji)
P. O. Box 298
Riverdale, GA 30274
Tel: (404) 461 3204

**India Cultural and
Religious Center**
1281 Cooper Lake Rd. S.E.
Smyrna, GA 30080
Tel: (404) 436 3719

HAWAII

Iraivan Temple
7345 Kuamoo Rd.
Kauai, HI 96746
Tel: (808) 822 3012

Kadavul Hindu Temple
107 Kaholalele Rd.
Kauai, HI 96746
Tel: (808) 822 3012

ILLINOIS

Balaji Temple
1745 W. Sullivan Road
P. O. Box 1536
Aurora, IL 60507
Tel: (312) 844 2252

Hindu Temple of Greater Chicago
See above: Hindu Temple of
Greater Chicago

Manav Seva Mandir
101 South Church Street
Bensenville, IL 60106
Tel: (312) 860 9797/8

Swaminarayan Temple
1 South 631 Milton Avenue
P. O. Box 2081
Glen Ellys, IL 60138
Tel: (312) 469 1484

Vivekananda Vedanta Society
5423 S. Hyde Park Blvd.
Chicago, IL 60615
Tel: (312) 363 0027

KENTUCKY

Hindu Temple of Kentucky
P. O. Box 22813
4430 Shenandoah Drive
Louisville, KY 40252
Tel: 429 8888

LOUISIANA

**Hindu Temple Society
of New Orleans**
P. O. Box 761
Kenner, LA 70063
Tel: (504) 466 0322
or 469 0910

MARYLAND

India House of Worship
1428 Chilton Dr.
Silver Spring, MD 20904
Tel: (301) 384 4090

Mangala Mandir
1120 Fairland Rd.
Silver Spring, MD 20904
Tel: (301) 384 6980

Mata's Darbar, VHP of America
17225 Founders Mill Drive
Rockville, MD 20855
Tel: (301) 869 3729

**Murugan Temple of
North America**
6300 Princess Garden Parkway
Lanham, MD 20706
Tel: (301) 552 4889

Sri Siva Vishnu Temple
6905 Cipriano Rd.
Lanham, MD 20706

MASSACHUSETTS

New England Hindu Temple
P. O. Box 157
Wellesley Hills, MA 02181

MICHIGAN

Bharatiya Temple
2212 Ridgeline Rd.
Lansing, MI 48912
Tel: (517) 485 1060

Bharatiya Temple
P. O. Box 61
Troy, MI 48099
Tel: (313) 879 2552

Paschima Sri Viswanatha Temple
1147 S. Elms Rd.
Flint, MI 48504

MINNESOTA

Geeta Ashram
10537 Noble Avenue N.
Brooklyn Park, MN 55443

Hindu Society of Minnesota
1835 Polk Street NE
Minneapolis, MN 55418

MISSISSIPPI

**Hindu Temple Society
of Mississippi**
139 Chinquipin Cove
Ridgeland, MS 39157
Tel: (601) 856 4783

NEW JERSEY

Hindu Mandir
1 Gaston Avenue
Garfield, NJ 07026
Tel: (201) 478 9886

Hindu Temple
25 E. Taunton Avenue
Berlin, NJ 08009

Shree Ram Mandir
10 Carlton Rd.
Metuchen, NJ 18840
Tel: (201) 949 0937
or 321 9470

Swaminarayan Temple
4 Louisa Place
Weehawkan, NJ 07087
Tel: (201) 333 5277

United Hindu Temple
208 Powder Mill Rd.
Morris Plains, NJ
Tel: (201) 285 0311

Ved Mandir
1 Ved Mandir Dr.
(off Riva Avenue)
E. Brunswick, NJ 08850
Tel: (201) 821 0404

NEW YORK

Arya Samaj
150-22 Hillside Avenue
Jamaica, NY
Tel: (718) 479 0152

**Capital District Hindu
Temple Society**
450 Albany-Shaker Road
P. O. Box 11650
Loudonville, NY 12211
Tel: (518) 459 7272

Ganesha Temple, Flushing
See above: Swaminarayan
Mission and Fellowship

**Hindu Cultural Society of
Western New York**
1595 North French
Getzville, NY 14068
Tel: (716) 688 6104

Ma Yogashakti Durga Mandir
114-23 Lefferts Blvd.
South Ozone Park, NY 11420
Tel: (718) 641 0402

Saivite Campus Ministry
Swami Lingaye Pasupati
University of Buffalo, NY
34 Embassy Square #1
Tonawanda, NY 14150
Tel: (716) 833 2507

Sri Rajarajeswari Peetam
33 Park Circle
Rochester, NY 14623
Tel: (716) 272 8081

USA Pandit's Parishad, Inc.
89-12 146 Street
Jamaica, NY 11435
Tel: (718) 526 0529

NORTH CAROLINA

Hindu Society of North Carolina
309 Aviation Parkway
Morrisville, NC 27560

OHIO

Bharatiya Temple of Central Ohio
Pres: Harish Chinai
3903 Westerville Road
Columbus, OH 43224
Tel: (614) 459 8673

**Hindu Society of Greater
Cincinnati**
524 Dixmyth Avenue
Cincinnati, OH 45220

Hindu Temple
2615 Lillian Lane
Beavercreek, OH 45324
Tel: (513) 429 4455

Hindu Temple of Toledo
2510 Cotswood Dr.
Toledo, OH 43617
Tel: (419) 841 3109

**Hindu Temple Society of Toledo
and of N.E. Ohio**
6464 Sodom Hutching Rd.
P. O. Box 8042
Youngstown, OH 44505
Tel: (216) 539 4077

Shiva Vishnu Temple
Priest: V. V. Shastri
7733 Ridge Rd.
Box 29508
Parma (Cleveland), OH 44129
Tel: (206) 888 9433

Sri Lakshmi Narayan Temple
6464 Sodom-Hutchings Rd.
Liberty, OH
Tel: (216) 539 4077

PENNSYLVANIA

H.A.R.I. Temple
301 Stigerwalt-Hollow Road
New Cumberland, PA 17070
Tel: (717) 774 7750

Hindu Temple Society
P. O. Box 56
Monroeville, PA 15146
Tel: (412) 327 1799

Pushti Margiya Vaishnav Samaj
R. R. 2, Box 1085
Schuylkill Haven,
PA 17972-9430
Tel: (717) 754 7067

**Sarva Dharma Temple
(Santini Ketan)**
Priest: A. R. Shukla
4200 Airport Road
Allentown, PA 18130
Tel: (215) 264 2810

Sri Dakshinamurti Temple
P. O. Box 1059
Saylorsburg, PA 18535
Tel: (717) 992 2339

Sri Rajarajeswari Peetam
RD 8, Box 8116
Stroundsburg, PA 18360
Tel: (717) 629 0481

Sri Shridi Sai Baba Temple
3744 Old William Penn Highway
Pittsburgh, PA 15235
Tel: (412) 823 1296

Sri Venkateswara Temple
P. O. Box 17280
Pittsburgh, PA 15235
Tel: (412) 373 3380

TENNESSEE

Hindu Temple
P. O. Box 17694
Memphis, TN 38187
Tel: (901) 682 0223

Sri Ganesh Temple
P. O. Box 121438
Nashville, TN 37212
Tel: (615) 356 4182

TEXAS

Hindu Temple of San Antonio
18518 Bandera Road
Helotes, TX 78023
Tel: (512) 695 9400
or 965 9141

Shree Meenakshi Temple
17130 McLean Rd.
Pearland, TX 77584
Tel: (713) 489 0358

HINDU PERIODICALS

The first Hindu periodicals in America were issued by the Vedanta Society. Since 1965, as the Hindu community has expanded, a number of periodicals have appeared, several of outstanding print quality, such as *Back to Godhead* and *Clarion Call*. Unlike the Buddhist periodicals which struggle with a number of languages spoken by their communities, Hindus have adapted quite quickly to English. Listed below are those currently being published, their address, and the name of their sponsoring organization.

The Ajapa Journal, Shri Janardan Ajapa, Yoga Ashram, Box 1731, Placerville, CA 95667, Ajapa Yoga Foundation

American Haidakhan Samaj Newsletter, 104 Blue Drive, Placerville, CA 95667, Haidakhan Samaj

American Meditation Society Newsletter, Box 314, Dresher, PA 19025, American Meditation Society

Aum Aeim Hreem Kleem Chamundayai Vichhe, Box 73, Harbor City, CA 90710-0073, Aum Namo Bhagavate Vasudevaya Foundation

Back to Godhead, Box 18928, Philadelphia, PA 19119-0428, International Society for Krishna Consciousness

Badarikashrama Sandesha, 15602 Maubert Avenue, San Leandro, CA 94578, Badarikashrama

Bulletin, Krishnamurti Foundation, Box 216, Ojai, CA 93023-0216, Krishnamurti Foundation

The Center News, The Vedantic Center, 3528 N. Triunfo Canyon Rd., Agoura, CA 91301, Vedantic Center

Chetana, Box 61, Troy, MI 48099, Bharatiya Temple

Clarity, 14618 Tyler Foote Rd., Nevada City, CA 95959, Ananda

Collaboration, Box 372, High Falls, NY 12440, Matagiri Sri Aurobindo Center

Contact With Vimala Thakar, Vimala Thakar Foundation, Huizerweg 46, 1261 AZ Balricum, Holland, Friends of Vimala Thakar

Crazy Wisdom, 750 Adrian Way, San Rafael, CA 94903, Laughing Man Institute

Darshan, SYDA Foundation, Box 600, South Fallsburg, NY 12779, Siddha Yoga Dham Associates

Dawn, R.R. 1, Box 400, Honesdale, PA 18431, Himalayan Institute Quarterly

Delaware Valley Prout News, Proutist Universal, 228 S. 46th Street, Philadelphia, PA 19139, Ananda Marga Yoga Society

Discover Bhagwan, Swami Anand Vibhaven, 13041 SW Knaus Rd., Lake Oswego, OR 97034, Osho International

The Eleutherian Advocate, 750 Adrian Way, San Rafael, CA 94903, Laughing Man Institute

The Flame of Kriya, 2414 N. Kedzie, Chicago, IL 60647, Temple of Kriya Yoga

The Gandhi Message, Gandhi Memorial Center, 4748 Western Avenue N.W., Box 9515, Washington, D.C. 20016, Self-Realization Church of Absolute Monism

Himalayan International Institute of Yoga Science and Philosophy, R.R. 1, Box 400, Honesdale, PA 18431, Himalayan Institute Quarterly

I Am News, R.D. 3, Box 141, Monroe, NY 10950, Intercosmic Center of Spiritual Awareness

Indian Youth Review, Box 17280, Pittsburgh, PA 15235-0280, Sri Venkateswara Temple

Integral Light, Yoga Research Foundation, 6111 S.W. 74th Avenue, Miami, FL 33143, Yoga Research Foundation

Integral Yoga Magazine, Satchidananda Ashram, Yogaville, Buckingham, VA 23921, Integral Yoga Institute

International Yoga Guide, Yoga Research Foundation, 6111 S.W. 74th Avenue, Miami, FL 33143, Yoga Research Foundation

The ISKCON World Review, 3764 Watseka Avenue, Los Angeles, CA 90034, International Society for Krishna Consciousness

Konarak, Dr. Raj P. Mishra, 1 Camp Court, W. Caldwell, NJ 07006, United Hindu Temple of New Jersey

The Kripalu Experience, P. O. Box 793, Lenox, MA 01242, Kripalu Center for Yoga and Health

The Laughing Man, 750 Adrian Way, San Rafael, CA 94903, Laughing Man Institute

Light of Consciousness, Sacred Mountain Ashram, 3305 County Road 96, Ward, CO 80481-1637, Truth Consciousness

Lila, Box 3384, Los Angeles, CA 90078, Center of Being

The Little Lamp, Nilgiri Press, Box 477, Petaluma, CA 94953, Blue Mountain Center of Meditation

Manadam, Sandeepany West, Box 9, Piercy, CA 9467, Chinmaya Mission (West)

The Mystic Cross, 4748 Western Avenue N.W., Washington, D.C. 20016, Self-Realization Church of Absolute Monism

News from Jain Ashram, 722 Tomkins Avenue, Staten Island, NY 10305, International Nahavir Jain Mission

Newsletter, Box 697, Lombard, IL 60148, Hindu Temple of Greater Chicago

Newsletter, 1600 Las Virgenes Canyon Rd., Calabasas, CA 91302, Hindu Temple Society of Southern California

New Vrindaban Worldwide, R.D. 1, Box 318A, Moundsville, WV 26041, International Society for Krishna Consciousness of West Virginia

Osho Times, 702 32nd Avenue So., Seattle, WA 98144, Osho International

Prana Yoga Life, Box 1037, Berkeley, CA 94701, Prana Yoga Ashram

Purna Yoga, 1291 Weber Street, Pomona, CA 91768, Atmaniketan Ashram

Reflections, Box 8080, Santa Cruz, CA 95061, Avadhut Ashram

Rudra, Box 1973, Cambridge, MA 02238, Nityananda Institute, Inc.

Saptagiri Vana, Box 17280, Pittsburgh, PA 15235-0280, Sri Venkateswara Temple

Satsang, Box 13, Randallstown, MD 21133, Fivefold Path

Sathya Sai Newsletter, 1800 East Garvey Avenue, West Civina, CA 91791, S. A. I. Foundation

Self-Realization, 3880 San Rafael Avenue, Los Angeles, CA 90065, Self-Realization Fellowship

Tawagoto, Box 25839, Prescott Valley, AZ 86312, Hohm

Transformation, SYDA Foundation, Box 600, South Fallsburg, NY 12779, Siddha Yoga Dham Associates

Truth Journal, Lake Rabun Rd., Box 7, Lakemont, GA 30552, Church of the Christian Spiritual Alliance

World Government News, Age of Enlightenment, Distribution, Box 186, Livingston Manor, NY 12758, World Plan Executive Council

Yogashakti Mission Newsletter, 114-23 Lefferts Blvd., South Ozone, NY 11420, Ma Yoga Shakti International Mission

ISLAM AND ISLAM-INSPIRED ORGANIZATIONS

The Islamic World reaches from China and Indonesia across southern Asia to Yugoslavia and West Africa. It is based upon the worship of Allah, the One God, as revealed by Muhammad, his Prophet. Muslims began to arrive in the United States in the nineteenth century and established early communities in the Midwest—Detroit, Toledo, Chicago. In the 1960s the community began to grow dramatically and is now approximately the same size as the Jewish community and is continuing to grow rapidly by immigration and proselytization. Significant in the growth of American Islam has been the conversion of a large number of black people attracted to Islam both as an alternative to Christianity and as a religion of equality and human rights.

While there is some variation in Islam, most noticeably in the division of Sunni and Shi'a, there is a strong sense of boundary. Groups which show some affinity with Islam, or claim membership in the community, but which deny essential beliefs are considered non-Muslim by orthodox Muslims. Sufis, the Muslim mystics, continually find themselves on the border between acceptance and non-acceptance. The various sects which have proclaimed the arrival of the Madhi, such as the Ahmadiyyas, have had to fight for any position in Muslim society. The Nation of Islam, which at one time proclaimed the return of Allah in the person W. Fard Muhammad, were plainly heretical, but have been accepted as they modified their beliefs to accord with orthodox Islam.

INTRAFAITH ORGANIZATIONS

American Muslim Council

The American Muslim Council works to protect the rights of Muslims in the United States.

Hq: 121 New York Avenue, N.W., Ste. 525, Washington, DC 20005

Council of Imams in North America

The Council of Imams was formed in the 1970s to provide fellowship and support among Muslim religious leaders.

Hq: 1810 Pfingsten Road, Northbrook, IL 60002
Tel: (312) 272 0319

179

Council of Islamic Organizations of America

The Council of Islamic Organizations of America is the most inclusive organization for Muslims in the United States.

Hq: Washington, D.C.

Council of the Masajid (Mosques) in the U.S.A.

The Council of the Masajid (Mosques) in the U.S.A. provides coordination for local mosques while promoting a spirit of unity.

Hq: c/o Dawud Assad, Gen. Sec., 99 Woodwiew Dr., Old Bridge, NJ 08857
Tel: (201) 679 8617

Federation of Islamic Associations in the United States and Canada

One of the oldest Muslim intrafaith groups, the Federation of Islamic Associations in the United States and Canada was founded in 1952 by Abdullah Ingram.

Hq: c/o Gen. Sec. Federation Nihad Hamid, 25351 Five Mile Rd., Redford Township, MI 48239

Muslim World League

The Muslim World League is an international association of Muslims with national organizations in many countries.

Hq: 134 W. 26th Street, P. O. Box 1674, New York, NY 10001-1674
Tel: (212) 627 4330
or
International Hq: Mecca, Saudia Arabia

THE ORTHODOX MUSLIM COMMUNITY

Shi'a Muslims

The Shi'a Muslims are the second largest Muslim group. They are the majority in Iran, Iraq, and Pakistan.

Hq: No central address. For information: Islamic Center of Detroit, 15571 Joy Rd., Detroit, MI 48228
Tel: (303) 831 9222
or
Shi'a Association of North America, 108 5363 62nd Dr., Forest Hills, NY 11375

Sunni Muslims

The majority of Muslims, both in the world and in the United States, are Sunnis Muslims.

Hq: No central headquarters. For information: Islamic Center, 2551 Massachusetts Av., N.W., Washington, D.C. 20008
Tel: (202) 332 8343
or
Council of Imams in North America, 1214 Cambridge Crescent, Sarnia, ON, Canada N7S 3W4
or
Federation of Islamic Associations in the U.S.A. and Canada, 25351 Five Mile Road, Redford Township, MI 48239
or
Islamic Society of North America, P. O. Box 38, Plainfield, IN 46168
Tel: (317) 839 8157
Fax: (317) 839 1840
or
The Islamic Circle of North America, P. O. Box 3174, Jamaica, NY 11432
Tel: (718) 658 1199
or
Institute of Islamic Information and Education, P. O. Box 41129, Chicago, IL 60641-0129
Tel: (312) 777 7443

ISLAMIC AND ISLAMIC-INSPIRED ORGANIZATIONS

African Islamic Mission

The African Islamic Mission is a predominantly black Muslim fellowship which emerged in the 1970s.

Hq: 806 St. Johns Pl., Brooklyn, NY
    11216
Tel: (718) 638 4610

Ahmadiyya Anjuman Ishaat Islam, Lahore, Inc.

The Ahmadiyya Anjuman Ishaat Islam, Lahore, Inc. was founded in 1908 by Maulawi Muhammad Ali, a follower of Muslim reformer Hazrat Mirza Ghulam Ahmad. Ali, and present-day Lahore Ahmadiyyas, denied Ahmad any status that would make him an equal of Muhammad and hence lead to the Ahmadiyya's being declared heretical.

Hq: 36911 Walnut Street, Newark, CA
    94560
or
International Hq: Darus Salaam, 5
    Usman Block, New Garden
    Town, Lahore, Pakistan

Ahmadiyya Movement in Islam

The Ahmadiyya Movement in Islam was founded in 1889 by Hazrat Mirza Ghulam Ahmad. It differs from Orthodox Islam in that the members believe Ahmad to be the Promised Messiah promised by Islam and other faiths.

Hq: 2141 Leroy Place, N.W.,
    Washington, D.C. 20008
Tel: (202) 232 3737
or
International Hq: Rabwah, Pakistan

The American Druze Society

The Druze began in the eleventh century when the group's founder, Darasi, proclaimed al-Hakim, the caliph of Egypt, to be God incarnate. The movement survived in Lebanon and was brought to the United States early in this century. The American Druze Society was formed in the 1940s.

Hq: 3718-4th St., N., Arlington, VA
    22203
Tel: (703) 525 8613

American Muslim Mission

The American Muslim Mission continues the Nation of Islam founded by Wallace Fard Muhammad and Elijah Muhammad. Beginning in the 1970s the organization decentralized and moved toward an orthodox Islam perspective.

Hq: Masjid Hon. Elijah Muhammad,
    7351 S. Stony Island Ave.,
    Chicago, IL 60649
Tel: (312) 643 0700
or
Sister Clara Muhammad Foundation,
    634 E. 79th Street, Chicago, IL
    60619

Ansaaru Allah Community

The Ansaaru Allah Community differs from most Muslims in their belief that Muhammad Ahmed Ibn Abdullah (1845-1885) was the Madhi, the successor to the Prophet Muhammad. The belief spread from the Sudan and has found support among American blacks. The Ansaaru Allah Community was founded in the late 1960s as the Nubian Islamic Hebrew Mission.

Hq: 716 Bushwick Avenue, Brooklyn,
    NY 11221
Tel: (718) 455 9749

Arica Institute

The Arica Institute, founded in 1971 by Oscar Ichazo, draws on the Sufi tradition through the teaching of Georgei Gurdjieff.

Hq: 150 Fifth Avenue, New York, NY 10011
Tel: (212) 807 9600

Association of Spiritual Training

The Association of Spiritual Training is a Pakistani-based sufi group.

Hq: c/o Mansoor Ahmad Hashmi, 1600 Plum Street, #33 E, University Village, Fort Collins, CO 80521
Tel: (303) 491 0851
or
International Hq: P. O. Allahhabad, District Rahimyar Khan, Pakistan

Bawa Muhaiyaddeen Fellowship

The Bawa Muhaiyaddeen Fellowship was founded in 1971 by followers of Sri Lankan Sufi master Shaikh Muhaiyaddeen M. R. Guru Bawa.

Hq: 5820 Overbrook Avenue, Philadelphia, PA 19131
Tel: (215) 879 8604

Beshara School of Intensive Esoteric Education

The Beshara School of Intensive Esoteric Education was founded in 1971 to study twelfth century Spanish Sufi master Muhyiddin Ibn'Arabi.

Hq: Box 42238, San Francisco, CA 94101
Tel: (415) 333 8403
or
International Hq: Frilford Grange, Frilford, Abingdon, Oxford, OX13 5NX U.K.

Chishti Order of America

The Chishti Order of America originated in what today is Iran, in the tenth century Persia, and moved its center to India several centuries later. The Chishti Order in America represents the Sabri, one of several important branches of the order. It was brought to America in 1972.

Hq: Current address unavailable for this edition

Claymont Society for Continuous Education

The Claymont Society for Continuous Education was founded in 1971 by students of John Godolphin Bennett, a student of Georgei Gurdjieff.

Hq: Box 112, Charlestown, WV 25414

Gurdjieff Foundation

The Gurdjieff Foundation grew out of the work of spiritual teacher Georgei Gurdjieff. Gurdjieff was in turn partially inspired by the Sufi teachers he met in his travels. The first Foundation was organized by Jeanne de Salzmann in Europe shortly after Gurdjieff's death in 1949. The first American Foundation was opened in 1953 under the leadership of John Pentland, who two years later founded the San Francisco Foundation.

Hq: Box 549, San Francisco, CA 93101
Tel: (415) 587 4951

Habibiyya-Shadhiliyya Sufic Order

The Habibiyya-Shadhiliyya Sufic Order is a Moroccan Sufi Order whose lineage began with Shaykh al-Kamil Sayyedina 'sh-Shaykh Muhammad ibn al-Habib.

4 Hq: c/o Diwan Press, Fields Books Store, 1419 Polk Street, San Francisco, CA 94109.

Hanafi Madh-Hab Center, Islam Faith

The Hanafi Madh-Hab Center, Islam Faith, a predominantly black Muslim group founded in 1958 by Hammas Abdul Khaalis, follows the Hanafi school of the Sunni Muslims. In the 1970s, the movement suffered a series of violent setbacks including an attempted assassination of its leader in which his wife was wounded and several of his children were killed.

Hq: 7700 16th Street, Washington, D.C. 10012

His Highness Prince Aga Khan Shia Imami Ismaili Council for the United States

The Ismaili Shi'a Muslims developed from a split in the Shi'a community in 765 C.E. over which of two claimants to being the chief Imam would be. The Ismailis followed the leadership of Ismail. A schism within the Ismaili community in 1094 resulted in the emergence of the Nizari branch. The leader of this branch is Prince Karim Shah, Aga Khan IV.

Hq: 3021 Margaret Mitchell Drive, Atlanta, GA 30327

Institute for Religious Development

W. A. Nyland, a student of Georgei Gurdjieff, founded the Institute for Religious Development as an independent teaching center in 1960.

Hq: Chardavogne Rd., Warwick, NY 19990

Institute for the Development of the Harmonious Human Being

The Institute for the Development of the Harmonious Human Being was founded in the early 1960s by E. J. Gold, a teacher inspired by the tradition of Georgei Gurdjieff.

Hq: Box 370, Nevada City, CA 95959
Tel: (916) 352 5518

International Association of Sufism

The International Association of Sufism is a Sufi organization which publishes *Sufism*, a quarterly journal.

Hq: P. O. Box 2382, San Rafael, CA 94912
Tel: (415) 472 6859

Jafari-Shadhiliyya Sufic Order

The Jafari-Shadhiliyya Sufic Order is a Pakistani Sufi order under the leadership of Shaykh Fadlalla Haeri.

Hq: c/o Zahra Trust, Box 730, Blanco, TX 78606

Jerrahi Order of America

The Jerrahi Order of America is a branch of a Turkish Sufi order, the Halveti-Jerrahi, currently headed by Sheikh Muzaffer Ozak Al-Jerrahi.

Hq: 864 S. Main St., Spring Valley, NY 10977

Khaniqahi-Nimatullahi

The Khaniqahi-Nimatullahi is an Iranian Sufi Order founded in the fourteenth century by Nur ad-din M. Ni'matullah.

Hq: c/o Leader Dr. Javad Nurbakhsh, 306 W. 11th St., New York, NY 10014
Tel: (212) 924 7739

Mevlana Foundation

The Mevlana Foundation was founded in 1976 by Sufi teacher Reshad Feild.

Hq: Current address unavailable for this edition

Moorish Science Temple of America

The Moorish Science Temple of America, the original modern Black Muslim group, was founded in 1925 by Timothy Drew (Noble Drew Ali).

Hq: 762 W. Baltimore St., Baltimore, MD 21201
Tel: (301) 366 3591

Moorish Science Temple, Prophet Ali Reincarnated, Founder

The Moorish Science Temple, Prophet Ali Reincarnated, Founder was founded in 1975 by Richardson Dingle-El, who claimed to be the reincarnation of Noble Drew Ali, the Temple's original founder.

Hq: 2119 Aiken St., Baltimore, MD 21218

M.T.O. Shahmaghsoudi (School of Islamic Sufism)

The Maktab Tarighat Oveyssi Shahmaghsoudi, or Oveyssi School of Islamic Sufism, traces its history to the prophet Muhammad. It is an Iranian Sufi Order which came to the West in the 1970s.

Hq: P. O. Box 209, Verdago City, CA 91046
Tel: (818) 957 2259

Naqshbandi Sufi Order

The Naqshbandi Sufi Order has its roots in Saudi Arabia and the teachings of Sheikh Nazim Al-Qubrusi.

Hq: c/o Abdal Haqq Sazonoft, 1718 Waukegan Rd., No. 60A, Glenview, IL 60025
Tel: (312) 729 7814
or
International Hq: Sheikh Nazim, c/o Baysal Gülboy, P. O. Box 80, Girne, Mersin, 10, Turkey

The Nation of Islam (The Caliph)

The Nation of Islam (The Caliph) was founded by Emmanuel Abdullah Muhammad, following the death of Elijah Muhammad in 1975. He rejected the changes made in the original Nation of Islam by Wallace D. Muhammad.

Hq: Muhammad's Temple of Islam, No. 1, Baltimore, MD

The Nation of Islam (Farrakhan)

The Nation of Islam (Farrakhan) was founded in 1978 by Abdul Haleem Farrakhan (Louis Eugene Wolcott), a prominent leader who rejected the changes made in Nation of Islam by Wallace D. Muhammad. This is the largest of the several Nation of Islam factions currently in existence.

Hq: 4855 S. Woodlawn Avenue, Chicago, IL 60615
Tel: (312) 324 6000
or
FCN Publishing Co., 734 W. 79th Street, Chicago, IL 60620
Tel: (312) 602 1230

Nation of Islam (John Muhammad)

The Nation of Islam (John Muhammad) was founded in 1978 by John Muhammad.

Hq: 16187 Hamilton Avenue, Highland
    Park, MI 48203
Tel: (313) 342 4574

Nation of Islam
(Silas Muhammad)

The Nation of Islam led by Silas Muhammad rejected the changes in the original Nation of Islam (now the American Muslim Mission) made by Wallace D. Muhammad.

Hq: 4475 Will Lee Road, College Park,
    GA

Prosperos

Prosperos, a group whose practices were inspired by the work of Georgei Gurdjieff, was founded in 1956 by Phez Kahlil and Thane Walker.

Hq: Inner Space Center, Box 5505, El
    Monte, CA 91734
Tel: (213) 438 5105, or 350 3293

Society for Islamic and
Eastern Mysticism

The Society for Islamic and Eastern Mysticism is a Sufi group.

Hq: c/o Society for Preservation and
    Propagation of Eastern Arts,
    Box 6362, Salt Lake City, UT
    84196

Society for the Development of
the Faculties of Man

The Society for the Development of the Faculties of Man is a Sufi group.

Hq: P. O. Box 70046, Los Angeles, CA
    90070

or
P. O. Box 343343, Coral Gables, FL
    33134

Subud

In his writings, Georgei Gurdjieff alluded to a Prophet of Consciousness as a person yet to come. Some felt that Bapak Subuh, an Indonesian teacher, fit the description and sponsored his travel to the West. Integral to his teachings was the practice of *latihan*, surrendering to the power of God.

Hq: 4 Pilot Rd., Carmel, CA 93924

Sufi Islamia Ruhaniat Society

The Sufi Islamia Ruhaniat Society was founded in 1962 by independent Sufi teacher Ahmed Murad Chisti (Samuel L. Lewis).

Hq: 410 Precita Avenue, San Francisco,
    CA
Tel: (415) 285 0562

Sufi Order in the West

The Sufi Order in the West was founded in 1910 by Pir Hazrat Inayat Khan, a representative of the Nizami branch of the Chishti Sufi Order, based in India. The Order is currently led by Pir Hazrat Vilayat Khan.

Hq: Secretariat, Box 574, Lebanon
    Springs, NY 12114
Tel: (518) 794 8181
    or
Omega Institute for Holistic Studies,
    Lake Drive, RD 2, Box 377,
    Rhinebeck, NY 12572
Tel: (914) 338 6030 or 266 4301

MUSLIM PERIODICALS

The Ahmadiyya Gazette, 2141 Leroy Place N.W., Washington, DC 20008, Ahmadiyya Movement in Islam

Al-Ittihad, Box 38, Plainfield, IN 46168 (Sunni)

Al-Nourl, 2551 Massachusetts Ave., Washington, D.C. 20008

The AMC Report, 121 New York Avenue, N.W., Ste. 525, Washington, DC 20005, American Muslim Council

The American Ismaili, 3021 Margaret Mitchell Drive, Atlanta, GA 30327, His Highness Prince Aga Khan Shia Imami Ismaili Council for the United States of America

Ansar Village Bulletin, 719 Bushwick Ave., Brooklyn, NY 11221, Ansaaru Allah Community

The Bulletin, 2551 Massachusetts Avenue, N.W., Washington, DC 20008, The Islamic Center (Sunni)

The Final Call, FCN Publishing Co., 734 W. 79th Street, Chicago, IL 60620, The Nation of Islam (Farrakhan)

God's Light, 5820 Overbrook Ave., Philadelphia, PA 19131, Bawa Muhaiyaddeen Fellowship

Hijrah, Hijrah Publications, P. O. Box 431062, Los Angeles, CA 90043

Husaini News, P. O. Box 6810, Chicago, IL 60645, Husaini Association of Greater Chicago (Shi'a)

187

Islamic Affairs, 172 Vine St. S.W., Atlanta, GA 30314, Islamic Society of Georgia (Shi'a)

Islamic Horizons, Box 38, Plainfield, IN 46168, Muslim Students' Association (Sunni)

The Islamic Review, 36911 Walnut St., Newark, CA 94560, Ahmadiyya Anjuman Ishaat Islam, Lahore, Inc.

The Islamic Review, 108 5363 62nd Dr., Forest Hills, New York, NY 11375, Shia Association of North America

Look and See, 7700 16th St., Washington, DC 20012, Hanafi Madh-hab Center, Islam Faith

The Message, 4380 N. Elston Avenue, Chicago, IL 60641, Muslim Community Center (Sunni)

The Message, Route 15, Box 270, Tucson, AZ 85715, Sufi Order in the West

The Minaret, 434 S. Vermont Avenue, Los Angeles, CA 90020, Islamic Center of Southern California (Sunni)

Moorish Guide, 3810 S. Wabash, Chicago, IL 60653, Moorish Science Temple, Prophet Ali Reincarnated, Founder

Muhammad Speaks, Muhammad's Temple of Islam 1, 1233 W. Baltimore St., Baltimore, MD 21223, The Nation of Islam (The Caliph)

Muhammad Speaks Continues, Muhammad Temple No. 1, 16187 Hamilton Avenue, Highland Park, MI 48203. Nation of Islam (John Muhammad)

The Muslim Journal, 7801 S. Cottage Grove Ave., Chicago, IL 60619, American Muslim Mission

Muslim Star, 25351 Five Mile Road, Redford Twp., MI 48239, Federation of Islamic Associations in the U.S.A. and Canada

The Muslim Sunrise, 2141 Leroy Place N.W., Washington, DC 20008, Ahmadiyya Movement in Islam

Newsletter, 235 Park Ave. South, New York, NY 10003, Arica Institute

Newsletter, Box 5505, El Monte, CA 91734, Prosperos

Our Heritage, 3718 4th Street N., Arlington, VA 22203. American Druze Society

Path of Righteousness, Council of Imams in North America, 1214 Cambridge Crescent, Sarnia, ON, Canada N7S 3W4

Sufi Islamia Ruhaniat Society Newsletter, Box 1066, San Rafael, CA 94915, Sufi Islamia Ruhaniat Society

Talk of the Month, Box 370, Nevada City, CA 95959, Institute for the Development of the Harmonious Human Being

Under the Wings, Route 15, Box 270, Tucson, AZ 85715, Sufi Order in the West

Ziraat, 22 Pillow Rd., Austin, TX 78745, Sufi Order in the West

JUDAISM

Judaism entered what would become the United States immediately after the Dutch lost control of Recife, Brazil, to the Portuguese. The initial group settled in New York City Tel: (then New Amsterdam) and a second group found their way to Newport, Rhode Island. By the time of the American Revolution there were six established congregations. During the nineteenth century, especially after the fall of Napoleon, German Jews within whom the spirit of reform blossomed, arrived and began to develop the Reform Jewish movement. The Germans dominated the community through the century, but their dominance was challenged when the 1881 pogroms in Russia set off a massive wave of immigration of Eastern European Jews. The community grew from several hundred thousand to several million by the time immigration was cut off in the 1920s.

Just as the Reform Jews had created a new form of Judaism, so the new immigrants from Russia Tel: (and other Eastern European countries) created a third form, Conservative Judaism, traditional yet not fully Orthodox. Throughout the twentieth century the Jewish community rallied around the three camps even as other new variations appeared. Two became of special importance. Reconstructionism slowly differentiated itself from Conservative Judaism and has gained a grudging respectability as a fourth form of the faith. Then after world War II, a new wave of Orthodox Jews, the Hassidic mystics, were introduced in great numbers. Thus like the other major religious communities, the Jewish community has had to come to grips with diversity and denominationalism.

While dealing with the divisions within traditional Judaism, the community has also had the problem of confronting non-ethnic Jews adopting Jewish religious beliefs and practices and declaring themselves Jews. The most visible groups are in the black community. Modern day prophets identified themselves and the black community in slavery with the Hebrews in ancient Egypt.

INTRAFAITH ORGANIZATIONS

American Association of Rabbis

The Association, founded in 1978, is a professional organization for rabbis whose ministry is variously located in a synagogue, an educational institution, or in social service.

Hq: 350 Fifth Avenue, Ste. 3308, New York, NY 10001
Tel: (212) 244 3350

Synagogue Council of America

The Synagogue Council provides a place for dialogue and cooperative action for Jewish religious leaders across the major traditions. Its work is supplemented by numerous local rabbinical councils which also cross the Reform, Conservative, orthodox, and Reconstructionist barriers.

Hq: c/o Pres. Rabbi Herbert M. Baumgard, 327 Lexington Avenue, New York, NY 10016
Tel: (212) 686 8670

World Council of Synagogues
Tel: (Conservative)

The World Council of Synagogues is an international fellowship of Conservative Jews.

Hq: Exec. Dir. Bernard Barsky, 155 Fifth Avenue, New York, NY 10010
Tel: (212) 533 7693

World Jewish Congress

The World Jewish Congress has set as its primary mission to foster the unity of the Jewish people worldwide.

Hq: 501 Madison Avenue, 17th Floor, New York, NY 10022
Tel: (212) 755 5770

World Union for Progressive Judaism

The World Union for Progressive Judaism provides a place for fellowship and cooperative action for liberal Jewish leaders worldwide.

Hq: Dir. Mr. Martin Strelzer, 838 Fifth Avenue, New York, NY 10021
Tel: (212) 249 0100

JEWISH CONGREGATIONAL AND RABBINICAL ORGANIZATIONS

Conservative Judaism

The Rabbinical Assembly

The Rabbinical Assembly was formed in 1919.

Hq: 3080 Broadway, New York, NY 10027
Tel: (212) 678 8060

United Synagogue of America

The United Synagogue of America was founded in 1913 by Rabbi Solomon Schechter.

Hq: Pres. Franklin D. Kreutzer, 155 Fifth Avenue, New York, NY 10010
Tel: (212) 533 7800
or
c/o Pres. Rabbi Kassel Abelson, Rabbinical Assembly, 3080 Broadway, New York, NY 10027
Tel: (212) 678 8060

Orthodox Judaism

Rabbinical Alliance of America (Orthodox)

The Rabbinical Alliance of America was founded in 1942.

Hq: c/o Pres. Rabbi Abraham B. Hecht, 156 Fifth Avenue, Ste. 807, New York, NY 10011
Tel: (212) 242 6420

Rabbinical Council of America, Inc. (Orthodox)

The Rabbinical Council of America started in the United States in 1935.

Hq: c/o Pres. Rabbi Milton H. Polin, 275 Seventh Avenue, New York, NY 10001
Tel: (212) 807 7888

Union of Orthodox Jewish Congregations of America

The Union of Orthodox Jewish Congregations in America was founded in 1898.

Hq: c/o Pres. Sidney Kwestel, 45 W. 36th Street, New York, NY 10018
Tel: (212) 563 4000

Union of Orthodox Rabbis of the United States and Canada

The Union of Orthodox Rabbis in the United States and Canada was formed in 1902 to serve the Orthodox rabbis of Eastern European descent.

Hq: c/o Dir. Rabbi Hersh M. Ginsberg, 235 E. Broadway, New York, NY 10002
Tel: (212) 964 6337

Union of Sephardic Congregations

The Union serves Jewish centers of Spanish and Portuguese origins.

Hq: 8 W. 70th Street, New York, NY 10023
Tel: (212) 873 0300

Reconstructionist Judaism

Federation of Reconstructionist Congregations and Havurot

The Federation of Reconstructionist Congregations and Havurot was founded in 1935 by Mordecai M. Kaplan.

194 Religious Bodies in the United States: A Directory

Hq: c/o Pres. Lillian S. Kaplan, 270 W. 89th Street, New York, NY 10024
Tel: (212) 496 2960

Reconstructionist Rabbinical Association (Federation of Reconstructionists and Havurot)

The Reconstructionist Rabbinical Association (Federation of Reconstructionists and Havurot) was founded by Mordecai M. Kaplan.

Hq: c/o Pres. Rabbi Ira Schiffer, Church Road and Greenwood Avenue, Wyncote, PA 19095
Tel: (215) 576 0800

Reform Judaism

Central Conference of American Rabbis (Reform)

The Central Conference of American Rabbis was founded in 1889.

Hq: c/o Pres. Rabbi W. Jack Stern, 21 E. 40th St., New York, NY 10016
Tel: (212) 684 4990

Union of American Hebrew Congregations (Reform)

The Union of American Hebrew Congregations was founded in 1824 by Rabbi Isaac Wise and others.

Hq: c/o Pres. Rabbi Alexander M. Schindler, 838 Fifth Avenue, New York, NY 10021
Tel: (212) 249 0100

OTHER JEWISH AND JEWISH-INSPIRED ORGANIZATIONS

Bluzhever Hasidism

The Bluzhever Hasidism was started by the Shapira family.

Hq: Belzer Bet Midrash, 662 Eastern Pkwy., Brooklyn, NY 11213

Bobov Hasidism

The Bobov Hasidism was founded by Rabbi Benzion Halberstamm.

Hq: Rabbi Solomon Halberstamm, Yeshiva Bnai Zion, 1501 48th Street, Brooklyn, NY 11219
Tel: (718) 853 0086

Bostoner Hasidism

The first Bostoner Hasidic center was opened in the 1920s by Grand Rabbi Pinchas D. Horowitz.

Hq: New England Chasidic Center, 1710 Beacon Street, Brookline, MA 02146
Tel: (617) 734 5100

Bratslav Hasidism

The Bratslav Hasidism was founded in the nineteenth century by the followers of Nachman of Bratslav.

Hq: Bratslav Research Institute, 3100 Brighton 3rd Street, Brooklyn, NY 11238
Tel: (718) 769 0086
or
International Hq: Bratslav Research Institute, c/o Rabbi Chaim Kromer, P. O. Box 3370, Jerusalem, Israel 91038

Chernobyl Hasidism

The Chernobyl Hasidism was founded in the eighteenth century by Mordecai Twersky.

Hq: Rabbi Israel Jacob Twersky, 1520
49th Street, Brooklyn, NY
11232

Church of God and Saints of Christ

The Church of God and Saints of Christ, the first of the black Jewish groups, was founded in 1896 by Elder William S. Crowdy

Hq: Bishop James R. Grant, 10703
Wade Park Avenue, Cleveland,
OH 44106

Church of God (Black Jews)

The Church of God (Black Jews), an early black Jewish nationalist group, was founded in the early twentieth century by F. S. Cherry.

Hq: Current address unavailable for this
edition

Commandment Keepers Congregation of the Living God

The Commandment Keepers Congregation of the Living God was founded in 1924 by Arnold Josiah Ford. It drew much of its inspiration and agenda from the modern rediscovery of the Falashas, the black Jews of Ethiopia.

Hq: 1 W. 123rd Street, New York, NY
10027

Congregation Kehillath Yaakov (Kehilat Jacob)

The Congregation Kehillath Yaakov (Kehilat Jacob), a Neo-Hassidic synagogue, is the center for the international work of Sholomo Carlebach.

Hq: 390 Fort Washington Avenue,
New York, NY 10033

Congregation of New Square (Skver Chasidism)

The Congregation of New Square (Skver Chasidism) was founded in the nineteenth century by Isaac Twersky.

Hq: North Main Street, New Square,
NY 10977

House of Judah

The House of Judah is a predominantly black group now headquartered in rural Alabama. Headquartered for many years in Chicago, it was founded in 1965 by William A. Lewis.

Hq: Current address unavailable for this
edition

Klausenburg Hasidism

The Klausenburg Hasidism was founded in the nineteenth century by the Halberstamm family.

Hq: Current address unavailable for this
edition

Little Synagogue

The Little Synagogue is a Neo-Hassidic/metaphysical center and seminary founded by Rabbi Joseph H. Gelbermann.

Hq: 7 W. 96th Street, New York, NY
11213

Lubavitch Hasidism

Lubavitch Hasidism, the largest of the Hassidic groups currently operating in North America, was brought from Europe in 1940 by Rabbi Joseph Isaac Schneersohn.

Hq: 770 Eastern Pkwy., Brooklyn, NY
11213
Tel: (718) 493 9250

Monastritsh Hasidism

The Monastritsh Hasidism was founded by Jacob Isaac Rabinowicz in the eighteenth century and came to the United States in the early 1920s under the leadership of Rabbi Joshua Hershal Rabinowicz.

Hq: Current address unavailable for this edition

Nation of Yahweh (Hebrew Israelites)

The Nation of Yahweh (Hebrew Israelites) is a predominantly black group founded in the 1970s by Hulon Mitchell Jr. (who is more popularly known by his religious name Yahweh ben Yahweh).

Hq: Temple of Love, 2766 N.W. 62nd St., Miami, FL 33147
Tel: (800) 347 5995

Novominsk Hasidism

The Novominsk Hasidism was founded by Jacob Perlow in the nineteenth century and came to the United States in 1925.

Hq: Rabbi Nahum M. Perlow, 1569 47th Street, Brooklyn, NY 11220
Tel: (718) 633 4861

Original Hebrew Israelite Nation

The Original Hebrew Israelite Nation was founded in the 1960s by G. Parker (Ben Ammi Carter) and Shaleah Ben-Israel.

Hq: Current address unavailable for this edition

Pan African Orthodox Christian Church

The Pan African Orthodox Christian Church is a predominantly black Christian group which draws heavily on Jewish nationalist themes. It was founded in 1953 by Albert B. Cleage, Jr., formerly a minister in the United Church of Christ.

Hq: 13535 Livernois, Detroit, MI 48238
Tel: (313) 491 0777

P'Nai Or Religious Fellowship

The P'Nai Or Religious Fellowship was founded in 1962 by Rabbi Zalman Schachter-Shalomi.

Hq: 6723 Emlen Street, Philadelphia, PA 19119
Tel: (215) 849 5385

Satmar Hasidism

The Satmar Hasidism was founded by Rebbe Yoel Teitelbaum in the early twentieth century and came to the U.S.A. in 1946.

Hq: Congregation Y L D'Satmar, 152 Rodney, Brooklyn, NY 11220

Sha'Arei Orah

The Sha'Arei Orah is a Neo-Hassidic center founded in 1982 by Rabbi David Din.

Hq: 15-A 73 St., New York, NY 10023

Sighet Hasidism

The Sighet Hasidism was founded in the nineteenth century by Rebbe Moses Teitelbaum.

Hq: 152 Hewes St., Brooklyn, NY 11211

Society for Humanistic Judaism

The Society for Humanistic Judaism, which advocates a non-theistic form of Judaism with great emphasis upon ethics, was founded in 1970 by Sherwin T. Wine & Daniel Friedman.

Hq: 28611 W. Twelve Mile Rd., Farmington Hills, MI 48018
Tel: (313) 477 1410

Society of Jewish Science

The Society of Jewish Science, a form of Judaism with some debt to Christian Science, was founded in 1922 by Rabbi Morris Lichtenstein.

Hq: 88 Sunnyside Blvd., Plainview, NY 11803
Tel: (516) 349 0022

Society of the Bible in the Hands of Its Creators, Inc.

The Society of the Bible in the Hands of Its Creators, Inc. was founded in 1943 by Moses Guibbory.

Hq: Current address unavailable for this edition

Stolin Hasidism

The Stolin Hasidism was founded in the early twentieth century by Rabbi Jacob.

Hq: Stolin Bet Midrash, 1818 54th St., Brooklyn, NY 11211

Talnoye (Talner) Hasidism

The Talnoye (Talner) Hasidism was founded in the nineteenth century by David Twersky.

Hq: Rebbe Alexander Twersky, Talner Beth David, 64 Corey Rd.. Brookline, MA 02146

United Hebrew Congregations

The United Hebrew Congregations, a predominantly black group, was founded in the mid-1970s by Rabbi Naphtali Ben Israel.

Hq: Current address unavailable for this edition

United Israel World Union

The United Israel World Union was founded in 1943 by David Horowitz.

Hq: 1123 Broadway, New York, NY 10010

JEWISH PERIODICALS

There are hundreds of periodicals serving the larger Jewish community. This list is limited to those of the religious Jewish community.

Conservative Judaism, 3080 Broadway, New York, NY 10027, Conservative Judaism

Humanistic Judaism, 28611 W. Twelve Mile Road, Farmington Hills, MI 48018, Society for Humanistic Judaism

Jewish Action, 45 W. 36th St., New York, NY 10018, Orthodox Judaism

Jewish Science Interpreter, Box 484, Plainview, NY 11803, Society of Jewish Science

Journal of Reform Judaism, 21 E. 40th St., New York, NY 10016, Reform Judaism

Kabbalah for Today, 7 W. 96th Street, Ste. 19B, New York, NY 10025, The Little Synagogue

The New Menorah, 6723 Emlen Street, Philadelphia, PA 19119, P'nai Or Religious Fellowship

The Reconstructionist, 270 W. 89th Street, New York, NY 10024

Reform Judaism, 838 Fifth Avenue, New York, NY 10021

Talks and Tales, 770 Eastern Parkway, Brooklyn, NY 11213, Lubavitcher Hassidism

Tradition, 275 Seventh Avenue, New York, NY 10001, Orthodox Judaism

The Uforatzto Journal, 700 Eastern Parkway, Brooklyn, NY 11213, Lubavitcher Youth Organization

United Synagogue Review, 155 Fifth Avenue, New York, NY 10010, Conservative Judaism

Yahweh Magazine, 2766 N.W. 62nd Street, Miami, FL 33147, Nation of Yahweh

LATTER-DAY SAINTS

The Latter-day Saint groups are all products of the new revelation received by Joseph Smith, Jr., beginning in the 1820s. The basic revelation is contained in the Book of Mormon, with supplementary material in several other books, the Doctrines and Covenant and the Pearl of Great Price. He also began a new edited version of the Bible, the Inspired Version, which is used by some of the groups that resulted from the new religious current he unleashed.

In 1944 Smith was assassinated. The largest percentage of his followers followed Brigham Young to Utah and created what we know today as the Church of Jesus Christ of Latter-day Saints. The great majority of Latter-day Saints are members of that single church body. Some of the Saints remained in the midwest and eventually reorganized and established headquarters at Independence, Missouri. Known today as the Reorganized Church of Jesus Christ of Latter Day Saints, they constitute the next largest church. A third significant faction settled in Independence where they purchased the lot Smith had designated as the cite for the building of the Saint's Temple. In both Utah and Missouri, numerous factions developed. The most important of the splinter groups are those which continue the practice of polygamy.

The majority of churches which have separated from the Missouri and Utah church have ceased to exist, however a number continue. The Reorganized Church has recently suffered the loss of a number of its more conservative members in protest of changes in the church.

Aaronic Order

The Aaronic Order is a communal group founded in 1942 by Dr. Maurice Lerrie Glendenning.

Hq: Box 7095, Murray, UT 84107
Tel: (801) 262 1668

Apostolic United Brethren

The Apostolic United Brethren is a polygamy-practicing group founded in 1975 by Joseph White Musser and former members of the United Order Effort.

201

Hq: 3139 W. 14700 S. #A. Bluffsdale, UT 84065

Center Branch of the Lord's Remnant

The Center Branch of the Lord's Remnant was founded in 1984 by Robert Baker and former members of the Reorganized Church of Jesus Christ of Latter Day Saints.

Hq: 709 W. Maple, Independence, MO 64050

Tel: (816) 224 3102

Christ's Church

Christ's Church is a polygamy-practicing church founded in 1978 by Gerald W. Peterson, Sr., and former members of the Apostolic United Brethren

Hq: Current address unavailable for this edition

Church of Christ at Halley's Bluff

The Church of Christ at Halley's Bluff (also known as the Church of Christ at Zion's Retreat) was formed in 1932 by former members of the Church of Christ (Temple Lot) led by Thomas B. Nerren and E. E. Long.

Hq: Schell City, MO 64783

Church of Christ (Fetting/Bronson)

The Church of Christ (Fetting/Bronson) is one of two groups which trace their history to Otto Fetting and accept the new revelations which were being received by him. In the 1950s the church split, in part due to the advocacy of sabbatarianism by S. T. Bronson. Bronson's followers organized as the Church of Christ (Fetting/Bronson).

Hq: 1138 East Gudgell, Independence, MO 64055

Tel: (816) 461 4844

Church of Christ Immanuel

The Church of Christ Immanuel was founded in 1975 by former members of the Church of Christ (Temple Lot) in Flint, Michigan.

Hq: 1308 Davison Rd., Davison, MI 48423

Church of Christ, Nondenominational Bible Assembly

The Church of Christ, Nondenominational Bible Assembly emerged during a period of trial between the Reorganized Church of Jesus Christ of Latter Day Saints and the Church of Christ (Temple Lot). Under the leadership of Pauline Hancock, a group of Temple Lot members began to meet and in their study developed numerous disagreements with the Latter-day Saint position. Over the next decade they formed a new congregation and grew ever more critical of the teaching in which they had been raised. Finally, they converted to evangelical Christianity and have actively proselytized among Latter-day Saint groups.

Hq: 1515 S. Harvard, Independence, MO 64052

Church of Christ (Restored)

The Church of Christ (Restored) was founded in 1929 by Otto Fetting, an apostle of the Church of Christ (Temple Lot), whose revelations had been rejected by that church's leaders. With his supporters, he founded another church and continued to receive new revelations.

Hq: Mr. Uel Sisk, 609 C Lilac Place, John Knox Village, Lee's Summit, MO 64063

Church of Christ (Temple Lot)

The Church of Christ (Temple Lot) was founded in 1866 by Granville Hedrick and other followers of Joseph Smith who did not join either the Utah church or the Reorganized Church of Jesus Christ of Latter Day Saints.

Hq: Apostle William A. Sheldon, 1011 Cottage, Independence, MO 64050
Tel: (816) 833 3995

Church of Christ "With the Elijah Message", Established Anew in 1929

The Church of Christ "With the Elijah Message", Established Anew in 1929 was founded in 1943 by W. A. Draves and former members of the Church of Christ (Restored) who accepted the new revelations Draves was receiving at the time.

Hq: 608 Lacy Road, Independence, MO 64050
Tel: (816) 252 2343

Church of Jesus Christ (Bickertonite)

The Church of Jesus Christ (Bickertonite) was founded in 1875 by William Bickerton and followers of Joseph Smith's revelation in the Eastern United States.

Hq: Sixth and Lincoln Sts., Monogahela, PA 15603
Tel: (412) 258 3066

Church of Jesus Christ (Bulla)

The Church of Jesus Christ (Bulla) was founded in the early 1980s by Art Bulla, a former member of the Church of Jesus Christ of Latter-day Saints.

Hq: Current address unavailable for this edition

Church of Jesus Christ (Cutlerite)

The Church of Jesus Christ (Cutlerite) was founded in 1853 by Alpheus Cutler, a Mormon leader at the time Joseph Smith was killed.

Hq: 819 S. Cottage St., Independence, MO 64050

Church of Jesus Christ of Latter-day Saints

The Church of Jesus Christ of Latter-day Saints is the largest branch of the movement which resulted from the prophetic work of Joseph Smith, Jr. The church has become an international body with more than six million members.

Hq: 50 E. North Temple, Salt Lake City, UT 64051

Church of Jesus Christ of Latter-day Saints (Strangite)

The Church of Jesus Christ of Latter-day Saints (Strangite) was founded in 1845 by James Jesse Strang, a church leader in Wisconsin at the time Joseph Smith, Jr., was killed. He received a set of revelations which became authoritative for his church.

Hq: Vernon Swift, Box 522, Artesia, NM 88210

Church of Jesus Christ of Latter-day Saints (Strangite, Drew)

See: Church of Jesus Christ (Strangite, Drew)

Church of Jesus Christ of the Saints in Zion

The Church of Jesus Christ of the Saints in Zion was founded in 1984 by Roger Billings, formerly a member of the Church of Jesus Christ of Latter-day Saints.

Hq: Current address unavailable for this edition

Church of Jesus Christ (Strangite, Drew)

The Church of Jesus Christ (Strangite, Drew) was founded in 1955 by Theron Drew and some members of the Church of Jesus Christ (Strangite) who were attracted to the work of Merl Kilgore, the leader of the Zion's Order of the Sons of Levi.

Hq: 35315 Chestnut, Burlington, WI 53105

Church of Jesus Christ (Toney)

The Church of Jesus Christ (Toney) was founded in the 1980s by Forrest Toney, a former member of the Reorganized Church of Jesus Christ of Latter Day Saints. Toney disagreed with some of the recent changes made by order of the President of the Reorganized Church

Hq: Box 3565, Kansas City, MO 64134

Church of Jesus Christ (Zion's Branch)

The Church of Jesus Christ (Zion's Branch) was founded in 1984 by Robert Cato, a former member of the Reorganized Church of Jesus Christ of Latter Day Saints.

Hq: 108 S. Pleasant, Independence, MO
Tel: (816) 254 7160

Church of the First Born of the Fullness of Times

The Church of the First Born of the Fullness of Times is a polygamy-practicing group founded in 1955 by Joel LeBaron and several of his brothers. The family had associated with Mormon polygamists who resided in Mexico (where the practice had been tolerated) for a number of years.

Hq: 5854 Mira Serana, El Paso, TX 79912

Church of the Lamb of God

The Church of the Lamb of God is a polygamy-practicing group founded in 1970 by Ervil LeBaron, the brother of Joel LeBaron and formerly the Patriarch of the Church of the First Born of the Fullness of Times. In an effort to exercise control of the whole polygamist community, mem-bers of this church became involved in a number of murders and the group's present status is in doubt.

Hq: Current address unavailable for this edition

Church of the New Covenant in Christ

The Church of the New Covenant in Christ was founded in the 1980s as the Evangelical Church of Christ by John W. Bryant, formerly a member of the Apostolic United Brethren. Over the years Bryant became convinced that the patriarchal nature of the polygamous life was wrong. His changed opinions led to a reorganization of his family and the church under its present name in the mid-1980s.

Hq: Box 3910, Salem, OR 97302

Churches of Christ in Zion

The Churches of Christ in Zion was founded in 1979 by Robert W. Chambers, formerly a member of the Reorganized Church of Jesus Christ of Latter Day Saints who disagreed with some of the recent changes in the Reorganized Church.

Hq: 18713 E. 30th Terrace, Independence, MO 64057

Confederate Nations of Israel

The Confederate Nations of Israel is a polygamy-practicing group founded in 1978 by Alexander Joseph, formerly a member of the Apostolic United Brethren.

Hq: Presiding King Alexander Joseph, Long Haul, Box 151, Big Water, UT 94741

Holy Church of Jesus Christ

The Holy Church of Jesus Christ was founded in the 1970s by Alexandre Roger Caffiaux, a Frenchman and a prophet who became a member of the Church of Jesus Christ of Latter-day Saints (Strangite). Rejected by the Strangite leadership, he reorganized his following into a new church.

Hq: Current address unavailable for this edition

Millennial Church of Jesus Christ

The Millennial Church of Jesus Christ was founded in the mid-1980s by Leo Peter Evoniuk LeBaron, who claimed succession to Ervil LeBaron's Church of the Lamb of God.

Hq: Leo Peter Evoniuk LeBaron, 177 Webster Street, Monterey, CA 93940

Reorganized Church of Jesus Christ of Latter Day Saints

The Reorganized Church of Jesus Christ of Latter Day Saints was founded in 1860 by Jason Briggs, Zenos Gurley, and William Marks and followers of Joseph Smith, Jr., who decided against migrating to Utah during the 1850s.

Hq: World Church Secretary, W. Grant McMurray, The Auditorium, Box 1059, Independence, MO 64051
Tel: (816) 833 1000

Restoration Branches Movement

The Restoration Branches Movement was founded in the mid-1980s by conservative members of the Reorganized Church of Jesus Christ of Latter Day Saints who rejected the "liberal" direction it was taking as it moved toward a Protestant theological perspective and approved the ordination of women.

Hq: No central address. For information: Price Publishing Company, 207 W. Southside Blvd., Independence, MO 64055
Tel: (816) 461 5659

Restored Church of Jesus Christ (Walton)

The Restored Church of Jesus Christ (Walton) was founded in 1977 by Eugene O. Walton, a former member of the Reorganized Church of Jesus Christ of Latter Day Saints.

Hq: Box 1651, Independence, MO 64055

Sons Ahman Israel

Sons Ahman Israel is a polygamy-practicing group which has some gnostic and magical ideas. It was founded in 1981 by Patriarch David

Israel and other former members of the Church of Jesus Christ of Latter-day Saints.

Hq: SAI Acres, Fredonia, AZ 86022

True Church of Jesus Christ Restored

The True Church of Jesus Christ Restored was founded in 1974 by David L. and Denise Roberts. Roberts, formerly associated with the Church of Christ (Temple Lot) experienced a series of revelations which have become the basis of the new church he founded.

Hq: 1533 E. Mechanic, Independence, MO 64050

United Order Effort

The United Order Effort, the largest of the polygamy-practicing groups, was founded in 1929 by Lorin C. Woolley. Its center is the community of Colorado City, Arizona.

Hq: Colorado City, AZ 86021

Zion's Order, Inc.

The Zion's Order, Inc. is a communal group founded in 1953 as Zion's Order of the Sons of Levi by Dr. Marl Kilgore, formerly a member of the Aaronic Order. The group assumed its present name in 1975.

Hq: Route 2, Box 104-7, Mansfield, MO 65704

LATTER-DAY SAINT PERIODICALS

Aaron's Star, P. O. Box 7095, Salt Lake City, UT 84197, Aaronic Order

The Church News, 30 E. 100 South, Salt Lake City, UT 84110, Church of Jesus Christ of Latter-day Saints

Deseret News, Box 1257, Salt Lake City, UT 84110, Church of Jesus Christ of Latter-day Saints

Ensign, 50 East Temple Street, Salt Lake City, UT 84150, Church of Jesus Christ of Latter-day Saints

Evening and Morning Star, 2/82 Banbury Road, Oxford, OX2 6JT England, Sons Ahman Israel

The Friend, 50 East Temple Street, Salt Lake City, UT 84150, Church of Jesus Christ of Latter-day Saints

The Gospel Herald, c/o Mr. Uel Sisk, 609 C Lilac Place, John Knox Village, Lee's Summit, MO 64063, Church of Christ (Restored)

Gospel News, 8423 Boettner Road, Bridgewater, MI 84115, Church of Jesus Christ (Bickertonite)

New Era, 50 East Temple Street, Salt Lake City, UT 84150, Church of Jesus Christ of Latter-day Saints

Restoration Voice, Box 1611, Independence, MO 64055, (unofficial) Restoration Branches Movement

Quarterly Report, Box 1774, Independence, MO 64055, (unofficial) Restoration Branches Movement

Saints Herald, Box 1059, Independence, MO, 64051, Reorganized Church of Jesus Christ of Latter Day Saints

Stone Magazine, c/o SAI Acres, Fredonia, AZ 86022, Sons Ahman Israel

Sunstone, 331 S. Rio Grande St., Ste. 30, Salt Lake City, UT 84101, Independent

The Voice of Eternal Life, 1533 East Mechanic, Independence, MO 64050, True Church of Jesus Christ Restored

The Voice of Peace, 608 Lacy Road, Independence, MO 64050, Church of Christ "With the Elijah Message," Established Anew in 1929

The Voice of Warning, 1138 E. Gudgell, Independence, MO 64055, Church of Christ (Fetting/Bronson)

The Witness, 410 N. Pleasant, Independence, MO 64050, Church of Jesus Christ (Zion's Branch)

Zion's Advocate, Box 492, Independence, MO 64051, Church of Christ (Temple Lot)

Zion's Trumpet, Box 1651, Independence, MO 64055, Restored Church of Jesus Christ (Walton)

METAPHYSICAL/ANCIENT WISDOM/NEW AGE

The term "metaphysical" refers to groups that share a basic characteristic in searching for a reality above and beyond the common sense phenomenal world, and having found it, to apply their discovery in a practical manner. The metaphysical quest is as old as humankind, but in the eighteenth century it received a newer and more practical twist in the work of such people as Franz Anton Mesmer and Emanuel Swedenborg. During the nineteenth century, numerous spiritual explorers expanded upon their basic insights and created a host of new movements and organizations—the Theosophical Society, the National Spiritualist Association, the Hermetic Order of the Golden Dawn—to mention a few.

From these older organizations literally hundreds of groups, mostly small, the largest reaching only a few hundred thousand, emerged. Waves of interest swept across the country like the ocean tide on the shore only to recede a few years later. The latest wave, to which the name New Age Movement has been given, has been the most successful of all in generating interest and pushing the metaphysical concerns into mainstream culture.

In considering the many groups produced by the metaphysical movement, it is helpful to know a few terms which are used in the descriptions:

—Channeling: A process for contacting spirit entities, the deceased or the Masters (evolved beings), which is substantively the same as what used to be called mediumship.

—Magic(k): Often spelled with a "k" to distinguish it from stage magic, magick is the ability to command the powers undergirding the cosmos and use them as one wills.

—New Age: The New Age movement is a metaphysical movement which developed in the 1970s that looks for both personal transformation and social transformation in the near future.

—Neo-Paganism: A religion based upon the worship of the ancient pre-Christian deities of Europe and the Mediterranean Basin. Wicca is the most popular but by no means the only form of Neo-Paganism.

—New Thought: A healing movement based in the search for oneness with the universe or God which developed out of Christian Science in the late nineteenth century.

—Occult: Literally "that which is hidden." Occult realities are those structures and forces believed to undergird the universe. They are perceived and utilized by the various occult practices.

—Satanism: The belief in Satan as the ruling force or deity in this world.

—Spiritualism: A movement which began in the 1840s centered upon the contact with the spirits of the deceased through the activity of special people called mediums.

—Theosophical: Refers to the occult teachings of Madame Helena P. Blavatsky, co-founder of the Theosophical Society (1875), and those who followed her.

—Wicca: A religion built on the worship of nature usually personified as the Great Mother Goddess and her consort the Horned God. Wicca, or Witchcraft is to be sharply distinguished from Satanism.

INTRAFAITH ORGANIZATIONS

International New Thought Alliance

The International New Thought Alliance was founded in 1906 though it has its roots in other attempts to create an umbrella organization for New Thought churches and centers.

Hq: 5003 E. Broadway Road, Mesa, AZ 85206
Tel: (602) 830 2461

METAPHYSICAL/ANCIENT WISDOM/NEW AGE ORGANIZATIONS

Abbey of Théleme

The Abbey of Théleme is a magical group based upon the teachings of Aleister Crowley.

Hq: P. O. Box 666, Old Greenwich, CT 06870

Academy for Future Science

The Academy for Future Science was founded by J. J. Hurtak as a community to conduct research into the ancient metaphysical communities (termed communities of "Light") as an aid in the process of self-realization.

Hq: 17532 Santa Cruz Hwy., Los Gatos, CA 95030

Adventures in Enlightenment, a Foundation

The Adventures in Enlightenment, a Foundation is a New Age ministry founded in 1985 by Terry Cole-Whitaker, formerly a leading minister with the United Church of Religious Science.

Hq: Box 258, Rochester, WA 98579
Tel: (206) 273 8861

Aetherius Society

The Aetherius Society is a UFO contactee organization founded in 1954 by George King, a channel for messages from extraterrestrial leadership.

Hq: 6202 Afton Place, Hollywood, CA 90028
Tel: (213) 465 9652 or 467 HEAL

African Theological Archministry

The African Theological Archministry has tried to create a place for the practice of the ancient polytheistic magical faith of the Yoruban (Nigeria) people. Centered upon the village of Oyotunji, in rural South Carolina, it is led by King Oba Efuntola Oseijeman Adelabu Adefunmi I (Walter Eugene King).

Hq: Oyotunji African Yoruba Village, Box 51, Sheldon, SC 29941
Tel: (803) 846 8900 or 846 9939

The Afro-American Social Research Association

The Afro-American Social Research Association was founded in the 1970s by a channel called "Spirit of Truth."

Hq: Box 2150, Jacksonville, FL 32203

Agasha Temple of Wisdom

The Agasha Temple of Wisdom was founded in 1943 by Spiritualist medium Rev. Richard Zenor.

Hq: Box 5012, West Hills, CA 91308
Tel: (818) 762 3862 or (213) 464 6252

Agni Yoga Society

The Agni Yoga Society was founded in the mid-1920s by theosophists Nicholas and Helena Roerich.

Hq: 319 W. 107th Street, New York, NY 10025
Tel: (212) 864 7752

Aletheia Foundation

The Aletheia Foundation was formed in 1958 by Jack Schwarz to assist people with the development of their psychic/spiritual self and to find total health.

Hq: 1809 N. Highway 99, Ashland, OH 97520
Tel: (503) 488 0209

Alexandrian Wicca

Alexandrian Wicca, a revised form of Gardnerian Wicca, was created in the 1960s by British witch Alexander Sanders.

Hq: No central address

Algard Wicca

The Algard Wicca was founded in 1972 by Mary Nesnick.

Hq: Current address unavailable for this edition

American Catholic Church

The American Catholic Church was founded as an independent Catholic jurisdiction in 1915 by Archbishop Joseph Rene Vilatte. It came under theosophical influence in the 1930s and moved into the theosophical Liberal Catholic Church orb, where it has remained.

Hq: Most Rev. Simon Eugene Talarczyk, 430 Park Avenue, Laguna Beach, CA 92651

American Gnostic Church

The American Gnostic Church is a thelemic magick group following the teachings of magician Aleister Crowley founded in 1985 by Rev. James M. Martin.

Hq: Box 1219, Corpus Christi, TX 78403

American Order of the Brotherhood of Wicca

The American Order of the Brotherhood of Wicca was founded in the 1970s by Lady Sheba (Jessie Wicker Bell). It was one of the first groups to publish its secret magical rituals.

Hq: Current address unavailable for this edition

American Raelian Movement

The Raelian movement grew out of the experience of Claude Vorilhon (Raël) who claims that in 1973 he was contacted by space beings and told to spread a message of Peace, Love, and Fraternity.

Hq: Griffith Station, P. O. Box 661218, Los Angeles, CA 90066
or
North American Hq: Canadian Raelian Movement, P. O. Box 86, Youville Station, PQ, Canada H2P 2V2
or
International Hq: CP225, CH-1441, Geneva 8, Switzerland

Amica Temple of Radiance

The Amica Temple of Radiance was founded in the 1930s by Ivah Bergh Whitten, a teacher who emphasized the metaphysical properties of color.

Hq: 763 S. 53rd Street, Tacoma, WA 98408

Ancient Mystical Order of the Rosae Crucis

The Ancient Mystical Order of the Rosae Crucis, the largest of the modern Rosicrucian orders, was founded in 1915 by H. Spencer Lewis.

Hq: Rosicrucian Park, San Jose, CA 95191
Tel: (800) 88 AMORC

Ann Ree Colton Foundation of Niscience

The Ann Ree Colton Foundation of Niscience, a New Age metaphysical group, was founded in 1953 by Ann Ree Colton and Jonathan Murro.

Hq: 336 W. Colorado Blvd., Glendale, CA 91209
Tel: (818) 244 0113

Anthroposophical Society

The Anthroposophical Society began in 1912 when Rudolf Steiner, the head of the German Section of the Theosophical Society, led a revolt that resulted in most of the Section reorganizing under his leadership. The Society follows the voluminous teachings of Steiner, one of the most learned and impressive of modern occult teachers.

Hq: 529 W. Grant Place, Chicago, IL 60614
Tel: (312) 248 5606
or

International Hq: Goetheanum, Postfach 98, 4143 Dornach, Switzerland

Aquarian Educational Group

The Aquarian Educational Group is a Christian theosophical group founded in 1963 by Haroutiun Saraydarian.

Hq: Box 267, Sedona, AZ 86336
Tel: (602) 282 2655

Aquarian Foundation

The Aquarian Foundation was founded in 1955 by Spiritualist medium Keith Milton Rhinehart.

Hq: Rev. Keith Milton Rhinehart, 315 - 15th Avenue E., Seattle, WA 98112
Tel: (206) 324 6046

Aquarian Tabernacle Church

The Aquarian Tabernacle Church is a Wiccan fellowship founded in 1979 by Rev. Pete Davis and others.

Hq: Box 85507, Seattle, WA 98145

Arcana Workshops

The Arcana Workshops is a full-moon meditation group based upon the teachings of theosophist Alice A. Bailey.

Hq: Box 605, Manhattan Beach, CA 90266-0506
Tel: (213) 379 9990 or 540 8689

Arcane School

The Arcane School was founded in 1923 by theosophists Alice and Foster Bailey. Its teachings were channeled from a master, The Tibetan.

Hq: 113 University Place, 11th Floor, Box 722, Cooper Station, New York, NY 10276
Tel: (212) 982 8770

The Asatru Alliance

The Asatru Alliance emerged in the late 1980s with the reorganization of former members of the Asatru Free Assembly, which had been disbanded in 1987.

Hq: P. O. Box 961, Payson, AZ 85547

Ascended Master Teachings Foundation

The Ascended Master Teachings Foundation was founded in 1980 by Werner Schroeder to perpetuate the teachings of the "I AM" movement.

Hq: Box 466, Mount Shasta, CA 96067

Association for Research and Enlightenment

The Association for Research and Enlightenment was founded in 1931 to carry forth the work begun by psychic Edgar Cayce. Its teachings are built around the transcripts of Cayce's trance sessions, which are on file at the Association headquarters.

Hq: Box 595, Virginia Beach, VA 23451
Tel: (804) 428 3588

Association of Sananda and Sanat Kumara

The Association of Sananda and Sanat Kumara was founded in 1965 by New Age channel Sister Thedra (Dorothy Martin).

Hq: Box 35, Mount Shasta, CA 96067

Astara

Astara is an occult fellowship built on hermetic perpsective founded in 1951 by Robert and Earlyne Chaney.

Hq: 800 W. Arrow Hwy., Box 5003, Upland, CA 91785
Tel: (714) 981 4941

Aurum Solis

The Aurum Solis is a magical order founded in 1897 by Charles Kingold and George Stanton and brought to the United States in the 1970s by popular occult authors Melita Denning and Osborne Phillips (Vivian and Leonard B. Barcynski).

Hq: c/o The Administrator General, Box 43383-OSV, St. Paul, MN 55164

Ausar Auset Society

The Ausar Auset Society was founded in the mid-1970s by R. A. Straughn. It began as a chapter of the Rosicrucian Anthroposophical League and operates primarily in the black community in the greater New York City metropolitan area.

Hq: c/o Oracle of Truth, Box 281, Bronx, NY 10462

Brotherhood of the White Temple

The Brotherhood of the White Temple is an occult order founded in 1930 by Morris Doreal.

Hq: Sedalia, CO 80135

Brothers of the Earth

The Brothers of the Earth is a Neo-Pagan brotherhood founded in 1983 by Gary Lingen.

Hq: Church of the Earth, Box 13158, Dinkytown Station, Minneapolis, MN 55414

Builders of the Adytum

The Builders of the Adytum grew out of the American branch of the Hermetic Order of the Golden Dawn. It was founded in the early twentieth century by Paul Foster Case.

Hq: 5105 N. Figueroa, Los Angeles, CA 90042
Tel: (213) 255 7141

The Catholic Church of the Antiochean Rite

The Catholic Church of the Antiochean Rite is a Christian gnostic theosophical jurisdiction founded in the 1980s by Most Rev. Roberto C. Toca, Archbishop Primate of the church.

Hq: Box 8473, Tampa, FL 33674-8473
Tel: (813) 248 9145

Chirotesian Church of Faith

The Chirotesian Church of Faith is a metaphysical church founded in 1917 by Rev. D. J. Bussell.

Hq: 1757 N. Normandie, Los Angeles, CA 90027
Tel: (213) 662 0657

Christ Ministry Foundation

The Christ Ministry Foundation is a metaphysical ministry founded in 1935 by Eleanor Mary Thedick.

Hq: c/o The Seivertsons, 2411 Roland Rd., Sacramento, CA 95821

Christ Truth League

The Christ Truth League is a metaphysical ministry perpetuating the teachings of early New Thought writer H. B. Jeffery. It was founded in 1938 by Alden and Nell Truesdell.

Hq: 2400 Canton Dr., Fort Worth, TX 76112
Tel: (817) 451 2612

Christian Assembly

The Christian Assembly began as the San Jose Home of Truth, a New Thought metaphysical center, founded in 1900 by William Farwell.

Hq: 72 N. 5th Street, San Jose, CA
  95112
Tel: (408) 280 0500

Christian Spirit Center

The Christian Spirit Center, a Brazilian Spiritist organization, was founded by S. J. Haddad.

Hq: Box 114, Elon College, NC 27244

Christward Ministry

The Christward Ministry is a New Age occult fellowship founded in 1940 by Flower A. Newhouse.

Hq: Route 5, Box 206, Escondido, CA
  92025

Church and School of Wicca

The Church and School of Wicca, one of the largest of Wiccan groups in America, was founded in the early 1970s by Gavin and Yvonne Frost.

Hq: Box 1502, New Bern, NC 28560

Church of All Worlds

The Church of All Worlds is a Neo-Pagan fellowship founded in 1968 by Tim Zell and Lance Christie.

Hq: Box 1542, Ukiah, CA 95482

Church of Antioch

The Church of Antioch, an independent theosophical Catholic church, was founded in the 1930s by Archbishop Robert Raleigh (Justin A. Boyle).

Hq: Most Rev. Herman Adrian Spruit,
  Box 1015, Mountain View, CA
  94042
Tel: (408) 249 7846

Church of Christ, Scientist

The Church of Christ, Scientist, known for its unique teachings on spiritual healing, was founded in 1879 (reorganized in 1892) by Mary Baker Eddy.

Hq: Christian Science Center, 175
  Huntington Avenue, Boston, MA
  02115
Tel: (617) 262 2300

Church of Circle Wicca

The Church of Circle Wicca is an eclectic Wiccan/Neo-Pagan network/ group founded in 1975 by Selena Fox.

Hq: Sanctuary, Box 219, Mt. Horeb, WI
  53572
Tel: (608) 924 2216

Church of Cosmic Origin and School of Thought

The Church of Cosmic Origin and School of Thought was founded in 1963 by medium Hope Troxell.

Hq: Box 257, June Lake, CA 93529

Church of Divine Man

The Church of Divine Man, a psychic fellowship, was founded in 1972 by Lewis Bostwick. The church teaches psychic and spiritual development.

Hq: Berkeley Psychic Institute, 2436
  Haste Street, Berkeley, CA
  94704
Tel: (206) 258 1449

Church of Divine Man of Washington

The Church of Divine Man of Washington separated from the Church of Divine Man in the late 1980s.

Hq: 2402 Summit Avenue, Everett, WA
  98201
Tel: (206) 258 1449

Church of Eductivism

The Church of Eductivism was founded in 1971 by Jack Horner, a former leader in the Church of Scientology.

Hq: 3003 Santa Monica Blvd., Santa Monica, CA 90404

Church of Essential Science

The Church of Essential Science was founded in 1965 by medium Kingdon L. Brown (now known as Brian Seabrook).

Hq: Rev. Brian Seabrook, Box 31129, Phoenix, AZ 85046

Church of General Psionics

The Church of General Psionics is a psychic fellowship founded in 1968 by John Douglas and Henry D. Frazier.

Hq: 204 N. Catalina, Redondo Beach, CA 90277

Church of Illumination

The Church of Illumination is a church associated with the Fraternitas Rosae Crucis to proclaim the arrival of the Manistic Age, a time for the recognition of the inherent equality of men and women.

Hq: c/o Dir. Gerald E. Poesnecker, P.O. Box 220, Quakerstown, PA 18951
Tel: (215) 536 1900

Church of Light

The Church of Light is an occult church founded in 1932 by Elbert Benjamin and based upon the teaching of the Brotherhood of Light.

Hq: 2341 Coral Street, Los Angeles, CA 90031
Tel: (213) 226 0453

Church of Mercavah

The Church of Mercavah is a New Age church founded in 1982 by Rev. James A. Montadon.

Hq: Box 66703, Baton Rouge, LA 70896

Church of Metaphysical Christianity

The Church of Metaphysical Christianity is a Christian Spiritualist church founded in 1958 by Rev. Dorothy Graff Flexer and Russell J. Flexer.

Hq: 2717 Browning Street, Sarasota, FL 33577

Church of Pan

The Church of Pan is a Neo-Pagan group founded in 1970 by Kenneth Walker and members of a rural Rhode Island nudist camp.

Hq: 114 Johnson Rd., Foster, RI 02825
Tel: (401) 397 3007 or 397 9927

Church of Revelation (California)

The Church of Revelation is a Spiritualist church founded in 1930 by Rev. Janet Stine Lewis (Wolford).

Hq: Box 53294, San Jose, CA 95153
Tel: (408) 972 1925 or 425 1945

Church of Satan

The Church of Satan was founded in 1966 by Anton Szandor LaVey.

Hq: Box 210082, San Francisco, CA 94121

Church of Scientology International

The Church of Scientology International was founded in 1954 by L. Ron Hubbard. During the last twenty years it has become one of the most controversial of religious groups.

Hq: 6331 Hollywood Blvd., Ste. 1200, Los Angeles, CA 90028-6329
Tel: (800) 367 8788
Fax: (213) 960 3508

Church of Seven Arrows

The Church of Seven Arrows is a Neo-Pagan group which has integrated Native American perspectives into its teachings. It was founded in the 1970s by Revs. George Dew and Linda Hillshafer.

Hq: 4385 Hoyt St., Apt. 201, Wheatridge, CO 80033

Church of the Eternal Source

The Church of the Eternal Source is an Egyptian Neo-Pagan group founded in 1970 by Donald D. Harrison and Harold Moss.

Hq: Box 7091, Burbank, CA 91510-7091

Church of the Spiritual Advisory Council

The Church of the Spiritual Advisory Council was founded in 1974 by Paul V. Johnson, Robert Ericsson, and several former leaders of Spiritual Frontiers Fellowship. The Council's purpose is to assist members in their personal advancement in spiritual and psychic awareness and in healing.

Hq: 2965 W. State Road 434, Longwood, FL 32779
Tel: (305) 774 6151

Church of the Tree of Life

The Church of the Tree of Life is one of several groups that considered psychedelics a sacramental substance, but differed in that it recommended only legal substances for ingestion by

members. It was founded in 1971 and its current status is in doubt.

Hq: Current address unavailable for this edition

Church of the Trinity (Invisible Ministry)

The Church of the Trinity (Invisible Ministry) is a New Thought metaphysical church founded in 1972 by A. Stuart Otto, known to church members as Friend Stuart.

Hq: c/o A. Stuart Otto, Box 37, San Marcos, CA 92069-0025
Tel: (618) 746 9430

Church of the White Eagle Lodge

The Church of the White Eagle Lodge was founded in 1934 by Grace and Ivan Cooke, medium channels. The church was named for their major spirit guide, an American Indian.

Hq: Rev. Jean Le Fevre, St. John's Retreat Center, Box 930, Montgomery, TX 77356
Tel: (409) 597 5757
or
International Hq: Newlands, Rake, Liss Hampshire, England GU33 7HY, U.K.

Church of Tzaddi

The Church of Tzaddi is a New Age Spiritualist church founded in 1962 by Amy Merritt Kees and named for a letter in the Hebrew alphabet.

Hq: Box 13729, Boulder, CO 80308-3

Church Universal and Triumphant

The Church Universal and Triumphant is an Ascended Master fellowship in the "I AM" tradition. It was founded in Washington, D.C., 1974 by Mark and Elizabeth Prophet.

Hq: Box A, Corwin Springs, MT 59021-0881
Tel: (406) 848 7441

City of the Sun Foundation

The City of the Sun Foundation (originally called Christ's Truth Church and School of Wisdom) is an Ascended Master fellowship in the "I AM" tradition. It was founded in 1968 by Rev. Wayne Taylor.

Hq: Box 370, Columbus, NM 88029

Congregational Church of Practical Theology

The Congregational Church of Practical Theology is a loosely-organized psychic fellowship founded in 1969 by Dr. E. Arthur Winkler.

Hq: 31916 Pat's Lane, Springfield, LA 70462
Tel: (504) 294 2129

Coptic Fellowship of America

The Coptic Fellowship of America is an esoteric Christian group founded in 1927 by Hamid Bey, an Egyptian who migrated to the United States in the 1920s.

Hq: 1735 Pinnacle, S.W., Wyoming, MI 48509
Tel: (616) 531 1339

Cosmic Awareness Communications

Cosmic Awareness Communications was founded in 1963 and built around the messages of an entity known as Cosmic Awareness channeled through William Ralph Duby.

Hq: Box 115, Olympia, WA 98507

Cosmic Circle of Fellowship

The Cosmic Circle of Fellowship was founded in 1954 by UFO contactee William Ferguson and two associates, Edward A. Surine and Edna I. Valverde.

Hq: Edna Valverde, 4857 N. Melvina Avenue, Chicago, IL 60630

The Course in Miracles

The Course in Miracles is a massive volume channeled by Helen Schucman, psychologist at Columbia University. In the mid-1970s, the Foundation for Inner Peace was founded to publish and circulate the book, and in the intervening years a number of organizations have arisen to perpetuate its metaphysical teachings.

Hq: Miracle Experiences, Inc., Box 158, Islip Terrace, NY 11752
Tel: (516) 277 0218
or
Hq: Foundation for Inner Peace, Box 635, Tiburon, CA 94920
or
Miracle-Distribution Center, 1141 East Ash, Fullerton, CA 92631
Tel: (714) 738 8380
or
California Miracles Center, 2269 Market Street, San Francisco, CA 94114
Tel: (415) 620 2556

Covenant of the Goddess

The Covenant of the Goddess is a national Wiccan fellowship founded in 1975 by Aiden Kelly, Alison Harlow, and others.

Hq: Box 1226, Berkeley, CA 94704

Cymry Wicca

The Cymry Wicca is a Neo-Pagan Wiccan founded in 1967 by Rhuddlwm Gawr.

Hq: Box 674884, Marietta, GA 30067

Dawn of Truth

The Dawn of Truth is a ministry founded in the mid-twentieth century by Mikkel Dahl, an independent teacher. It has founded its most stable organizational center in Shepherdsfield, a community in Missouri.

Hq: Shepherdsfield, R.R. 4, Box 399, Fulton, MO 65251
Tel: (314) 642 1439

Dianic Wicca

Dianic Wicca is a Wiccan teaching that emerged in the early 1970s that sees Witchcraft as a basically female religion centered upon the Greek goddess Diana. Its major exponent has been Zsuzsanna Emese Budapest (in California), high priestess of the Susan B. Anthony Coven No. 1.

Hq: Susan B. Anthony Coven No. 1, Box 11363, Oakland, CA 94611
Tel: (415) 420 1454

Divine Science Federation International

Divine Science, one of the major forms of New Thought metaphysics, was first articulated in the 1880s by Melinda Cramer, a teacher in San Francisco. The Divine Science Federation grew out of the Divine Science Association she founded.

Hq: 1819 E. 14th Avenue, Denver, CO 80218
Tel: (303) 322 7730

Divine Word Foundation

The Divine Word Foundation was founded in 1962 by Dr. Hans Nordwin von Koerber to perpetuate the revelations of Jakob Loeber, an Austrian mystic.

Hq: 26648 San Felipe Rd., Warner Springs, CA 92086

Earthstar Temple

The Earthstar Temple is a magical/ Wiccan group founded in the 1970s by Ed Buczynski.

Hq: 35 W. 19th Street, New York, NY 10011
Tel: (212) 242 7182

Ecclesia Gnostica

The Ecclesia Gnostica is an independent gnostic Catholic church founded by Archbishop Stephen A. Hoeller, formerly a bishop in the Pre-Nicene Church.

Hq: Most Rev. Stephan Hoeller, 4516 Hollywood Blvd., Los Angeles, CA 90027
Tel: (213) 467 2685

Ecclesia Gnostica Mysterium

The Ecclesia Gnostica Mysterium is an independent gnostic Catholic church founded in the 1970s by Bishop Rosa Miller.

Hq: Most Rev. Rosa Miller, 3437 Alma, #23, Palo Alto, CA 94306
Tel: (415) 494 7412

Eclesia Catolica Cristiana

The Eclesia Catolica Cristiana is an independent esoteric Catholic juris-diction founded in 1969 by Delfin Roman Cardona.

Hq: 2112 Grand Avenue, Bronx, NY 10453

Ecumenical Ministry of the Unity of All Religions

The Ecumenical Ministry of the Unity of All Religions and the associated World University of America were founded in the 1970s by Filipino-American theosophists Dr. Benito Reyes and his wife Dominga L. Reyes.

Hq: 107 N. Ventura Street, Ojai, CA 93023
Tel: (805) 646 1440

Edta Ha Thoma

Edta Ha Thoma is an independent gnostic Catholic jurisdiction founded in 1984 by Archbishop James A. Dennis.

Hq: Mar Petros, 578 Green, No. 5-20, San Bruno, CA 94066

Embassy of the Gheez-Americans

The Embassy of the Gheez [Ethiopian]-Americans is a predominantly black metaphysical organization under the leadership of Mysikiitta Fa Senntao, believed by her followers to be an extraterrestrial entity seeking her lost people.

Hq: c/o Mt. Helion Sanctuary, Rock Valley Rd., Box 53, Long Eddy, NY 12760

Emissaries of Divine Light

The Emissaries of Divine Light is a New Age metaphysical communal group founded in 1932 by Lloyd Arthur Meeker.

Hq: 5569 N. Country Rd. 29, Loveland, CO 80537
Tel: (303) 669 2166

ESP Laboratory

The ESP Laboratory is an occult organization founded in 1966 by psychic Al G. Manning. Manning teaches a form of magick and Witchcraft.

Hq: Box 216, 219 Southridge Dr., Edgewood, TX 75117

Etherian Religious Society of Universal Brotherhood

The Etherian Religious Society of Universal Brotherhood was founded in 1965 by visionary E. A. Hurtienne.

Hq: Box 446, San Marcos, CA 92069

Ethiopian Zion Coptic Church

The Ethiopian Zion Coptic Church was founded by black nationalist Marcus Garvey in Jamaica in 1914. Among the practices it developed over the years was the smoking of ganja (marijuana) as a sacramental act. Reintroduced into the United States in the 1970s, the church ran into conflict with legal authorities and its leaders were arrested on drug charges and convicted in 1981.

Hq: Current address unavailable for this edition

The Farm

The Farm is a New Age communal group founded in the 1960s by Stephen Gaskin.

Hq: 1256-C Drakes Ln., Summertown, TN 38483
Tel: (615) 964 3574

Federation of St. Thomas Christian Churches

The Federation of St. Thomas Christian Churches is an independent esoteric Christian church founded in 1963 by Archbishop Joseph L. Vredenburgh.

Hq: 134 Dakota Avenue #308, Santa Cruz, CA 95060
Tel: (408) 423 4952

Fellowship of the Inner Light

The Fellowship of the Inner Light was founded in 1972 by psychic channel Paul Solomon who has modeled his career somewhat after that of Edgar Cayce.

Hq: c/o The Fellowship Center, 620 14th Street, Virginia Beach, VA 23451
Tel: (804) 428 5782

First Christians' Essene Church

The First Christians' Essene Church was founded in 1937 by Hungarian mystic and teacher Edmond Bordeaux Szekely.

Hq: 2536 Collier Ave., San Diego, CA 92116
Tel: (619) 298 1809

First Church of Divine Immanence

The First Church of Divine Immanence is a New Thought fellowship founded in 1952 by Dr. Henry Milton Ellis.

Hq: Current address unavailable for this edition

Foundation, a Hermetic Society

The Foundation, a Hermetic Society was founded in 1971 by W. E. Stone. Its most recent publications have carried no current address.

Hq: Current address unavailable for this edition

Foundation Church of Divine Truth

The Foundation Church of Divine Truth was founded in the 1980s by former members of the disbanded Foundation Church of the New Birth (originally founded in 1958). The Church is built around the channeled material of medium James Edward Padgett (1852-1923).

Hq: Box 66003, Washington, D.C. 20035-6003

Foundation Faith of God

The Foundation Faith of God was founded in 1974 by former members of the Process Church of the Final Judgment, which had been disbanded by its leadership. After several name changes in theological emphases and a move toward traditional Christianity, it assumed the present name in 1980.

Hq: Faith Center, 3055 S. Bronco, Las Vegas, NV 89102
Tel: (702) 258 9012

Foundation for Science of Spiritual Law

The Foundation for Science of Spiritual Law is a Spiritualist church founded in 1968 by Dr. Alfred Homer and Rev. Gladys A. Homer.

Hq: Current address unavailable for this edition

Foundation for Self Realization Beyond the Human Potential

The Foundation for Self Realization is built around the work of channel Penny Torres and Mafu, the entity she channels. In 1989 Torres visited India where she took the vows for the renounced life (sannyas) and is now known as Swami Paramananda Saraswatti.

Hq: Box 2094, Vacaville, CA 95696-2094
Tel: (707) 447 5005

Foundation of Human Understanding

The Foundation of Human Understanding is a New Age fellowship founded in 1961 by Roy Masters who began his teaching career as a hypnotist.

Hq: c/o Tall Timber Ranch, 1980 Deer Creek Rd., Selma, OR 97538
Tel: (503) 597 4360

Fraternitas L. V. X. Occulta [Fraternity of the Hidden Light]

The Fraternitas L. V. X. Occulta [Fraternity of the Hidden Light] is a hermetic magical order founded in the mid-1980s by former members of the Builders of the Adytum.

Hq: Paul A. Clark, Box 5094, Covina, CA 91723

Fraternitas Rosae Crucis

The Fraternitas Rosae Crucis, the original Rosicrucian group in the United States, was founded in 1868 by author and occult pioneer, Pascal B. Randolph.

Hq: Beverly Hall, Quakertown, PA 18951
Tel: (215) 536 1900

Future Foundation

The Future Foundation was founded in 1969 by Gerard W. Gottula for the purpose of sharing spiritual healing and life readings.

Hq: Box 26, Steinauer, NE 68441

Gardnerian Wiccan

The initial thrust of the revival of Wicca (Witchcraft) in the late-twentieth century originated with Gerald Gardner, a retired British civil servant and amateur occultist. Gardnerian Wiccan is the name given to those groups (covens) which follow the rituals he devised and derived from the lineage of his coven in England.

Hq: Lady Rhiannon, Box 6896, FDR Station, New York, NY 10150

General Assembly of Spiritualists

The General Assembly of Spiritualists was founded in 1930 as a split from the National Spiritualist Association of Churches.

Hq: Rev. Rose Ann Erickson, Ansonia Hotel, 2107 Broadway, New York, NY 10023

General Church of the New Jerusalem

The General Church of the New Jerusalem was founded in 1882 by William Benade and other former members of the General Convention of the New Jerusalem.

Hq: Bryn Athyn, PA 19009
Tel: (215) 947 4660

General Convention of the New Jerusalem in the United States of America

The General Convention of the New Jerusalem in the United States of America was founded in 1817 and follows the teaching of eighteenth century Swedish seer Emanuel Swedenborg.

Hq: c/o Office Dir. Ethelwyn Worden, 48 Sargent Street, Newton, MA 02158

General Convention of the Swedenborgian Church

See: General Convention of the New Jerusalem in the United States of America

George Adamski Foundation

The George Adamski Foundation was founded in 1965 to perpetuate the teachings of George Adamski, the first of the modern UFO contactees. Adamski had taught metaphysics for years prior to his UFO claims.

Hq: Current address unavailable for this edition

The Georgian Church

The Georgian Church is a Neo-Pagan Wiccan group founded in the 1970s by George Patterson. Its rituals follow a variation of the Gardnerian Wicca

Hq: 1908 Verde St., Bakersfield, CA 93304

Gnostic Association of Cultural and Anthropological Studies

The Gnostic Association of Cultural and Anthropological Studies is a gnostic esoteric group founded in 1952 by Samuel Aun Weor, a native of Columbia.

Hq: Box 291488, Los Angeles, CA 90029
Tel: (213) 483 6839

Gnostic Orthodox Church

The Gnostic Orthodox Church is an independent gnostic Eastern Orthodox group originally founded in 1968 by Abbot-Bishop George Burke. After several shifts of program and name, the group assumed its present stance and name in 1984.

Hq: Abbot-Bishop George Burke, RR 1, Box 75, Geneva, NE 68361
Tel: (402) 759 4952

Grail Movement of America

The Grail Movement of America was founded in the 1930s to perpetuate the esoteric teachings of Austrian Oskar Ernest Bernhardt (pen name: Abd-ru-shin).

Hq: 2081 Partridge Lane, Binghamton, NY 13903
Tel: (607) 723 4501

Hallowed Grounds Fellowship of Spiritual Healing and Prayer

The Hallowed Grounds Fellowship of Spiritual Healing and Prayer is a Spiritualist center founded in 1961 by Rev. George Daisley.

Hq: Rev. George Daisley, 629 San Ysidro Rd., Montecito, CA 93108
Tel: (805) 969 3353

Holy Grail Foundation

The Holy Grail Foundation is a Spiritualist church founded in the 1940s by Rev. Leona Richards.

Hq: Rev. Leona Richards, 1344 Pacific Avenue, Suite 100, Santa Cruz, CA 94501

Home of Truth

The Home of Truth is an early New Thought metaphysical church founded in 1888 by Annie Rix Militz.

Hq: 1300 Grand Street, Alameda, CA 94501
Tel: (415) 522 3346

Huna Research Associates

The Huna Research Associates was founded in 1950 by Max Freedom Long to research and practice the teachings of Huna, the ancient religion of Hawaii.

Hq: 126 Camilia Dr., Cape Girardeau, MO 63701
Tel: (314) 334 3478

"I AM" Religious Activity

The "I AM" Religious Activity was founded in the 1930s by Guy W. and Edna W. Ballard, the Messengers of the Ascended Masters, especially Master Saint Germain, who contacted Guy Ballard in 1929.

Hq: Saint German Foundation, 1120 Stonehedge Dr., Schaumberg, IL 60194
Tel: (312) 882 7400

Independent Associated Spiritualists

The Independent Associated Spiritualists is a Spiritualist church founded in 1925.

Hq: Rev. Marion Owens, 124 W. 72nd Street, New York, NY 10023

Independent Church of Antioch

The Independent Church of Antioch was founded in the 1960s by Bishop Robert Branch and former members of the Church of Antioch.

Hq: The New Church Center, 350 Santa Cruz Street, Boulder Creek, CA 95006
Tel: (408) 338 7130

Independent Spiritualist Association of the United States of America

The Independent Spiritualist Association of the United States of America was founded in 1924 by Amanda Flowers and other former members of the National Spiritualist Association of Churches.

Hq: Rev. Harry M. Hilborn, 5130 W. 25th Street, Cicero, IL 60650

Infinite Way

The Infinite Way was founded in 1954 by former Christian Science practitioner Joel S. Goldsmith. A circle of students who listen to Goldsmith's tapes and study his material has remained active.

Hq: Box 215, Youngstown, AZ 85363
Tel: (602) 974 9763

Inner Circle Kethra E'Da Foundation, Inc.

The Inner Circle Kethra E'Da Foundation was founded in 1945 to perpetuate the teaching brought forth by medium/channel Mark Probert.

Hq: Box 1722, San Diego, CA 92112

Inner Light Foundation

The Inner Light Foundation is a New Age group founded in 1969 by Betty Berthards.

Hq: Box 761, Novato, CA 94948
Tel: (415) 382 1040

Inner Peace Movement

The Inner Peace Movement is a New Age group founded in 1964 by Francisco Coll.

Hq: Box 4897, Washington, D.C. 20008

Institute of Cosmic Wisdom

The Institute of Cosmic Wisdom, founded in the early 1950s by Rev. Clark Wilkerson, is based upon Huna, the ancient religion of Hawaii.

Hq: 3528 Franciscan Lane, Las Vegas, NV 89121

Institute of Divine Metaphysical Research

The Institute of Divine Metaphysical Research is an esoteric Christian group founded in 1958 by Dr. Henry Clifford.

Hq: Box A877, Los Angeles, CA 90019
Tel: (213) 733 0672

Institute of Mentalphysics

The Institute of Mentalphysics was founded in 1927 by Edwin John Dingle to perpetuate the teachings he had gained in his travels in the East.

Hq: 59700 - 29 Palms Hwy., Joshua
Tree, CA 92252
Tel: (619) 365 8371

International Alliance of Churches of the Truth

The International Alliance of Churches of the Truth is a New Thought metaphysical fellowship of churches founded in 1987 by Judi D. Warren. It continues the work of the Church of the Truth founded in 1913 in Spokane, Washington, by Albert C. Grier.

Hq: Pastor Judi D. Warren, 690 E.
Orange Grove Blvd., Pasadena,
CA 91104
Tel: (818) 795 6905

International General Assembly of Spiritualists

The International General Assembly of Spiritualists was founded in 1936 by Rev. Arthur Ford and other mediums formerly with the National Spiritualist Association of Churches.

Hq: 1809 E. Bayview Blvd., Norfolk,
VA 23503
Tel: (804) 588 6833

International Metaphysical Association

The International Metaphysical Association was founded in 1955 by former members of the Church of Christ, Scientist. It is associated with the Rare Book Company which reprints old Christian Science titles.

Hq: 20 E. 68th Street, New York, NY
10021

International Spiritualist Alliance

The International Spiritualist Alliance is a Canadian-based Spiritualist church with congregations in the United States.

Hq: Current address unavailable for this
edition

Johannine Catholic Church

The Johannine Catholic Church is an independent esoteric Catholic church founded by J. Julian and Rita Anna Gillman in 1968 and incorporated in 1971.

Hq: Archbishop J. Julian Gillman, Box
227, Dulzura, CA 92107
Tel: (619) 468 3810

Joy Foundation, Inc.

The Joy Foundation is an eclectic theosophical group founded in 1977 by Rev. Dr. Elizabeth Louise Huffer.

Hq: 2821 De La Vina, Santa Barbara,
CA 93105

Lama Foundation

The Lama Foundation is a New Age center/community founded in the 1960s by Steve Durke and his family.

Hq: Box 44, San Cristobal, NM 877564
Tel: (505) 586 1269

Law of Life Activity

The Law of Life Activity was founded in the 1960s as an independent teaching center and focus of a study group network in the "I AM" tradition.

Hq: c/o A. D. K. Luk, 8575 S. Crow
Cutoff, Rye Star Rte., Pueblo,
CO 81004

Lectorium Rosicrucianum

The Lectorium Rosicrucianum was founded in 1924, and reorganized after the disruptions of World War II, in Holland by Jan Van Rijckenborgh and Catharose de Petri, former members of the Rosicrucian Fellowship.

Western North American Hq: Box 9246,
Bakersfield, CA 93389
Tel: (805) 327 2827
or
International Hq: Bakenessergracht 11-
15, 2011JS The Netherlands

Lemurian Fellowship

The Lemurian Fellowship is a communal group founded in 1936 by esoteric teacher Robert D. Stelle.

Hq: Box 397, Ramona, CA 92065

Liberal Catholic Church International

The Liberal Catholic Church International is a theosophical Catholic church founded in 1983 by the merger of two Liberal Catholic jurisdictions.

Hq: 1736 Holly Oaks Ravine Dr.,
Jacksonville, FL 32225

Liberal Catholic Church, Province of the United States

The Liberal Catholic Church is an independent theosophical Catholic church founded in England in 1916 and brought to the United States the following year.

Hq: Rt. Rev. Lawrence J. Smith, 9740
S. Avers, Evergreen Park, IL
60642
Tel: (312) 424 8329

Life Study Fellowship Foundation, Inc.

The Life Study Fellowship Foundation is a New Thought metaphysical mail-order organization founded in 1939.

Hq: Noroton, CT 06820

Light of the Universe

The Light of the Universe was founded in 1969 by psychic/channel Maryona (the religious name of Helen Spitler).

Hq: 161 N. Sandusky Rd., Tiffin, OH
44883

Lighted Way

The Lighted Way is a New Age group founded in 1966 by Muriel Isis (Muriel R. Tepper).

Hq: P. O. Box 1749, Pacific Palisades,
CA 90272
Tel: (212) 472 5942 or (818) 789 0913

Lord's New Church Which is Nova Hierosolyma

The Lord's New Church Which is Nova Hierosolyma was founded in 1937 by H. D. G. Groeneveld, a former member of the General Church of the New Jerusalem in Holland.

Hq: Rev. Phillip Odhner, Box 4, Bryn
Athyn, PA 19009

Lotus Ashram

The Lotus Ashram was founded in 1971 by Spiritualist medium Noel Street and his wife Coleen Street.

Hq: Rev. Noel Street, 264 Mainsail, Port
St. Lucie, FL 33452

Love Project

The Love Project was founded in 1972 by Arleen Lorrance and Diane Pike, widow of Episcopal Bishop James Pike.

Hq: Box 7601, San Diego, CA 92107
Tel: (619) 225 0133

Mark-Age

Mark-Age is a New Age UFO group founded in 1960 by Gentzel Boyd and Pauline Sharpe to channel messages from the "Hierarchical Board" (the spiritual rulers of the solar system).

Hq: Box 290368, Fort Lauderdale, FL 33329
Tel: (305) 587 5555

Mayan Order

The Mayan Order is an occult group that teaches the secrets of the ancient Mayans.

Hq: Box 2710, San Antonio, TX 78299

Meditation Groups, Inc.

Meditation Groups, Inc., is a theosophical group in the Alice Bailey tradition founded in 1950 by Florence Garrique and former members of the Arcane School.

Hq: Box 566, Ojai, CA 93023
Tel: (805) 646 5508

Metropolitan Spiritual Churches of Christ, Inc.

The Metropolitan Spiritual Churches of Christ, Inc., is a predominantly black Christian Spiritualist church founded in 1925 by Bishop William Frank Taylor and Leviticus Lee Boswell.

Hq: Dr. I. Logan Kearse, 4329 Park Heights Avenue, Baltimore, MD 21215

Mindstream Church of Universal Love

The Mindstream Church of Universal Love is a New Age group founded in 1979 by Rev. Kenneth and Wendie Glimour Donabie-Dixon.

Hq: Current address unavailable for this edition

Monastery of the Seven Rays

The Monastery of the Seven Rays is one of several names for the magical activities under the guidance of thelemic magician Michael Bertiaux. He is also the leading American bishop for the Neo-Pythagorean Church.

Hq: Box 1554, Chicago, IL 60690-1554

Morningland-Church of the Ascended Christ

The Morningland-Church of the Ascended Christ is a New Age church founded in 1973 by Daniel Mario Sperato.

Hq: 2600 E. 7th Street, Long Beach, CA 90804

Mu Farm

The Mu Farm is a communal group founded in 1971 by Fletcher Fist.

Hq: Yoncalla, OR 97499

National Colored Spiritualist Association of Churches

The National Colored Spiritualist Association of Churches is a predominantly black Spiritualist church founded in 1922 by former members of the National Spiritualist Association of Churches.

Hq: Rev. Nellie Mae Taylor, 1245 West Watkins Rd., Phoenix, AZ 85007

National Spiritual Aid Association

The National Spiritual Aid Association is a fellowship founded in 1937 for independent Spiritualist mediums.

Hq: 5239 40th Street, N., St. Petersburg, FL 33714

National Spiritual Alliance of the U.S.A.

The National Spiritual Alliance of the U.S.A. is a Spiritualist association founded in 1913 by Rev. G. Tabor Thompson.

Hq: RFD 1, Lake Pleasant, MA 01347

National Spiritual Science Center

The National Spiritual Science Center is a Spiritualist church founded in 1941 by Alice W. Tindall.

Hq: 5605 16th St., N.W., Washington, D.C. 20011
Tel: (202) 723 4510

National Spiritualist Association of Churches

The National Spiritualist Association of Churches was founded in 1893 by Harrison Barrett, James M. Peebles, and Cora L. Richmond.

Hq: P. O. Box 128, Casadega, FL 32706
Tel: (904) 228 2506

Native American Church

The Native American Church is the organizational nexus of a movement among American Indians which includes the sacramental use of the psychedelic cactus peyote. It was founded in 1906.

Hq: Current address unavailable for this edition

New Age Bible and Philosophy Center

The New Age Bible and Philosophy Center was founded in the 1930s by Corinne S. Heline, formerly a leader in the Rosicrucian Fellowship.

Hq: 1139 Lincoln Blvd., Santa Monica, CA 90403
Tel: (213) 395 4346

New Age Church of the Christ

The New Age Church of the Christ was founded in the early 1950s by Geraldine Innocente and former members of the "I AM" Religious Activity. It was originally known as the Bridge to Freedom.

Hq: Box 333, Kings Park, NY 11754

New Age Church of Truth

The New Age Church of Truth was founded in the mid-1960s by psychic Gilbert N. Holloway.

Hq: Star Route 2, Box CLC, Deming, NM 88030

New Age Teachings

The New Age Teachings movement was founded in 1967 by New Age channel Anita Afton [better known by her religious name, Illiana].

Hq: Box 346, Brookfield, MA 01506
Tel: (508) 867 3754

New Order of Glastonbury

The New Order of Glastonbury is an independent esoteric Catholic order founded in 1979 by a group of independent Old Catholic priests.

Hq: Box 324, Rialto, CA 92376

New, Reformed, Orthodox Order of the Golden Dawn

The New, Reformed, Orthodox Order of the Golden Dawn is a Wiccan group founded in 1969 by a small group of Neo-Pagans in the San Francisco Bay Area.

Hq: Rowan Fairgrove, Box 360607, Milpitas, CA 95035

New Wiccan Church

The New Wiccan Church is an independent Neo-Pagan Wiccan church in the Gardnerian Wiccan tradition.

Hq: Box 162046, Sacramento, CA 95816

Noohra Foundation

The Noohra Foundation is a New Thought metaphysical center founded in 1970 by Bible scholar Dr. Rocco A. Errico, student of Assyrian Bible-translator George Lamsa.

Hq: Dr. Rocco A. Errico, 720 Paularino Avenue, Costa Mesa, CA 92626

Oasis Fellowship

The Oasis Fellowship was founded by mediums/channels George and Alice White.

Hq: Box 0, Florence, AZ 85232

Old Catholic Episcopal Church

The Old Catholic Episcopal Church is a theosophically-oriented Catholic jurisdiction founded in 1951 by Bishop Jay Davis Kirby.

Hq: Most Rev. John Charles Maier, 489 Jasmine Street, Laguna Beach, CA 92651

Old Holy Catholic Church, Province of North America

The Old Holy Catholic Church, Province of North America is a theosophically-oriented independent Liberal Catholic jurisdiction founded in 1979 by Bishop George W. S. Brister.

Hq: Most Rev. Alvin Lee Baker, 705 North 5th, Weatherford, OK 73096
Tel: (405) 772 7080

Open Way

The Open Way is a New Age group founded by Lovie Webb Gasteiner.

Hq: Lovie Webb Gasteiner, Box 217, Celina, TN 38551

Order of Thelema

The Order of Thelema is an independent magical order which follows the tradition of magician Aleister Crowley.

Hq: Box 551, Chula Vista, CA 92012
Tel: (619) 427 4191

Ordo Adeptorum Invisibilium

The Ordo Adeptorum Invisibilium was founded by three thelemic ritual magicians in 1979 in England and came to the United States in 1981.

International Hq: c/o Gerry Ahrens, 18 Crampton House, Patmore Street, London, England SW8 4JQ

Ordo Lux Kethri [Order of the Kethric Light]

The Ordo Lux Kethri [Order of the Kethric Light] was founded in 1982 by April Schadler Bishop and Michael Albion Macdonald, former members of the Builders of the Adytum.

Hq: 584 Castro Street, San Francisco, CA 94114

Ordo Templi Astarte
Order of the Temple of Astarte
OTA
Church of Hermetic Science

The Ordo Templi Astarte (Order of the Temple of Astarte or the OTA), also known as the Church of Hermetic Science, was founded in 1970 by Carroll R. Runyon, Jr.

Hq: P. O. Box 40094, Pasadena, CA 91114

Ordo Templi Orientis

The Ordo Templi Orientis was founded in the 1890s in Germany by Karl Kellner. It was brought into the English-speaking world by Aleister Crowley. Following the death of Crowley's successor Karl Germer in the 1960s, the order became disorganized. The most prominent claimant to succession (one recognized by American courts) was that of Grady McMurtry. This branch of the O.T.O. is now headed by McMurtry's successor.

Hq: JAF Box 7666, New York, NY 10116-4632

or

Office Grand Treasurer General, Box 430, Fairfax, CA 94930

Tel: (415) 454 5176

Ordo Templi Orientis (Grant)

One claimant to leadership of the Ordo Templi Orientis was British magician Kenneth Grant (Grant). During the 1970s he began to establish a following in the United States.

Hq: Ruth Keenan, P. O. Box 450867, Miami, FL 33245-0867

The Original Neo-Kleptonia Neo-American Church

The Original Neo-Kleptonia Neo-American Church, one of several churches which believes that the psychedelic drug LSD is a sacramental substance, was founded in 1964 by Arthur Kleps.

Hq: Box 11, Mandalit Elk Ridge, Redway, CA 95560

Our Lady of Enchantment, Church of the Old Religion

The Our Lady of Enchantment, Church of the Old Religion, a Wiccan church, was founded in 1978 by Lady Sabrina.

Hq: Box 1366, Nashua, NH 03061
Tel: (603) 880 7237

The Path of Light

The Path of Light is a New Age group founded in 1972 by channel Mary Myers.

Hq: 3427 Denson Pl., Charlotte, NC 28215
Tel: (704) 536 8159

Phoenix Institute

The Phoenix Institute is a New Thought metaphysical group founded in 1966 by Kathryn Breese-Whiting.

Hq: Current address unavailable for this edition

Planetary Light Association

The Planetary Light Association is a New Age group founded in 1983 by channel Jann Weiss.

Hq: Box 180786, Austin, TX 78718

Pre-Nicene Church (De Palatine)

The Pre-Nicene Church (De Palatine) is a gnostic Catholic church founded in 1953 by Ronald Powell.

Hq: Most Rev. Seiji Yamauchi, 23301 Mobile Street, Canoga Park, CA 91307-3322

Progressive Spiritual Church

The Progressive Spiritual Church was founded in 1907 by Rev. G. V. Cordingley.

Hq: Current address unavailable for this edition

Pyramid Church of Truth and Light

The Pyramid Church of Truth and Light is a Spiritualist church founded in 1941 by Revs. John and Emma Kingham.

Hq: Current address unavailable for this edition

Quartus Foundation for Spiritual Research

The Quartus Foundation is a New Age organization founded by popular metaphysical author John Randolph Price in 1981.

Hq: P. O. Box 1768, Boerne, TX 78006
Tel: (512) 537 4689

Quimby Center

The Quimby Center is a New Age center founded in 1946 by Dr. Neva Dell Hunter.

Hq: Box 453, Alamogordo, NM 88310

Rainbow Family of Living Light

The Rainbow Family of Living Light is a loosely-organized New Age fellowship founded in 1960s by Rev. Barry Adams.

Hq: Route 1, Box 6, McCall, ID 83638

Reformed Druids of North America

The Reformed Druids of North America is a Neo-Pagan fellowship originally founded in 1963 by students at Carlton College, Northfield, Minnesota.

Hq: Live Oak Grove, 616 Minor Rd., Orinda, CA 94563

Religious Science International

Religious Science International is one of two New Thought churches which traces its origins to metaphysical teacher Ernest Holmes in 1949 and took the present name in 1954.

Hq: 3230 5th Avenue, San Diego, CA 92103
Tel: (619) 298 4175

Renaissance Church of Beauty

The Renaissance Church of Beauty is a New Age community founded by Michael Repunzal (Michael Metelica) in 1969. It assumed its present name in 1974.

Hq: Box 112, Turner's Falls, MA 01376

Rosicrucian Anthroposophical League

The Rosicrucian Anthroposophical League was founded in 1932 by Samuel Richard Parchment, a former member of the Rosicrucian Fellowship.

Hq: Current address unavailable for this edition

Rosicrucian Fellowship

The Rosicrucian Fellowship was founded in 1907 by Max Heindel (Carl Louis Van Grasshof), a student of Rudolf Steiner, the founder of the Anthroposophical Society.

Hq: 2222 Mission Avenue, Box 713, Oceanside, CA 92054
Tel: (714) 757 6600

Roosevelt Spiritual Memorial Benevolent Association

The Roosevelt Spiritual Memorial Benevolent Association was founded in 1949 by independent Spiritualists.

Hq: Rev. Nellie M. Pickens, Box 68-313, Miami, FL 33138

Ruby Focus of Magnificent Consummation

The Ruby Focus of Magnificent Consummation is devoted to Ascended Masters of the "I AM" tradition. It was founded in the mid-1960s by Garman and Evangeline Van Polen.

Hq: P. O. Drawer 1188, Sedona, AZ 86336

Sabaean Religious Order of Amen

The Sabaean Religious Order of Amen is a Neo-Pagan fellowship founded in the 1960s by Frederic de Arechaga.

Hq: El Sabarum, 3221 N. Sheffield, Chicago, IL 60657
Tel: (312) 248 0791

Sabian Assembly

The Sabian Assembly is an astrological occult fellowship founded in 1923 by Marc Edmund Jones.

Hq: Sabian Publishing House, Box 7, Stanwood, WA 98292

Sacred Society of the Eth, Inc.

The Sacred Society of the Eth, Inc. is an occult group growing out of the "I AM" tradition. It was founded in 1967 by Jo'el of Arcadia (Walter W. Jecker).

Hq: Box 3, Forks of Salmon, CA 96031

School for Esoteric Studies

The School for Esoteric Studies is a theosophical group founded in 1956 by former members of the Arcane School.

Hq: 40 E. 49th Street, Suite 1903, New York, NY 10017
Tel: (212) 755 3072

School of Light and Realization (Solar)

The School of Light and Realization (Solar) is a theosophic group in the Alice Bailey tradition. It was founded in 1969 by Norman and Katy Creamer.

Hq: Box 2276, North Canton, OH 44720

School of Natural Science

The School of Natural Science is an occult group founded in 1883 by John E. Richardson.

Hq: 25355 Spanish Ranch Rd., Los Gatos, CA 95030

Seed Center

The Seed Center was founded in 1968 by independent Christian practitioner William Samuel.

Hq: c/o Mountain Brook Publications, Box 7474, Mountain Brook, AL 35253

Seicho-No-Ie [Home of Infinite Life, Wisdom and Abundance]

The Seicho-No-Ie [Home of Infinite Life, Wisdom and Abundance] is a Japanese New Thought metaphysical movement founded in 1930 by Masaharu Taniguchi, a student of Religious Science.

Hq: 14527 S. Vermont Avenue, Gardena, CA 90247
Tel: (213) 321 4833

Semjase Silver Star Center

The Semjase Silver Star Center was founded in the 1970s by followers of the messages received by Eduard "Billy" Meier, a Swiss who claims contact with a being from the Pleiades star system.

Hq: Box 797, Alamogordo, NM 88311
or
International Hq: Freie Interessengemeinschaft für Grenz- und Geistwissenschaften und Ufologie-Studien [Free Community of Interests in the Border and Spiritual Sciences and UFO Studies], Hinterschmidruti, Switzerland

SM Church

The SM Church grew out of the Temple of the Goddess, a San Francisco group dedicated to both the worship of a female deity and the practice of sado-masochism.

Hq: Priestess Robin Stewart, Box 1407, San Francisco, CA 94101

Societas Rosicruciana in Civitatibus Foederatis

The Societas Rosicruciana in Civitatibus Foederatis was founded in 1880 by Charles E. Meyer as an order within Freemasonry.

Hq: Current address unavailable for this edition

Society of Christ, Inc.

The Society of Christ is a spiritualist church founded by Bishops Dan Boughan and Harriette Leifeste.

Hq: Bishop Dan Boughan, 3061 Harrington Street, Los Angeles, CA 90006

Society Ordo Templi Orientis in America

The Society Ordo Templi Orientis in America, one of several competing O.T.O. ritual magick groups, was founded in 1975 by Marcelo Ramos

Motta, a Brazilian magician. It subsequently has developed a following in the United States.

Hq: Box 2573, Stillwater, OK 74076

Solar Light Center

The Solar Light Center was founded in the mid-1960s by UFO contactee Marianne Francis.

Hq: 7700 Avenue of the Sun, Central Point, OR 97501

Soulcraft

Soulcraft is an occult association built upon the experiences and teachings of William Dudley Pelley.

Hq: Box 192, Noblesville, IN 46060

Sovereignty, Inc.

Sovereignty, Inc. is a New Age group built around the channeling of J. Z. Knight. Knight channels an entity named Ramtha.

Hq: Box 909, Eastsound, WA 98245

Spiritual Science Mother Church

The Spiritual Science Mother Church is a Spiritualist church with roots in Christian Science. It was founded by Mother Julia O. Forrest and Dr. Carl H. Pieres.

Hq: Spiritual Science Center of New York, 360 E. 72nd Street, New York, NY 10016
Tel: (212) 628 2276

Spiritualist Episcopal Church

The Spiritualist Episcopal Church was founded in 1941 by Revs. Clifford Bias, John Bunker, and Robert Chaney, mediums at Camp Chesterfield, a Spiritualist camp in Indiana.

Hq: Current address unavailable for this edition

Starborne Unlimited

Starborne Unlimited is a New Age group built around the channeled teachings of Solara Antara Amaa-Ra.

Hq: Route 7, Box 191B, Charlottesville, VA 22901
Tel: (804) 974 7771
Fax: (804) 974 7807

Stelle Group

The Stelle Group is an occult community founded in 1963 by Richard Kieninger. It is named for Robert Stelle, the founder of the Lemurian Fellowship.

Hq: 405 Mayfield Avenue, Garland, TX 75041
Tel: (214) 864 0799
or
Stelle, IL 60919
Tel: (815) 256 2200

Superet Light Doctrine Church

The Superet Light Doctrine Church is a Spiritualist church founded in 1925 by Dr. Josephine De Croix Trust, who developed a unique perspective on the spiritual nature of color.

Hq: 2516 W. Third Street, Los Angeles, CA 90057
Tel: (213) 288 8145

Tara Center

The Tara Center was founded in 1980 by Benjamin Creme, a student of the Alice Bailey teachings, to proclaim the imminent appearance of Maitreya, the coming World Savior.

Hq: Box 6001, North Hollywood, CA 91603
Tel: (818) 785 6300

Tayu Fellowship

The Tayu Fellowship is a Neo-Pagan fellowship primarily operating within the homosexual community. It was founded in the 1970s by Daniel Inesse and others.

Hq: Box 11554, Santa Rosa, CA 95406

Teaching of the Inner Christ, Inc.

The Teaching of the Inner Christ is a metaphysical group founded in 1965 by Revs. Ann Meyer Makeever and Peter Victor Meyer. Though agreeing with the perspective of New Thought metaphysics, the group also practices channeling.

Hq: "Inner Christ" Administrative Center, 3150 Main Street, Lemon Grove, CA 92045
Tel: (619) 934 2595

Temple of Nepthys

The Temple of Nepthys was formed by former members of the Temple of Set.

Hq: P. O. Box 4603, San Francisco, CA 94101

Temple of Set

The Temple of Set was founded in 1975 by former members of the Church of Satan under the leadership of Michael A. Aquino.

Hq: P. O. Box 470307, San Francisco, CA 94147
Tel: MCI-Mail: (415) 314 3953
Telex: 650 314 3953

Temple of the Goddess Within

The Temple of the Goddess Within is a feminist Wicce (Witchcraft) group founded in the 1970s by Ann For Freedom.

Hq: 2441 Cordova Street, Oakland, CA 94602

Temple of the Pagan Way

The Temple of the Pagan Way is a Neo-Pagan group founded in 1966 by Herman Enderle and Virginia Brubaker.

Hq: Box 60151, Chicago, IL 60660

Temple of the People

The Temple of the People, formerly the Syracuse, New York, chapter of the Theosophical Society, was founded in 1898 by William H. Dower and Francis A. LaDue.

Hq: Box 7095, Halcyon, CA 93420
Tel: (805) 489 2822

Temple of Truth

The Temple of Truth, a ritual magick order, was founded in 1973 by Nelson and Anne White.

Hq: Box 93124, Pasadena, CA

Temple of Universal Law

The Temple of Universal Law is a Spiritualist church founded in 1936 by Rev. Charlotte Bright.

Hq: 5030 N. Drake, Chicago, IL 60625

Theocentric Foundation

The Theocentric Foundation is a hermetic occult group. It was founded in 1959 but had roots in previous organizations reaching back into the 1920s.

Hq: 3341 E. Cambridge Avenue, Phoenix, AZ 85008

Theosophical Society

The Theosophical Society was founded in New York City in 1875 by Helena P. Blavatsky, Henry S. Olcott,

and William Q. Judge. In 1895, the majority of the American lodges separated from the international Theosophical Society, then headquartered in India.

Hq: Post Office Bin C, Pasadena, CA 91109
Tel: (818) 797 7817
Fax: (818) 791 0319

The Theosophical Society in America

The Theosophical Society in America was founded in 1875 by Helena Petrovna Blavatsky, Col. Henry Steel Olcott, and William Judge. In 1895 the American branch of the Society split. Those lodges which remained in connection with the international movement head-quartered in Adyar, India, reorganized and eventually became known as the Theosophical Society in America.

Hq: Box 270, Wheaton, IL 60189
Tel: (312) 668 1571
or
International Hq: Adyar, Madras, India 600 020

Theosophical Society (Hartley)

The Theosophical Society (Hartley) was founded in 1951 by William Hartley, a former leader in the Theosophical Society headquartered in Pasadena, California. The group currently has no centers in the United States, but has developed a following in Holland.

International Hq: Blavatskyhius, De Ruyterstratt 74, 2518 A V Gravenhage 07023, 17776 Netherlands

The Tibetan Foundation, Inc.

The Tibetan Foundation is a New Age group built around the

channeling of Kathlyn L. Kingdon. She channels Djwhal Khul, an Ascended Master often referred to as the Tibetan.

Hq: P. O. Box 27364, Santa Ana, CA 92799
Tel: (714) 533 0755 or 758 3729

Today Church

The Today Church was founded in 1970 by Bud and Carmen Moshier, both former ministers with the Unity School of Christianity.

Hq: 13531 N. Central Expwy., Bldg. 2100, Suite 2133, Box 832366, Dallas, TX 75243
Tel: (214) 458 8550

T.O.M. Religious Foundation

The T.O.M. Religious Foundation is a Spiritualist church founded in the 1960s by Rev. Ruth Johnson.

Hq: Box 52, Chimayo, NM 87522

True Church of Christ, International

The True Church of Christ, International is a Christian Spiritualist church founded by Christian Weyand.

Hq: Box 2, Station G, Buffalo, NY 14213

Truth Center, a Universal Fellowship

The Truth Center, a Universal Fellowship was founded in 1970 by W. Norman Cooper, a former Christian Science practitioner.

Hq: 6940 Oporto Dr., Los Angeles, CA 90068

Unarius—Science of Life

The Unarius—Science of Life is a UFO contactee group founded in 1954 by Ernest L. Norman and his wife, Ruth Norman.

Hq: 143 S. Magnolia, El Cajon, CA 92022
Tel: (619) 447 4170

United Christian Scientists

The United Christian Scientists was founded in 1975 by a group of independent students of Christian Science.

Hq: Box 8048, San Jose, CA 95155

United Church and Science of Living Institute

The United Church and Science of Living Institute is a predominantly black New Thought metaphysical group founded in 1966 by Rev. Frederick Eikerenkotter II, popularly known as Rev. Ike.

Hq: Rev. Frederick Eikerenkotter II, Box 1000, Boston, MA 02103

United Church of Religious Science

The United Church of Religious Science is one of two organizations tracing their origin to the life and teachings of Ernest S. Holmes. The United Church was formally established in 1957 and grew out of the Institute of Religious Science and School of Philosophy originally founded in 1927.

Hq: 3251 W. 6th Street, Box 75127, Los Angeles, CA 90075
Tel: (213) 388 2181

United Lodge of Theosophists

The United Lodge of Theosophists was founded in 1909 by Robert Crosbie, who was originally a member of the Theosophical Society (Pasadena).

Hq: 245 W. 33rd Street, Los Angeles, CA 90007
Tel: (213) 748 7244 or 457 7397

United Spiritualist Church

The United Spiritualist Church was founded in 1967 by Rev. Floyd Humble, Edwin Potter, and Howard Mangan.

Hq: 813 W. 165th Place, Gardena, CA 90247

Unity School of Christianity

The Unity School of Christianity and its associated Association of Unity Churches is the largest New Thought metaphysical organization in the United States. Unity was founded in the 1880s by Charles S. and Myrtle Fillmore.

Hq: Unity Village, MO 64065
Tel: (816) 524 7414
or
Association of Unity Churches, Box 610, Lee's Summit, MO 64063

Universal Association of Faithists

The Universal Association of Faithists is a Spiritualist group based upon the teachings of John Ballou Newbrough, who created the Faithist movement in the 1880s. Newbrough was the author of a book, *Oahspe*, referred to as a "New Age Bible."

Hq: Universal Faithists of Kosmon, Box 664, Salt Lake City, UT 84110-0664
Tel: (801) 254 6903

Universal Church of Scientific Truth

The Universal Church of Scientific Truth is a New Thought metaphysical church founded by Dr. Joseph T. Ferguson.

Hq: Dr. Joseph T. Ferguson, 1250 Indiana Street, Birmingham, AL 35224
Tel: (205) 786 9980

Universal Church of the Master

The Universal Church of the Master, one of the larger Spiritualist churches operating in the United States, was founded in 1908 by Dr. B. J. Fitzgerald.

Hq: 501 Washington Street, Santa Clara, CA 95050
Tel: (408) 248 3624

Universal Foundation for Better Living

The Universal Foundation for Better Living is a predominantly black New Thought metaphysical church founded in 1974 by Johnnie Coleman, formerly a minister with the Unity School of Christianity.

Hq: 11901 Ashland Avenue, Chicago, IL 60643
Tel: (312) 568 2282

Universal Great Brotherhood

The Universal Great Brotherhood is a theosophical occult group founded in 1948 by Frenchman Serge de la Ferriere.

Hq: Administrative Council of the U.S.A., Box 9154, St. Louis, MO 63117

Universal Harmony Foundation

The Universal Harmony Foundation is a Spiritualist church founded in 1942 (as the Universal Psychic Science Association) by Rev. Helene and J. Bertram Gerling.

Hq: Rev. Helene Gerling, 5903 Seminole Blvd., Seminole, FL 33542
Tel: (813) 392 7725

Universal Industrial Church of the New World Comforter

The Universal Industrial Church of the New World Comforter was founded in 1947 by Allen Michael Noonan, who has claimed contact with entities from space.

Hq: 1868 Princeton Avenue, Stockton, CA 95204

Universal Life - The Inner Religion

The Universal Life - The Inner Religion was founded in Germany in 1977 by Gabriele Wittek.

Hq: Box 3379, New Haven, CT 06525
Tel: (203) 281 7771
or
International Hq: Postfach 5643, 8700 Wurzburg, Germany

Universal Link

The Universal Link, founded in England by Richard Grave in 1961, came to the U.S. in the late 1960s.

International Hq: 1, St. George Square, St. Annes, Lancashire, England, U.K.

Universal Religion of America

The Universal Religion of America was founded in 1958 by Rev. Marnie Koski.

Hq: Christ Universal Church, 295 N. Tropical Trail, Merritt Island, FL 32952

Universal Spiritualist Association

The Universal Spiritualist Association was founded in 1956 by Mabel Riffle.

Hq: Maple Grove, 5848 Pendleton Avenue, Anderson, IN 46013
Tel: (317) 644 0371

Universal White Brotherhood

The Universal White Brotherhood was founded in 1937 by theosophist Omraam Mikhal Aivanhov, a student of Bulgarian theosophist Peter Deunov.

Hq: Prosveta U.S.A., Box 49614, Los Angeles, CA 90049
or
International Hq: 2 Rue du Belvedere de la Ronce, 82310 Serves, France

Universalia

The Universalia began as a New Age channeling group in Denver in 1981. It was formally organized in 1985.

Hq: Box 6243, Denver, CO 80206

Universariun Foundation

The Universariun Foundation was founded in 1958 by Zelrun and Daisy Karsleigh.

Hq: Box 890, Taylor, AZ 85939

Universe Society Church

The Universe Society Church was founded by Hal Wilcox in 1951 (as Institute of Parapsychology) and took the present name in the early 1980s.

Hq: Box 38132, Los Angeles, CA 90038
Tel: (213) 464 3524

University of Life Church

The University of Life Church was founded in the 1960s by Richard Ireland.

Hq: Rev. Richard Ireland, 5600 Sixth Street, Phoenix, AZ 85040

URANTIA Foundation

The URANTIA Foundation, founded in 1950, publishes and

disseminates the teachings of *The URANTIA Book*, a channeled book.

Hq: 533 Diversey Pkwy., Chicago, IL 60014
Tel: (312) 327 0424

Venusian Church

The Venusian Church is a Neo-Pagan group with a strong emphasis on sexual freedom founded in 1975 by Ron Peterson.

Hq: c/o The Longhouse, 23301 Remond-Fall City Hwy., Redmond, WA 98053
Tel: (206) 391 1787

White Star

White Star is a UFO contactee group founded in 1950s by Doris C. LeVesque.

Hq: Box 307, Joshua Tree, CA 92252

Wisdom Institute of Spiritual Education

The Wisdom Institute of Spiritual Education is a New Thought organization founded by Frank and Martha Baker.

Hq: 1236 S. Marlborough, Dallas, TX 75208

Witches International Craft Associates

The Witches International Craft Associates is a Neo-Pagan Wiccan group founded in 1970 by Dr. Leo Louis Martello. W.I.C.A. follows a Sicilian Pagan tradition of Goddess worship.

Hq: 153 W. 80th St., New York, NY 10024

Word Foundation

The Word Foundation was founded in 1950 by theosophists Harold W. Percival. Percival is the author of a massive volume, *Thinking and Destiny*, which the Foundation publishes and whose teachings it espouses.

Hq: Box 18235, Dallas, TX 75218
Tel: (214) 348 5006

World Understanding

The World Understanding is a metaphysical organization founded in 1955 by Daniel Fry, who has claimed contact with entities from outer space (flying saucer beings) and also to have taken rides in their space ships.

Hq: Box 614, Alamagordo, NM 88311

METAPHYSICAL/ANCIENT WISDOM/NEW AGE PERIODICALS

ABRAXAS, 45516 Hollywood Blvd., Hollywood, CA 90027, Ecclesia Gnostica

Action, Box 1000, Boston, MA 02103, United Church and Science of Living Institute

Advance, Advanced Organization of Los Angeles, 1306 N. Berendo St., Los Angeles, CA 90027, Church of Scientology

Agape, Box 2057, Glendale, CA 91209, Ann Ree Colton Foundation of Niscience

Agasha Temple Newsletter, 460 N. Western Av., Los Angeles, CA 90004, Agasha Temple of Wisdom

Akbar Journal, 12212 N. 58th Place, Scottsdale, AZ 85254, Aquarian Educational Group

Aletheia Newsletter, 1809 N. Highway 99, Ashland, OR 97520, Aletheia Foundation

The American Theosophist, Box 270, Wheaton, IL 60189, The Theosophical Society in America

Aquarian Lights, Box 502, Wyalusing, PA 18853, International Church of Ageless Wisdom

As It Is, 2634 E. 7th St., Long Beach, CA 90804, Morningland-Church of the Ascended Christ

Attain: Health, Happiness, and Success, 31916 Pat's Lane, Springfield, LA 70462, Congregational Church of Practical Theology

The Auditor, Church of Scientology, Western United States, 1413 N. Berendo St., Los Angeles, CA 90027, Church of Scientology

Aura Flamma, Box 1219, Corpus Christi, TX 78403, American Gnostic Church

Avasthology Journal, 107 N. Ventura St., Ojai, CA 93023, Ecumenical Ministry of the Unity of All Religions

The Banner of Light, Maple Grove, 5848 Pendleton Avenue, Anderson, IN 46013, Universal Spiritualist Association

Bark Leaf, 451 Columbus Avenue, San Francisco, CA 94133, Church of the Tree of Life

Basor, Basor Press, 578 Green, No. 5-20, San Bruno, CA 94066, Edta Ha Thoma

The Beacon, Lucis Publishing Company, 113 University Place, 11th Floor, Box 722, Cooper Station, New York, NY 10276, Arcane School

Brothersong, c/o Church of the Earth, Box 13158, Dinkytown Station, Minneapolis, MN 55414, Brothers of the Earth

Bulletin, New Age Bible and Philosophy Center, 1139 Lincoln Blvd., Santa Monica, CA 90403, New Age Bible and Philosophy Center

Cause, American Saint Hill Organization, 1413 N. Berendo St., Los Angeles, CA 90027, Church of Scientology

The Channel, 1300 Grand Street, Alameda, CA 94501, Home of Truth

The Christian Science Journal, One Norway Street, Boston, MA 02115, Church of Christ, Scientist

The Christian Science Monitor, One Norway Street, Boston, MA 02115, Church of Christ, Scientist

Christian Science Quarterly, One Norway Street, Boston, MA 02115, Church of Christ, Scientist

Christian Science Sentinel, One Norway Street, Boston, MA 02115, Church of Christ, Scientist

Church of Light Quarterly, Box 76862, Los Angeles, CA 90076, Church of Light

Church of Truth Newsletter, 690 East Orange Grove Blvd., Pasadena, CA 91104, International Alliance of Churches of the Truth

Circle Network Bulletin, Box 219, Mt. Horeb, WI 53572, Church of Circle Wicca

Circle Network News, Box 219, Mt. Horeb, WI 53572, Church of Circle Wicca

The Cloven Hoof, Box 210082, San Francisco, CA 94121, Church of Satan

The Coming Revolution, Box A, Livingston, MT 59047, Church Universal and Triumphant

Communion, Box 169, Spaulding, MI 49886, Liberal Catholic Church International

Contact, Association of Unity Churches, Box 610, Lee's Summit, MO 64063, Unity School of Christianity

Contributor's Bulletin, 3910 Los Feliz Blvd., Los Angeles, CA 90027, Philosophical Research Society

Cosmic Frontiers, Box 257, June Lake, CA 93529, Church of Cosmic Origin and School of Thought

Cosmic Voice, 6202 Afton Place, Hollywood, CA 90028, Aetherius Society

The Covenant of the Goddess Newsletter, Amber K., Box 176, Blue Mounds, WI 53517, Covenant of the Goddess

Creative Thought, 3130 5th Avenue, San Diego, CA 92103, Religious Science International

Daily Inspiration for Better Living, 11901 Ashland Avenue, Chicago, IL 60643, Universal Foundation for Better Living

Daily Meditation, Box 2710, San Antonio, TX 78299, Mayan Order

Daily Meditation, Prosveta Inc., 1565 Montee Masson, Duvernay Est, Laval, PQ H7E 4P2, Canada, Universal White Brotherhood

Daily Studies, 1819 E. 14th Avenue, Denver, CO 80218, Divine Science Federation International

Daily Word, Unity Village, MO 64065, Unity School of Christianity

Divine Truth Commentary, Box 66003, Washington, DC 20035-6003, Foundation Church of Divine Truth

Druid Missal-any, 616 Minor Rd., Orinda, CA 94563, Reformed Druids of North America

Ensenzas de la Neuva Era, Box 346, Brookfield, MA 01506, New Age Teachings

Equinox, Box 90018, Nashville, TN 37209, Society Ordo Templi Orientis in America

Esoteric Review, 533 E. Anapamu St., Santa Barbara, CA 93013, Independent Church of Antioch

E.S.P. Laboratory Newsletter, Box 216, 219 S. Ridge Drive, Edgewood, TX 75119, E.S.P. Laboratory

The Etherian Bulletin, Box 446, San Marcos, CA 92069, Etherian Religious Society of Universal Brotherhood

Expression, Box 4897, Washington, DC 20008, Inner Peace Movement

Faith, Noroton, CT 06820, Life Study Fellowship Foundation, Inc.

The Faithist Journal, 2324 Suffolk Av., Kingman, AZ 86401, Universal Association of Faithists

Fiery Synthesis, Box 267, Sedona, AZ 86336, Aquarian Educational Group

Foundation Newsletter, Tonapah, AZ 85354, Foundation for Science of Spiritual Law

Freedom, Church of Scientology, Western United States, 1404 N. Catalina St., Los Angeles, CA 90027, Church of Scientology

Gateways, Box 324, Rialto, CA 92376, New Order of Glastonbury

Georgian Newsletter, 1908 Verde St., Bakersfield, CA 93304, The Georgian Church

The Gnostic, 3437 Alma, No. 23, Palo Alto, CA 94306, Ecclesia Gnostica Mysterium

The Gnostic Arhat, Box 291488, Los Angeles, CA 90029, The Gnostic Association of Cultural and Anthropological Studies

The Golden Dawn, Box 356, Columbus, NM 88029, City of the Sun Foundation

Grail World, Grail World Publishing Co., 512 Fairlawn Dr., Urbana, IL 61801, Grail Movement of America

The Green Egg, Box 982, Ukiah, CA 95482, Church of All Worlds

The Herald of Christian Science, One Norway Street, Boston, MA 02115, Church of Christ, Scientist

Hermes, Universal Theosophy Fellowship, Box 1085, Santa Barbara, CA 92101, United Lodge of Theosophists

The Hidden Light, Box 5094, Covina, CA 91723, Fraternitas L. V. X. Occulta

The Hidden Path, Windwalker, Box 793 F, Wheeling, IL 60090, Gardnerian Wicca

The Huna Work, Huna Research Inc., 126 Camillia Dr., Cape Girardeau, MO 63701, Huna Research Associates

The I.G.A.S. Journal, 1809 East Bayview Blvd., Norfolk, VA 23503, International General Assembly of Spiritualists

In the Continuum, Box 415, Oroville, CA 95965, Ordo Templi Orientis

Independent Christian Science Quarterly, 20 East 68th Street, New York, NY 10021, International Metaphysical Association

The Infinite Way Letter, Box 215, Youngtown, AZ 85363, Infinite Way

Inner Light Foundation Newsletter, Box 761, Novato, CA 94948, Inner Light Foundation

Inner Peace, Coleman Publishing, 99 Milbar Blvd., Farmingdale, NY 11735, Miracle Experiences Inc.

Integrity International, Box 9, 100 Mile House, British Columbia, Canada V0K 2E0, Emissaries of Divine Light

International Spiritualist News Review, 3371 Findlay Street, Vancouver, BC, Canada, International Spiritualist Alliance

Journal for Anthroposophy, 211 Madison Av., New York, NY 10016, Anthroposophical Society

Kosmon Voice, Box 664, Salt Lake City, UT 84110-0664, Universal Association of Faithists

The Lamp, Box 60235, Oklahoma, OK 73146, Old Holy Catholic Church, Province of North America

Law of Life Enlightener, A. D. K. Publications, 8575 S. Crow Cutoff, Rye Star Route, Pueblo, CA 81044, Law of Life Activity

Lemurian View Point, Box 397, Ramona, CA 92065, Lemurian Fellowship

Life in Action, 25355 Spanish Ranch Road, Los Gatos, CA 95030, School of Natural Science

Life Times, Santa Barbara, CA, Independent Church of Antioch

The Light Beyond, Box 366, Grand Central Station, New York, NY 10017, Universal Brotherhood

Light of the Logos, 59700, 29 Palms Highway, Box 640, Yucca Valley, CA 92286-0640, Institute of Mentalphysics

Light on the Path, Sedalia, CO 80135, Brotherhood of the White Temple

Longhouse Calendar, 23301 Redmond-Fall, City Rd., Redmond, WA 98053, Venusian Church

The L.O.T.U.S., 161 N. Sandusky, Tiffin, OH 44883, Light of the Universe

Lotus Leaves, Box 39, Fabins, TX 79838, Lotus Ashram

Lucifer, Blavatsyhuis, de Ruyterstraat 74, 2518 A V Gravenhage, 070231776 The Netherlands, Theosophical Society (Hartley)

The Madre-Grande Journal, Box 227, Dulzura, CA 92017, Johannine Catholic Church

The Magical Link, JAL Box 7666, New York, NY 10116, Ordo Templi Orientis

Mark-Age Inform Nations (MAIN), Box 290368, Ft. Lauderdale, FL 33329, Mark-Age

Master Thoughts, Box 37, San Marcos, CA 92069-0025, Church of the Trinity (Invisible Ministry)

The Mentor, Two Larkin Rd., Scarsdale, NY 10583, Sanctuary of the Master's Presence

Mercury, 321 W. 101th St., New York, NY 10025, Societas Rosicruciana in America

The Messenger, 2107 Lyon St., San Francisco, CA 94115, The Swedenborgian Church

The Metaphysical Messenger, 2717 Browning Street, Sarasota, FL 33577, Church of Metaphysical Christianity

Metu Neter, c/o Oracle of Thoth Inc., Box 281, Bronx, NY 10462, Ausar Auset Society

Minister's Tips, 31916 Pat's Lane, Springfield, LA 70462, Congregational Church of Practical Theology

Miracle News, Box 158, Islip Terrace, NY 11752, Miracle Experiences Inc.

Miracles, San Francisco Miracles Foundation, 1040 Masonic Avenue 2, San Francisco, CA 94117, Miracle Experiences Inc.

The National Spiritualist Reporter, 1245 West Watkins Rd., Phoenix, AZ 85007, National Colored Spiritualist Association of Churches

The National Spiritualist Summit, 668 E. 62nd Street, Indianapolis, IN 46220, National Spiritualist Association of Churches

Network News, Box 6001, North Hollywood, CA 91603, Tara Center

The New Age Forum, Box 31129, Phoenix, AZ 85046, Church of Essential Science

New Age Teachings, Box 346, Brookfield, MA 01506, New Age Teachings

New Church Home, Bryn Athyn, PA 19009, General Church of the New Jerusalem

New Church of Life, Bryn Athyn, PA 19009, General Church of the New Jerusalem

New Dimensions, 8780 Venice Blvd., Los Angeles, CA 90034, Foundation for Human Understanding

The New Spirit, 21475 Summit Rd., Los Gatos, CA 95030, Church of Revelation (Hawaii)

New York Newsletter, The Christian Community, 309 West 74th St., New York, NY 10023, Anthroposophical Society

Newsletter, Box 367, Laguna Beach, CA 92652-0367, Old Catholic Episcopal Church

Newsletter, 3055 S. Bronco, Las Vegas, NV 89102, Foundation Faith of God

Newsletter, Star Route 2, Box CLC , Deming, NM 80030, New Age Church of Truth

Newsletter for the Americans, Box 930, Montgomery, TX 77356, Church of the White Eagle Lodge

Newsletter of the Superetist Brotherhood and Sisterhood, 1516 W. 3rd Street, Los Angeles, CA 90057, Superet Light Doctrine

Noohra Light, 720 Paularino Avenue, Costa Mesa, CA 92626, Noohra Foundation

Of a Like Mind, Box 6021, Madison, WI 53704, Dianic Wicca

Open Letter, c/o Ruby Focus of Magnificent Consummation, P. O. Drawer 1188, Sedona, AZ 86336, Ruby Focus of Magnificent Consummation

Our Daily Bread, Swedenborg Book Center, 2129 Chestnut Street, Philadelphia, PA 19103, The Swedenborgian Church

Outer Court Communications, Box 1366, Nashua, NH 03061, Our Lady of Enchantment, Church of the Old Religion

Pagan Spirit Alliance Newsletter, Box 219, Mt. Horeb, WI 53572, Church of Circle Wicca

Panegyria, Box 85507, Seattle, WA 98145, Aquarian Tabernacle Church

The Path of Truth, Box 5582, Johannesburg, South Africa 2000, School of Truth

Pathways to Health, The A.R.E. Clinic, 4018 N. 40th St., Phoenix CA 85018, Association for Research and Enlightenment

Pearls of Wisdom, Box A, Livingston, MT 59047, Church Universal and Triumphant

Pentegram, Box 9246, Bakersfield, CA 93389, Lectorium Rosicrucianum

The Philosophers' Stone, Administration Building, Stelle, IL 60919, Stelle Group

Planetary Beacon, Box 180786, Austin, TX 78718, Planetary Light Association

Prism, Church of Antioch, Box 1015, Mountain View, CA 94042, Church of Antioch

Prisms of Joy, 2821 De La Vina, Santa Barbara, CA 93105, Joy Foundation

PRS Journal, 3910 Los Feliz Blvd., Los Angeles, CA 90027, Philosophical Research Society

P.R.S. News, 3910 Los Feliz Blvd., Los Angeles, CA 90027, Philosophical Research Society

The Quest, Box 270, Wheaton, IL 60189, The Theosophical Society in America

Quimby Center Newsletter, Box 453, Alamogordo, NM 88310, Quimby Center

Radiance, Box 83, Hinniker, NH 03242, Universal Association of Faithists

Rays from the Rose Cross, 2222 Mission Avenue, Box 913, Oceanside, CA 92054, Rosicrucian Fellowship

Red Garters, Box 162046, Sacramento, CA 95816, New Wiccan Church

Reflections on the Inner Light, Route 1, Box 141, Timberville, VA 22853, Fellowship of the Inner Light

Revelation of Awareness, Box 115, Olympia, WA 98507, Cosmic Awareness Communications

Rosicrucian Digest, Rosicrucian Park, San Jose, CA 95191, Ancient and Mystical Order of the Rosae Crucis

Rosicrucian Forum, Rosicrucian Park, San Jose, CA 95191, Ancient and Mystical Order of the Rosae Crucis

Royal Teton Ranch News, Box A, Livingston, MT 59047, Church Universal and Triumphant

The Sabian News Letter, 1324 Tulane Rd., Wilmington, DE 19803, Sabian Assembly

Science of Mind, Box 75127, Los Angeles, CA 90075, United Church of Religious Science

Scroll, Box 16103, San Diego, CA 92116, First Christians' Essene Church

Scroll of Set, P. O. Box 29271, San Francisco, CA 94129, Temple of Set

The Seeker Newsletter, Box 7601, San Diego, CA 92007, Love Project

The Seeker's Quest Newsletter, Box 8188, San Jose, CA 95155 Christ Ministry Foundation

Seicho-No-Ie Truth of Life, 14527 S. Vermont Avenue, Gardena, CA 90247, Seicho-No-Ie

Seshen, Ram-it-ka Isa-hotep, 2922 S. Marvin Ave., Tucson, AZ 85730, Church of the Eternal Source

Share International, Box 971, North Hollywood, CA 91603, Tara Center

The Solarian, Route 1, Box 71, Sutton's Bay, MI 49682, School of Light and Realization (Solar)

Source, Church of Scientology, Flag Service Org., Inc., P. O. Box 31751, Tampa, FL 33631-3751, Church of Scientology

The Spiritual Digest, 5903 Seminole Blvd., Seminole, FL 33452 Universal Harmony Foundation

Spiritual Healing Bulletin, 6202 Afton Place, Hollywood, CA 90028, Aetherius Society

The Spiritual Outlook, 809 W. 165th St., Place Gardena, CA 90247, United Spiritualist Church

S.P.M. Newsletter, 200 E. 58th Street, New York, NY 10019, Society of Pragmatic Mysticism

St. Thomas Journal, 159 Mission St., No. B, Santa Cruz, CA 95060, Federation of St. Thomas Christian Churches

Starcraft, 7700 Avenue of the Sun, Central Point, OR 97501, Solar Light Center

Stella Polaris, Newlands, Rake, Liss, Hampshire, England GU33 7HY, United Kingdom, Church of the White Eagle Lodge

The Stelle Group Newsletter, Box 75, Quinlan, TX 75474, Stelle Group

Studia Swedenborgiana, 48 Sargent Street, Newton, MA, The Swedenborgian Church

Sunrise, P. O. Bin C, Pasadena, CA 91109, Theosophical Society

Survival, Box 1502, New Bern, NC 28560, Church and School of Wicca

The Sword of Dyrnwyn, 1029 Peachtree St., Ste. 218, Atlanta, GA 30309, Cymry Wicca

The Temple Artisan, Box 7095, Halcyon, CA 93420, Temple of the People

Temple Messenger, 5030 N. Drake, Chicago, IL 60625, Temple of Universal Law

Theologia 21, Box 37, San Marcos, CA 92069-0025, Church of the Trinity (Invisible Ministry)

The Theosophical Movement, Theosophy Hall, 40 New Marine Lane, Bombay 400 001, India, United Lodge of Theosophists

Theosophy, 245 W. 33rd St., Los Angeles, CA 90007, United Lodge of Theosophists

Thesmophoria, Susan B. Anthony Coven No. 1, Box 11363, Oakland, CA 94611, Dianic Wicca

Tidings, Box 37, San Marcos, CA 92069-0025, Church of the Trinity (Invisible Ministry)

Times of the Signs, Box 307, Joshua Tree, CA 92252, White Star

Ubique, The Liberal Catholic Church, Box 1117, Melbourne, FL 32901, Liberal Catholic Church, Province of the United States

U.C.C. Spokesman, 1704 Venice Blvd., Los Angeles, CA 90006, Universal Christ Church, Inc.

U.C.M. Magazine, 45 North 1st St., San Jose, CA 95113, Universal Church of the Master

Unarius Light, 145 S. Magnolia, El Cajon, CA 92020, Unarius-Science of Life

Understanding, Box 614, Alamagordo, NM 88311, World Understanding

UNISOC Newsletter, Box 38132, Hollywood, CA 90038, Universe Society Church

Unity, Unity Village, MO 64065, Unity School of Christianity

The Universalian, Box 6243, Denver, CO 80306, Universalia

URANTIA Brotherhood Bulletin, 533 Diversey Parkway, Chicago, IL 60614, Urantia Brotherhood

The URANTIAN Journal of URANTIA Brotherhood, 533 Diversey Parkway, Chicago, IL 60614, Urantia Brotherhood

URANTIAN News from URANTIA Foundation, 533 Diversey Parkway, Chicago, IL 60614, Urantia Brotherhood

USRS Newsletter, Unity Village, MO 64065, Unity School of Christianity

Venture Inward, Box 595, Virginia Beach, VA 23451, Association for Research and Enlightenment

Vision, 3150 Main St., Lemon Grove, CA 92045, Teachings of the Inner Christ, Inc.

The Voice, Box 4765, San Jose, CA 95126, Church of Inner Wisdom

Voice of Astara, 800 Arrow Hwy., Box 5003, Upland, CA 91785, Astara

The Voice of the "I AM", 1120 Stonehedge Drive, Schaumburg, IL 60194, "I AM" Religious Activity

The Voice of the Synod, Very Rev. William Holme, Box 7042, Rochester, MN 55903, Liberal Catholic Church, Province of the United States

The Voice of Universarius, Box 890, Taylor, AZ 92020, Universariun Foundation

The Voyager, Box 832366, Richardson, TX 75083-2366, Today Church

Waves of Joy, 2821 De La Vina, Santa Barbara, CA 93105, Joy Foundation

The Way, Box 333, Kings Park, NY 11754, New Age Church of the Christ

Wee Wisdom, Unity Village, MO 64065, Unity School of Christianity

The White Light, Box 93124, Pasadena, CA 91109-3124, Temple of Truth

The Wise Woman, 2441 Cordova St., Oakland, CA 94602, Temple of the Goddess Within

The World, Box 333, Kings Park, NY 11754, New Age Church of the Christ

World Goodwill Newsletter, World Goodwill, 113 University Place, 11th Floor, Box 722, Cooper Station, New York, NY 10276, Arcane School

The World Wide Messenger, Universelles Leben, Postfach 5643, 8700 Wurz, Germany, Universal Life - The Inner Religion

Young Ideas, Box 5582, Johannesburg, South Africa 2000, School of Truth

SHINTO

Shinto is the state religion of Japan. It is based upon the worship of Nature, often personified in a number of deities. The central deity is Kami, the life force. Frequently identified with the nationalistic aspiration of pre-World War II Japan, it was not popular in the United States but did find its way to Hawaii which had the largest Japanese population. During World War II most of the Shinto shrines in America were confiscated and all but one destroyed. The older Shinto groups survived in Hawaii and reformed after the war. Very little has been written about the variations in Shinto organization and practice.

After World War II, with the declaration of religious freedom, Japan experienced a blossoming of what were termed "new religions." Some of these new religions were basically variations on Shinto and they began to make their way to the West in the wake of their rapid expansion in Japan. Religions like Konko Kyo and Tenreikyo were suppressed during the early twentieth century.

Church of World Messianity

The Church of World Messianity (also known as Sekai Kyusei Kyo) was founded in Japan by Mokichi Okada in 1934. It assumed its present name in 1950.

Hq: 3068 San Marino Street, Los Angeles, CA 90006
Tel: (213) 387 8366

Honkyoku Shinto

Honkyoku Shinto is a traditionalist form of Shinto. It was brought to Hawaii in 1906 by Rev. Masasato Kawasaki.

Hq: Honkyoku-Daijingu Temple, 61 Puiwa Rd., Honolulu, HI 96817

Inari Shinto

Inari Shinto was founded in Hawaii in 1912 by Rev. Yoshio Akizaki.

Hq: Hawaii Inari Taisha, 2132 S. King Street, Honolulu, HI 96817

Jinga Shinto

The Jinga Shinto was founded in Hawaii in 1913 by Rev. Shina Miyake.

Hq: Hawaii Ichizuchi Jinga, 2020 S. King Street, Honolulu, HI 96817

Jinsha Shinto

Jinsha Shinto was brought to Hawaii in 1913.

Hq: Kotohira Jinshan Temple, 1045 Kana Lane, Honolulu, HI 96817

Konko Kyo

The Konko Kyo, a Japanese new religion, was founded in 1859 by Bunjiro Kawate. It came to America in 1919.

Hq: Rev. Alfred Y. Tsyyuki, 2924 E. 1st Street, Los Angeles, CA 90033
Tel: (213) 268 6980

Mahikari of America

Mahikari of America (Divine True Light) was founded in Japan in 1959 by Kotama Okada.

Hq: Los Angeles Dojo, 6470 Foothill Blvd., Tujunga, CA 91042
Tel: (818) 353 0071
or
International Hq: 1517-8 Yamada-oho, Takayama City, Gifu Japan

Shinreikyo

Shinreikyo is a Shinto movement which emphasizes healing. It came to Hawaii in 1963.

Hq: c/o Mr. Kameo Kiyota, 310C Uulani St., Hilo, HI 96720

Society of Johrei

The Society of Johrei was founded in 1971 by former members of the the Church of World Messianity.

Hq: Box 1321, Brookline, MA 02146
Tel: (617) 739 9042

Taishakyo Shinto

Taishakyo Shinto was founded in 1873 in Japan by Sonfuku Senge. It was brought to Hawaii in 1906.

Hq: 215 N. Kukui Street, Honolulu, HI 96817
Tel: (213) 261 3379

Tenrikyo

Tenrikyo, one of Japan's new religions, was founded by Miki Nakayama in 1838 and was officially recognized in 1908.

Hq: Tenrikyo Mission, 2727 E. First Street, Los Angeles, CA 90033
Tel: (213) 261 3379
or
International Hq: Tenri-san, Nara-ken 632, Japan

Tensho-Kotai-Jingu-Kyo

The Tensho-Kotai-Jingu-Kyo was founded in 1947 by Ogamisama (Kitamura Sayo).

Hq: Hawaii Dojo, 888 N. King Street, Honolulu, HI 96817
Tel: (808) 841 7162

Third Civilization

Third Civilization, a new religion, was founded in the nineteenth century by Sen-sei Koji Ogasawara.

Hq: Box 1836, Santa Fe, NM 87501

SHINTO PERIODICALS

Konko Review, 2924 East First Street, Los Angeles, CA 90033, Konko Kyo

MOA Newsletter, Mokichi Okada Association, 369 Junipero Avenue, Long Beach, CA 90814, Church of World Messianity

Tenrikyo Newsletter, 2727 E. First Street, Los Angeles, CA 90033, Tenrikyo

Third Civilization Monthly, Box 1836 , Santa Fe, NM 87501, Third Civilization

True Light, 6470 Foothill Blvd., Tujunga, CA 91042, Mahikari of America

Voice from Heaven, Tensho-Kotai-Jingu-Kyo, Tabuse, Yamagushi Pref., Japan, Tensho-Kotai-Jingu-Kyo

World Messianity Newsletter, 369 Junipero Avenue, Long Beach, CA 90814, Church of World Messianity

SIKHISM/SANT MAT

Sikhism was developed by Guru Nanak, a sixteenth century religious reformer in India (and thus a contemporary of Martin Luther). Nanak faced the problem of the intense conflict between Muslims, who had conquered part of northern India and the Hindus. Spurred by a vision of God's presence, he created a new religion which, by combining the best features of each, he hoped might bring reconciliation. Instead, it added a new faith to those already present. Nanak emphasized a monotheistic God, which he called the True Name, and advocated as a major religious practice the repetition of the Name of God. Following Nanak's death, nine gurus (teachers) followed him in succession. After the last guru's death, their writings were combined in a book, the *Siri Guru Granth Sahib*, the holy book of the Sikhs, which became their new and permanent guru. Administrative leadership for the faith was invested in a collective of senior leaders in Amritsar, where the Golden Temple became the center of the world Sikh community.

Sikhism's strength was in northern India, especially the Punjab. There in the eighteenth century a new religious impulse developed which drew heavily from Sikhism but differed from it in several important respects. Most importantly, Sant Mat (the Way of the Saints) reintroduced the living guru and thus set aside the *Siri Guru Granth Sahib* as the ultimate authority. The repetition of the Name of God was developed into *surat shabd yoga*, the yoga of the sound current. The guru initiates the believer into the techniques, primarily the repetition of mantras, particular sounds, which lead one back to union with God. While Sikhism remained a religion of Punjabis, at the beginning of the twentieth century Sant Mat began to find an audience in the West. In the years since the abandonment of the Oriental exclusion act, several Sant Mat teachers (most importantly Kirpal Singh) have developed followings in the United States, and a set of Westernized Sant Mat groups shorn of their Indian cultural trapping have appeared (ECKANKAR, Movement of Inner Spiritual Awareness).

Divine Science of Light and Sound

The Divine Science of Light and Sound was founded in 1980 by Jerry Mulvin, a former teacher with ECKANKAR.

Hq: 2554 Lincoln Blvd., Box 620, Marina del Rey, CA 90291
Tel: (213) 306 3322

ECKANKAR

The ECKANKAR was founded in 1965 by Paul Twitchell, formerly a disciple of Kirpal Singh. It has become the source of other Westernized Sant Mat groups.

Hq: Box 27300, Minneapolis, MN 55427
Tel: (612) 544 0066

Elan Vital

The Elan Vital, a Sant Mat group, was founded in the early 1980s by Guru Maharaj Ji. Originally called the Divine Life Mission, it reorganized as Elan Vital in the 1980s.

Hq: Box 6130, Malibu, CA 90264

Kirpal Light Satsang

The Kirpal Light Satsang was founded in 1974 by Thakar Singh, one of several teachers who claimed a succession from Kirpal Singh.

Hq: Merwin Lake Rd., Kinderhook, NY 12106
Tel: (518) 758 1906

Master Path

Master Path was founded in the late 1980s by Gary Olson, formerly associated with Darwin Gross and the Sounds of Soul.

Hq: 1231 South Bender, Glendora, CA 91740

Movement of Spiritual Inner Awareness, Church of the

The Church of the Movement of Spiritual Inner Awareness was founded in 1968 by Sri John-Roger Hinkins, formerly a leader with ECKANKAR.

Hq: 3500 W. Adams Blvd., Los Angeles, CA 90018
Tel: (213) 737 4055

Nirankari Universal Brotherhood Mission

The Nirankari Universal Brotherhood Mission is a Sant Mat group founded in 1929 by Boota Singh.

Hq: Current address unavailable for this edition

Radha Soami Satsang Beas

The Radha Soami Satsang Beas, an early Sant Mat group, developed around the work of Jaimal Singh (1838-1903) who developed a following at Beas.

Hq: Roland G. de Vries, 10901 Mill Springs Dr., Nevada City, CA 95959
Tel: (916) 262 5772
or
International Hq: Dera Baba Jaimal Singh, Dist. Amritsar 143, 204 Punjab, India

Sant Bani Ashram

The Sant Bani Ashram was founded by Ajaib Singh, one of the claimants to the succession of Kirpal Singh.

Hq: Franklin, NH 03235

Sawan Kirpal Ruhani Mission

The Sawan Kirpal Ruhani Mission is the primary organization carrying on the lineage of Kirpal Singh. It recognized the succession of Darshan Singh, Kirpal Singh's son.

Hq: 8605 Village Way, No. C, Alexandria, VA 22309-1605
or
International Hq: Kirpal Ashram, 2 Canal Rd., Vijay Magar, Delhi, India 110009

Sikh Council of North America

The Sikh Council of North America seeks to provide coordination of and communication among American Sikh centers, primarily those of Punjabi-Americans.

Hq: 95-30 118th St., Richmond Hill, NY 11419

Sikh Dharma

The Sikh Dharma is the primary Sikh group operating among non-Punjabis in the West. It was founded in Los Angeles in 1968 by Yogi Bhajan.

Hq: Chancellor to the Siri Singh, Sahib: M.S.S. Guru Terath, Singh Khalsa, Box 845, Santa Cruz, NM 87567

Sounds of Soul

Sounds of Soul was founded in Oregon by Sri Darwin Gross, the successor to Paul Twitchell and formerly the leader of ECKANKAR.

Hq: Box 68290, Oak Grove, OR 97268

SIKHISM/SANT MAT PERIODICALS

Beads of Truth, 3HO Foundation, 1620 Pruess Rd., Los Angeles, CA 90035, Sikh Dharma

ECKANKAR Journal, Box 27300, Minneapolis, MN 55427, ECKANKAR

Kirpal Light Satsang Newsletter, Merwin Lake Rd., Kinderhook, NY 12160, Kirpal Light Satsang

The Movement Newspaper, Box 19458, Los Angeles, CA 90019, Church of the Movement of Spiritual Inner Awareness

Radha Soami Greetings, 18 Country Dr., Hutchinson, KS 67501, Radha Soami Satsang Beas

Sant Bani: The Voice of the Saints, Sant Bani Ashram, Franklin, NH 03235, Sant Bani Ashram

Sant Nirankari, Nirankari Colony, Delhi 1100009, India, Nirankari Universal Brotherhood Mission

Sat, Merwin Lake Rd., Kinderhook, NY 12160, Kirpal Light Satsang

Sat Sandesh, Rte. 1, Box 24, Bowling Green, VA 22427, Sawan Kirpal Ruhani Mission

Sawan Kirpal Ruhani Mission Newsletter, Rte. 1, Box 24, Bowling Green, VA 22427, Sawan Kirpal Ruhani Mission

TAOISM

Taoism is one of the ancient religions of China. It urges the harmonization of the individual with Nature which leads to an ethical stance of doing nothing contrary to Nature. Taoism is possibly best known in the West for its philosophy of Yin and Yang (male and female) and the desire to find health and happiness by balancing these two basic realities of nature. Taoism first found acceptance in the West, through the I Ching, a popular Chinese divinatory practice, but more recently has experienced its greatest success through its association with the martial arts, especially kung fu. Taoist religious groups, often in connection with martial arts centers, began to appear in the 1960s, and while not as popular as Buddhism, it is finding a small but dedicated following.

Chung Fu Kuan (Taoist Sanctuary)

The Taoist Sanctuary (Inner Truth Looking Place) was founded in the 1960s by Dr. Khigh Alx Dhieh, best known as a character actor on television.

Hq: Phoenix, AZ

East West Foundation

Macrobiotics, which developed in Japan from underlying Chinese taoist principles, has been widely accepted as a diet system, but also includes a complete metaphysical system. The East West Foundation founded in 1972 by Michio Kushi is the most successful macrobiotic association in the United States.

Hq: 17 Station Street, Brookline, MA 02147
Tel: (617) 232 1000

Foundation of Tao

The Foundation of Tao was founded by Dr. Stephen Chang, a Chinese-American physician.

Hq: 1015 Lakeview Way, Redwood City, CA 94062
Tel: (415) 365 0835

George Ohsawa Macrobiotics Foundation

The George Ohsawa Macrobiotics Foundation was founded in the 1950s by Herman Aihara. Aihara was a student of George Ohsawa, the founder of Macrobiotics

265

Hq: 1511 Robinson Street, Oroville, CA
    95965
Tel: (916) 533 7702

Shrine of the Eternal Breath of Tao

The Shrine was founded in the 1970s by Master Ni, Hua-Ching, the author of a number of books on Taoism.

Hq: 117 Stonehaven Way, Los Angeles,
    CA 90049
Tel: (213) 472 9970

Taoist Esoteric Yoga Center and Foundation

The Taoist Esoteric Yoga center and Foundation was established by Mantak Chia and Maneewan Chia, who moved to the United States from Thailand in the 1970s. From the original center, the Foundation has spread across the United States and Europe.

Hq: P. O. Box 1194, Huntington, NY
    11743
Tel: (516) 367 2701

TAOIST PERIODICALS

East West Journal, 17 Station Street, Brookline, MA 02147, East West Foundation

The Healing Tao Journal, P. O. Box 1194, Huntington, NY 11743, Taoist Esoteric Yoga Center and Foundation

Macrobiotics Today, 1511 Robinson Street, Oroville, CA 95965, George Ohsawa Macrobiotics Foundation

UNCLASSIFIED RELIGIOUS ORGANIZATIONS

The diversity of American religion pictured in the preceding chapters is even more evident as this last chapter is approached. The groups listed below do not fit into any of the major divisions of American religion as described in the preceding chapters. Included below not only are a number of unique perspectives to religion, but a variety of "non-religious" organizations for whom atheism functions much as religion does for believers. A number of mail order churches, those which offer ordination through the mail for a small fee to any who ask, which have little or no doctrinal position are also listed in this chapter. Finally, this last chapter includes a number of international movements which as yet have not developed a large diverse following in America (Zoroastrianism) or have been able to keep most of their followers in a single organization (Bahais, Unitarians).

All-One-Faith-in-One-God State

The All-One-Faith-in-One-God State was founded in 1959 by Rev. Henry Corey and Dr. E. H. Bonner. A soapmaker, Bonner advertises his faith on the soap's labels.

Hq: Dr. E. H. Bonner, Box 28, Escondido, CA 92025
Tel: (619 745 7069

American Association for the Advancement of Atheism

The American Association for the Advancement of Atheism was founded in 1925 by Charles Lee Smith, a popular lecturer and advocate of a nontheistic philosophy.

Hq: Box 2832, San Diego, CA 92112

American Atheists, Inc.

American Atheists, Inc. was founded in 1963 by Madalyn Murray O'Hair, who became famous for filing a suit against public recitation of the Bible and the Lord's Prayer in the public schools.

Hq: Jon G. Murray, Box 2117, Austin, TX 78767
Tel: (512) 458 1244

American Ethical Union

The American Ethical Union was founded in 1876 (as Ethical Cultural Society) by ethicist Felix Adler.

Hq: Pres. Ron Solomon, 2 West 64th Street, New York, NY 10023

Tel: (212) 873 6500

or

International Hq: International Humanist and Ethical Union, Ouderhof 11, 2512 GH Utrecht, The Netherlands

American Fellowship Church

The American Fellowship Church was founded in 1975 (as Mother Earth Church) by T. H. Swenson.

Hq: Box 4693-G, Rolling Bay, WA 98061

American Humanist Association

The American Humanist Association was founded in 1929 by Charles Francis Potter and Theodore Curtis Abell who attempted to articulate a non-theistic religion.

Hq: 7 Harwood Dr., Box 146, Amherst, NY 14226-0146

Tel: (716) 839 5080

American Rationalist Federation

The American Rationalist Federation was founded in 1955 by former members of the United Secularists of America in protest of its secretive financial policies. Rationalism is defined as a commitment to the supremacy of reason.

Hq: 2001 St. Louis Avenue, St. Louis, MO 63144

Atheists United

Atheists United was founded in 1981 by atheists in the greater Los Angeles area.

Hq: Suite 211, 14542 Ventura Blvd., Sherman Oaks, CA 91403

Baha'i Faith

The Baha'i Faith grew out of the teachings of Baha'u'llah and his son Abdu'l-Baha, two religious teachers from Persia who had been exiled to Palestine, from whence the Faith has spread worldwide. The Faith was established in America with its initial converts in the 1890s.

Hq: c/o Gen. Sec. Robert Henderson, 536 Sheridan Road, Wilmette, IL 60091

Tel: (312) 869 9039

Calvary Grace Christian Church of Faith

The Calvary Grace Christian Church of Faith is a mail-order church founded in 1961 by Rev. Dr. Herman Keck Jr.

Hq: Current address unavailable for this edition

Calvary Grace Churches of Faith

The Calvary Grace Churches of Faith is a mail-order church founded in 1954 by Angelo C. Spern. It was one of the first of the mail-order churches and also provided educational degrees.

Hq: Box 333, Rillton, PA 19140

Church of Holy Light

The Church of Holy Light is one of several mail order churches.

Hq: Box 4478, Pittsburgh, PA 15205

Church of Nature

The Church of Nature, described as a libertarian humanist church, was founded in 1979 by Rev. Christopher L. Brockman.

Hq: Box 407, Dryden, MI

Church of the Creator

The Church of the Creator, founded in 1973 by Ben Klassen, is an atheist racialist church with strong beliefs about the superiority of white people.

Hq: Box 400, Otto, NC 28763

Church of the Holy Monarch,

The Church of the Holy Monarch is a mail order church founded in 1976 by Robert Walker and Archbishop R. M. LeRoux.

Hq: Current address unavailable for this edition

Church of the Humanitarian God

The Church of the Humanitarian God is a pro-life church founded by Ron Libert in 1969.

Hq: Box 13236, St. Petersburg, FL 33733

Church of the New Song

The Church of the New Song, founded in 1970 by Bishop Harry W. Theriault, operates primarily with the national prison system.

Hq: World Faith Exchange, Box 3472, West Palm Beach, FL 33402

Confraternity of Deists, Inc.

The Confraternity of Deists, a modern Deist church, was founded in 1967 by Paul Englert.

Hq: Current address unavailable for this edition

Crown of Light Fellowship

The Crown of Light Fellowship is a mail order church founded in 1967 by Rev. D. H. Howard.

Hq: Current address unavailable for this edition

Ethical Culture Movement

See: American Ethical Union

Freedom from Religion Foundation

The Freedom from Religion Foundation was founded in 1978 by Anne Nicol Gaylor and former members of American Atheists, Inc.

Hq: Box 750, Madison, WI 53701

Gay and Lesbian Atheists

The Gay and Lesbian Atheists, founded in 1978 by Daniel Curzon, argues against religion in part because of religion's role in oppressing gay people.

Hq: Box 14142, San Francisco, CA 94114

Holy Spirit Association for the World Unification of World Christianity

The Holy Spirit Association for the World Unification of World Christianity was founded by Rev. Sun Myung Moon in 1954. It is based upon his many revelations. It came to the USA in 1959 where it has become one of the most controversial religious bodies.

Hq: 4 W. 43rd Street, New York, NY 10036
Tel: (212) 768 7022

Kerista Commune

The Kerista Commune is a commune best known for its practice of polyfidelity, a form of group marriage. It was founded in 1956 by Brother Jud (John Presmont).

Hq: 543 Frederick Street, San Francisco, CA 94117
Tel: (415) 759 9508

Life Science Fellowship
The Life Science Fellowship is a mail order church founded by Archbishop Gordon L. Cruikshank.

Hq: Current address unavailable for this edition

Mazdaznan Movement
The Mazdaznan Movement, one of two Zoroastrian groups in America, was founded in 1902 in Chicago by Rev. Otoman Zar-Adhust Hanish.

Hq: 1701 Aryana Dr., Encinitas, CA 92024
Tel: (619) 942 9855

Moral Re-Armament
The Moral Re-Armament was a spiritual movement founded in 1938 by Dr. Frank N. Buchman.

Hq: 1707 H St., N.W. #900, Washington, D.C. 20006
or
International Hq: Mountain House, 1824 Caux, Switzerland

Omniune Church
The Omniune Church is a mail order church founded in the 1970s by Rev. M. S. Medley.

Hq: 309 Breckenridge, Texarkana, TX 75501

Orthodox Baha'i Faith, Mother Baha'i Council of the United States
The Orthodox Baha'i Faith, Mother Baha'i Council of the United States was founded in the 1950s by former members of the Baha'i faith.

Hq: 3111 Futura, Roswell, NM 88201

Orthodox Baha'i Faith under the Regency
The Orthodox Baha'i Faith under the Regency was founded in the 1970s by Reginald B. (Rex) King and former members of the Orthodox Baha'i Faith, Mother Council of the United States.

Hq: National House of Justice of the U.S. and Canada, Box 1424, Las Vegas, NV 87701

Perfect Liberty Kyodan
The Perfect Liberty Kyodan was founded in 1946 by Tokuchika Miki.

Hq: 700 S. Adams St., Glendale, CA 91205
Tel: (818) 956 7516

Rastafarians
The Rastafarian movement was founded in the 1930s in Jamaica and brought to the USA in the 1960s.

Hq: Current address unavailable for this edition

Remey Society
The Remey Society was founded in 1968 by former members of the Orthodox Baha'i Faith, Mother Baha'i Council of the United States.

Hq: 80-46 234 St., Jamaica, NY 11427-2116

Summum
The Summum is an Egyptian-based religion founded in 1975 by Claude Rex Nowell.

Hq: 707 Genesee Avenue, Salt Lake City, UT 84104

Unitarian Universalist Association

The Unitarian Universalist Association was formed in 1961 by a merger of the American Unitarian Association and Universalist Church in America.

Hq: 25 Beacon Street, Boston, MA 02108
Tel: (617) 742 2100

United Libertarian Fellowship

The United Libertarian Fellowship, based upon principles of libertarian philosophy, was founded in 1975 by William C. White.

Hq: Pres: Will Barkley, 1220 Larnel Place, Los Altos, CA 94022

Universal Life Church

The Universal Life Church, one of the first of the mail order churches, was founded in 1962 by Kirby J. Hensley who is said to have ordained several million people.

Hq: 601 Third Street, Modesto, CA 95351

Universal Life Mission Church

The Universal Life Mission Church (also known as Apostolic Sabbatarian Baptist Churches of America) was founded in 1977 by Kenneth Russell Lyons. It grew out of the Universal Life Church.

Hq: Current address unavailable for this edition

World Union of Universal Religion and Universal Peace

The World Union of Universal Religion and Universal Peace was founded after World War II. In the 1920s, independent Baha'is began to organize and gradually came together to form the World Baha'i Union. Decimated in the War, it reorganized after peace was declared.

International Hq: Schwabstrasse 10, 7050 Waiblingen bei Stuttgart, Germany

Zoroastrian Associations in North America

The Zoroastrian Associations in North America serve as a national network for Zoroastrian centers, primarily in the Iranian-American community.

Hq: For Information: Center for Zoroastrian Research, 3270 E. Robinson Rd., Bloomington, IN 47401-9301

PERIODICALS OF THE UNCLASSIFIED RELIGIOUS GROUPS

AEU Reports, 2 W. 64th Street, New York, NY 10023, American Ethical Union

The American Atheist, Box 2117, Austin, TX 78768, American Atheists, Inc.

Atheist United Newsletter, 12542 Ventura Blvd., Ste. 211, Sherman Oaks, CA 91403

Breakthroughs, 1707 H. Street, N.W., #900, Washington, DC 20006, Moral Re-Armament

Culture Sculpture, 543 Frederick Street, San Francisco, CA 94117, Kerista Commune

Ethical Platform, 2 W. 64th Street, New York, NY 10023, American Ethical Union

Exegesis, Box 407, Dryden, MI 48428, Church of Nature

For a Change, c/o The Good Road, Ltd., 12 Palace Street, London, SW1E 5JF, England, Moral Re-Armament

Freethought Today, Box 750, Madison, WI 53701, Freedom from Religion Foundation

GALA Review, Box 14142, San Francisco, CA 94114, Gay and Lesbian Atheists

The Humanist, 7 Harwood Dr., Box 146, Amherst, NY 14226, American Humanist Association

Kerista, 543 Frederick Street, San Francisco, CA 94117, Kerista Commune

The Node, 543 Frederick Street, San Francisco, CA 94117, Kerista Commune

Perfect Liberty, 700 S. Adams St., Glendale, CA 91205, Perfect Liberty Kyodan

Racial Loyalty, Box 400, Otto, NC 28763, Church of the Creator

The Truth Seeker, Box 2832, San Diego, CA 92112, American Association for the Advancement of Atheism

The ULC News, 601 Third Street, Modesto, CA 95351, Universal Life Church

UU World, 25 Beacon Street, Boston, MA 02108, Unitarian Universalist Association

U. S. Baha'i Report, 536 Sheridan Road, Wilmette, IL 60091, Baha'i Faith

Utopian Class Room, 543 Frederick Street, San Francisco, CA 94117, Kerista Commune

World Order, 536 Sheridan Road, Wilmette, IL 60091, Baha'i Faith

BIBLIOGRAPHY

The selective bibliography includes only the major sources consulted in the process of preparing this directory. Not listed are the many yearbooks produced by different religious groups, and the vast files in the American Religions Collection at the University of California-Santa Barbara from which the basic directory list was originally compiled.

Body Mind Spirit Magazine, Editors of. *The New Age Catalogue: Access to Information and Sources*. New York: Doubleday, 1988. 244pp.

Clark, Francis, ed. *Interfaith Directory*. New York: International Religious Foundation, 1987. 178pp.

Directory of Sabbath-Observing Groups. Fairview, OK: The Bible Sabbath Association, 1986. 231pp.

Finding Friends Around the World: Being the Handbook of the Religious Society of Friends. London: Friends World Committee for Consultation (Quakers), 1982. 128pp.

FWCC Friends Directory of Meetings and Churches in the Section of the Americas, 1987/88. Philadelphia: Friends World Committee for Consultation, 1988. 153pp.

Geisendorfer, James V., ed. *A Directory of Religious and Parareligious Bodies and Organizations in the United States*. Lewiston, NY: The Edwin Mellen Press, 1989. 427pp.

Haiek, Joseph R. *Arab American Almanac*. Glendale, CA: News Circle Publishng Co., 1984. 322pp.

Ingenito, Marcia Gervase, ed. *National New Age Yellow Pages*. Fullerton, CA: Highgate House, 1988. 252pp.

Israelowitz, Oscar. *Guide to Jewish Canada & U.S.A., Vol. 1: Eastern Provinces.* Brooklyn, NY: Israelowitz Publishing, 1990. 326pp.

———. *Guide to Jewish U.S.A., Vol. 2: The South.* Brooklyn, NY: Israelowitz Publishing, 1988. 175pp.

Jacquet, Constant H., Jr., ed. *Yearbook of American & Canadian Churches, 1989.* Nashville, TN: Abingdon Press, published annually.

Khalsa, Dharam Kaur, ed. *The New Consciousness Sourcebook: Spiritual Community Guide.* 6th ed. Pomona, CA: Arcline Publications, 1985. 207pp.

Lichdi, Diether Goetz, ed. *Mennonite World Handbook: Mennonites in Global Witness, 1990.* Carol Stream, IL: Mennonite World Conference, 1990. 440pp.

MacPhail, Carolyn Cott, ed. *Choices and Connections: The First Catalog of the Global Family.* Boulder, CO: Human Potential Resources, Inc., 1987. Various pagination.

Melton, J. Gordon, ed. *The Encyclopedia of American Religions*, 3rd ed. Detroit, MI: Gale Research, 1989. 1102pp.

Morreale, Don, ed. *Buddhist America: Centers, Retreats, Practices.* Santa Fe, NM: John Muir Publications, 1988. 349pp.

The 1990/91 Directory of Intentional Communities: A Guide to Cooperative Living. Evansville, IN: Fellowship for Intentional Community, 1990. 310pp.

Pruter, Karl, ed. *A Directory of Autocephalous Anglican, Catholic and Orthodox Bishops.* Highlandville, MO: St. Willibrord Press, 1958. *Supplement.* Highlandville, MO: St. Willibrord Press, 1990. 64pp. *Supplement.* Highlandville, MO: St. Willibrord Press, 1991. 16pp.

Rosen, Oded, ed. *The Encyclopedia of Jewish Institutions: United States and Canada.* Tel Aviv, Israel: Mosadot Publications, 1983. 501pp.

Singer, David, ed. *American Jewish Yearbook 1987.* Vol. 87. New York: The American Jewish Committee; Philadelphia: The Jewish Publication Society, published annually.

Ward, Gary L., ed. *Independent Bishops: An International Directory.* Detroit, MI: Apogee Books, 1990. 524pp.

World Methodist Council. *Handbook of Information 1987-1991.* Biltmore Press, 1987. 101pp.

INDEX

A

Aaronic Order 201
Abbey of Théleme 210
Academy for Future Science 210
Adhyatma Yoga Dharma 153
Adhyatmic Sadhana Sangh, U.S.A. 154
Advaita Fellowship 154
Advent Christian Church 13, 94
Adventures in Enlightenment, a Foundation 211
Aetherius Society 211
African-American Catholic Congregation 13
African Islamic Mission 181
African Methodist Episcopal Church 14, 96
African Methodist Episcopal Zion Church 14
African Orthodox Church 14
African Orthodox Church in the West 14
African Theological Archministry 211
African Union First Colored Methodist Protestant Church 14
African Universal Church 14
The Afro-American Social Research Association 211
Agasha Temple of Wisdom 211
Agni Dhatu Samadhi Yoga 154

Agni Yoga Society 211
Ahmadiyya Anjuman Ishaat Islam, Lahore, Inc. 181
Ahmadiyya Movement in Islam 181
Ajapa Yoga Foundation 154
Akshar Purushottam Sanstha 165
Alaska Yearly Meeting (of Friends) 14
Albanian Orthodox Archdiocese of America 14
Albanian Orthodox Diocese of America 14
Aletheia Foundation 211
Alexandrian Wicca 211
Algard Wicca 211
All Faiths Ecumenical Diocese of the South and Southwest 15
Allegheny Wesleyan Methodist Episcopal Connection (Original Allegheny Conference) 15
Alliance World Fellowship 9
All-One-Faith-in-One-God State 269
All Saints Episcopal Church (Nashville, TN) 101
Alpha and Omega Christian Church 15
Alpha and Omega Pentecostal Church of God 15
Amana Church Society (Church of True Inspiration) 15, 45
Amended Christadelphians See: Christadelphians: Amended

American Association for the
Advancement of Atheism
269
American Association of Lutheran
Churches 15
American Association of Rabbis
192
American Atheists, Inc. 269
American Baptist Association 15,
28
American Baptist Churches in the
U.S.A. 16, 49, 62, 78, 101,
112
American Buddhist Congress 133
American Buddhist Movement 134
American Carpatho-Russian
Orthodox Greek Catholic
Church 16
American Catholic Church 211
American Catholic Church
See: Orthodox Catholic
Church in America (Verra)
American Catholic Church of
Antioch 16
American Catholic Church–Old
Catholic 16
American Catholic Church (Syro-
Antiochean) 16
American Coalition of Unregistered
Churches 16
American Council of Christian
Churches 9, 71
American Druze Society 181
American Eastern Orthodox
Catholic Church 16
American Episcopal Church 16
American Episcopal Diocese, South
16
American Ethical Union 269
American Evangelical Christian
Churches 17
American Evangelistic Association
17
American Fellowship Church 270
American Forum for Jewish-
Christian Cooperation 3
American Gnostic Church 212
American Haidakhan Samaj 154

American Hebrew Eastern Orthodox
Greek Catholic Church 17
American Humanist Assn. 270
American Indian Evangelical Church
17
American Institute for the Study of
Racial and Religious
Cooperation 3
American Lutheran Church 27, 55
American Meditation Center 154
American Mission for Opening
Churches 17
American Muslim Council 179
American Muslim Mission 181
American National Baptist
Convention 81
American Order of the Brotherhood
of Wicca 212
American Orthodox Catholic Church
17
American Orthodox Catholic Church
(Irene) 17
American Orthodox Catholic Church
(Propheta) 17
American Orthodox Catholic Church-
Western Rite Mission,
Diocese of New York 18
American Orthodox Catholic Church
(Zaborowski)
See: Mariavite Old Catholic
Church, Province of North
America
American Orthodox Church 18
American Orthodox Church (Russell)
See: Holy Orthodox Catholic
Church
American Orthodox Exarchate,
Archdiocese of North
America 18
American Prelature 18
American Raelian Movement 212
American Rationalist Federation 270
American Rescue Workers 18
American Vegan Society 154
American World Patriarchs 18
American Zen College 134
Amica Temple of Radiance 212
Amrita Foundation 155

Ananda 155
Ananda Ashrama and Vedanta
Centre 155
Ananda Marga Yoga Society 155
Anchor Bay Evangelistic Association
18
Ancient British Church 60
Ancient Mystical Order of the
Rosae Crucis 212
Ancient Tridentine Catholic Church
18
Anglican Catholic Church 18
Anglican Church of North America
19
Anglican Consultative Council 9
Anglican Episcopal Church of N.
America 19
Anglican Orthodox Church 19
Anglican Rite Jurisdiction
19
Anglo-Catholic Church in America
19
Anglo-Saxon Federation of America
19
Ann Ree Colton Foundation of
Niscience 212
Ansaaru Allah Community 181
Anthroposophical Society 212
Antiochian Orthodox Archdiocese of
North America 19
Apostolic Assemblies of Christ, Inc.
19
Apostolic Catholic Assyrian Church
of the East, North
American Diocese 20
Apostolic Catholic Church of the
Americas 20
Apostolic Christian Church
(Nazarean) 20
Apostolic Christian Churches,
International 20
Apostolic Christian Churches of
America 20, 63
The Apostolic Church 20
Apostolic Church of Christ 20
Apostolic Church of Christ in God
21, 80, 100, 108
Apostolic Church of Jesus 21

Apostolic Church of Jesus Christ 21
Apostolic Episcopal Church (Holy
Eastern Catholic and
Orthodox Church) 21
Apostolic Faith Church 20, 61
Apostolic Faith Church of America
21
Apostolic Faith Church of God 21,
22
Apostolic Faith Church of God and
True Holiness 22
Apostolic Faith Church of God Live
On 22
Apostolic Faith Church of God's
Giving Grace 22
Apostolic Faith Churches of God in
Christ 22
Apostolic Faith (Hawaii) 21
Apostolic Faith (Kansas) 21
Apostolic Faith Mission 21
Apostolic Faith Mission Church of
God 22
Apostolic Faith Mission of Portland,
Oregon 22
Apostolic Gospel Church of Jesus
Christ 22
Apostolic Holiness Church of
America 22
Apostolic Lutheran Church of
America 23, 26
Apostolic Lutherans (Church of the
First Born) 23
Apostolic Lutherans (Evangelicals
No. 1) 23
Apostolic Lutherans (Evangelicals
No. 2) 23
Apostolic Lutherans (The
Heidemans) 23
Apostolic Lutherans (New
Awakening) 23
Apostolic Methodist Church 23
Apostolic Old Catholic Church 23
Apostolic Orthodox Catholic Church
23
Apostolic Orthodox Old Catholic
Church 24
Apostolic Overcoming Holy Church
of God 24

Apostolic United Brethren 201
Aquarian Educational Group 213
Aquarian Foundation 213
Aquarian Tabernacle Church 213
Arcana Workshops 213
Arcane School 213
Archdiocese of the Old Catholic
    Church of America
    See: Orthodox Catholic
    Church in America
    (Brown)
Arica Institute 182
Armenian Apostolic Catholic Church
    of America 24
Armenian Church of America,
    Diocese of 24
Armenian Evangelical Brethren 24
Armenian Evangelical Church 24
Arsha Vidya Pitham 155
Arunchala Ashrama 155
Arya Samaj 173
The Asatru Alliance 213
Asbury Bible Churches 25
Ascended Master Teachings
    Foundation 213
Assemblies of God, General Council
    25, 33
Assemblies of God International
    Fellowship
    (Independent/Non
    Affiliated) 25
Assemblies of the Called Out Ones
    of Yah 25
Assemblies of the Church of Jesus
    Christ 25
Assemblies of the Lord Jesus Christ,
    Inc. 25
Assemblies of Yahweh 25, 79, 113
Assemblies of Yahweh (Easton,
    Michigan) 25
Assembly of Christian Soldiers
    25
Assembly of Yahweh 25
Assembly of YHWHHOSHUA 26
Associate Reformed Presbyterian
    Church 26
Associated Brotherhood of
    Christians 26

Associated Churches, Inc. 26
Associated Churches of Christ
    (Holiness) 26
Associated Gospel Churches 10, 26
Associates for Religion and
    Intellectual Life 3
Associates for Scriptural Knowledge
    26
Association for Research and
    Enlightenment 213
Association of American Leastadian
    Congregations 26
Association of Evangelical Gospel
    Assemblies 26
Association of Evangelical Lutheran
    Churches 55
Association of Evangelicals for Italian
    Missions 26
Association of Free Lutheran
    Congregations 27
Association of Friends Meetings
    See: Lake Erie Yearly
    Meeting (of Friends)
Association of Fundamental Gospel
    Churches 27
Association of Fundamental
    Ministries and Churches
    27
Association of Independent
    Methodists 27
Association of Occidental Orthodox
    Parishes 27
Association of Sananda and Sanat
    Kumara 213
Association of Seventh-day
    Pentecostal Assemblies 27
Association of Spiritual Training 182
Association of Unity Churches 237
Association of Vineyard Churches
    27
Astara 213
Atheists United 270
Atmaniketan Ashram 155
Aum Namo Bhagavate Vasudevaya
    Foundation 155
Aurobindo, Disciples of 156
Aurum Solis 214
Ausar Auset Society 214

Autocephalous Slavonic Orthodox Catholic Church (in exile) 27
Autocephalous Syro-Chaldean Church of North America 28
Avadhut Ashram 156

B

Babaji Lingam Temple 169
Badarikashrama 169
Baha'i Faith 270
Balaji Temple 171
Baptist Bible Fellowship 28
Baptist Bible Union 62
Baptist General Conference 28
Baptist Missionary Association of America 28
Baptist National Education Convention 81
Baptist World Alliance 10
Bawa Muhaiyaddeen Fellowship 182
Beachy Amish Mennonite Churches 28
Bellflower Vedic Dharma Samaj 169
Berachah Church 28
Berean Bible Fellowship 28
Berean Bible Fellowship (Chicago) 28
Berean Fundamental Church 29
Berkeley Zen Center 134
Beshara School of Intensive Esoteric Education 182
Bethany Bible Church and Related Independent Bible Churches of the Phoenix, Arizona, Area 29
Bethel Ministerial Association 29
Bethel Temple 29
Bharatiya Temple 172
Bharatiya Temple of Central Ohio 173
Bhavana Society 134

Bible Brethren 29
Bible Church of Christ 29
Bible Churches (Classics Expositor) 29
Bible Fellowship Church 29
Bible Holiness Church 29
Bible Methodist Church 29
Bible Methodist Connection of Churches 29
Bible Methodist Connection of Tennessee 29, 30
Bible Missionary Church 30, 111
Bible Presbyterian Church 30, 112
Bible Way Church of Our Lord Jesus Christ World Wide 30, 109
Bible Way Pentecostal Church 30
Biblical Church of God 30
Black Primitive Baptists 30
Blue Mountain Center of Meditation 156
Bluzhever Hasidism 194
B'Nai Shalom 30
Bobov Hasidism 194
Bodaiji Mission 134
Body of Christ Movement 31
Boston Church of Christ 31, 47
Bostoner Hasidism 194
Brahma Kumaris World Spiritual University 156
Branch SDA's 31
Branham Tabernacle and Related Assemblies 31
Bratslav Hasidism 194
Brethren Church (Ashland, Ohio) 31, 57
Brethren in Christ Church 31, 32, 86, 110
Bridge to Freedom 228
Brotherhood of the White Temple 214
Brothers of the Earth 214
Buddha's Universal Church 135
Buddhist Association of the United States 135
Buddhist Brotherhood of America 135
Buddhist Churches of America 135

Buddhist Churches of Canada 135

Buddhist Fellowship of New York
     135

Buddhist Lodge of the Theosophical
     Society in Los Angeles
     See: Buddhist
     Brotherhood of America

Buddhist Sangha Council of
     Southern California
     133

Buddhist Society of America
     See: First Zen Institute of
     America

Builders of the Adytum 214, 222

Bulgarian Eastern Orthodox Church,
     Diocese of North and
     South America 31

Bulgarian Eastern Orthodox Church
     (Diocese of North and
     South America and
     Australia) 31

Byelorussian Autocephalous
     Orthodox Church in the
     U.S.A. 32

Byelorussian Orthodox Church 32

Byzantine Catholic Church 32

Byzantine Old Catholic Church 32

Byzantine Orthodox Church 32

C

California Bosatsukai 135

California Evangelistic Association
     32

California Institute of Integral
     Studies 156

Calvary Chapel Church 32

Calvary Fellowship, Inc. 32

Calvary Grace Christian Church of
     Faith 270

Calvary Grace Churches of Faith
     270

Calvary Holiness Church 32

Calvary Ministries Inc., International
     33

Calvary Pentecostal Church 33

Cambodian Buddhists 135

Cambridge Buddhist Association 136

Capital District Hindu Temple
     Society 173

Carolina Evangelistic Association 33

Catholic Apostolic Church 82

Catholic Apostolic Church at Davis
     33

Catholic Apostolic Church in Brazil
     33, 66

Catholic Apostolic Church in North
     America (Patriarchate of
     Brazil) 33

The Catholic Church of the
     Antiochean Rite 214

Catholic Life Church 33

Celtic Evangelical Church 33

Centennial Parliament of Religions 4

Center Branch of the Lord's
     Remnant 202

Center for Religious Experience and
     Study 4

Center of Being 156

Central Conference of American
     Rabbis 194

Central Yearly Meeting of Friends
     33

Chagdud Gonpa Foundation 136

Sri Chaitanya Saraswat Mandal 156

Ch'an Meditation Center 136

Chapori-Ling Foundation Sangha
     136

Charismatic Catholic Church:
          Independent Rite of America
          33

Charismatic Catholic Church of
     Canada 34

Chernobyl Hasidism 194

Children of God
     See: Family of Love

Chinese Buddhist Association 136

Chinmaya Mission (West) 157

Sri Chinmoy Centres 157

Chirotesian Church of Faith
     214

Chishti Order of America 182

Cho Ko Long Buddhist Mahayana
     Center 136

Chowado Henjo Kyo 136

Christ Catholic Church 34
Christ Faith Mission 34
Christ Family 34
Christ Holy Sanctified Church of
     America 34
Christ Ministry Foundation 214
Christ Truth League 214
Christadelphians-Amended 34
Christadelphians-Unamended 34
Christian Alliance 37
Christian and Missionary Alliance 9,
     37, 79
Christian Apostolic Church (Forest,
     Illinois 34
Christian Apostolic Church
     (Sabetha, Kansas) 35
Christian Assemblies (Gene
     Edwards) 35
Christian Assemblies (George
     Geftakys) 35
Christian Assembly 214
Christian Brethren (Plymouth
     Brethren) 35, 47
Christian Catholic Church
     (Evangelical-Protestant) 35
Christian Church (Disciples of
     Christ) 35, 71, 104
Christian Church of North America,
     General Council 35
Christian Churches and Churches of
     Christ 35
Christian Congregation 36
Christian Conservative Churches of
     America 36
Christian Convention Church 36
Christian Faith Band
     See: Church of God
     (Apostolic)
Christian Holiness Association 10
Christian Identity Church 36
Christian International Network of
     Prophetic Ministries 36
Christian Israelite Church 36
Christian Methodist Episcopal
     Church 36
Christian Millennial Fellowship 37
Christian Mission
     See: Salvation Army

Christian Nation Church U.S.A. 37
Christian Orthodox Catholic Church
     37
Christian Pilgrim Church 37
Christian Prophets of Jehovah
     37
Christian Reformed Church in North
     America 37, 95
Christian Research, Inc. 37
Christian Spirit Center 215
Christian Union 37, 45
Christian Union (Cleveland,
     Tennessee) *See*: Church of
     God (Cleveland, Tennessee)
Christian Unity Baptist Association
     38
Christ's Ambassadors 38
Christ's Assembly 38
Christ's Church 202
Christ's Sanctified Holy Church
     (Louisiana) 38
Christ's Sanctified Holy Church
     (South Carolina) 38
Christ's Truth Church and School of
     Wisdom 218
Christward Ministry 215
Chung Fu Kuan (Taoist Sanctuary)
     265
Church and School of Wicca 215
Church for the Fellowship of All
     People 38
Church of All Worlds 215
Church of Antioch 215
Church of Bible Understanding 38
Church of Christ
     See: Churches of Christ
Church of Christ at Halley's Bluff
     42, 202
Church of Christ at Zion's Retreat
     202
     See: Church of Israel
Church of Christ (Fetting/Bronson)
     202
Church of Christ Holiness unto the
     Lord 38
Church of Christ (Holiness) U.S.A.
     38, 54
Church of Christ Immanuel 202

Church of Christ,
    Nondenominational Bible
    Assembly 202
Church of Christ (Non-
    Instrumental) 31
Church of Christ (Restored) 202
Church of Christ, Scientist
    215
Church of Christ (Temple Lot)
    202, 203
Church of Christ "With the Elijah
    Message", Established
    Anew in 1929 203
Church of Christian Liberty 39
Church of Circle Wicca 215
Church of Cosmic Origin and
    School of Thought 215
Church of Daniel's Band 39
Church of Divine Man 215
Church of Divine Man of
    Washington 215
Church of Eductivism 216
Church of Essential Science 216
Church of General Psionics 216
Church of God and Saints of Christ
    195
Church of God and True Holiness
    39
Church of God (Anderson, Indiana)
    27, 39, 40
Church of God (Apostolic) 20, 21,
    39
Church of God (Black Jews) 195
Church of God, Body of Christ 39
Church of God by Faith, Inc. 39,
    67
Church of God (Cleveland,
    Tennessee) 39, 56, 64, 88,
    107
Church of God Evangelistic
    Association 39
Church of God General Conference
    (Abrahamic Faith) 40
Church of God (Guthrie,
    Oklahoma) 40
Church of God (Holiness) 40
Church of God (Huntsville,
    Alabama) 40

Church of God in Christ 40, 59, 63,
    104
Church of God in Christ,
    Congregational 40
Church of God in Christ,
    International 40
Church of God in Christ, Mennonite
    40
Church of God in the Lord Jesus
    Christ
    See: American Orthodox
    Catholic Church
Church of God International 41
Church of God (Jerusalem) 41, 112
Church of God (Jerusalem Acres)
    41
Church of God (Jesus Christ the
    Head) 41
Church of God (O'Beirn) 41
Church of God of Prophecy 40, 41,
    78
Church of God of the Apostolic
    Faith 41
Church of God of the Mountain
    Assembly 42
Church of God of the Original
    Mountain Assembly 41, 42
Church of God of the Union
    Assembly 42
Church of God (Sabbatarian) 41, 42
Church of God (Sanctified Church)
    42
Church of God, Seventh Day 100
Church of God (Seventh Day,
    Denver, Colorado) 42
Church of God (Seventh Day, Salem,
    West Virginia) 42
Church of God, Seventh Era
    See: Congregation of Yah
Church of God, the Eternal 39
Church of God, the House of Prayer
    42
Church of God (Which he Purchased
    with His Own Blood) 42
Church of God with Signs 42
Church of Greece 105
Church of Holy Light 270
Church of Illumination 216

Church of Israel 42
Church of Jesus
    See: Yahweh's Temple
Church of Jesus Christ
    (Bickertonite) 203
Church of Jesus Christ (Bulla) 203
Church of Jesus Christ Christian
    See: Church of Jesus
    Christ Christian, Aryan
    Nations
Church of Jesus Christ Christian,
    Aryan Nations 43
Church of Jesus Christ (Cutlerite)
    203
Church of Jesus Christ of Latter-
    Day Saints 203
Church of Jesus Christ of Latter-
    Day Saints (Strangite) 203
Church of Jesus Christ of Latter-
    Day Saints (Strangite,
    Drew) 203
Church of Jesus Christ of the Saints
    in Zion 204
Church of Jesus Christ (Strangite,
    Drew) 203
Church of Jesus Christ (Toney) 204
Church of Jesus Christ (Zion's
    Branch) 204
Church of Light 216
Church of Mercavah 216
Church of Metaphysical Christianity
    216
Church of Nature 270
Church of Our Lord Jesus Christ of
    the Apostolic Faith 30, 43,
    44, 107, 111
Church of Pan 216
Church of Revelation (California)
    216
Church of Satan 216
Church of Scientology International
    216
Church of Scotland 26, 96
Church of Seven Arrows 217
Church of St. Joseph 43
Church of the Bible Covenant 43
Church of the Brethren 29, 31, 38,
    43, 52, 61, 70

Church of the Christian Crusade 43
Church of the Christian Spiritual
    Alliance 157
Church of the Creator 271
Church of the East in America
    See: Orthodox Church of
    the East
Church of the Eternal Source 217
Church of the Everlasting Gospel
    See: The Neverdies
Church of the First Born of the
    Fullness of Times 204
Church of the Full Gospel, Inc. *See*:
    General Conference of the
    Evangelical Baptist Church,
    Inc.
Church of the Gospel 43
Church of the Holy Monarch 271
Church of the Holy Trinity 43
Church of the Humanitarian God
    271
Church of the Kingdom of God 43
Church of the Lamb of God 204
Church of the Little Children
    43
Church of the Living God (Christian
    Workers for Fellowship) 42,
    44, 67, 68
Church of the Living God (Hawaii)
    44
Church of the Living God (North
    Carolina) 44
Church of the Living God, The Pillar
    and Ground of Truth 44,
    58, 107
Church of the Living Gospel *See*:
    The Neverdies
Church of the Living Word 44
Church of the Lord Jesus Christ 25
Church of the Lord Jesus Christ of
    the Apostolic Faith 44
Church of the Lutheran Brethren of
    America 44
Church of the Lutheran Confession
    44
Church of the Mennonite Brethren
    in Christ 29
Church of the Nazarene 30, 45, 48

Church of the New Covenant in Christ 204
Church of the New Song 271
Church of the Spiritual Advisory Council 217
Church of the Tree of Life 217
Church of the Trinity (Invisible Ministry) 217
Church of the United Brethren in Christ 45, 68
Church of the White Eagle Lodge 217
Church of True Inspiration 45
Church of Truth 225
Church of Tzaddi 217
Church of Universal Light 143
Church of Universal Triumph/the Dominion of God 45
Church of World Messianity 255
Church on the Rock North America 45
Church Universal and Triumphant 217
The Church Which Is Christ's Body 45
Churches in the Lord Jesus Christ of the Apostolic Faith 45
Churches of Christ in Christian Union 45
Churches of Christ in Zion 205
Churches of Christ (Non-Instrumental) 46, 47
Churches of Christ (Non-Instrumental, Conservative) 46
Churches of Christ (Non-Instrumental, Discipling) 46
Churches of Christ (Non-Instrumental, Ecumenical) 46
Churches of Christ (Non-Instrumental, Non-Class, One Cup) 46
Churches of Christ (Non-Instrumental, Non-Sunday School) 47

Churches of Christ (Non-Instrumental, Premillennial) 47
Churches of Christ (Pentecostal) 47
Churches of God, General Conference 47
Churches of God, Holiness 47
Churches of God (Independent Holiness People) 47
Churches of God in the British Isles and Overseas (Needed Truth) 47
Churches Under the Cross 82
Cimmarron Zen Center in Los Angeles 143
City of the Sun Foundation 218
Claymont Society for Continuous Education 182
Coalition for Religious Freedom, U.S.A. 4
College of Buddhist Studies, Los Angeles 133
Colonial Tabernacle of Long Beach, California
    See: California Evangelistic Association
Colonial Village Pentecostal Church of the Nazarene 48
Colorado Reform Baptists 48
Colored Methodist Church
    See: Christian Methodist Episcopal Church
Commandment Keepers Congregation of the Living God 195
Community Chapel and Bible Training Center 48
Community Churches, International Council of
    See: International Council of Community Churches
Community of Catholic Churches 48
Community of the Good Shepherd Eastern
    See: Western Orthodox Church in America

Community of the Love of Christ
(Evangelical Catholic) 48
Concilio Olazabal de Iglesias Latino
Americano 48
Concordant Publishing Concern 48
Concordia Lutheran Conference 48
Confederate Nations of Israel 205
Conference of the Evangelical
Mennonite Church 49
Confraternity of Christian Doctrine,
Saint Pius X 49
Confraternity of Deists, Inc. 271
Congregation Kehillath Yaakov 195
Congregation of Mary Immaculate
Queen 77
Congregation of New Square 195
Congregation of Yah 49
Congregational Bible Church 49
Congregational Christian Churches,
National Association of
49, 78, 81, 107
Congregational Church 99, 103
Congregational Church of Practical
Theology 218
Congregational Holiness Church 49
Congregational Mennonite Church
See: Congregational Bible
Church
Congregational Methodist Church
49
Connecticut Valley Hindu Temple
Society 170
Conservative Baptist Association of
America 49, 61
Conservative Congregational
Christian Conference 49
Conservative German Baptist
Brethren 50
Conservative Lutheran Association
See: World Confessional
Lutheran Assn.
Conservative Mennonite Conference
50
Conservative Mennonite Fellowship
(Non-Conference) 50
Consultation on Church Union
10
Continuing Episcopal Church 50

Cooneyites
See: Christian Convention
Church
Coptic Fellowship of America 218
Coptic Orthodox Church 50
Coptic Orthodox Church (Western
Hemisphere) 50
Cosmic Awareness Communications
218
Cosmic Circle of Fellowship 218
Council for the World's Religions 4,
6
Council of Bible Believing Churches
International 9, 10
Council of Imams in North America
179, 180
Council of Islamic Organizations of
America 180
Council of the Masajid (Mosques) in
the U.S.A. 180
Council on Religion and International
Affairs 4
Course in Miracles 218
Covenant of the Goddess 218
Covenanters 96
Crossroads Church of Christ
(Gainesville, Florida) 31
Crown of Light Fellowship 271
Cumberland Presbyterian Church
50, 99, 111
Cymry Wicca 218

D

Dai Bosatsu Zendo 148
Damascus Christian Church 51
Datta Yoga Centers 157
Davidian Seventh-Day Adventist
Association 51
Dawn Bible Students Association 51
Dawn Horse Fellowship 158
Dawn of Truth 219
Defenders of the Truth 51
Deliverance Evangelistic Centers 51
Deva Foundation 157
Devatma Shakti Society 157
Devi Mandir 169
Dharma Friendship Foundation 136

Dharma Rain Zen Center 136
Dharma Realm Buddhist
    Association 137
Dharma Sangha 137
Dharma Zen Center of Hawaii
    137
Dhiravamsa Foundation 137
Dhyanyoga Centers 157
Diamond Sangha 137
Dianic Wicca 219
Diocese of Christ the King 51
Disciples of the Lord Jesus Christ
    51
Divine Life Society 165
Divine Science of Light and Sound
    260
Divine Word Foundation 219
Door of Faith Church and Bible
    School 51
Drikung Dharma Centers 137
Duck River (and Kindred)
    Association of Baptists 51
Dunkard Brethren Church 38, 50,
    52

E

Earthstar Temple 219
East West Cultural Center 156
East West Foundation 265
Eastern Orthodox Catholic Church
    in America 52
Eastern States Buddhist Association
    of America 137
Ecclesia Gnostica 219
Ecclesia Gnostica Mysterium 219
ECKANKAR 260
Eclesia Catolica Cristiana 219
Ecumenical Catholic Church 52
Ecumenical Catholic Diocese of
    America 52
Ecumenical Methodists Conferences
    12
Ecumenical Ministry of the Unity of
    All Religions 219
Ecumenical Orthodox Catholic
    Church-Autocephalous

    See: Holy Eastern Orthodox
        Catholic and Apostolic
        Church in North America
Edta Ha Thoma 220
Eheiji Monastery 143
Elan Vital 260
Elim Fellowship 52
Elim Minister Fellowship
    See: Elim Fellowship
Elk River Baptist Association
    51
Embassy of the Gheez-Americans
    220
Embrace Foundation 4
Emissaries of Divine Light 220
Emmanuel Association 52
Emmanuel's Fellowship 52
Emmanuel Holiness Church 52
Epiphany Bible Students Association
    52
Episcopal Church 16, 18, 19, 21, 50,
    51, 53, 95
ESP Laboratory 220
Estonian Evangelical Lutheran
    Church 53
Estonian Orthodox Church in Exile
    53
Etherian Religious Society of
    Universal Brotherhood 220
Ethical Culture Movement *See*:
    American Ethical Union
Ethiopian Orthodox Church in the
    United States of America 53
Ethiopian Orthodox Coptic Church,
    Diocese of North and South
    America 53
Ethiopian Zion Coptic Church 220
Eucharistic Catholic Church 53
Evangelical Alliance
    See: World Evangelical
        Fellowship
Evangelical and Reformed Church
    107, 111
Evangelical Association 54
Evangelical Bible Church 53
Evangelical Catholic Church 54
Evangelical Catholic Communion
    54

Evangelical Christian Church
(Wesleyan) 54
Evangelical Church of Christ
(Holiness) 54
Evangelical Church of North
America 54
Evangelical Congregational Church
54
Evangelical Covenant Church of
America 54
Evangelical Episcopal Church 54
Evangelical Free Church of America
55
Evangelical Friends Church, Eastern
Division 55
Evangelical Lutheran Church in
America 55
Evangelical Lutheran Church in
America (1988) 15
Evangelical Lutheran Synod 55
Evangelical Mennonite Brethren
Conference
See: Fellowship of
Evangelical Bible Churches
Evangelical Methodist Church
55
Evangelical Methodist Church of
America 55
Evangelical Ministers and Churches,
International 56
Evangelical Mission Alliance 37
Evangelical Orthodox (Catholic)
Church in America (Non-
Papal Catholic) 56
Evangelical Presbyterian Church 56
Evangelical Synod 95
Evangelical Union of Bohemian and
Moravian Brethren in
North America 110
Evangelical United Brethren 54, 65
Evangelical Wesleyan Church 56
Evangelistic Church of God 56
Ewam Choden 138

F

Faith Assembly 56

Faith Mission Church 56
Faith Tabernacle Corporation of
Churches 56
Family of Love (Children of God)
48, 56
The Farm 220
Federal Council of Churches 11
Federation of Islamic Associations in
the U.S.A. and Canada 180
Federation of Reconstructionist
Congregations and Havurot
193
Federation of St. Thomas Christian
Churches 220
Fellowship in Prayer 4
Fellowship of Christian Assemblies
57
Fellowship of Evangelical Bible
Churches 57
Fellowship of Fundamental Bible
Churches 57
Fellowship of Grace Brethren
Churches 57
Fellowship of Independent
Evangelical Churches 57
Fellowship of the Inner Light 220
Filipino Assemblies of the First Born
57
Filipino Community Churches 57
Finnish Orthodox Church 57
Fire-Baptized Holiness Church of
God of the Americas 57
Fire-Baptized Holiness Church
(Wesleyan) 58
First Assembly Holiness Church of
God in Christ 58
First Born Church of the Living God
58
First Christians' Essene Church
221
First Church of Divine Immanence
221
First Congregational Methodist
Church of the U.S.A. 58
First Deliverance Church of Atlanta
58
First Interdenominational Christian
Association 58

First Zen Institute of America 138
Five Years Meeting of Friends
    See: Friends United
    Meeting
Fivefold Path 157
Fo Kuang Shan Buddhist Society
    138
Followers of Christ 58
For My God and My Country 58
Foreign Mission Baptist Convention
    of the U.S.A. 81
Foundation, a Hermetic Society
    221
Foundation Church of Divine Truth
    221
Foundation Faith of God 221
Foundation for Biblical Research
    59
Foundation for Inner Peace 218
Foundation for Science of Spiritual
    Law 221
Foundation for Self Realization
    Beyond the Human
    Potential 221
Foundation for the Preservation of
    the Mahayana Tradition
    146
Foundation of Human
    Understanding 211
Foundation of Revelation 158
Foundation of Tao 265
Fountain of Life Fellowship 59
Fraternitas L.V.X. Occulta
    [Fraternity of the Hidden
    Light] 222
Fraternitas Rosae Crucis 216, 222
Free and Old Christian Reformed
    Church of Canada and
    America 59
Free Anglican Church in America
    59, 82
Free Christian Zion Church of
    Christ 59
Free Church of God in Christ 59
Free Church of God in Christ in
    Jesus' Name 59
Free Church of God True Holiness
    59

Free Daist Communion 158
Free Gospel Church, Inc. 59
Free Lutheran Congregations,
    Association of
    See: Association of Free
    Lutheran Congregations
Free Magyar Reformed Church in
    America *See*: Hungarian
    Reformed Church in
    America
Free Methodist Church of North
    America 60, 108
Free Protestant Church of England
    60
Free Protestant Episcopal Church
    60
Free Reformed Church
    See: Free and Old Christian
    Reformed Church of Canada
    and America
Free Serbian Orthodox Church-
    Diocese for the U.S.A. and
    Canada 60
Free Will Baptist Church of the
    Pentecostal Faith 60
Freedom from Religion Foundation
    271
Friends General Conference 60
Friends of Buddhism—Washington,
    D.C. 138
Friends of the Western Buddhist
    Order 138
Friends United Meeting 33, 60
Friends World Committee for
    Consultation 10
Full Gospel Assemblies International
    60
Full Gospel Church Association 61
Full Gospel Evangelistic Association
    61
Full Gospel Fell. of Churches and
    Ministers International 61
Full Gospel Pentecostal Association
    61
Full Salvation Union 61
Fundamental Baptist Fellowship 61
Fundamental Baptist Fellowship
    Association 61

Fundamental Brethren Church 61
Fundamental Methodist Church 61
Future Foundation 222

G

Ganden Tekchen Ling 138
Ganesha Temple, Flushing 173
Gardnerian Wiccan 222
Gaudiya Vaishnava Society 158
Gay and Lesbian Atheists 271
Gedatsu Church of America 138
Geeta Ashram 172
General Assemblies and Church of the First Born 62
General Assembly of Spiritualists 222
General Association of Davidian Seventh-Day Adventists 62
General Association of General Baptists 62
General Association of Regular Baptist Churches 61, 62
General Church of the New Jerusalem 222
General Conference of Mennonite Brethren Churches
    See: Mennonite Brethren Church of North America
General Conference Mennonite Church 62
General Conference of the Church of God (Seventh Day) 42, 62, 63
General Conference of the Evangelical Baptist Church, Inc. 62
General Convention of the New Jerusalem 222
General Convention of the New Jerusalem in the United States of America 222
General Convention of the Swedenborgian Church 222

General Council of the Churches of God 63
General Six-Principle Baptists 63
George Adamski Foundation 222
George Ohsawa Macrobiotics Foundation 265
The Georgian Church 223
German Apostolic Christian Church 34, 35, 63
German Reformed Church 47, 95
Global Congress of the World's Religions 4
Glorious Church of God in Christ Apostolic Faith 63, 88
Gnostic Association of Cultural and Anthropological Studies 223
Gnostic Orthodox Church 223
God's House of Prayer for All Nations 63
God's Missionary Church 63
Golden Lotus Inc. 158
Gospel Assemblies (Jolly) 63
Gospel Assemblies (Sowders/Goodwin) 63
Gospel Harvesters Evangelistic Association 64
Gospel Mission Corps 64
Gospel Spreading Church 64
Grace Brethren Churches, Fellowship of
    See: Fellowship of Grace Brethren Churches
Grace and Hope Mission 64
Grace Gospel Fellowship 64
Grail Movement of America 223
Greek Archdiocese of Vasiloupolis 64
Greek Orthodox Archdiocese of North and South America 64, 65
Greek Orthodox Church of America 65
Greek Orthodox Diocese of New York 65
Gurdjieff Foundation 182

H

Habibiyya-Shadhiliyya Sufic Order 182
Hall Deliverance Foundation 65
Hallowed Grounds Fellowship of Spiritual Healing and Prayer 223
Hanafi Madh-Hab Center, Islam Faith 183
Hanuman Foundation 158
H.A.R.I. Temple 174
Hawaii Buddhist Council 133
Hawaii Chinese Buddhist Society 138
Healing Temple Church 65
Hebrew Israelites
    See: Nation of Yahweh
Hermetic Order of the Golden Dawn 214
Higashi Hongwanji Buddhist Church 139
Highway Christian Church of Christ 65, 95
Himalayan International Inst. of Yoga Science and Philosophy 158
Hindu Community and Cultural Center (Livermore, CA) 170
Hindu Cultural Society of Western New York 173
Hindu Mandir (Garfield, NJ) 172
Hindu Sanatan Dharma of America (Orlando, FL) 170
Hindu Society of Arizona 169
Hindu Society of Greater Cincinnati 173
Hindu Society of Minnesota 172
Hindu Society of North Carolina 173
Hindu Temple (Augusta, GA) 171
Hindu Temple (Beaver Creek, OH) 173
Hindu Temple (Berlin, NJ) 172
Hindu Temple Cultural Center (Fremont, CA) 170
Hindu Temple (Memphis, TN) 174

Hindu Temple of Atlanta 171
Hindu Temple of Greater Chicago 171
Hindu Temple of Kentucky 171
Hindu Temple of San Antonio 174
Hindu Temple of South Florida 171
Hindu Temple of Toledo 173
Hindu Temple Society (Monroeville, PA) 174
Hindu Temple Society of Colorado 170
Hindu Temple Society of Mississippi 172
Hindu Temple Society of New Orleans 171
Hindu Temple Society of North E. Ohio 173
Hindu Temple Society of Southern California 170
Hindu Temple Society of Toledo of N. E. Ohio 173
Hindu Vishwa Parishad of America 153
His Highness Prince Aga Khan Shia Imami Ismaili Council for the United States 183
Hohm Community 158
Holiness Baptist Association 65
Holiness Church of God Inc. 65
Holiness Gospel Church 65
Holy Alamo Christian Church Consecrated
    See: Music Square Church
Holy Apostolic-Catholic Church of the East (Chaldean-Syrian) 65
Holy Catholic Church, Anglican Rite Jurisdiction of the Americas 19, 66
Holy Church of Jesus Christ 205
Holy Eastern Orthodox Catholic and Apostolic Church in North America 66
Holy Eastern Orthodox Church in the United States 66, 88
Holy Episcopal Church in America 66
Holy Grail Foundation 223

Holy Orthodox Catholic Apostolic Church in the Philippines 66
Holy Orthodox Catholic Church 66
Holy Orthodox Catholic Church, Eastern and Apostolic 32, 66
Holy Orthodox Catholic Church in America 66
Holy Orthodox Church, American Jurisdiction 67
Holy Orthodox Church in America 67
Holy Orthodox Old Catholic Church 67
Holy Shankaracharya Order 158
Holy Spirit Association for the Unification of World Christianity (i.e., the Unification Church) 4, 6, 271
Holy Temple of God, Inc. 67
Holy Ukrainian Autocephalic Orthodox Church in Exile 67
Home of Truth 223
Honkyoku Shinto 255
Honpa Hongwanji Mission of Hawaii 135
Hoomana Naauoa O Hawaii 44, 67, 73
Hoomana O Ke Akua Ola 44
Hope Center for Interfaith Understanding 5
House of God, Holy Church of the Living God, The Pillar and Ground of Truth, The House of Prayer for All People 67
House of God Which Is the Church of the Living God, The Pillar and Ground of Truth, Inc. 67
House of God Which Is the Church of the Living God, The Pillar and Ground of Truth, Inc. (Tate) 68

House of God Which Is the Church of the Living God, The Pillar and Ground of Truth without Controversy (Keith Dominion) 68
House of Judah 195
House of Prayer, Church of God 68
House of Prayer for All People 68
House of the Lord 68
House of the Lord Pentecostal Church 68
House of Yahweh (Abilene, Texas) 69
House of Yahweh (Odessa, Texas) 69
Huna Research Associates 223
Hungarian Reformed Church in America 69
Hutterian Brethren-Dariusleut 69
Hutterian Brethren-Lehreleut 69
Hutterian Brethren of New York, Inc. 69
Hutterian Brethren-Schmiedeleut 69

I

"I AM" Religious Activity 223
Inari Shinto 255
Independent Anglican Church
See: Anglican Church of North America
Independent Assemblies of God
See: Fellowship of Christian Assemblies
Independent Assemblies of God, International 70
Independent Assemblies of God of the U.S. 25
Independent Assemblies of God (Scandinavian) 25
Independent Associated Spiritualists 224
Independent Baptist Church of America 70
Independent Bible Church Movement 70
Independent Brethren Church 70

Independent Catholic Church in
Montana 70
Independent Catholic Church
International 70
Independent Catholic Church of
America 71
Independent Christian Churches,
International 70
Independent Church of Antioch 88,
224
Independent Fundamental Churches
of America 70, 84
Independent Fundamentalist Bible
Churches 70
Independent Old Roman Catholic
Hungarian Orthodox
Church of America 71
Independent Spiritualist Association
of the United States of
America 224
India Cultural and Religious Center
171
India House of Worship 172
Indo-American Yoga-Vedanta
Society 159
Infant Jesus of Prague Catholic
Church 71
Infinite Way 224
Inner Circle Kethra E'Da
Foundation, Inc. 224
Inner Light Foundation 224
Inner Peace Movement 224
Insight Meditation Society 139
Institute for Religious Development
183
Institute for the Development of the
Harmonious Human Being
183
Institute of Cosmic Wisdom 224
Institute of Divine Metaphysical
Research 224
Institute of Islamic Information and
Education 180
Institute of Mentalphysics 224
Integral Yoga International
159
Integrity Communications (and
Related Ministries) 71

Intercosmic Center of Spiritual
Awareness 159
Interfaith, Inc. 5
Interfaith Movement 5
Intermountain Yearly Meeting of the
Society of Friends 71
International Alliance of Churches of
the Truth 225
International Association for
Religious Freedom 5
International Association of Lutheran
Churches 71
International Association of Sufism
183
International Babaji Kriya Yoga 159
International Buddhist Meditation
Center 139
International Christian Churches 71
International Church of the
Foursquare Gospel 44, 71
International Convention of Faith
Churches and Ministers 71
International Council of Christian
Churches 10
International Council of Community
Churches 72
International Council of Religions 5
International Council of Unitarians
and Other Liberal Religious
Thinkers and Workers
See: International
Association for Religious
Freedom
International Deliverance Churches
72
International Evangelical Church and
Missionary Association 72
International Evangelism Crusades 72
International Foundation for Spiritual
Unfoldment 154
International General Assembly of
Spiritualists 225
International Metaphysical
Association 225
International Minister Association
72
International Ministerial Federation,
Inc. 72

International Ministerial Fellowship
       72
International Nahavir Jain Mission
       159
International New Thought Alliance
       210
International Pentecostal Assemblies
       73
International Pentecostal Church of
       Christ 72
International Pentecostal Holiness
       Church 51, 73, 91
International Society for Krishna
       Consciousness 156, 159
International Society for Krishna
       Consciousness of West
       Virginia 160
International Society of Divine Love
       160
International Spiritualist Alliance
       225
International Zen Institute of
       America 139
Iowa Yearly Meeting of Friends 73,
       84
Iraivan Temple 171
Islamic Center of Detroit 180
Islamic Center (Washington, D.C.)
       180
Islamic Circle of North America
       180
Islamic Society of North America
       180
Israelite House of David 73
Israelite House of David as
       Reorganized by Mary
       Purnell 73

J

Jafari-Shadhiliyya Sufic Order 183
Jain Meditation International Center
       160
Jean Klein Foundation 160
Jehovah's Witnesses 73, 90
Jemez Bodhi Mandala (Jemez
       Springs, NM) 144

Jerrahi Order of America 183
Jesus Only Church of God 25
Jesus People Church 73
Jetsun Sakya Center 139
Jinga Shinto 255
Jinsha Shinto 256
Jodo Mission 139
Johannine Catholic Church 225
John Wesley Fellowship and Francis
       Asbury Society of Ministers
       73
Joy Foundation, Inc. 225

K

Kadavul Hindu Temple 171
Ka Hale Hoano Hou O Ke Akua 73
Kagyu Dharma 139
Kansas Yearly Meeting (of Friends)
       78
Kanzeonji Zen Buddhist Temple
       140
Karma Kagya 140
Karma Triyana Dharmachakra 140
Kawaiaho (Congregational) Church
       74
Kealaokamalamalama 73
Kentucky Mountain Holiness
       Association 74
Kerista Commune 271
Keshavashram International
       Meditation Center 160
Khaniqahi-Nimatullahi 183
King David Spiritual Temple of
       Truth Association 110
Kirpal Light Satsang 260
Klausenburg Hasidism 195
Kodesh Church of Emmanuel 74
Kongosatta-In Tendai Buddhist
       Temple 140
Konko Kyo 256
Korean Buddhist Bo Moon Order
       140
Korean Buddhist Chogye Order 140
Korean Buddhist Sangha Association
       of the Western Territory in
       the U.S. 134

Korean Presbyterian Church in
    America, General Assembly
    of 74
Kripalu Center for Yoga and Health
    160
Krishnamurti Foundation of
    America 160
Kriya Yoga Ashrama, Inc. 160
Kundalini Research Foundation
    161
Kunzang Osdal Palyul Changchub
    Choeling/The World Prayer
    Center 140
Kwan Um Zen School 141
Kwan Yin Temple 141
Kyova Association of Regular
    Baptists 74

L

Lake Erie Yearly Meeting (of
    Friends) 74
Lakshmi 163
Sri Lakshmi Narayan Temple
    174
Lama Foundation 225
Lamaist Buddhist Monastery of
    America *See*: Tibetan
    Buddhist Learning Center
Lamb of God Church 74
Lao Buddhist Sangha of the U.S.A.
    141
Laodician Home Missionary
    Movement 74
Last Day Messenger Assemblies 74
Latin-American Council of the
    Pentecostal Church of God
    75
Latin-American Council of the
    Pentecostal Church of God
    of New York 74
Latter House of the Lord for All
    People and the Church of
    the Mountain, Apostolic
    Faith 75
Latvian Evangelical Lutheran
    Church in America 75

Law of Life Activity 225
Layman's Home Missionary
    Movement 74, 75
Lectorium Rosicrucianum 225
Ledeboerian Churches 82
Lemurian Fellowship 226
Leroy Jenkins Evangelistic
    Association 75
Liberal Catholic Church 212
Liberal Catholic Church International
    226
Liberal Catholic Church, Province of
    the United States 226
Liberty Baptist Fellowship 75
Liberty Fellowship of Churches and
    Ministers 75
Life Science Fellowship 272
Life Study Fellowship Foundation,
    Inc. 226
Lighted Way 226
Lighthouse Gospel Fellowship 75
Light of the Universe 226
Lithuanian Evangelical Lutheran
    Church in Exile 76
Little River Baptist Association 65
The Little Synagogue 5, 195
Little Synagogue 195
Living Dharma Center 141
The (Local) Church 35, 76
Longchen Nyingthig Buddhist Society
    141
Lord's New Church Which is Nova
    Hierosolyma 226
Los Angeles Buddhist Church
    Federation 134
Los Gatos Zen Group 141
Lotus Ashram 226
Love Project 226
Lower Lights Church 76
Lubavitch Hasidism 195
Lumber River Annual Conference of
    the Holiness Methodist
    Church 76
Lutheran Church in America 55
Lutheran Church—Missouri Synod
    48, 76
Lutheran Churches of the
    Reformation 76

Lutheran Free Church 27
Lutheran World Convention 10
Lutheran World Federation 10
Lutheran's Alert National
　　See: World Confessional
　　Lutheran Association

M

Ma Yogi Shakti International
　　Mission 161
Ma Yogashakti Durga Mandir 173
Macedonian Orthodox Church 76
Mages Creek Assn. of Regular
　　Baptists 97
Mahasiddha Nyingmapa Center 141
Mahayana Sutra and Tantra Center
　　141
Mahikari of America 256
Maitreya Institute 141
Malankara Orthodox (Syrian)
　　Church 76
Manav Seva Mandir 171
Mandala Buddhist Center 141
Mangal Mandir (Washington, DC)
　　170
Mangala Mandir 172
Manujothi Ashram 161
Maranatha Christian Churches 77
Mariavite Old Catholic Church,
　　Province of N. Am. 77
Mark-Age 227
Mary Immaculate Queen of the
　　Universe Center 77
Master Path 260
Mata Amritanandamayi Mission
　　161
Mata's Darbar, VHP of America
　　172
Matri Satsang 161
Mayan Order 227
Mazdaznan Movement 272
Meditation Groups, Inc. 227
Megiddo Mission 77
Meher Baba, Lovers of 161
Mennonite Brethren Ch. of N. Am.
　　(Bruedergemeinde) 77

Mennonite Church 49, 50, 77, 96,
　　102
Mennonite Church, General
　　Conference *See*: General
　　Conference
Mennonite World Conference 11
Mercian Rite Catholic Church 77
Methodist Church (1939-1968) 27,
　　55, 57, 62, 78, 109
Methodist Church in the Caribbean
　　and the Americas 110
Methodist Episcopal Church 14, 21,
　　39, 58, 60, 78, 92, 98, 102
Methodist Episcopal Church, South
　　23, 36, 49, 76, 78, 83, 92,
　　102
Methodist Protestant Church 57, 62
　　78 *See also:* Fellowship of
　　Fundamental Bible Churches
Metropolitan Church Association 78
Metropolitan Community Churches,
　　Universal Fellowship of
　　78
Metropolitan Holiness Church
　　See: Metropolitan Church
　　Association Metropolitan
　　Spiritual Churches of Christ,
　　Inc. 227
Mevlana Foundation 184
Mexican National Catholic Church
　　78
Mid-American Yearly Meeting (of
　　Friends) 78
Middle East Dialogue Group 5
Midwest Congregational Christian
　　Church 78
Midwest Holiness Association 56
Millennial Church of Jesus Christ
　　205
Mindstream Church of Universal
　　Love 227
Ministry of Christ Church 78
Minnesota Baptist Association 78
Minnesota Convention
　　See: Minnesota Baptist
　　Association
Minnesota Zen Meditation Center
　　141

Miracle Life Fellowship Intl. 79
Miracle Life Revival 79
Missionary Christian and Soul
    Winning Fellowship 79
Missionary Church 79
Missionary Church Association
    79
Missionary Diocese of the Holy
    Spirit 79
Missionary Dispensary Bible
    Research 79
Missionary Methodist Church of
    America 79
Mississippi Conference of the
    Methodist Protestant
    Church 78
Missouri Valley Friends Conference
    79
Mita Movement 79
Moksha Foundation 162
Molokan Spiritual Christians
    (Postojannye) 80
Molokan Spiritual Christians
    (Pryguny) 80
Monastery of the Seven Rays
    227
Monastery of Tibetan Buddhism
    141
Monastritsh Hasidism 196
Moody Church 80
Moorish Science Foundation of
    America 184
Moorish Science Temple, Prophet
    Ali Reincarnated, Founder
    184
Moral Re-Armament 272
Moravian Church in America
    (Unitas Fratrum) 80
Morningland-Church of the
    Ascended Christ 227
Mount Baldy Zen Center 143
Mount Calvary Holy Church in
    America 80
Mount Calvary United Church of
    God 80
Mount Hebron Apostolic Temple of
    Our Lord Jesus of the
    Apostolic Faith 80

Mount Sinai Holy Church 81
Mt. Zion Sanctuary 81
Mountain and River Order (Zen)
    148
Mountain Union Regular Baptist
    Association 38
Movement of Spiritual Inner
    Awareness, Church of the
    260
M.T.O. Shahmaghsoudi (School of
    Islamic Studies) 184
Mu Farm 227
Murugan Temple of North America
    172
Music Square Church 81
Muslim World League 180

N

Nada-Brahamananda Ashram 159
Naqshbandi Sufi Order 184
Narayanananda Universal Yoga Trust
    162
Nation of Islam (The Caliph) 184
Nation of Islam (Farrakhan) 184
Nation of Islam (John Muhammad)
    184
Nation of Islam (Silas Muhammad)
    185
Nation of Yahweh (Hebrew
    Israelites) 196
National Anglican Church 81
National Association of
    Congregational Christian
    Churches 50, 81
National Association of Evangelicals
    11
National Association of Free Will
    Baptists 81, 88, 108
National Association of Holiness
    Churches 81
National Baptist Convention 81,
    94
National Baptist Convention of
    America 81
National Baptist Convention of the
    U.S.A., Inc. 81

National Baptist Evangelical Life and Soul Saving Assembly of the U.S.A. 82
National Camp Meeting Association for the Promotion of Holiness
See: Christian Holiness Association
National Colored Spiritualist Association of Churches 227
National Conference of Christians and Jews 5
National Council of Community Churches
See: International Council of Community Churches
National Council of the Churches of Christ in the United States of America 6, 11
National David Spiritual Temple of Christ Church Union (Inc.) U.S.A. 110
National Ecumenical Coalition, U.S.A. 5
National Primitive Baptist Convention, Inc. 82
National Spiritual Aid Association 227
National Spiritual Alliance of the U.S.A. 228
National Spiritual Science Center 228
National Spiritualist Association of Churches 222, 224, 228
National Workshops on Christian-Jews Relations 6
Native American Church 228
Nazarene Episcopal Ecclesia 60
Nebraska Yearly Meeting (of Friends) 97
Nechung Drayang Ling 142
Nestorian Apostolic Church 82
Netherlands Reformed Congregations 82
The Neverdies 82
New Age Bible and Philosophy Center 228

New Age Church of the Christ 228
New Age Church of Truth 228
New Age Teachings 228
New Apostolic Church of North America 82
New Bethel Church of God in Christ (Pentecostal) 82
New Christian Crusade Church 82
New Congregational Methodist Church 82
New Covenant Churches of Maryland 83
New Ecumenical Research Association 6
New England Evangelical Baptist Fellowship 83
New England Hindu Temple 172
New Life Fellowship 83
New Order of Glastonbury 228
New, Reformed, Orthodox Order of the Golden Dawn 228
New Salem Association of Regular Baptists 74, 96
New Testament Assn. of Independent Baptist Churches 83
New Testament Church of God 83
New Wiccan Church 229
Nichiren Mission 142
Nichiren Shoshu 142
Nipponzan Myohoji 142
Nirankari Universal Brotherhood Mission 260
Nityananda Institute, Inc. 162
No-name Church
See: Christian Convention Church
Noohra Foundation 229
North American Baptist Association
See: Baptist Missionary Association of America
North American Baptist Conference 83
North American Baptist Fellowship 11
North American Episcopal Church
See: Anglican Church of North America

North American Interfaith Network
Project 6
North American Old Roman
Catholic Archdiocese of
Saint Mary Orthodox
Catholic Churches 83
North American Old Roman
Catholic Church 83,
84
North American Old Roman
Catholic Church–Utrecht
Succession, 37, 84
North American Traditional Old
Roman Catholic Church
(Chicago) 84
North Carolina Yearly Meeting of
Friends (Conservative)
84
North Pacific Yearly Meeting of the
Religious Society of
Friends 84
Northern Baptist Convention
See: American Baptist
Churches in the U.S.A.
Northwest Yearly Meeting of
Friends Church 84
Norwegian-Danish Evangelical Free
Church 55
Norwegian Lutheran Church 55
Norwegian Seaman's Church
(Mission) 84
Novominsk Hasidism 196
Nyingmapa Institute Center 142

O

Oasis Fellowship 229
Office of Christian-Muslim Concerns
6
Ohio Bible Fellowship 84
Ohio Yearly Meeting of the Society
of Friends 84
Old Brethren Church 85
Old Brethren German Baptist
Church 85
Old Catholic Church,
Archepiscopate of Healing

Arts, Missionaries and
Chaplains of America 85
Old Catholic Church in America 85
Old Catholic Church in North
America (Catholicate of the
West) 85
Old Catholic Episcopal Church 229
Old Episcopal Church 85
Old Episcopal Church of Scotland
85
Old German Baptist Brethren 85,
86
Old Holy Catholic Church of the
Netherlands 86
Old Holy Catholic Church, Province
of North America 229
Old Order Amish Mennonite Church
86
Old Order German Baptist Church
86
Old Order (or Yorker) River
Brethren 52, 86
Old Order (Reidenbach) Mennonites
86
Old Order (Wenger) Mennonites
86
Old Order (Wisler) Mennonites 86,
111
Old Orthodox Catholic Patriarchate
of America 86
Old Roman Catholic Church 53, 87
Old Roman Catholic Church
Archdiocese of Chicago 87
Old Roman Catholic Church-English
Rite
See: Old Roman Catholic
Church in North America
Old Roman Catholic Church (English
Rite) and the Roman
Catholic Church of the
Ultrajectine Tradition
87
Old Roman Catholic Church in
North America 87
Old Roman Catholic Church-Utrecht
Succession 87
Om Guru Narayanaya Ashram 170
Omniune Church 272

Open Bible Evangelistic Association 87
Open Bible Standard Churches 87
Open Way 229
Order of Buddhist Contemplatives 142
Order of St. Francis 87
Order of Thelema 229
Ordinary Dharma 142
Ordo Adeptorum Invisibilium 229
Ordo Lux Kethri [Order of the Kethric Light] 229
Ordo Templi Astarte [Order of the Temple of Astarte - OTA] [Church of Hermetic Science] 229
Ordo Templi Orientis 230
Ordo Templi Orientis (Grant) 230
Oregon Yearly Meeting of Friends *See*: Northwest Yearly Meeting of Friends Church
Oriental Missionary Society Holiness Church of North America 88
(Original) Church of God, Inc. 88
Original Free Will Baptists, North Carolina State Convention 88
Original Glorious Church of God in Christ Apostolic Faith 88
Original Hebrew Israelite Nation 196
The Original Neo-Kleptonia Neo-American Church 230
Original Pentecostal Church of God 88
Original United Holy Church International 88
Orthodox Baha'i Faith, Mother Baha'i Council of the United States 272
Orthodox Baha'i Faith under the Regency 272
Orthodox Catholic Archdiocese of Philadelphia *See*: Holy Eastern

Orthodox Church in the United States
Orthodox Catholic Autocephalous Church (USA) 88
Orthodox Catholic Church 79, 88
Orthodox Catholic Church in America (Brown) 89
Orthodox Catholic Church in America (Verra) 89
Orthodox Catholic Church of America 89
Orthodox Catholic Church of North and South America 89
Orthodox Catholic Diocese of Connecticut and New England *See*: Orthodox Catholic Church of North and South America
Orthodox Catholic Synod of the Syro-Chaldean Rite 89
Orthodox Church in America 89, 98
Orthodox Church of America 89
Orthodox Church of the East 89
Orthodox Episcopal Church of God 90
Orthodox Presbyterian Church 90
Orthodox Reformed Church 90
Osho International 162
Our Lady of Enchantment, Church of the Old Religion 230
Our Lady of Fatima Cell Movement 77
Our Lady of Fatima Crusade 77
Our Lady of the Roses, Mary Help of Mothers Shrine 90
Overcoming Saints of God 90
Oveyssi School of Islamic Sufism 184
Oyidan 142

P

Pacific Coast Association of Friends *See*: Pacific Yearly Meeting of Friends
Pacific Yearly Meeting of Friends 90
Paia Montukuji Mission 143

Palaniswami Sivan Temple 170
Palolo Kwannon Temple (Tendai
    Sect) 143
Pan African Orthodox Christian
    Church 196
Pansophic Institute 143
Paschima Sri Viswanantha Temple
    172
Pastoral Bible Institute 51, 90
The Path of Light 230
Pentecostal Assemblies of Jesus
    Christ 109
Pentecostal Assemblies of the World
    21, 43, 65, 90, 91
Pentecostal Church, Inc. 109
Pentecostal Church of Christ 73
Pentecostal Church of God 91
Pentecostal Church of God of
    America 91
Pentecostal Church of the Living
    God, The Pillar and
    Ground of Truth 91
Pentecostal Church of Zion 91
Pentecostal Churches of Apostolic
    Faith 19, 91
Pentecostal Evangelical Church 91
Pentecostal Evangelical Church of
    God, National and
    International 91
Pentecostal Fellowship of North
    America 11
Pentecostal Fire-Baptized Holiness
    Church 52, 91
Pentecostal Free Will Baptist
    Church 91
Pentecostal Holiness Church
    See: International
    Pentecostal Holiness
    Church
Pentecostal World Conference 11
People of Destiny International 91
People's Christian Church 92
People's Methodist Church 92
Perfect Liberty Kyodan 272
Philadelphia Buddhist Assn. 143
Philanthropic Assembly 92
Philippine Independent Catholic
    Church 85, 92

Philippine Independent Church
    92
Phoenix Institute 230
Pilgrim Assemblies International 92
Pilgrim Holiness Church
    See: Wesleyan Church
Pilgrim Holiness Church of New
    York 92
Pilgrim Holiness Church of the
    Midwest 92
Pillar of Fire 64, 92
Planetary Light Association 230
Plymouth Brethren
    See: Christian Brethren
Plymouth Brethren (Exclusive: Ames
    Brethren) 93
Plymouth Brethren (Exclusive: Ex-
    Taylor Brethren) 93
Plymouth Brethren (Exclusive:
    Raven-Taylor Brethren) 93
Plymouth Brethren (Exclusive:
    Reunited Brethren) 93
Plymouth Brethren (Exclusive:
    Tunbridge Well Brethren)
    92
Plymouth Brethren (Ex-Taylor
    Brethren) 93
P'nai Or Religious Fellowship 196
Polish National Catholic Church of
    America 93
Polish Old Catholic Church
    See: Old Orthodox Catholic
    Patriarchate of America
Prana Yoga Ashram 162
Prayer Band Fellowship Union 93
Pre-Nicene Church (De Palatine)
    230
Presbyterian Church in America 93
Presbyterian Church in the United
    States 93, 94
Presbyterian Church in the U.S.A.
    30, 50, 90
Presbyterian Church (U.S.A.) 94
Primitive Advent Christian Church
    94
Primitive Baptists 82
Primitive Baptists-Absolute
    Predestinarians 94

Primitive Baptists-Moderates 94
Primitive Baptists-Progressive 94
Primitive Catholic Church
    Evangelical Catholic
    See: Community of the
    Love of Christ (Evangelical
    Catholic)
Primitive Methodist Church 94
Progressive National Baptist
    Convention, Inc. 94
Progressive Spiritual Church 230
Prosperos 185
The Protes'tant Conference 95
Protestant Episcopal Church in the
    U.S.A.
    See: Episcopal Church
Protestant Orthodox Western
    Church
    See: Evangelical (Catholic)
    Church in America (Non-
    Papal Catholic)
Protestant Reformed Churches in
    America 90, 95
Puerto Rican National Catholic
    Church
    See: Confraternity of
    Christian Doctrine, Saint
    Pius X
Pure Holiness Church of God
    95
Pushti Margiya Vaishnav Samaj
    174
Pyramid Church of Truth and Light
    231

Q

Quartus Foundation for Spiritual
    Research 231
Quimby Center 231

R

Rabbinical Alliance of America
    (Orthodox) 193
Rabbinical Assembly 193

Rabbinical Council of America, Inc.
    (Orthodox) 193
Radha-Raman Vedic Temple 170
Radha Soami Satsang Beas 260
Rainbow Family of Living Light
    231
Rajneesh International 162
Raj-Yoga Math and Retreat 162
Ram Ananda Ashram 162
Shri Ram Chandra Mission 162
Rama Seminars 162
Rastafarians 272
Reconstructionist Rabbinical
    Association 194
Redeemed Assembly of Jesus Christ,
    Apostolic 95
Reform Catholic Church 95
Reformed Church in America 95
Reformed Church in the United
    States 69, 95
Reformed Druids of North America
    231
Reformed Episcopal Church 95
Reformed Mennonite Church 96
Reformed Methodist Union
    Episcopal Church 96
Reformed Orthodox Church in
    America 96
Reformed Orthodox Church
    (Slavonic) 96
Reformed Presbyterian Church of
    North America 96
Reformed Zion Union Apostolic
    Church 96
The Registry 96
Regular Baptists 96, 107
Regular Baptists (Predestinarian) 97
Reiyukai America 143
Religious Liberty Association of
    America 6
Religious Science International 231
Religious Youth Service 6
Remey Society 272
Remnant Church 97
Remnant of Israel 97
Renaissance Church of Beauty 231
Reorganized Church of Jesus Christ
    of Latter Day Saints 205

Restoration Branches Movement 205
Restored Church of Jesus Christ (Walton) 205
Restored House of Israel 97
Restored Israel of Yahweh 97
Rex Humbard Ministry 97
Rigpa Fellowship 143
Rinzai-Ji, Inc. 143
Rissho Kosei Kai 144
Rocky Mountain Yearly Meeting (of Friends) 97
Roman Catholic Church 13, 16, 52, 77, 87, 93, 97, 101, 103
Romanian Orthodox Church in America 97
Romanian Orthodox Episcopate of America 98
Roosevelt Spiritual Memorial Benevolent Association 231
Rosicrucian Anthroposophical League 214, 231
Rosicrucian Fellowship 225, 228, 231
Rosicrucian Society in America 67
Ruby Focus of Magnificent Consummation 232
Russian Orthodox Church 19, 64, 89, 98, 106
Russian Orthodox Church in the U.S.A., Patriarchal Parishes of the 98
Russian Orthodox Church Outside of Russia 98
Russian-Ukrainian Evangelical Baptist Union of the U.S.A. 98

S

Sabaean Religious Order of Amen 232
Sabian Assembly 232
Sacramento Hindu Temple 170
Sacred Society of the Eth, Inc. 232
Sadhana Ashram 163

Sahaja Yoga 163
S.A.I. Foundation 163
Saint Paul's Spiritual Church Convocation 110
Saiva Siddhanta Church 163
Saivite Campus Ministry 173
Sakya Monastery of Tibetan Buddhism 144
Sakya Phuntsok Ling Center for Tibetan Buddhist Studies and Meditation 144
Sakya Tegchen Choling See: Monastery of Tibetan Buddhism
Sakya Thupten Dargye Ling 144
Sakyadhita 134
Salvation Army 18, 98, 11
Sanbo Kyodan (Order of the Three Treasures) 137
Sanctified Church of Christ 98
Sandlick Association of Regular Baptists 97
Sanskrit Classics 163
Sant Bani Ashram 260
Saravamangala Mission 163
Sarva Dharma Temple (Santini Ketan) 174
Sat Yoga Self Transformation Center 163
Satmar Hasidism 196
Satyananda Ashrams, U.S.A. 164
SAVC Sri Radha-Krishna Temple 170
Sawan Kirpal Ruhani Mission 260
Scandinavian Assemblies of God in the U.S. Canada and Other Lands 70
Scandinavian Free Baptist Society of the U.S.A. 70
Scandinavian Independent Assemblies 70
Scandinavian Independent Baptist Denomination in the U.S.A. 70
R. W. Schambach Revivals 99
School for Esoteric Studies 232
School of Light and Realization (Solar) 232

School of Natural Science 232
School of the Natural Order 164
Schwenkfelder Church in America 99
Scripture Research Association 99
Seceder Movement 26
Second Cumberland Presbyterian Church in U.S. 99
Seed Center 232
Seicho-No-Ie [Home of Infinite Life, Wisdom, and Abundance] 232
Self-Enlightenment Meditation Society 162
Self-Realization Church of Absolute Monism 164
Self-Realization Fellowship 155, 164
Semjase Silver Star Center 232
Separate Baptists 107
Separate Baptists in Christ 99
Serbian Eastern Orthodox Church for the U.S.A. and Canada 99
Serbian Orthodox Church in America 60
Serbian Orthodox Church in Yugoslavia 76
Servant Catholic Church 99
Seventh-day Adventist Church 6, 31, 62, 92, 96, 99, 100, 106
Seventh-Day Adventist Church, Reform Movement 100
Seventh Day Baptist General Conference USA and Canada Ltd. 100
Seventh-Day Baptists (German) 100
Seventh Day Christian Conference 100
Seventh Day Church of God 100
Seventh Day Pentecostal Church of the Living God 100
Sha'Arei Orah 196
Shanti Mandir 164
Shanti Temple 164
Shanti Yoga Institute and Yoga Retreat 164
Shi'a Association of North America 180

Shi'a Muslims 180
Shiloh Apostolic Temple 100
Shiloh True Light Church of Christ 100
Shingon Mission 144
Shinnyo-en 144
Shinreikyo 256
Shinshu Kyokai Mission 144
Shiva-Shakti Ashram 164
Shiva Vishnu Temple 174
Shree Gurudev Rudrananda Yoga Ashram 162
Shree Meenakshi Temple 174
Shree Ram Mandir 172
Shree Venkateswara Swami Temple 170
Shri Mangal Mandir 179
Shri Ram Chandra Mission 162
Shri Shiva Balayogi Maharaj Trust 164
Shri Vishnu Scva Ashram 165
Shrine of the Eternal Breath of Tao 266
Siddha Yoga Dham Associates 165
Sighet Hasidism 196
Sikh Council of North America 261
Sikh Dharma 261
Sino-American Buddhist Association *See*: Dharma Realm Buddhist Association
Siva Ashram Yoga Center 140
Sivananda Yoga Vedanta Centers 165, 171
SM Church 233
Social Brethren 100
Societas Rosicruciana in Civitatibus Foederatis 233
Society for Humanistic Judaism 196
Society for Islamic and Eastern Mysticism 185
Society for the Development of the Faculties of Man 185
Society of Christ, Inc. 233
Society of Friends 10, 14, 60, 71, 73, 74, 78, 79, 84, 90, 97, 101
Society of Jewish Science 197
Society of Johrei 256
Society of Pius V 101

Society of Pius X 101
Society of the Bible in the Hands of
    Its Creators 197
Society Ordo Templi Orientis in
    America 233
Soka Gakkai 142
Sokoji Temple 147
Solar Light Center 233
Soldiers of the Cross of Christ,
    Evangelical International
    Church 101
Solomon Korteniemi Lutheran
    Society
    See: Apostolic Lutheran
    Church of America
Sonoma Mountain Zen Center 144
Sons Ahman Israel 205
Soto Mission 145
Sought Out Church of God in
    Christ 101
Soulcraft 233
Sounds of Soul 261
South Carolina Baptist Fellowship
    101, 102
South Carolina Pentecostal Free
    Will Baptist Church 60
Southeast Kansas Fire Baptized
    Holiness Associations
    See: Fire-Baptized
    Holiness Church
    (Wesleyan)
Southeastern Yearly Meeting (of
    Friends) 101
Southern Appalachian Yearly
    Meeting and Association
    (of Friends) 101
Southern Baptist Convention 101,
    112
Southern Episcopal Church 101
Southern Methodist Church 25, 73,
    102
Southwide Baptist Fell. 101, 102
Sovereign Grace Baptist Churches
    102
Sovereignty 233
Spiritual Frontiers Fellowship 217
Spiritual Science Mother Church
    233

Spiritualist Episcopal Church 233
Sri Aurobindo Association 156
Sri Dakshinamurti Temple 174
Sri Ganesh Temple 174
Sri Lakshmi Narayan Temple 174
Sri Lankan Sangha Council of North
    America 145
Sri Rajarajeswari Peetam (NY)
    173
Sri Rajarajeswari Peetam (PA) 174
Sri Rama Foundation 165
Sri Shridi Sai Baba Temple 174
Sri Siva Vishnu Temple 172
Sri Venkateswara Temple 174
Standing Conference of Canonical
    Orthodox Bishops in the
    Americas 12, 14
Starborne Unlimited 234
Stauffer Mennonite Church 102, 111
Stelle Group 234
Stillpoint Institute 145
Stolin Hasidism 197
Subramuniya Yoga Order 163
Subud 185
Sufi Islamia Ruhaniat Society
    185
Sufi Order in the West 185
Summit: A Forum for Inter-Religious
    Dialogue 6
Summum 272
Sunni Muslims 180
Sunray Meditation Society 145
Superet Light Doctrine Church
    234
Susana Yeiktha Meditation Center
    and Buddhist Society
    See: Stillpoint Institute
Swami Kuvalayananda Yoga (SKY)
    Foundation 165
Swaminarayan Mission and
    Fellowship 165
Swaminarayan Temple (IL) 171
Swaminarayan Temple (NJ) 172
Swedish Evangelical Free Church 55
Swedish Lutheran Asgarius Synod
    54
Swedish Lutheran Mission Synod 54
Swiss Reformed Church 20

Synagogue Council of America 192
Syrian Orthodox Church of Antioch
(Archdiocese of the United
States and Canada)
(Jacobite) 102
Syrian Orthodox Church of Malabar
102

T

Tabernacle of Prayer for All People
103
Taishakyo Shinto 256
Talnoye (Talner) Hasidism 197
Taoist Esoteric Yoga Center and
Foundation 266
Tara Center 234
Tassajara Mountain Center 147
Taungpupu Kaba-aye Dharma
Center 145
Tayu Fellowship 234
Teaching of the Inner Christ, Inc.
234
Temple of Cosmic Religion 166
Temple of Kriya Yoga 166
Temple of Nepthys 234
Temple of Set 234
Temple of the Goddess Within
234
Temple of the Pagan Way 235
Temple of the People 235
Temple of Understanding 6
Temple of Universal Law 235
Tenrikyo 256
Tensho-Kotai-Jingu-Kyo 256
Thai-American Buddhist Association
146
Thee Orthodox Old Roman Catholic
Church 103
Theocentric Foundation 235
Theosophical Society 235
Theosophical Society (Hartley)
235
The Theosophical Society in
America 235
Third Civilization 256
Thubten Dhargye Ling 145

Tibetan Buddhist Learning Center
146
The Tibetan Foundation, Inc. 235
Timely Messenger Fellowship 103
Tioga River Christian Conference
103
Todaiji Hawaii Bekkaku Honzan
146
Today Church 23
T.O.M. Religious Foundation 236
Tomlinson Church of God
See: Church of God of
Prophecy
Traditional Catholics of America 103
Traditional Christian Catholic Church
103
Traditional Episcopal Church 103
Traditional Protestant Episcopal
Church 103
Traditional Roman Catholic Church
in the Americas 103
Tridentine Catholic Church 104
Tridentine Old Roman Community
Catholic Church 104
Triumph the Church and Kingdom
of God in Christ (Int.) 104
Triumph the Church in
Righteousness 104
True Church 236
True Church of Christ, Intl. 236
True Church of Jesus Christ
Restored 206
True Fellowship Pentecostal Church
of God in America 104
True Grace Memorial House of
Prayer 104
True Jesus Church 104
True Light Church of Christ
105
True Light Church of God 105
True (Old Calendar) Orthodox
Church of Greece (Synod of
Metropolitan Cyprian),
American Exarchate 105
True Vine Pentecostal Churches of
Jesus 105
True Vine Pentecostal Holiness
Church 105

Truth Center, a Universal
Fellowship 236
Truth Consciousness 166
Truth for Today Bible Fellowship
105
Twentieth Century Church of God
105
The Two-by-Twos
See: Christian Convention
Church

U

Ukrainian Autocephalous Orthodox
Church of America and
Europe 105
Ukrainian Evangelical Alliance of
North America 105
Ukrainian Evangelical Baptist
Convention 106
Ukrainian Missionary and Bible
Society
See: Ukrainian Evangelical
Baptist Convention
Ukrainian Orthodox Church in
America (Ecumenical
Patriarchate) 106
Ukrainian Orthodox Church of the
U.S.A. 106
Unamended Christadelphians
See: Christadelphians:
Unamended
Unarius–Science of Life
236
Undenominational Church of the
Lord 106
Unification Association of Christian
Sabbath Keepers 106
Unification Church
See: Holy Spirit Association
for the Unification of
World Christianity
Union Association of Regular
Baptists 97
Union of American Hebrew
Congregations 194

Union of Messianic Jewish
Congregations 106
Union of Orthodox Jewish
Congregations of America
193
Union of Orthodox Rabbis of the
United States and Canada
193
Union of Sephardic Congregations
193
Unitarian Universalist Association
273
United American Orthodox Catholic
Church 106
United Anglican Church in North
America 106
United Baptists 107
United Brethren in Christ 45, 107
United Christian Church 107
United Christian Church and
Ministerial Association 107
United Christian Church of America
107
United Christian Scientists 236
United Church and Science of Living
Institute 236
United Church of Christ 50, 78, 81,
107
United Church of Jesus Christ
(Apostolic) 107
United Church of Religious Science
236
United Church of the Living God,
the Pillar and Ground of
Truth 107
United Churches of Jesus Christ,
Apostolic 107, 108
United Crusade Fellowship
Conference 108
United Episcopal Church (1945)
Anglican/Celtic 108
United Episcopal Church of America
103
United Episcopal Church of North
America 108
United Evangelical Brethren 109
United Evangelical Church 54

United Free Gospel and Missionary
    Society
    See: Free Gospel Church,
    Inc.
United Free-Will Baptist Church
    108
United Full Gospel Ministers and
    Churches 108
United Fundamentalist Church 108
United Hebrew Congregations 197
United Hindu Temple 173
United Holiness Church of North
    America 108
United Holy Church of America
    80, 81, 88, 108
United House of Prayer for all
    People 68, 69, 109
United Israel World Union 197
United Libertarian Fellowship 273
United Lodge of Theosophists 236
United Methodist Church 54, 109
United Missionary Church 79
United Old Roman Catholic Church
    109
United Order Effort 206
United Pentecostal Church
    International 72, 109
United Pentecostal Council of the
    Assemblies of God 109
United Presbyterian Church in the
    U.S.A. 93, 94
United Seventh-Day Brethren 109
United Spiritualist Church 237
United Synagogue of America
    193
United Way of the Cross Churches
    of Christ of the Apostolic
    Faith 109
United Wesleyan Methodist Church
    of America 110
United Zion Church 110
Unity of the Brethren 110
Unity School of Christianity 237
Universal Association of Faithists
    237
Universal Christian Spiritual Faith
    and Churches for All
    Nations 110

Universal Church of Christ 110
Universal Church of Scientific Truth
    237
Universal Church of the Master 237
Universal Church, the Mystical Body
    of Christ 110
Universal Foundation for Better
    Living 237
Universal Great Brotherhood 237
Universal Harmony Foundation 237
Universal Industrial Church of the
    New World Comforter 238
Universal Life Church 273
Universal Life Mission Church
    273
Universal Life - The Inner Religion
    238
Universal Link 238
Universal Religion of America 238
Universal Shrine of Divine Guidance
    110
Universal Spiritualist Association 238
Universal White Brotherhood 238
Universal World Church 110
Universalia 238
Universariun Foundation 238
Universe Society Church 238
University of Life Church 238
Upper Cumberland Presbyterian
    Church 111
URANTIA Foundation 238
USA Pandit's Parishad, Inc. 173

           V

Vajradhatu 146
Vajrapani Institute for Wisdom
    Culture 146
Valley Light Center 166
Vedanta Society 155, 166
Vedanta Society of Sacramento 170
Vedantic Center 166
Ved Mandir 173
Venusian Church 239
Vietnamese United Buddhist
    Churches in the United
    States 146

Vimala Thakar, Friends of 166
Viniyoga America 167
Vipassana Fellowship of America
   See: Dhiravamsa
   Foundation
Shri Vishva Seva Ashram 167, 170
Vivekananda Vedanta Society 171
Voice of the Vedas 171
Volunteers of America 111

W

Washington Buddhist Vihara 134
Watchtower Bible and Tract Society
   See: Jehovah's Witnesses
The Way International 111
Way of the Cross Church of Christ
   109, 111
Weaver Mennonites 111
Weaverland Conference Old Order
   (Horning or Black
   Bumper) Mennonites 111
Wesleyan Church 30, 63, 92, 111
Wesleyan Church of North America
   56
Wesleyan Connection of Churches
   29
Wesleyan Holiness Association of
   Churches 111
Wesleyan Methodist Church 15, 30,
   79, 92, 111
Wesleyan Tabernacle Assn. 112
Western Orthodox Church 18, 112
Western Orthodox Church in
   America 24, 112
Western Son Academy 146
Westminster Biblical Fellowship 112
White Star 239
Wisconsin Evangelical Lutheran
   Synod 45, 94, 112
Wisdom Institute of Spiritual
   Education 239
Witches International Craft
   Associates 239
Witness and Testimony Literature
   Trust and Related Centers
   112

Won Buddhism 147
Word Foundation 239
Workers Together with Elohim 112
World Alliance of Reformed
   Churches (Presbyterian and
   Congregational) 12
World Baptist Fellowship 28, 112
World Community 167
World Community Service 167
World Conference on Religion and
   Peace 7
World Confessional Lutheran
   Association 113
World Council of Churches 11, 12
World Council of Synagogues 192
World Evangelical Fellowship 12
World Fellowship of Religions 7
World Insight International 113
World Jewish Congress 192
World Methodist Council 12
World Parliament Of Religions-
   Centenary Celebration
   Planning Group 7
World Plan Executive Council 167
World Understanding 239
World Union for Progressive Judaism
   192
World Union of Universal Religion
   and Universal Peace 273
Worldwide Church of God 26, 30,
   39, 41, 49, 59, 105, 113

Y

Yahweh Assemblies in Messiah 113
Yahweh's Temple 113
Yasodhara Ashram Society 168
Yeshe Nyingpo 142, 147
Yoga Research Foundation 168
Yoga Society of San Francisco 159
Yogi Gupta Association 168

Z

Zen Buddhist Temple of Chicago 147
Zen Center of Los Angeles 147
Zen Center of Rochester 147
Zen Center of San Francisco 137, 144, 147
Zen Center of Sonoma Mountain 147
Zen Lotus Society 147

Zen Mountain Monastery 148
Zen Studies Society 148
Zen Studies Society of Philadelphia 148
Zen Temple of Cresskill 148
Zen Wind 148
Zenshuji Soto Mission of Los Angeles 147
Zion's Order, Inc. 206
Zoroastrian Associations in North America 273